OUR HERITAGE OF THOUGHT

OUR HERITAGE
OF
THOUGHT

A Religious and Philosophical Study

By

BARCLAY LEWIS DAY

Bharatiya Kala Prakashan
DELHI (INDIA)

Indian First Edition : 2000

Published by **C.P. Gautam**
BHARATIYA KALA PRAKASHAN
3421-A, IInd Floor, Narang Colony, Tri Nagar,
Delhi-110035. Phone : 7153083

ISBN : 81-86050-58-2

Printed at
EXCELPRINTS
New Delhi

PREFACE

THIS book is simply an earnest endeavour to find out facts: in writing it my one object was to clear my own mind, not to influence the minds of others. It is published only because friends assured me that the matter collected for my own use would be very helpful to others who have no time for individual research.

It will be seen that I advance no special theories. I merely offer to my readers material for thought, from which each must deduce his own inferences and draw his own conclusions.

The chief quotations are taken as follows, viz.:—those from the *Iliad* from the prose translation of Andrew Lang, Walter Leaf, and Ernest Myers; those from the Sacred Books of China from the translation by James Legge; those from the *Ethics* of Spinoza from the translation by R. Willis; those from Kant's *Critique of Pure Reason* from the translation by F. Max Müller; those from Schopenhauer's *World as Will and Idea* from the translation by R. B. Haldane and J. Kemp; those from Comte's *Positive Philosophy* from the free translation of Harriet Martineau, of which Comte himself so highly approved.

BARCLAY LEWIS DAY.

CONTENTS

Our Heritage of Thought

CHAPTER I

EGYPTIAN THOUGHT

WHO has not longed to know the origin of our current ideas on all those subjects of thought which have for us the deepest interest? To me, this longing was so strong, some twenty years ago, that I undertook the labour of love of which this volume is the result. My aim was not to study the world's religions, and still less to waste time over the many superstitions which have clouded thought from age to age. I have simply tried to track the world's thought as far back as was possible to me. This being so, perhaps some of my readers, who rely upon authority in all matters of belief, may think that it was scarcely necessary to have included in my survey the chapter which I have called "Confusion of Thought." But, knowing how much the collation of the material of this particular chapter helped to clear my own mind, I let it go with the rest, in the hope that it may be, as Maimonides quaintly says, somewhat of "a guide to the perplexed."

There seems no doubt at all that our ethical and

philosophical thought has come to us originally from the East, though it is still uncertain whether civilisation began earlier in the broad valley of the Euphrates or in the narrower valley of the Nile. On the whole, it seems best to begin the review of past thought with that of Egypt, because of the greater reliability of the Egyptian records. One naturally asks, who were the Egyptians? and to this question there seems to be no quite satisfactory answer. Of late years, indeed, implements and weapons of worked flint have been found in the burial-places of some prehistoric race, or races, along the banks of the Nile; but to us these earlier people are less interesting than the much more civilised race which undoubtedly occupied Egypt several thousand years previous to the time of Mena, who was probably the first civilised monarch who reigned in Egypt. From whence these civilised races came into Egypt is by no means certain. Dr Lepsius, after long study of the skulls and skeletons of numerous mummies, thinks that the early civilised Egyptians were a mixed race of Arabian-Kushite and Ethiopian origin, who made their first settlements in the country near the very ancient city of Meroë. The earliest records found of this district speak of it as being "the Land of Punt" and "the Land of Râ." Amun, the chief deity at Apé (Thebes), was invoked as "King of Punt," and Hâthor, his goddess, as "Queen of Punt," whilst the god Horus was adored as the "Holy Morning-Star, rising west of the Land of Punt." Dr Flinders Petrie considers Punt to be the country lying on both sides of the southern end of the Red Sea, and that the earliest civilised settlers in

Egypt were a Semitic race, akin to the Phœnicians, which had slowly wandered westwards towards the Mediterranean, mingling, as they came, with the Ethiopian tribes through whose country they passed. Dr Petrie rests his theory that these Semites came from the Red Sea on the fact that, when he was "clearing out the temple of Koptos, in search of prehistoric remains," he came upon portions of three colossal statues which were "of an earlier style than any yet known," and on which he found represented "the figures of shells, sawfish, ostrich, and elephants, indicating that the people who carved them came from the south." Koptos was, he says, "the early terminus of the Koser road." He adds that "the resemblance in features" between Egyptians and Semites, as seen on the monuments, "shows that they may well be of the same race"—a remark with which all who have studied the monuments will readily agree. Dr Brügsch supports the theory of Lepsius, whilst Benfey, De Rouget, and Ebers all agree that the earliest civilised Egyptians were a mixed Semitic race. Dr Wallis Budge, writing in 1893, says: "It is quite as impossible to show that the Egyptian was a Semite, as that he was a Negro."

Be their origin what it may, there can be no doubt that the early Egyptians were already a highly civilised people when we have our first historical record of them, at the time of the First Dynasty, which, according to the most recent estimate of Professor Flinders Petrie, was founded by Mena about 4777 B.C. The state of their civilisation is shown by the many objects of gold, copper, engraved rock-crystal, porphyry, alabaster, diorite, and granite found in 1899 by Dr Petrie in the tombs of this dynasty at Thinis, near Abydos. There is no record, indeed, of the dynasties of the Pharaohs on the monuments; but Egyptologists have found it convenient to adopt the classification of the successive kings of Egypt which was compiled by Manetho, a priest of Sebennytos, from temple records, during the reign of Ptolemy I.—the general of Alexander the Great—who founded the Greek dynasty. That the Egyptians of this epoch had trading relations with the tribes living along the upper reaches of the Nile, is proved by the fact of the finding in these tombs of a quantity of ebony and ivory and fragments of rhinòceros-horn; whilst the presence also of many objects carved in obsidian shows that they had intercourse with Mesopotamia. The theory of the introduction of Babylonian civilisation into Egypt is supported by the similarity of the brick building at Negada, identified as the tomb of Mena, with some of the royal sepulchres found along the lower Euphrates. The tomb of Mena is a rectangular mass of brickwork, of which the four corners point to the four chief points of the compass, and which is buttressed at regular intervals, much after the manner of the massive brick tombs at Tello and Nippur. Recent discoveries at Nippur show that it was part of the burial-ceremony of the early Babylonian chiefs to set fire to their tombs, and the calcined bricks at Negada show that the tomb of Mena has also been exposed to the action of intense heat.

Mena appears to have been born at Tena (Thinis), near Abtu (Abydos), and to have built a new city at the point where the Nile broadens out to the Delta, as the most suitable spot from which he could control both Upper and Lower Egypt. This city was known as Men-nefer (the Good Abode). The Assyrians called it Mimpi, and the Greeks later knew it as Memphis. Most of the stone of Memphis is built into the modern city of Cairo, so that all that can now be seen of the city of Mena is the great embankment which he made to divert the course of the river and give more building-space, and a few ruined walls half-buried in the soil. The next Pharaoh of whom we have much definite knowledge was known as Sneferu, whose tomb, rising from a lofty mound, at Medûm, thirty miles south of Cairo, is one of the most striking objects along the Nile. Dr Flinders Petrie has found the name of Sneferu engraved both on the walls of the tomb and in the adjoining temple, in which also he found "fragments of Sneferu's wooden coffin." It was customary for the king's courtiers to erect their own "mastabas," or burial-chambers, round about the tomb of the monarch. The sepulchral chambers of the court of Sneferu, found at Medûm, show, says Dr Petrie, that "all the essentials of an advanced architecture seem to have been quite familiar to the Egyptians under Sneferu." The most beautifully decorated of these mastabas is that of Nefert, supposed to have been a daughter of the Pharaoh, and of her husband Rahotep. There are now in the museum of Cairo strikingly lifelike statues of Nefert and Rahotep, which were found in their mastabas. These statues are carved with great skill out of limestone, and of equal artistic merit is a decorative panel, painted in fresco, of a group of Nile geese, which reveals not only a keen appreciation of nature, but also excellent knowledge of form. Equally lifelike, and probably of still earlier date, is a smaller statue of carved wood, also in the Cairo museum, which was found near Medûm, and is supposed to be the portrait of the overseer who looked after the building of the pyramid, because of the long stick which he carries in his hand. "The inscriptions on the tombs at Medûm," says Dr Petrie, "are the earliest traceable evidence" of the civilisation of the Egyptians between 3998 B.C. and 3969 B.C., the date ascribed by him to this Pharaoh. But the artistic excellence already attained shows, as Professor Sayce remarks, "that it is the climax of long years of growth." The construction and workmanship of the Great Pyramid at Gizeh, which is the burial-place of "Kufui" (Kheops), a successor of Sneferu, is another proof of their great architectural skill, some of the great slabs of polished granite, in what is known as the Queen's Chamber, being so finely fitted that their joints are scarcely perceptible. Herodotus says that this immense pyramid, which rises 480 feet above the sand, was built by relays of one hundred thousand men, who worked for three months at a time, and that it took twenty years to build. This, Dr Petrie thinks, indicates that work went on only during the three months of the year when the annual inundation made it necessary for all agricultural labour to cease.

But, perhaps, more than any other monument, the Sphinx, now all but buried beneath the desert sand, bears witness to the antiquity of Egyptian art. Dr Petrie considers that it was carved at some period between 3908 B.C. and 3845 B.C. As Professor Maspero remarks, "the art which could conceive and hew this gigantic statue out of the mountain-side was an art in its maturity, master of itself and sure of its effects." The Sphinx lies at no great distance from the site of the very ancient city of Annu, also called Pi-Ra (House of the Sun), and later known to the Greeks as Heliopolis. When uncovered in 1816 A.D., this statue was found to measure 190 feet in length, the face being 14 feet wide. A granite tablet was discovered, let into the breast of the man-lion, which records that, in the year 1533 B.C., Thutmes IV., son of Thutmes the Great, had previously cleared away the sand which in those far-off days already half-buried the monster. On the tablet Thutmes engraved the following inscription:—"A great enchantment rests on this place from the beginning of time. . . . The king's son, Thutmes, had arrived here on his journey about mid-day . . . and had stretched himself to rest in the shade of the great god, and it happened that sleep overtook him. He dreamed at his slumber, at the moment when the sun was at the zenith, and it seemed to him as if this great god spoke to him with his own mouth, 'Behold me, thou, my son Thutmes, I am thy father Hormaku, Kephr, Râ, Tûm.'" This inscription, therefore, is one more link in the chain of evidence which leads students to consider that most of the names of the "great gods" were, after a certain epoch, merely regarded as synonyms for the aspects of the One Supreme Deity; for "Kephr" is the Rising Sun, or the Future, "Râ" is the Noonday Sun, or the Present, "Tûm" is the Setting Sun, or the Past. According to Professor Maspero, the earliest doctrine of the origin of the "the great gods" is that they all emanated simultaneously from Horus. Mariette, Maspero, Sayce, and Flinders Petrie think that the Sphinx symbolises the god Horus in his aspect as Herû-Kuti (Herû of the two Horizons), or, as the name is also translated, "Horus in the circle of Light." If this be so, the Sphinx was an emblem, not only of the sun's daily course through the sky, but also of the sun's annual course through the circle of the zodiac. Dr Wallis Budge reads the name as "Herû-em-chat," which he translates as "Horus in the Horizon," the rising sun, the conqueror of darkness. The figure of the Sphinx, he says, has been hewn as a whole out of the natural rock, but has been built up here and there, where necessary. The worship of Herû appears to have been one of the most ancient cults in the Nile valley. The name Herû is translated as meaning "the one above." All that part of the sky through which the sun appears daily to travel was personified as Het-Herû, or Hâthor, and thus the god is fabled to rise from and sink into "the bosom of Hâthor," who was usually invoked as "the Great Mother." On the monuments Hâthor is always represented as a woman, generally crowned with the horns of a cow, between which rests the solar disc.

The pyramids, the Sphinx, and the remarkable statues found in the mastabas near Medûm show us clearly the artistic and engineering skill attained at that early period in Egypt. The next Pharaoh after Khufu who stands most clearly out from the misty past is Amen-em-hat, who ruled Egypt from Thebes, and who gained for himself the epithet of "Amen-em-hat the Good" by cutting a canal at Dahshur to lead off some of the yearly overflow of the Nile into a vast amphitheatre among the Libyan hills, thus turning a desert into the fertile oasis known as the Fayum. The first obelisk ever erected in Egypt was placed by Amen-em-hat's son, Usurtasen, in front of the temple of Amen-Râ, the sun-god, at Thebes. The great architectural skill of this epoch is shown by the ruins of the magnificent monuments built by the Pharaohs of this dynasty, at Karnak, Luxor, Tanis, Abydos, and Bubastis. In the entrance-courts of their rock-hewn tombs, which look down upon the Nile, at Beni Hassan, we can clearly trace the evolution from the simple four-sided shaft, through the octagon column, to the perfect "Doric" column. These columns at Beni Hassan are identical with the Doric shafts first erected in Greece a thousand years afterwards. The five centuries subsequent to this flourishing epoch in Egypt were times of great unrest, due in some degree to invasions by surrounding Semitic races. It was during this period that the Khâr (Phœnicians) founded their first settlements in the Eastern Delta, especially about Tanis. Dr Brügsch says that on the shores of Lake Menzaleh, near Port Said, the race of fishermen and sailors still show all the facial and physical characteristics of their Phœnician descent. The Semitic race known as the Shasû, the Bedawîn of the Syrian desert, were ultimately driven out of Lower Egypt by a vigorous Pharaoh named Aahmesu, who was known to the Greeks as Amosis.[1] His grandson, Thutmes, also waged constant war with various Semitic races, and boasts, on his monuments, of the costly chariots and the splendid armour of which he despoiled the chieftains of Canaan, as well as of the immense number of Semites whom he brought back prisoners to Egypt. His grandson again, Thutmes III., also records fifteen victorious campaigns in Syria and Phœnicia, and tells us of the multitude of Semitic slaves whom he set to labour at his vast monuments. On one of these we find the portrait of his overseer of works, with the suggestive inscription, "The stick is in my hand; be not idle!" It was this same Thutmes who erected the two colossal sitting statues of himself, carved in sandstone, which are still to be seen near Thebes.

At Tel-el-Amarna, midway between Thebes and Memphis, Dr Lepsius, in 1878, discovered the ruins of a forgotten city, built by Khu-n-Aten, the son-in-law of this Thutmes. These ruins were excavated in 1891 by Dr Flinders Petrie, and show us a very remarkable and distinct style of decoration, the pavement of the great hall of the palace of Khu-n-Aten being covered with paintings of animals, birds, fish,

[1] It may be that a Jewish perversion of this historical fact was the real origin of the "leading out" of the Israelites by the legendary "Moses."

and vegetation, not done in the conventional manner usual on the monuments, but all treated with observation of nature, and executed with a freedom of touch somewhat suggestive of Japanese work. Khu-n-Aten appears to have attempted to reform not only art but religion. He adored the sun's disc, as being the most suggestive of all visible symbols of the unseen ruler of the universe. One of the prayers of Aten, quoted by Dr Brügsch, runs:—"Thou, O God, who art in truth the living One, thou art he who created that which never was, who formest all in the universe." Another prayer, quoted by Dr Flinders Petrie, runs: —"Thou makest the seasons of the year to create all thy works: the winter making them cool, the summer giving warmth. . . . Thou makest the far-off heaven, that thou mayest rise in it, that thou mayest see all that thou hast made when thou wert alone. . . . Thou art very brilliant, beautiful, and exalted. Thy beams encompass all the lands that thou hast made. . . . How excellent are thy ways, thou Lord of Eternity!"

Carl Niebuhr (1903) quotes a hymn to Aten which runs partly thus:—

"Glorious dost thou appear on the horizon, Aten, thou living creator of all life, when thou risest in the east, filling all countries with thy splendour. But, when thou goest to repose in the west, the earth sinks into darkness, like unto that of death. Then, each man lies in his house with covered face and closed eyes, and knows not what happens to him. . . .

"When Aten brings on the day the darkness flees before thy rays, and both lands of Egypt rejoice. . . .

Thy rays descend to the depths of the sea. By thee the woman conceives, and the man is made to beget, the child quickens within the womb. . . .

"Thou didst create the seasons for the completion of thy work, the cool winter and the hot summer. Thou alone didst build the vault of heaven, the lofty path whence thou surveyest all that thou hast made. Thou, Aten, the day of the world, my heart turns to thee! . . ."

But the gentle Khu-n-Aten, who, according to Niebuhr, probably died in 1365 B.C., ruled his empire with so little firmness that his successors, the Pharaohs of the famous nineteenth dynasty, had to fight hard to regain Egypt's lost political power. They built as energetically as they fought. Seti, who founded the family in 1327 B.C., built at Karnak a hall still more magnificent than the Hall of Thutmes, the roof of which was supported by one hundred and sixty-five columns, some of them 66 feet high. He also engraved on the temple-wall at Abydos an elaborate table showing the cartouches of all his royal ancestors, from Mena downwards.

Rameses II. commemorated his victories in Nubia by hewing a great rock-temple in the cliffs at Abu-Simhel, at the entrance of which we see to-day the four huge sitting statues of this Pharaoh, who was known to the Greeks as Sesostris. His grandson, Rameses III., was the last of the strong rulers of Egypt, which, under the feeble sway of his successors, became a province of the great Assyrian Empire. But the invasion of Assyria by the king of Elam gave the opportunity to Nakû—called Necho by the

Greeks—to free the country from the Assyrian yoke, by the aid of a large number of paid troops from Caria and Ionia. Necho afterwards retained his Greek mercenaries in permanent camps at Neucratis, in the Delta, and did his utmost to attract Greek colonists to Egypt. Thus the harbours of Egypt became full of Greek ships, Greek temples were built, and it was not long before the Greek culture and language preponderated throughout Lower Egypt. Then, after passing successively under the sway of Nebuchadnezzar of Babylon, of Cambyses and Darius of Persia, and of Alexander of Macedon, Egypt enjoyed another three centuries of national life under the Greek dynasty of the Ptolemies, before it at length lost its identity as a mere province of the great Roman Empire.

The priests of Heliopolis boasted that their city, known as the "Holy City," was the oldest in the land Be that as it may, it is evident that more doctrines can be traced back to the priests of Heliopolis than to any other of the many hierarchies of Egypt. Amongst other theories, the thinkers of Heliopolis postulated a moist, homogeneous essence, or fluid substance, called "the Nû," as the source and origin of the universe. Initiates of the priestly brotherhood of this city were taught that, "when as yet there was neither heaven nor earth," there arose in the Nû a god, whom they variously called Tem, Tûm, Atmû, and finally Atmû-Râ, a name which signifies "existing alone in the abyss." Tem personifies the "Hidden Sun," or the power of latent heat, and was invoked as "the Great Father."

He is the only one of the great gods who is represented invariably with a human head. The Heliopolitan theory of creation was that from Tem emanate the twin pair Shû and Tefnût. The god Shû personifies the atmosphere, the goddess Tefnût personifies moisture. From their union proceeds a second pair of deities, Seb and Nût. The god Seb personifies the earth, the goddess Nût the sky. These two deities remain locked in each other's embrace until Nût (the sky) is lifted up and separated from Seb (the earth) by Shû (atmosphere). It is worth noticing here that, though at both Heliopolis and Memphis Shû invariably personifies the atmosphere, at Thebes he personifies light. The "children" born of Nût are said to be dawn, daylight, twilight, and darkness, personified respectively by Isis, Osiris, Nephtys, and Typhon.

The Osiris mythos is an allegory of the apparent daily and yearly birth, growth, decline, and death of the sun, personified by the god Ausêt, or, as the Greeks afterwards called him, Osiris, who is slain by his brother Set (Typhon) or darkness, only to be re-born as Het (Horus), the son of his sister-wife, Isis. Thus the young Horus[1] is the symbol both of re-birth and of everlasting life. After his setting, or death, the sun is hidden below the horizon: Osiris is then said to be in the underworld, and in this

[1] Horus, the son of the sun, is symbolised on the monuments by the winged solar disc. The death of Osiris was celebrated on the 17th day of the third month, Athyr. The Egyptian year began on July 20, with the rising of the Nile, when also the star Sirius—called Sopdit by the Egyptians, and Sothis by the Greeks—re-appeared in the east at daybreak.

phase of his course he becomes "Lord of Eternity" and "Judge of the Dead." As the various local cults gradually became more and more amalgamated throughout Egypt, most of the deities assumed a more and more complex character. Isis became identified with Hâthor, "the Great Mother" of Upper Egypt, and also with the goddess who personified the soil, yearly fertilised by its union, so to speak, with the river, which, in Upper Egypt, was personified as Osiris. The desert sand was symbolised as his brother, Typhon. Between these two brothers the conflict is everlasting: it is the struggle between the life-sustaining and the life-destroying forces of nature. In the Delta, Osiris and Isis were also worshipped as the first teachers to men of civilisation and art. The knowledge of the cultivation of barley and wheat was especially held to be due to Isis, so that the Greeks easily identified this deity with their own goddess Demeter, and Osiris with Dionysos. At different times, and in different districts, every one of the great gods was, in his turn, held to be the Supreme Deity, until at length Râ was recognised throughout Egypt as the chief god. He is represented on the monuments under a threefold aspect—as Kephr-Râ, the morning sun; Râ, the sun of noon; and Atûm-Râ, the evening sun. We see him sailing through "the watery abyss," on his "bark of millions of years." At the court of Egypt it was the custom to consider the Pharaoh as the representative of Râ on earth, and to address the reigning monarch as Râ, the royal life of to-day; the heir-apparent, the royal life of the future, was addressed as Horus; whilst the deceased Pharaoh, the royal life of yesterday, was always spoken of as Osiris.

To the unthinking many no doubt Râ was merely the sun-god, but to the thinking few Râ personified all life, physical and metaphysical. Exoterically considered, Kephr-Râ was the rising sun, but esoterically he symbolised the awakening to life of inert matter, and also the entry of the spirit on a glorified existence beyond the tomb. In this relation his emblem was the beetle. We get a fairly good idea of what Râ meant to the Egyptians from some of the hymns to Râ translated by Dr Wallis Budge in his lately published version of the Book of the Dead:—

"Oh thou beautiful Being, thou dost renew thyself in thy season. . . . Every heart swelleth with joy at thy rising, eternally. . . . Oh Râ, the divine man-child, the heir of eternity, self-begotten and self-born. . . . Thou god of life, thou lord of love, all men live when thou shinest. . . . Thou king of right and truth!"

. . . .

"Thou risest, thou risest, thou shinest, thou shinest: thou art crowned king of the gods; thou art lord of heaven; thou art lord of earth; thou art the creator of beings celestial and of beings terrestrial. Thou art the one god who came into being in the beginning of time. . . . Oh thou, who didst give thyself birth! oh One! Mighty, of myriad aspects and forms! Thou art unknown, and no tongue is worthy to declare thy likeness: only thou thyself!"

. . . .

A papyrus found in the tomb of Neri Khonsu, priestess of Amen about 1000 B.C., shows us the idea of Râ at that epoch:—

"This holy god, the lord of all gods, Amen-Râ! The holy soul who came into being in the beginning. The great god who liveth by (or upon) Mâat, the first divine substance, which gave birth to subsequent divine substance. . . . The being whose births are hidden, and whose growths are unknown: the holy Form, beloved, terrible and mighty in his risings, Khepher-Râ, who created every evolution of his existence, except whom, at the beginning, none other existed . . . the beneficent god who is untiring, . . . whose substitute is the divine disc: the unknown One, who hideth himself from that which cometh forth from him. He is the flame which sendeth forth rays of light with mighty splendour; but, though observation can be made of him at his appearance, yet he cannot be understood, and at dawn men make supplication to him . . . Amen-Râ, the king of the gods!"

. . . .

"Homage to thee, oh thou who art Râ when thou risest, and Temû when thou settest. . . . Worshipped be thou whom the goddess Mâat embraceth at morn and at eve. . . . Homage to thee who dost rest upon Mâat, oh Amen-Râ! Thou dost pass over and dost travel through untold spaces. . . . Thou passest through them in peace, and thou dost steer thy way through the watery abyss to the place which thou lovest. This thou dost in one little moment of time, and then thou dost sink down and dost make an end of the hours. . . . Grant that I may behold thee at dawn, each day!" (Papyrus of Hu-nefer, British Museum, No. 9901.)

. . . .

"Homage to thee, oh thou glorious being, oh Tem-Heru-Khuti! When thou risest in the horizon of heaven a cry of joy cometh forth to thee from the mouth of all peoples. Oh thou beautiful being, who dost renew thyself in thy season in the form of the Disc within thy mother, Hâthor. Oh Râ, thou art Heru-Khuti, the divine Man-child, the heir of eternity, self-begotten and self-born. . . . Thou king of right and truth!" (Papyrus of Nekht, British Museum, No. 10,471.)

. . . .

"I am he who cometh forth advancing, whose name is unknown. I am yesterday, and seer of millions of years is my name. . . . I am Horus . . . the only one who proceedeth from the Only One. . . . I open the doors of heaven; I open up the way for the births of to-day; I am the child who marcheth along the roads of yesterday. . . . I myself am not known, but I am he who knoweth thee. . . . I am Horus, who live for millions of years, whose flame shineth upon you and bringeth your hearts to me." (Papyrus of Nû, British Museum, No. 10,477.)

. . . .

It is the opinion of Professor Rawlinson that, behind the exoteric religion symbolised on the monuments, there was an esoteric meaning divulged only to the thoughtful at initiation, and that this esoteric religion distinctly recognised one supreme First Cause of all things. One sacred text says: "He is not graven in marble, his abode is not known, there is no building which can contain him; he is not seen, he doth not manifest his form, vain are all representations." Another text says: "All gods came into being when he began."

In some of the earlier cults we find that the primordial substance of the universe was symbolised as "the Divine Mother," and exoterically worshipped under many names—Mâat, Maut, Mut, Hâthor, and Isis. The generative force of nature was personified as the god Khem; the creative idea—the Logos of the later Greeks—as the god Nûm; the creative act as the god Phtah; divine mystery was personified as the god Amûn, or Amen; divine wisdom as the god Thoth; and divine justice as the god Osiris.[1] But the names of all these deities became in time interchangeable, showing that the later thinkers at least in ancient Egypt regarded them merely as so many manifestations of one Supreme Deity.

Although Râ became chief god throughout Egypt generally, at Hermapolis, one of the oldest cities in Central Egypt, the chief deity was Tehuti, better known to us by his Greek name Thoth. With Thoth was associated Mâat, "the Great Mother." According to Hermapolitan texts, "when the Great God first awoke in the Nû," he cried with a loud voice, "Come

[1] Dr Wallis Budge, the Curator of the Egyptian Antiquities at the British Museum, is of opinion that a drama representing the death and resurrection of the god Osiris was annually performed in certain temples.

unto me!" and immediately, at his command, there sprang forth from north, south, east, and west the four great gods who rule "the four Houses of the world." But practically Thoth appears to be, like Râ, the synthesis of all the gods. All creation is his work. He is "the Voice," he is "the Law-giver"; Phtah, "the Opener," and Knemû, "the Fashioner," execute his commands. Thoth is "the Master of Words," the "Possessor of Magic Writings," who taught men the art of "speaking to the eye." Thoth seems to have all the attributes ascribed by the Greeks to Apollo, for he is said to have revealed to men the arts of carving, engraving, painting, and writing. The art of "speaking to the eye" began in early Egypt with the use of signs, which were the representations of actual objects. Then, for the sake of brevity, only parts of objects were indicated; for instance, the head of an ox became the recognised sign for the whole animal. Then the signs evolved into ideograms, which conveyed ideas by suggestion. Thus, supremacy and command were indicated by the paw of a lion; a stone battle-axe, used only by the king, indicated the king himself; an ostrich feather, worn only by the king, was the sign of justice; whilst the idea of immense multitude was suggested by a tadpole.

Thoth was also fabled to be the originator of medicine, music, and astronomy. He is said to have divided the year into twelve months of thirty days, and the gods of the Osirian cycle are held to have been born during the five extra days which it was afterwards found necessary to add to the original

360. The name Thoth is given to the first month in the year,[1] which begins on the 20th of July, when the star Sirius, called Sothis by the Greeks, and by the Egyptians Sopdit, rises at sunrise on the horizon, and when the yearly inundation of the Nile is about at its highest. Three days previously every family in ancient Egypt kept the festival by lighting new lamps fed with oil saturated with salt, whilst the priests kindled new fire for the sanctuaries. It seems probable that the Chaldæans were earlier students of the stars than the Egyptians. But Professor Maspero says that at the dawn of the historic period—which Professor Flinders Petrie tells us dates back about six thousand years—there was no temple in Egypt "which did not possess its official 'Watchers of the Night,' or Urshû." It was the duty of these watchers to observe all the movements of the thirty-six constellations, and to make notes of any fresh phenomena. There is still in existence a mutilated chart of the heavens which was drawn at Thebes, showing that at least five of the planets were well known and distinguished by their characteristic colours, viz. Jupiter (Uapshetatûi), Saturn (Kahiri), Mercury (Sobku), Mars (Doshiri), and Venus (Bonû), whose double aspect of morning-star (Tiu Nutiri) and evening-star (Uati, the Lonely One) was also familiar to the Egyptian astronomers. All the Egyptian temples were built with their front façade facing the exact point in the heavens at which, on a special day in

[1] The Egyptian months were called: 1, Thoth; 2, Phaophi; 3, Athyr; 4, Choiak; 5, Jybi; 6, Mechir; 7, Phamenoth; 8, Pharmuti; 9, Pachons; 10, Payni; 11, Epiphi; 12, Mesori.

the year, the star emblematic of the god to whom the temple was dedicated rose at sunrise.

We derive our knowledge of Egyptian thought partly from the voluminous inscriptions engraved on the monuments, partly from the very large number of papyri that have been found wrapped within the linen swathings of the mummies. In 1893, Dr Wallis Budge published a translation of the principal of these papyri, which, as they have mostly to do with the dead, are collectively known as "The Book of the Dead." Though grouped as a whole, these ancient texts appear to have had no regular sequence, until they "were copied and arranged" by the priests of Amen, during the reign of the twenty-sixth dynasty. Dr Budge tells us that, as early as 4200 B.C., or during the time of the second dynasty, these Egyptian texts not only "take the fact of a future life for granted, but assume its duration to be infinite"; and he brings evidence to show that the section known to students as Chapter 64, which dates from about this period, was "edited" five centuries later, or about 3733 B.C., by a son of the Pharaoh who built the Great Pyramid, who was called Herutatef, and "who is known from other sources as the author of various works." We get a good idea of the ethical thought of ancient Egypt from the 125th Chapter of the Book of the Dead, which is generally spoken of by Egyptologists as the Negative Confession. The form in which the text has come down to us dates only from the time of the eighteenth dynasty, but Dr Budge tells us that "the ideas that it contains are as old as the third dynasty."

From it we learn how thoroughly the Egyptian thinkers believed in the power of their good deeds to gain for them the enjoyment of life after death. The deceased therefore pleads that not only is he no murderer or manslaughterer, but has never incited others to commit murder, has stirred up no strife, and has given way to anger only "in a just cause." He asserts that he is neither an adulterer, nor unchaste. He pleads further that he has never "behaved insolently," nor "spoken haughtily," and that he has "abused no man." Further, that he has not sworn, has "not multiplied speech overmuch," has "not shut his ears to the words of right and wrong," has committed no kind of robbery, has "not sought to enrich himself at his neighbour's expense," has "not wasted his neighbour's ploughed land, nor defiled his running water." It is difficult, says Dr Budge, to render the exact shades of meaning of the Egyptian texts, but he assures us that "the general sense is well made out."

Dr Lepsius has translated a well-known papyrus, now at Berlin, from which we are able to gather some of the thoughts of an Egyptian about death. The writer says:—"I say to myself every day: As is the convalescence of a sick person who goes to Court after his affliction, such is death. . . .

"I say to myself, every day: As is the inhaling of the scent of a perfume, as is a seat beneath the shelter of an outstretched curtain, on that day, so is death. . . .

"I say to myself, every day: As is a road which passes over the flood of the inundation, as a man who goes as a soldier, whom nothing resists, such is death. . . ."

From the well-known Prisse papyrus in the Paris National Library we gather some Egyptian proverbs which are believed to have been written by Phtah-Hotep, whose tomb was discovered at Saqqâra. He says:—"Let thy countenance shine joyfully as long as thou livest. . . . Did a man ever leave the coffin, after having once entered it? . . . And if thou hast become great, after thou hast been lowly, and if thou hast amassed riches after poverty, so that, because of this, thou hast become the first in the city, . . . let not thy heart be lifted up because of thy riches, for the author of them is God. Despise not thy neighbour who is as thou wast, but treat him as thy equal."

Carl Niebuhr (1903) quotes also the song from the tomb of King Antef, composed by "the Harper":—"... Ruined are the dwellings of ancestors; they are as if they had never been, and no man returns from beyond to tell us what has become of them. . . . Adorn thyself as beautifully as may be, and let not thine heart fail thee so long as thou remainest on earth. Trouble not thyself until the day of mourning breaks. For he whose heart has ceased to beat hears no lamentation, he who rests in the grave shares not thy grief. Therefore, let your days be glad, your countenance joyful; and be not idle, for no man takes his possessions with him, nor does he ever return."

It was the conviction of the Egyptians that every word, spoken or written, must surely produce its result. Hence the practice of placing sacred texts in the tombs and coffins with the mummies: it being hoped that these texts, in some mysterious way, would aid the deceased during his progress through the underworld. The practice of "mummifying" the dead was, according to Dr Wallis Budge, adopted in Egypt "certainly as early as 4500 B.C." The process was tedious and costly, sometimes costing as much as £240. But, although the dead were preserved with such care, there is nothing to show us that the Egyptians expected any actual reanimation of the man's physical body, or Khât. Their hope and expectation appears to have been, that the Khât would, as they expressed it, "germinate," and that from it, in due course, would emanate the Kâ, that which the Greeks called the "eidolon," and which we call "the double." The Kâ was the vehicle, or medium, through which the deceased would enjoy a quasi-life, similar to the life he had enjoyed before his death. The Kâ was supposed to animate the effigy or statue of the deceased, which was placed in the sepulchral chamber adjacent to the tomb, and therefore it was the aim of all who could afford it to secure, before death, as accurate a likeness of themselves as possible. This accounts for the remarkably lifelike Kâ-statues found in some of the Egyptian tombs, which may now be seen in the museum at Cairo. These portrait-statues reveal to us a phase of Egyptian art very different from the conventional sculptures on the monuments. Kings and very rich men always had one or more replicas carved of their Kâ-statues, which replicas were concealed in or near the chamber of the Kâ, which might serve the Kâ as a resting-place in case of accident: it was thought that any injury, accidental or wilful, inflicted on the statue would be felt by the Kâ, whilst, if there existed only one portrait of the deceased, its complete destruction would be disastrous. In most of "the houses of the Kâ" we find the walls covered with engraved or painted scenes, illustrating the past life of the deceased. We see him surrounded by his servants and by everything that made his life worth having. These illustrations, says Professor Maspero, had all "a magical purpose," the purpose being that this pictured world of men and things around the Kâ should help him to enjoy his phantom-life. In some way also it was believed that fresh air, food, and drink were necessary to the proper existence of the Kâ, and therefore it was the custom of wealthy Egyptians to endow their sepulchral-chapels with "priests of the Kâ," whose constant duty it was, at certain intervals of time, to place before the Kâ-statue offerings of food and drink, whilst the Kâ-chamber was always kept properly ventilated. In some of the texts buried with the mummy, we find the deceased expressing the hope that he may enjoy "the sweet breath of the north wind," and also that "I may eat my food under the sycamore of my lady the goddess Hâthor."

But we find that the Kâ, important as it was held to be, did not constitute the whole of the spiritual element in man. On the contrary, the individual was thought to be made up of no less than seven constituent elements, viz. the Khât (physical body), the Kâ (double), the Bâ (soul), the Khû (luminous vehicle), the Sekhem (vital force), the Ren (name), and the Khaibil (shadow). So far, Egyptologists have not been able to fix the exact relation of these seven postulated elements to one another. Dr Wallis Budge suggests that they "probably represented several stages of intellectual development"; but, at any rate, he says that they were "accepted as a fact" at least as early as the fifth and sixth dynasties. That the Kâ and the Bâ were not considered to be identical is clear, because, whilst the Kâ was held to animate the Kâ-statues, the Bâ was supposed to pass directly after death to the Judgment of Osiris, in the "Hall of Truth." Here the soul of the deceased witnessed the process of balancing all the good thoughts and good deeds of its past life against the standard of normal human virtue—the man was, in fact, his own judge of his future fate. If the balance (which on the monuments is represented as a feather) dipped ever so little in his favour, the soul passed joyfully onward to find rest in Aahlû (Pools of Peace). But, if the sum of the man's good thoughts and good deeds did not reach the normal standard, Osiris ordered the soul to pass through a series of transmigrations, which gave it many chances of becoming more spiritual; and if it failed to seize these opportunities of improving its condition, it was ultimately condemned to annihilation. The earliest versions of the texts contain no reference to this judgment of the soul by Osiris, but they are very frequent in the papyri about 1550 B.C.

Although the ancient Egyptians took so much thought about the long and shadowy existence which they hoped to enjoy after death, and did everything they could to ensure the preservation of their mummies and Kâ-statues, on which they thought so much depended, they appear to have been by no means a melancholy people, but thoroughly to have enjoyed their short span of human life. This is the opinion of Brügsch Bey, who lived so long in the country and had the opportunity of the most exhaustive study of the monuments and inscriptions. "Travel," he says, "through the land of the old Pharaohs, look at the pictures carved and painted on the walls of the sepulchral chapels, read the words cut in stone, or written in black ink on papyrus, and you will be obliged to admit that (instead of being reflective, serious, reserved, religious, occupied only with the other world, and caring little or nothing about this lower life) no people could be gayer, more lively, of more childlike simplicity than these old Egyptians. They loved life with all their hearts, and found the deepest joy in their mere existence. . . . Above all things they regarded justice, and virtue had in their eyes the highest value. The law which ordered them to 'pray to the gods, to honour the dead, to give bread to the hungry, water to the thirsty, clothing to the naked,' reveals to us the finest qualities of the old Egyptian character—pity towards the unfortunate." And indeed, when we think of the climate of Egypt, where frost and snow are unknown, and rain is of very rare occurrence, we need not be surprised to find the people depicted on their monuments as a joyous, light-hearted race, who lived in the present, leaving the morrow to take care of itself. Many a droll caricature found on the walls also indicates such a temperament. And this also was the opinion of Herodotus, who spent a long time at Memphis about 550 B.C. He tells us with what gaiety the Egyptians of his day kept all their festivals, and he has preserved for us a popular song of the period which says:—

> "Men are aye passing away,
> And youths are taking their place.
> As Râ rises up every morn,
> As Tûm every evening doth set,
> So women conceive and bring forth,
> So men without ceasing beget.
> Each soul in its turn draweth breath:
> Each man born of woman sees death.
> Take thy pleasure to-day,
> Mind thee of joy and delight;
> Soon life's pilgrimage ends,
> And we pass into silence and night. . . .
> Let all then think of the day
> Of departure without a return.
> 'Twill be well to have lived
> Spurning injustice and sin;
> For he who has loved the right,
> In the hour which none can flee,
> Enters upon the delight
> Of a glad eternity. . . .
> Give freely out of thy store,
> And thou shalt be blest evermore!"

CHAPTER II

BABYLONIAN THOUGHT

TO-DAY, as we look down the broad valley of the lower Euphrates, the aspect of the country is that of a succession of swamps. But there was a time when, owing to an admirable system of irrigation, this region was the most fertile in the then known world, and attracted immigrants from far and near—from the Persian Gulf on the east, from the mountain-region beyond Susa on the north, and from the Arabian highlands on the south. Even now, the rich alluvial soil of Babylonia produces in places splendid crops: palm-trees flourish, and also apricots, oranges, vines, and nuts. Herodotus tells us that, as late as 550 B.C., the yield of corn was commonly two hundred-fold, and he describes "the blades of the wheat-plant" as measuring "four fingers broad." Therefore, knowing that mankind everywhere has always been wandering down from the keen air and hard living in the highlands to the softer air and easier life in the lowlands, we need not wonder that all sorts of nomadic tribes flocked into this "paradise." As far as we can find out, however, no people ever appear to have been the first anywhere. Each nomadic race has always found some other race already settled in any region into which it wandered. The earlier comers generally gave way to the later, being already softened by their residence in the plains, and the more energetic among them moved on farther, whilst the indolent only remained behind to become the vassals and slaves of the more vigorous strangers. But occasionally the two races settled down quietly side by side, and more or less intermingled, each adopting some of the civilisation, customs, and language of the other. And this, as our discoveries of the primitive language of the ancient inscriptions show, is just what happened, over and over again, in the country watered by the Tigris and Euphrates.

We derive our knowledge of ancient Babylonia from the monuments and inscriptions which have been found there, chiefly during the last half-century. Some of these take us back to about 4500 B.C., the date ascribed to them by Dr Wallis Budge, the Curator of Egyptian Antiquities at the British Museum, in the handbook to the collection of Chaldæan and Babylonian antiquities which he published in 1900. The earliest inscriptions yet discovered come from Largash, Ur, and Uruk. It was at Largash that M. de Sarzec made those valuable discoveries in 1881, of the statues and inscriptions now to be seen in the Louvre. The records we have of the very earliest civilisation of Lower Babylonia are inscriptions in a non-Semitic language, which are engraved in cuneiform characters. This language, now called the Sumerian or Akkadian, is the oldest civilised speech known; and, long after it ceased to be spoken, it was used in Babylonia as a sacred or learned language, just as Latin was used in Europe in mediæval times. The Akkadian is one of those dialects known as "agglutinative," because the words are, so to say, simply "stuck together," thus avoiding any kind of grammatical change. François Lenormant thinks that Akkadian is akin not only to the language spoken at ancient Shushan, but also to other still earlier Turanian dialects. The name Akkadian or Sumerian was given to this language because it was discovered that the earliest known Semitic rulers in Lower Babylonia styled themselves in their inscriptions, after their conquest of the country, "king of the Sumerians and Akkadians." The word "Akkad" means "mountain," whilst the word "Sumir" means "plain." From this fact it is inferred that, in prehistoric times, the Akkadians came down from the highlands beyond Shushan (later known as Elam) and amalgamated with the lowland race of Sumerians whom they found there. In support of this theory François Lenormant points out that many of the signs which are found in the cuneiform Akkadian writing must have been invented by a people who not only had copper and gold, and conifers, but who were also familiar with wolves and bears, none of which metals, trees, or animals are to be found in the low country by the Euphrates. The number of implements, weapons, and ornaments of gold, copper, and iron found in Akkadian tombs distinctly show us that this people were skilful workers in metal.

During his excavations in the great mound at Koyunjik, on the Tigris, formed by the ruins of the vast palace of Asshurbanipal, king of Assyria, Layard came upon a very remarkable collection of tablets of baked clay, mostly engraved in the language of Akkad. Our experts have since deciphered a large proportion of these tablets, and have gained from them a very considerable knowledge of the history of early Babylonia. It appears that the collection was begun by Sargon of Assyria, 722 B.C., and added to later by both Sennacherib and Esarhaddon. But it was Asshurbanipal, 668 B.C., who resolved to make the records of the early history of his realm as complete as possible, by commanding that copies of all tablets and inscriptions preserved in the various temples of Lower Babylonia should be sent to Nineveh. Asshurbanipal says, in his own inscriptions: "I have inscribed upon tablets the noble products of the work of the scribe, which none of the kings who have gone before me had learned, together with the wisdom of Nabû, so far as it existeth. I have arranged them in classes, I have placed them in my palace." The result is that to-day, as Dr Wallis Budge tells us, we find among the twenty thousand cuneiform tablets now in the British Museum "lists of cuneiform signs with their phonetic values," as well as "vocabularies of the old, disused Akkadian language," placed side by side, on the same tablets with the Assyrian language of the time of Asshurbanipal. The amount of early Babylonian thought which has thus come down to us is, Dr Sayce says, "greater than that contained in the whole of the Old Testament." And this is all the more valuable since these early Akkadian "texts present us with the actual words of the original writer, whereas the text of the Old Testament has come to us through the hands of successive generations of copyists, who have corrupted many passages."

The outcome of the study of all these ancient records is the theory that the earliest civilisation of Lower Babylonia was that of the Akkadians, who appear to have been one of the many yellow-skinned Turanian races which came down from their highlands into the plain near the Persian Gulf, and mingled with the dark-skinned Kushite or Ethiopian race which they found there. After a time this early civilisation was invaded by an olive-skinned Semitic race of Bedawîn from the Arabian highlands. We learn from the inscriptions that all the Akkadian towns had earlier Turanian names, and that later these Akkadian names were translated into Semitic names. And when we get our first glimpse, about 4500 B.C., of the four chief Akkadian cities—Largash, Uruk, Ur, and Larsa—we find that each is very populous, that its inhabitants are employed in many industries and carry on a thriving trade, and that records are kept in a complete system of hieroglyphic writing. Each of these cities is surrounded by a tract of highly cultivated agricultural land, and each, even at this early epoch, seems already to have been more or less Semitised. Who then, we ask, were these conquering Semites?—and the only answer seems to be that they belonged to that ancient

Arabian race whose later representatives are known to history as Assyrians, Aramæans, Phœnicians, and Jews. The name Semite, or Shemite, is due to our biblical commentators, who derive it from Shem, the legendary son of the legendary Noah. In Eastern languages the terms "son" and "father" were picturesquely used to indicate that the one thing was the outcome of the other. For instance, Sidon, the earliest known seaport of importance on the Mediterranean, was called "the first-born of Canaan." Most early races liked to boast of a divine ancestor, whose name was usually derived from that of the race itself. Thus the name "Heber" was invented as that of the divine ancestor of the Hebrews, and the name "Aram" as that of the divine progenitor of the Aramæans, whilst the divine ancestor of the Assyrians was known as Asshur. This, it will be seen, was an easy way to explain difficult things to the unthinking. Then, to carry the idea of this divine ancestry further back, Heber, Aram, and Asshur were fabled to be the "sons" of the legendary Shem. Thus our modern historians have got into the way of grouping together the kindred races—Assyrians, Aramæans, Phœnicians, and Jews—as "Shemites," or Semites. Professor Sayce says that the expression sons of Shem, sons of Ham, or sons of Japhet is merely a figurative way of saying that they belonged to one of the lighter- or darker-skinned races of Western Asia. And he explains that "Shem" is identical with the Assyrian word "samu," which means "olive-coloured"; that "Ham" is the Assyrian word "khamma," which means "burnt black"; and that "Japhet" is the Assyrian word "ippat," which means "white race."

All the recent discoveries made by Botha, Layard, De Sarzec, George Smith, Sayce, Flinders Petrie, and others bear out the statement made in 261 A.D. by Berosus, that the inhabitants of Babylonia were a much mixed race. In his *Istoria Kaldaika*, which Berosus compiled from ancient temple-records at the command of Alexander the Great, who wanted to know the past history of his new realm, he says: "There were originally in Babylon a multitude of men of foreign race who settled there." An interesting fact about the early rulers of Babylonia is their passion for leaving records of themselves and their doings for posterity. They not only had their names stamped on the bricks with which they built their palaces and temples, but whenever they restored an ancient temple they took care to place in some safe spot in the basement carefully protected cylinders of hard stone or baked clay, on which were engraved a record of the chief facts of their reign. It is from these that we derive so much of our information.

Starting from Eridu, the city nearest to the Persian Gulf, the traveller comes successively to the ancient sites of Ur, Largash, Nippur, Uruk, and Babylon. Still higher up the Euphrates are the sites of Agadê and Sippar. We gather from the records that all these old Sumerian or Akkadian towns were constantly at war with each other, and nearly each of them seems, at one time or another to have been paramount in the country. Of the kings who ruled them we often know little more than the names.

Gudea, who ruled at Largash, tells us that in building his palace he got stone from Magan (Arabia) and cedar-wood from Amanus. We know, indeed, that Ur-Gur, and Dungi, his son, were kings of Ur, but the first king, as far as we know, who assumed the title of "king of Sumir and Akkad" is the ruler of Agadê, Shargani-sha-Ali, generally called Sharrukin, and better known to us by his later Hellenised name, "Sargon." He began to reign about 3795 B.C. Dr Flinders Petrie found monuments and inscriptions of his both at Nippur and Largash. In the British Museum may be seen his cylinder-signet, and that of his son, Naram-Sin, who succeeded him in 3750 B.C. Though engraved about 5700 years ago, the signet-cylinder of Sharrukin is really a work of art. It represents the legendary hero Gilgamesh and the sacred oxen: the figure of the man is archaic, but the long-horned oxen are carved with much observation of nature, with spirit, and with technical skill.

In the records of his achievements, engraved on his monuments and cylinders, Sharrukin relates his warlike expeditions westwards as far as Phœnicia, and tells of the great spoil which he brought back from "the sea of the setting sun." The historical value of these records is amply confirmed by the recent discoveries made by Professor Hilprecht, more especially the account of Sharrukin's expedition to the Mediterranean coast, and that of his son, Naram-Sin, against the Bedawîn of Magan, the district now known as the Peninsula of Sinai; whilst still more recent excavations, made by the American exploring party under Mr

Haines, have "unearthed monuments," says Dr Sayce, "of older date than those of Sargon of Akkad" (Sharrukin). Speaking of his achievements, Sharrukin says: "For forty-five years the kingdom I have ruled, and have governed the black-headed race. In multitudes of bronze chariots I rode over rugged lands: I ruled the upper countries." And he gives us a graphic picture of his own early life. He tells us that, as an infant, he was abandoned by his mother, the "princess" who gave birth to him, near the river Euphrates, "in an inaccessible place: in a basket of rushes she placed me: with bitumen the door of my ark she closed: on the river she launched me, which drowned me not: the river bore me along: to Akki, the water-carrier, it brought me: Akki, the water-carrier, in the tenderness of his heart, lifted me up: Akki made me his gardener: in my gardenership the goddess Ishtar loved me" (translated by Professor Sayce). When one reads this picturesque account of the desertion of Sharrukin, it is impossible to avoid the inference that it was the original source from which three thousand years later Ezra, in Babylon, derived his story of the finding of Moses.

About 1500 years after the time of Sharrukin, as we learn from the ancient temple-records preserved to us by Asshurbanipal, a king of Shushan, named Khudur-Nank-hundi or Kudur-Mabuk, pillaged the city of Uruk and subdued the whole of Lower Babylonia. Eighty years later, however, Khammurabi, the Bedawîn ruler at Bab-Il, higher up the Euphrates, was powerful enough to drive out the invaders; and from the time of Khammurabi (2250 B.C.) Bab-Il—

better known to us under its Greek name, Babylon —became the governing centre of the whole of Babylonia, which the Assyrians called Kaldu and the Greeks Chaldæa. Bab-Il, the Semitic name, is a direct translation of its earlier Akkadian name, Ka-Râ (Gate or House of God), but the earliest name of this ancient city was Tin-Tir (Place of the Tree of Life). Of all ancient allegories which attempt to set forth the ever-attractive mystery of the source and origin of life, the allegory of the "tree of life" is probably the oldest. We find it engraved on the earliest tablets and monuments yet discovered in the valley of the Euphrates. Many of these pictures of the tree of life are very archaic in character: they always show us the typical male and female, sometimes sitting, sometimes standing, one on each side of the tree, and generally reaching forth a hand to pluck the fruit, whilst behind them, erect like a staff, rises the serpent. The serpent is depicted sometimes between the pair, sometimes behind the woman, and in some instances seems almost emerging from her back. Dr Sayce tells us that the river Euphrates was called the stream of Heâ, the serpent-god of the tree of life. He also says that "Adam was a Babylonian word, and had the general sense of 'man,'" and he adds that "the 'Adamites,' in the old Babylonian legends, were the white race of Semitic descent, who stood in marked contrast to the 'Black-heads' or Akkadians"; whilst Professor Rawlinson aptly suggests that the Jewish legend of the "sons of God" taking to wife "the daughters of men" is an allegory of the intermingling of the Semites with the Sumir-Akkadians. A number of the official documents of Khammurabi are among the Chaldæan tablets in the British Museum, and quite recently, amid the ruins of Shushan, there has been found a very remarkable tablet engraved with the code of laws enacted by him. The sculptures on this tablet show Khammurabi standing before a god, who is surrounded by flames and who is evidently dictating to him the laws. Here again it is difficult to avoid the inference that we have the probable origin of the idea of the Jewish writer who lived in Babylon nearly a thousand years later,[1] and who describes the delivery of the Tablets or Tables of the Law to the legendary Moses by Yahveh amidst the thunder and lightning of Sinai. We have in the British Museum, at present, no Babylonian relic earlier than 4500 B.C.; but there are tablets in the museum at Constantinople, discovered lately by Professor Hilprecht, which are covered with cuneiform inscriptions believed to be quite two thousand years earlier. Be that as it may, there can be no question that the inhabitants of Babylonia, whether Akkadian or Semitic, must be considered to be the earliest literary people of whom we have any record. We find on one of their engraved tablets, indeed, that their idea of chaos was "the time when as yet no tablets were written"; or, as Professor Maspero puts it, "in Chaldæa nothing was supposed to have real existence until it received a name." The earliest Babylonian

[1] Khammurabi reigned from 2267 to 2213 B.C., according to Dr Winckler, who suggests that the strong wave of Semitic immigration which entered Babylonia about this time, and left such permanent traces in Syria and Canaan, may perhaps account for the appearance of the Semites known as "Hyksos" in Egypt.

code of laws was called "the Writings of Hoâ" (or Heâ). In later times, the name of this deity was Hellenised as Oë. Hence the name of "Oannes" (Oâ-ana, the god Hoâ), whom Berosus describes in his *Istoria Kaldaika* as emerging from the Persian Gulf to teach civilisation to men.

There are two early Akkadian laws, recorded in "the Writings of Hoâ," which show us that, in some respects, the Akkadian civilisation was higher than the Semitic. One of these laws protects a slave from the tyranny and cruelty of his master, the other asserts the precedence of the wife to her husband in all matters pertaining to the family life. Any son who denied his father was fined a sum of money; but if he denied his mother, he was banished from the country. It is typical of the Semitic race that they reversed all laws of this kind when once their power was supreme in Babylonia. Thus, a later law enacts that any son who denies his mother should be driven forth with execration, but that the son who denies his father should be branded and sold as a slave in the market. The desire to have a son was always great in the East, so that it was a frequent custom to adopt one. There is a tablet in the British Museum which recites that "Abd-Iskhara, son of Ibni-Samas, has Ibni-Samas adopted as his son. If Abd-Iskhara to his father shall say, 'Thou art not my father,' he shall cast him in fetters and sell him. But, if Ibni-Samas to Abd-Iskhara shall say, 'Thou art not my son,' he shall leave the house and estate, but shall take his portion, and carry it away as one of the children."

According to Professor Sayce, the Akkadian texts

always read "woman and man," but the Assyrian texts always read "man and woman." He says: "It is curious to find the Semitic translator of an Akkadian text invariably changing the order in which the words man and woman, male and female occur in the original." The Babylonian woman became more and more degraded as the country became more and more Semitised, till, at last, not only were marriageable girls sold at public auction to the highest bidders, but the still grosser ordinance was practised of religious prostitution. This ordinance compelled every woman, whatever her rank, to offer herself once in her life to the embrace of a stranger in the temple of the goddess Ishtar. The marriage of every Semitic woman was practically a sale, the bridegroom receiving from the father of his wife a formal receipt for the stipulated sum. This was sometimes "a golden mina," although the average price paid for a wife was "ten shekels of silver." When tired of his wife, the husband could easily rid himself of her, and, in certain cases, might sell her. Women of the higher ranks, however, were partially protected by a dower from their father; the dower being always somewhat in excess of the price paid for the wife by the husband. This sum served to support the woman in case of widowhood or repudiation.

Innumerable tablets of baked clay attest that, from a very early date, usury was a recognised business in Babylonia. We have also a large collection of promissory notes, contracts of sale. and cunningly worded deeds of all kinds. Bargains were written out by a public scribe, and duly witnessed. In the case of a loan, the amount borrowed, the time of repayment, and the interest agreed upon, with a penal clause in case of non-payment, were inscribed on a tablet of soft clay, and stamped with the signet-cylinders of both the contracting parties. The tablet, after having been baked in a kiln, was enclosed in a clay box, on the outside of which the chief facts of the contract were also engraved, and then the outer case also was baked, as a safeguard against tampering with the legal document within. Several of such contracts are preserved in the British Museum. Both duodecimal and decimal systems were used in reckoning, all values being calculated upon the standard value of corn. Agriculture was carried to great perfection in Babylonia, treatises on the best methods of corn-culture being kept for public reference in every temple. Systematic observations of the sun, moon, and stars were habitually made, from the topmost platforms of the Babylonian Ziggurats. These Ziggurats consisted of a series of rectangular mounds, or platforms, raised one above the other, decreasing in size as they ascended, with a temple crowning the topmost mound. From a distance, the appearance of a Ziggurat was that of a pyramid, or rather pyramidal hill. The literal translation of the word "Ziggurat" is "mountain"; hence we may infer that the Babylonian Ziggurats symbolised the "Holy Mountain," or "Mountain of the Lord," mentioned in many of the earliest inscriptions. This mountain was fabled to be sometimes in the north, sometimes in the east, sometimes in the north-east, and was also revered as "Father of Countries" and as "Mountain of Countries." Ziggurats differed in the number of their platforms or stages, according to the special idea of which each Ziggurat was symbolical. A Ziggurat of three tiers only was an emblem of the highest Divine Triad, viz. Anu, Heâ, and Bel; or of the lower Divine Triad—Sin, Shamash, and Ramân. A Ziggurat of five stages was emblematic of the five planets, whilst one consisting of seven platforms was a symbol of the sun, moon, and five planets.[1] The great Ziggurat built, as the inscription tells us, by Nebuchadnezzar in 600 B.C., at Bars-Nimroud, on the west bank of the Euphrates, was measured by Rawlinson. It rises in seven tiers to the height of 156 feet above the river, and on its highest platform once stood the temple of Nebo. This temple was also called "the temple of the Seven Lights of the Earth." Traces remain of the colours symbolic of the sun, moon, and planets, with which the several platforms were decorated. The tier which represented the sun was faced with plates of beaten gold.

In earlier times the year was divided into thirteen lunar months of twenty-eight days each; but the Chaldæan or Babylonian astronomers divided the year into twelve months, each of thirty days, and, in order to bring their calendar periodically into harmony with the course of the sun, they added an extra month every sixth year. Time was reckoned in ancient Babylonia by three different cycles, called

[1] "We know of Ziggurats," says Professor Maspero, "at Uru, Eridhu, Uruk, and Babylon." Ziggurats were so placed that either their four corners or their four sides faced exactly north, south, east, and west.

"sos," "ner," and "sar." The "sos" was a cycle of sixty years; the "ner" was a cycle of six hundred years; whilst the "sar" was a great cycle of three thousand six hundred years. These early astronomers calculated the exact time of the winter and summer solstices, and autumn and spring equinoxes. François Lenormant thinks there is evidence also that they calculated the precessions of the equinoxes. They certainly divided the apparent course of the sun through the heavens into twelve "houses" corresponding to the later "signs of the zodiac." When Alexander of Macedon went to Babylon, he took in his train of followers Calisthenes, the nephew of Aristotle, who, whilst there, sent home to his uncle numerous copies of Babylonian records of observations made by the magi, two thousand years earlier, of the aspects of the constellations, of the movements of the planets towards and away from the earth, of the relative brightness of the fixed stars, and of the eclipses of sun and moon. The sun-dial also was well known in Babylon.

In the Akkadian dialect a priest was called "imga," which was Semitised into "mag," from which word come the Latin "magus" and our own words "magic" and "magician." The chief-priest was the "Rab-mag," the seer, the knower, the man who both saw and foresaw more than his fellow-men. Divination was practised by the magi, and astrological tables were kept in every temple library which all might consult at will. A collection of seventy astronomical and astrological tablets has been discovered, which experts attribute to the time of Sharrukin.

Akkadian religious thought is based on the idea that the universe is ruled by spirits, which are immanent throughout nature. These spirits were supposed to guide the course of sun, moon, and stars, to bring sunshine and rain, to cause vegetation to germinate and bring forth fruit, and to watch over and protect the lives of animals and men. These were beneficent spirits. But there were also spirits of evil, who caused storms, drought, earthquakes, pestilence, and death, and against these the Chaldæans practised a system of magical incantations. By day, the evil spirits might be ignored, but they were to be dreaded when once the protecting sun had sunk below the horizon. Therefore, of all the good spirits, the most popular was Gibir or Gibil,[1] the Spirit of Fire. "O Gibil, valiant son of the Abyss! Thy clear flame, breaking forth, lightens the darkness. . . . Thou art he who exposes his breast to the mighty enemy!" The Semites brought with them into Chaldæa their own Sabæan worship, and thus the adoration of sun, moon, and stars gradually modified the earlier belief in nature-spirits, so that, as time went on, three great spirits only were invoked, viz. the rulers of "the Three Spheres." The first "Sphere" was the realm of the god Anu: it was "the Highest Heaven," the far-off region of the fixed stars. The second "Sphere" was the realm of the god Heâ: it was "the Lower Heaven," the region traversed by the sun, moon, and planets. The third

[1] "Gibil" was the name specially given to the sacred fire which was produced by friction from an instrument of reeds similar to the "arani" or fire-drill of Vedic India.

"Sphere" was the realm of the god Im—also called Vul, Mulge, and Mermer: it was "the Heavenly Ocean" or "the Great Deep," the storehouse of winds and storms and fertilising showers—in fact, the atmosphere of the earth.

These three great Akkadian gods, with the Semitic sun- and moon- and star-gods, constituted the objects of Chaldæan worship. But, beyond these, the later thinkers of Chaldæa postulated a Supreme Principle of the universe, which they spoke of simply as "the God" (Ilu). But, though "Ilu" gave its name to Bab-Ilu, the chief city, no temple was ever erected in Chaldæa to this abstract deity, nor was Ilu ever an object of the popular worship.

The temple at Uruk was dedicated to Anu, and that at Ur to Heâ. But both these deities became, in course of time, mere symbols or personifications of abstract ideas. Anu, who was invoked as "the Ancient One," "the Progenitor," and "the One," symbolised undifferentiated cosmic substance. Heâ, who was invoked as "He who raises the dead to life," "God of pure Life," "the fatherless One," who is eternally reproduced within the bosom of "the Great Deep" or "the Heavenly Ocean," symbolised the spirit of universal life. François Lenormant says that Heâ "is the intelligence which animates matter and renders it fertile, which penetrates the universe, and inspires it with life." Exoterically, Heâ was regarded as the god who assumed an earthly form—that of "the Divine Fish"—in order to teach mankind the arts of civilisation. His most popular emblem, especially at the "holy city" of Eridhu, was the serpent. Here was the sacred grove or "garden of Heâ," which was fabled to be the centre of the world, in which "the tree of life and knowledge" has its roots. The last of the three great dieties of the "Spheres" is Im, or Mermer, who personified the earth's atmosphere. He was invoked as "Lord of the Air" and "Lord of Fruitfulness." He is said to carry a flaming sword, and is represented on the monuments with a stone battle-axe or hammer, like the Scandinavian god Thor, or with three forked flames suggestive of lightning. In Chaldæa his name was Semitised as Rammân; but in Aramæa, or Syria, he was worshipped as chief deity under the name of Rimmon.

The deities inferior to the three "Rulers of the Spheres" were the rulers of the sun, moon, and five planets. The sun-god was called Ud, Babba, and Meridug, his later Semitic name being Shamash. At Babylon he was worshipped as Merodach, or Marduk, and at last simply as Bel ("the Lord"), which, in Syria and Phœnicia, became Baal. He is perhaps most frequently called Merodach, and adored as "Healer of Disease" and "Friend of Man." He is of course the "son" of Heâ, and is said to be continually passing from heaven to earth, and back again from earth to heaven, as the divine messenger of his father. "In a considerable number of hymns," says Professor Sayce, "Merodach is invoked as 'Restorer to Life,' 'Redeemer of Mankind,' 'Intercessor.'" He is, in fact, the earliest expression in Chaldæan thought of the idea of a mediator or saviour. Merodach is also called "the Avenger" who crushes Tiamat. On one of the tablets we read: "The neck of Tiamat swiftly shalt thou trample under foot." The moon-god was called Uriki. His Semitic name was Sin. The ruler of the planet Saturn was called Adar; the ruler of Jupiter, Marduk; the ruler of Mars, Nergal; the ruler of Venus, Ishtar; and the ruler of Mercury, Nebo. It is confusing to find that "Marduk" is also one of the later names of the sun-god, until we realise the fact that all the "great gods" are held to form a hierarchy of co-equal powers, that all in turn are invoked as "Chief of the Gods," and that each of the eight is credited, at times, with all the particular attributes of the others. Layard found inscriptions in the palace of Nebuchadnezzar at Babylon, in which Marduk is invoked as "Lord of Lords" and "Elder of the Gods."

In course of time Chaldæan thinkers made the discovery that all action is followed by reaction, and that force may be passive as well as active, or, as they expressed it, feminine as well as masculine. Therefore, to give expression to this idea, they postulated a "goddess" as the natural and necessary complement to every "god." Sometimes the goddess is suggestively invoked as the "reflection" of the god. The three chief goddesses, as popularly worshipped, were Nanâ (wife of Anu), Davkina (wife of Heâ), and Belit (wife of Bel). The goddesses, like the gods, became in time all practically merged into one, who was the personification of the passive, productive force of nature, and who was adored as "the Great Mother," and as "Queen of Fertility." Her Semitic name was Ishtar, and her symbol in the heavens was the planet Venus, "the Star of Love," at whose rising, after sunset, "man and woman are drawn together by mutual desire." But, when the Chaldæan astronomers had discovered that Venus was also, at times, the morning-star, it became necessary to credit the goddess with other attributes. Thus she was also invoked as Belit-Anunit, the chaste warrior-queen, who scorned all sexual love, like the Artemis of the later Hellenes. Ishtar had therefore a twofold aspect: in one she personified chastity and war, in the other love and lasciviousness. Under her latter aspect she was chiefly worshipped at Babylon by the name of Mulita, which later was Hellenised as Mylitta.

The fact that each spring the earth receives anew the warm caresses of the sun, that under his stimulating force she once more unveils her beauty of verdure and blossom, and once more bears fruit, was poetised by early Chaldæan bards as the love of Ishtar and Dumuzi.[1] The ancient mythos relates how the goddess first saw Dumuzi, the beautiful young shepherd, the son of Heâ and Davkina (Heaven and Earth), as he was tending his flock beneath the shade of the "tree of life" at Eridhu, and how their love came to an untimely end when Dumuzi[2] was killed by a wild boar—the synonym for the frost of winter—and passed away to the "realm of Allat," to "the land without return." Ishtar determines to follow her lover. But all who

[1] Dumuzi is an early Akkadian name for Shamash, the sun-god.

[2] The festival of Dumuzi was held, in Chaldæa, at the time of the summer solstice. It lasted for the first six days of the month Dûz (June-July).

enter the kingdom of Allat, queen of the underworld, must do so "naked as they were born," and we see on the old Chaldæan tablets that even Ishtar is forced to obey this law. At length she succeeds in reaching Dumuzi, called on one of the tablets "the only son, taken away before his time," and once more wakes him to life and love. In course of time this ancient mythos travelled westwards from Chaldæa. The Semites of Syria called the young son-god Dumuzi "Tammuz," whilst the Hellenes later called him "Adonis."

Inscriptions relating to Chaldæan sun-worship are very numerous; but the most picturesque record yet discovered of it is contained on a series of twelve tablets which were first deciphered by George Smith in 1872. At present the first tablet of the series is wanting, but of the other eleven we have two copies of each, which were found in the library of Asshurbanipal. These tablets relate the adventures of a prehistoric hero named Gilgamesh, who lived at the ancient city of Surippak (Uruk). "Gilgamesh" is, according to Professor Rawlinson, an earlier form of "Shamash," the Semitic name of the Chaldæan sun-god, and there can be no doubt that he is the original type of the later Greek "Herakles," and still later Jewish "Samson." The twelve tablets correspond, not only to the months of the Chaldæan year, but also to the twelve "signs" of the zodiac. Professor Sayce fixes the date of this Chaldæan epic at about 2500 B.C., when, owing to the precession of the equinoxes, the sign "Taurus," which had previously been the first sign in the zodiac, became the second;

but he says that, whatever may be the date of the poem in its present form, it certainly "embodies much older legends." He considers that the "Nemean lion," slain by Herakles in the later Greek legend, is identical with the lion[1] slain by Gilgamesh, and that the "deadly sickness" with which the hero is afflicted is identical with the raging fever which prostrated Herakles when he put on "the poisoned tunic" of Nessos. Sayce also suggests that the "winged bull" of Crete—a legend of a still later date—may perhaps also be identical with the monster created by special desire of Ishtar to revenge the refusal of her love.

Like Dumuzi, Gilgamesh is beloved by Ishtar, but unlike him, the hero flies from the embraces of the insatiable goddess of nature. In consequence of his refusal of her love the angry Ishtar smites him with a dire disease, to cure himself of which Gilgamesh starts on a journey to the "Mountain of the Sunset," at the uttermost confines of the world. After a series of adventures, the hero crosses "the Waters of Death" and reaches "the Island of the Blessed." Here he finds not only the "Fountain of Perpetual Youth" and the "Tree of Life," but also his own immortal grandsire, "Shamash-naphistim," or, as the British Museum authorities prefer to call him, "Tsît-naphistim." Of him Gilgamesh asks the secret of immortality. In reply, his grandsire relates to him

[1] This is the subject of the fifth tablet, which corresponds to the sign "Leo" of the zodiac. The lion was the symbol throughout the East for the scorching sun-heat. The old Chaldæan name for this month is "Fire making fire": it is the month of the summer solstice.

the story of the great deluge which once overwhelmed the city of Surippak, and tells him how the god Heâ ordered him to build a great ship to save himself and his family, which, when the flood subsided, was left grounded on the great mountains of the land of Nitsir. The story of this deluge forms the subject of the eleventh tablet of the epic of Gilgamesh. The tablet corresponds to the zodiacal sign "Aquarius," and to the eleventh month of the Chaldæan calendar—our January-February—which is the rainy season in the valley of the Euphrates. Haupt's translation of this tablet leaves no doubt that it was the origin of the Pentateuch version of the legendary Flood. "This city was already very ancient when the gods were moved in their hearts to command a great flood," says Shamash-naphistim to Gilgamesh. Then he relates to his grandson how he was warned by the god Heâ that the other "great gods" had resolved "to destroy the seed of life: but, do thou preserve it. Bring into the ship seed of every kind of life . . . and close the door, when the time comes. . . ." "Then, when Shamash brought round the appointed time, a voice spoke to me: 'This evening the heavens will rain destruction. Wherefore, go thou into the ship, and close the door.' . . . Then a great black cloud rises in the depths of the heavens, and Ramân thunders in the midst, while Nebo and Nergal encounter each other. . . . Light is changed to darkness, confusion and devastation fill the earth. . . . For six days and seven nights wind, storm, and flood reign supreme. . . . But, at the dawn of the seventh day, the storm decreased. . . .

The mountains of the land of Nazir held the ship fast. . . . At the dawn of the seventh day I took out a dove, and sent it forth. The dove went forth to and fro, but found no resting-place, and returned. Then I took out a raven and sent it forth. The raven went forth, and when it saw that the waters had abated, it came near again, cautiously wading through the water; but it did not return. Then I let out all the animals to the four winds of heaven, and offered sacrifice." Then the grandsire tells how the god Heâ rebuked the other gods for bringing about this deluge, and how he said to "the warlike Bel": "Why hast thou acted thus recklessly and brought on this deluge? Let the sinner suffer for his sin, and the evil-doer for his misdeeds; but to this man be gracious . . . that he may be preserved. . . . Until now Shamash-naphistim was only human, but now he shall be raised to be equal with the gods!"

The twelfth tablet of the Gilgamesh epic corresponds to the twelfth Chaldæan month, called "Deposit of Seed," and to the sign "Pisces" of the zodiac, and relates how "the Fishes of Heâ" accompany the revived hero in his ascent from "the cleansing waters." The first tablet has not yet been found. But, as the first month of the Chaldæan year is called "the Altar of Heâ," and is the month of the spring equinox—our March-April—François Lenormant surmises that, when discovered, it will be found to describe how Gilgamesh—the sun-god—offers sacrifice to Heâ for his restored strength, how Ishtar is appeased, and how, under the genial warmth of the reviving sun, life is once more renewed on the earth.

One of the tablets found in the library at Nineveh gives us a glimpse of the old Chaldæan idea of the beginning of the universe. It tells us how, "when the heaven above and the earth beneath were as yet unnamed, Apsu (the abyss) and Mummu-Tiamat (the billowy sea) alone existed. . . . The gods, as yet, were unnamed, and ruled not the destinies. . . . The days stretched themselves out. And the god Anû appointed the Houses of the Gods (signs of the zodiac), established the stars, ordered the months of the year, and limited the beginning and the end thereof, and established the planets, so that none should swerve from its appointed course. . . ."

The Arab dynasty, which reigned at Babylon from about 1500 B.C. to about 1300 B.C., no doubt greatly Semitised Babylonia; but, when the country became a province of the Assyrian Empire, Semitic ideas and customs were still more prevalent. When Nineveh was besieged, for the second time, by the Medes, under Kyaxares, the Assyrian viceroy at Babylon allied himself to the invaders, and thus, after the fall of Nineveh, he became the independent ruler of Babylon. During the reign of his son, Nebuchadnezzar, from 604 to 561 B.C., Babylon became the largest and richest city of the world. Nebuchadnezzar followed the Assyrian custom of transporting the prisoners taken in war, and brought to Babylon large numbers of Jews, Phœnicians, and Aramæans to labour at his immense buildings. With the idea of enclosing as much land as would grow corn enough to feed the whole population during a siege, he erected round the city a wall 40 miles in circumference, which fact, says Professor Rawlinson, "is established by a weight of testimony which we rarely possess in such a matter." According to Strabo, the ramparts were 32 feet wide and 75 feet high; whilst Herodotus tells us that the walls were sufficiently wide at the top for a chariot and horses to turn round on them. The palace of the king occupied a quadrangle of 760 yards, and, according to Layard, the base of its ruined walls is 70 feet above the Euphrates. The bricks of which the palace was built are, he says, "of a pale yellow colour, and of the best possible quality, nearly resembling our 'fire-bricks,' each brick bearing the name of Nebuchadnezzar"; the mortar with which they were built is, he says, "equal to Roman." The famous hanging gardens, near the palace, were raised on a series of vast terraces, supported by arches of the most massive construction. Nebuchadnezzar had them planted with forest trees and with such shrubs and flowers as should remind his Median wife of her early home among the mountains, and the queen's gardens were kept constantly fresh by a very ingenious system of watering. Besides restoring the temples of Bel and Nebo, Nebuchadnezzar constructed an immense reservoir near Sippara, which, according to some authorities, measured no less than 140 miles in circumference and was 180 feet deep. He also built a great reservoir at Babylon, and dug a broad and deep channel, known as "Nahr-Malcha," to connect the Euphrates with the Tigris. On the shore of the

Persian Gulf he built the seaport of Diridotis, with ample quays and breakwaters; for, though chiefly devoted to agriculture, the Babylonians carried on a large trade, not only overland with Media, Arabia, and Phœnicia, but by sea with India. We find proof of this commerce with India in the fact that, on the old tablets of vocabularies, "muslin" is called "Sindhu," which is the ancient name of India itself, from whence the muslin was imported. Quite lately also teak, a wood which grows only on the mountain-slopes of Lower India, has been found among the ruins of Ur in Chaldæa. The Babylonian carpets were largely exported to Western Asia. Many a record is extant of the beauty of these carpets, as well as of the rich hangings used by the wealthy Babylonians, of their luxurious dress and ornaments, and of the costly banquets served on dishes of gold and silver, with rare wines, perfumes, and music. Babylon, indeed, at the death of Nebuchadnezzar, in 561 B.C., might justly claim to be "the wonder of the world." The prize fell, during the following centuries, successively into the hands of Cyrus, Darius, and Alexander; but, when Augustus Cæsar died, in 14 A.D., the mighty Babylon was but a mass of ruins, deserted by all but a few Jews, whose descendants now inhabit the modern town of Hillah. Layard tells us that when he explored the site of Babylon, in 1853, he looked down from the ruins over "a boundless plain through which winds the Euphrates with its dark belt of evergreen palms. Rising in the distance high above all surrounding objects is the mound known by the

Arabs as 'Bab-Il.' Southwards of Bab-Il, for nearly three miles there is an almost uninterrupted line of mounds, the ruins of vast edifices, collected together as in the heart of a great city. They are enclosed by earthen ramparts, the remains of a line of walls leaving the foot of Bab-Il and stretching inland about two and a half miles from the present bed of the Euphrates, which to this day has a tendency to change its course and to lose itself in marshes to the west of its actual bed. . . . The great ruin, called by the Arabs 'Bars-Nimroud,' has for ages been a mine from which builders of cities, rising after the fall of Babylon, have obtained their material. To this day there are men who have no other trade than that of getting bricks from this vast heap, and taking them for sale to the neighbouring towns and villages, even as far as Baghdad. There is scarcely a house in Hillah which is not built of them. . . . Fragments of glass, Babylonian gems, cylinders, and small bronze figures are occasionally found by the Arabs on the mounds, and bought by the Jews of Hillah."

Quite recently German exploration has excavated the great gate of the palace of Nebuchadnezzar amid the debris of ancient Babylon, and also found there two hundred and twenty-five closely engraved cuneiform inscriptions which appear to belong to a public library, and date from a very early period. These, with the glazed tiles which decorated the gate of the palace, have been sent to Germany.

CHAPTER III

SEMITIC THOUGHT

One after another, tribes of warlike Semites descended from the Arabian highlands into the rich Babylonian country from a very early period. About 3000 B.C., a Semitic king of Harran, in Shubari, assumed the sonorous title of Shar-Kishati (Ruler of the World), and appears to have been constantly at war with the king of Bab-Il, lower down the Euphrates. Harran seems to have been, at this time, the chief centre of Semitic power, and it is probable that those very characteristic monuments of the Semitic ruler Mushesh-Ninib, which were found by Layard at Arbon, on the Chabur, the chief affluent of the Euphrates, belong to this epoch.

The city of Aushar, Semitised as Asshur, at the confluence of the Zab and the Tigris, built about 2500 B.C., is thought to have been of Akkadian origin, being mentioned in inscriptions of the time when the rulers of Shushan (Elam) were paramount in Lower Babylonia. The city of Ninua (Nineveh) was built somewhat later, about seventy miles higher up the Tigris. So far, the earliest stamped bricks which have been found at Asshur are stamped with the name of Ishmi-Dagan, who about 1840 B.C. was a feudatory of the ruler of Bab-Il. But by 1500 B.C. the Semitic ruler of Asshur was strong enough to have reversed the position, so that Bab-Il paid tribute to Asshur. The purely Semitic race was so much more vigorous and warlike than the mixed Babylonian race that it rapidly extended its dominion in all directions, and in course of time the Semitic capital was moved higher up the Tigris, to Nimroud. From Nimroud, military colonies were pushed farther northwards and westwards; and the kings of Aturia began to demand tribute from all their neighbours. If the tribute was paid, well and good; but if not, "the great king" marched an army against the defaulters, enforced an increased tribute, and also a contingent of soldiers for his army. As a proof of the great distances to which these Assyrian kings penetrated in their marauding expeditions, Mr John Taylor discovered in 1862, in the mountain district near the source of the Tigris, a little west of Lake Van, a rock-tablet which was set up before 1100 B.C. by Tiglath-Pileser to mark the limit of his sovereignty in that direction. Tiglath-Pileser, like most of the Assyrian kings, was very proud of his skill as a hunter, and boasts in his inscriptions: "One hundred and twenty lions I killed on my own feet, and from my chariot I killed eight hundred lions." Asshur-nazir-pal, who died about 860, boasts that he is "a destroyer of cities, a trampler of foes. . . . I dyed the mountains with their blood. . . . The children, male and female, I burnt in flames. . . . The nobles, as many as rebelled, I skinned alive. . . . Some I walled up inside the pillar." All the Assyrian kings were enthusiastic builders. The so-called "North-West Palace," excavated by Layard, at Nimroud, and the palace of Sharrukin II., called "Sargon" by the Greeks, show us the gigantic scale of their buildings. Sargon, indeed, built a new city higher up the Tigris, called "Dur-Sharrukin" (city of Sargon). When finished in 707 B.C., Sargon tells us how he peopled it. He says: "People from the four quarters of the earth, of foreign speech, of many tongues, who had dwelt in mountains and valleys, . . . whom I, in the name of Asshur, by the might of my arms had carried into captivity, I commanded to speak one tongue . . . and them I settled therein. Over them I placed sons of Asshur of wise insight in all things."[1] This wholesale deportation of their captives from one country to another was the constant policy of the Assyrian conquerors. Tiglath-Pileser II. records the removal of 72,950 Armenians from their mountains round Lake Van, and that he replaced them with the inhabitants of Hamath and the Syrian plains. Sargon, in speaking of similar deportations, laconically says: "I changed their abodes"; whilst Sennacherib tells us that, after his campaign against Hezekiah and his Aramæan and Phœnician allies, in 703 B.C., he transported two hundred thousand captives, chiefly Jews, to various parts of Assyria, "and Hezekiah himself I shut up, like a bird in a cage, in his capital city

[1] It is in the time of Sargon we find the first record of intercourse between Greece and Babylonia, when the rulers of seven Ionian cities sent presents, asking the help of the Assyrian king to drive the Tyrian Phœnicians out of Cyprus.

Jerusalem." Nineveh was practically rebuilt during the last ten years of the reign of Sennacherib: "I greatly enlarged the dwellings of Nineveh my royal city: its streets I rebuilt, and those that were too narrow I widened. I made it brilliant as the sun. . . . Murmurings ascended high, drinking-water the people knew not, and to the rains from the vault of heaven their eyes were directed. . . . Then I, Sennacherib, resolved in my mind to complete this work," which he did by constructing sixteen canals to supply the city with the water of the mountain-stream Khuzur, which may be seen to-day flowing amidst the ruins. The great palace of Sennacherib, says Professor Fergusson, was "surpassed in size only by the great palace-temple at Karnak in Egypt."

Vast as was the empire of Assyria at various epochs, nothing like settled government was ever established, and whenever the occasion seemed favourable the vassal provinces reasserted their independence. Each spring, therefore, "at the time when kings go forth to battle," as the monuments phrase it, the Assyrian monarch marched against some vassal who had not sent him the usual tribute, or against any other king whom he thought himself strong enough to reduce to vassaldom. We hear how Esarhaddon marched to the Mediterranean, to punish the "king of Sidon" and the "prince of Lebanon," and how he "cut off their heads," as a warning to the two-and-twenty other vassal-kings whom he summoned to pay him homage and tribute at Nineveh. Baal, king of Tyre, and Manasseh, king of Judah, head the list. "I passed them in review before me," he says, and tells us of the tribute they brought him—"great beams and rafters of cedar, cypress, and ebony," and alabaster and other precious stones, which "from the mountain quarries and places of their origin, for the adornment of my palace, with labour and difficulty unto Nineveh they brought"; and then he says that he entertained them all right royally.

Having plundered Memphis in 671 B.C., Esarhaddon assumed the title of "King of the Kings of Muzar" (Egypt), and carved an effigy of himself on the same rock[1] on which Rameses II., six hundred years earlier, had commemorated his victory over the Khatti, at Kadesh. When, five years later, the Egyptian feudatory princes had revolted, his son and successor Asshurbanipal plundered Thebes. "That city," he says, "the whole of it, in the service of Asshur and Ishtar, my hands took, and spoils unnumbered I carried off." Whilst the Assyrian king was engaged in Egypt, the king of Shushan took the opportunity to invade Babylonia. But Asshurbanipal hastened back, defeated him, and "cut off his head," and his chief officers were treated with great cruelty: "Who against Asshur uttered great curses, their tongues I pulled out, and their skins I tore off." As Layard points out, representations of all these revolting punishments, and many others, are to be seen graphically sculptured on the monuments at Nineveh.

Asshurbanipal had placed his brother as viceroy at Babylon, and he, after a time, allied himself with the king of Shushan, thinking himself strong enough to make himself independent. After a vigorous

[1] The stele of the two kings may still be seen side by side.

resistance, Asshurbanipal took Babylon, and made an example of all the chief rebels. Some, he tells us, he "put into pits," some had their tongues pulled out, some had their limbs hacked off and thrown to dogs and vultures; and, "after I had done those things and appeased the hearts of the gods, my lords, the corpses of the people whom the pestilence-god had overthrown, out of the midst of Babylon, Kuth, and Sippar I brought, and into heaps I threw." Then came the turn of Shushan. After an arduous campaign, he sacked and burned all the towns, and then destroyed the capital. In his record of this expedition, Asshurbanipal boasts of the rich treasure he found in the temple and palace at Shushan, "where," as he says, "no other enemy before me had ever put his hand." He tells us also how he found there, and took back to Uruk, in Lower Babylonia, the ancient statue of the goddess Nana, which an earlier king of Shushan had carried off from that city many centuries before. Asshurbanipal winds up his record with a characteristic description of his method of warfare. He says: "For a journey of a month and twenty-five days the districts of Shushan I laid waste, the wells of drinking-water I dried up, . . . the springing up of good trees I burnt off the fields, wild asses, serpents, and beasts of the field I caused safely to lie down in them."

Whilst Asshurbanipal was thus fully occupied on his eastern frontier, his vassal provinces, Media, Syria, Phœnicia, and Egypt, seized the opportunity to assert their independence, which Asshurbanipal had no longer the energy to contest, but spent apparently the remainder of his life quietly at home, restoring the palace of his grandfather Sennacherib, and collecting that valuable series of the ancient records of his empire which was discovered in his library by Layard nearly two thousand five hundred years later. After the death of Asshurbanipal, the Medes, led by Uvakshatra — better known by his Hellenised name, Kyaxares — besieged and took Nineveh after a siege of two years, aided by the Semitic viceroy of Babylon.

The ample records of these vainglorious kings of Assyria give us vivid pictures of this vigorous race of Semites, which at one time no other people of the ancient world could withstand. Merciless fighters, daring hunters, self-indulgent sensualists, they dominated the more cultured Babylonians, and then adopted much of their civilisation. The method of building adopted by the Assyrians shows how little able they were to invent a style of their own. Although Assyria is close to the Zagros Mountains, where plenty of good stone is to be had for the quarrying, they built their palaces even of soft, sun-dried bricks, which they faced with harder bricks, baked in the kiln. They even placed their chief buildings on artificial mounds, just like the Babylonians, who were obliged to raise their temples and palaces on similar mounds, to keep them above the level of the constant inundations of the Euphrates, and who had no other building material but clay. Thus built, the walls of the great palaces of the Assyrian kings began to crumble before they were completed, so that the successive kings found it better to erect new palaces than to restore those of their predecessors. But, though the walls were always built of brick, later kings adorned the inside walls of their state-apartments with great slabs of sculptured stone and alabaster. Many of these slabs, wrought from the tenth to the seventh centuries B.C., are now in the British Museum, and show us that, although the Assyrian artists could not treat the human figure otherwise than conventionally, they observed nature closely when depicting animals, rendering lions, and especially horses, with character and spirit. Some of the enamelled bricks found in Assyrian ruins are technically excellent, and many of the earthenware vases and bronze lamps also found in Assyria are of elegant form. Opaque glass has also been found in ruins of the fifteenth century B.C., but no clear glass earlier than the eighth century B.C. Most of the bronze objects show that the Assyrians were skilful workers in metal—unless indeed these articles in bronze were the work of their Phœnician captives, which seems not unlikely, considering that the bronze used in them is composed of ten parts of copper and one part of tin, exactly like the bronze worked by the ancient Greeks. But, however much influenced Assyrian art may have been by that of Phœnicia and Greece, most of our experts think that, on the whole, the art of Assyria, like its culture and its religion, practically had its origin in Babylonia.

Like Ilu, the supreme deity of Babylonia, Asshur, the chief god of Assyria, had nowhere any temple dedicated to his worship. Asshur was, in fact, the personification of the Assyrians, just as Britannia may be said to personify Britain. He was invoked as "Lord of the legions of earth and heaven," and as "the great Lord who rules the host of the gods"; and the warrior-kings of Assyria were always the "chief-priests of Asshur." Like the Jewish Yahveh, Asshur was "Lord of Hosts" and "God of Battles," who led his "sons" to victory, and his emblem was always carried on the battle-standards of Assyrian armies. This emblem varied at different times. At one epoch it was a winged disc or circle, below which expanded the tail of a bird, probably the dove, sacred to Ishtar; at another epoch the emblem consisted of a circle filled with five small discs, suggestive of the sun and five planets known to the Assyrians; but in a later form of the emblem we see the god himself within the circle, drawing his bow at his enemies. The god's body below the waist ends in the outspread tail of a bird, like the earlier winged globe. In many of the symbols sculptured on the monuments the winged disc and the tail of the dove are seen immediately above the "tree of life." When placed in this connection the signification is obvious. The Assyrian symbol of the "tree of life" is a most conventionally treated palm-tree, which springs from an equally conventional pair of ram's horns. Generally from each side of the stem of the tree spring branches having terminal fruits suggestive of fir-cones. As Professor Rawlinson aptly remarks, "the emblem which combines the horns of the ram, an animal noted for procreative power, with the image of a fruit- or flower-producing tree," can be taken only to symbolise "the prolific or generative power in nature."

After Asshur and Nin, who was the patron deity of Ninua (Nineveh), the deities most adored in Assyria were the goddesses Ishtar and Beltis—the "Great Mother" and the "Queen of Fecundity"—and the gods Bel, Sin, Shamash, and Nergal. According to Professor Rawlinson, the emblem of Nin was the winged bull, the winged lion being the emblem of Nergal. From inscriptions on some of the ancient Akkadian tablets, we learn that many of the sculptured figures placed on the palaces had talismanic value. This was the case as regards the great winged bulls seen on each side of the chief entrances, who were guardian spirits called "Kirubu" (Hebrew, "Kerubim"), from which come our words "cherub" and "cherubim." Esarhaddon tells us that, at the gates of his palace, he "placed bulls and colossi, who, according to their fixed command, turn themselves against the wicked: they protect the footsteps, making peace to be upon the path of the king, their creator." A statue frequently placed at the chief entrances of temples and palaces was that of the god Ea, "the divine fish" of Babylonia, the friend, protector, and instructor of mankind. The Assyrians called this god "Dagon," and portrayed him as a colossal man clothed, as it were, with a fish. Sometimes the fish-garment reaches to the god's ankles, sometimes it stops short at his waist. But, in every case, the head of the great fish, with the wide-open mouth uppermost, always forms the terminal covering of the god's head, and irresistibly suggests that it is probably the real origin of the mitre which, many centuries afterwards, was adopted as the symbolic head-gear of the bishops of the early Christian Church.

Nothing definite, so far, is known of the actual origin of the Phœnicians. One of the recent theories is that they entered Babylonia from the Barein Islands, at the upper end of the Persian Gulf. This coincides with the information given by Herodotus, who says: "According to their own account the Phœnicians came from the Eurythræan Sea." Another theory is that they belong to the dark-skinned race known to the Egyptians as the people of Punt, and whom they called "Keft," in later times, when, after long intermixture with the light-coloured Semites in the valley of the Euphrates, they settled in the Delta of the Nile for trading purposes. Professor Sayce considers the Phœnicians to be identical with the Caphtorim of the Jewish Scriptures. They were probably of kindred race to the people called Hyksos by the Greeks. We know that it was during the time when the Hyksos kings ruled in Lower Egypt that the chief settlements of the Phœnicians were made in the Nile Delta. Sidon was then the chief Phœnician trading port, and "Sidonians" one of the earliest historical names by which they are mentioned. The name "Phœnika" (Palm-land) was a later name given to this strip of coast by the Greeks.

In any case, the Phœnicians seem to have been one of the many mixed Semitic races which wandered up the valley of the Euphrates to the Mediterranean. But we have no record of the actual founding of any of the chief Phœnician towns—Arvad, Gebal, Sidon, Tyre; nor is it till early in the third millennium B.C. that these Phœnician ports on "the Sea of the Setting Sun" are mentioned in inscriptions of Gudea of Largash, of Sharrukin of Agadê, and of Khammurabi of Bab-Il.

The soil of Phœnicia is most fertile: even under the poor farming of to-day, the gardens are luxuriant with the scarlet and gold of pomegranate and orange, and the slopes of the lower hills are covered with mulberry, fig, olive, and vine, backed by forests of chestnut, sycamore, oak, and pine, leading up to the stately cedars of Lebanon. But this fertile land is a mere narrow strip of country between the sea and the mountains, and, as population increased, the inhabitants developed a remarkable faculty for seamanship, for commerce, and for colonisation. The Phœnicians were indeed a bold, self-reliant race, but, unlike their kinsmen, the Assyrians, they avoided fighting whenever possible: they preferred, in all cases, the path of least resistance. Whenever they were brought to bay in their own strongholds, however, by Assyrians, Persians, Greeks, or Romans, they invariably fought with fierce and persistent courage. Professor Deutsch, himself a Semite, sums up the Phœnicians in these words:—"By industry, perseverance, and unscrupulousness, adaptability and pliability, and a disregard for the rights of others, they obtained a foremost place in the history of their times. . . . They were the first systematic traders, the first miners and metallurgists, the greatest inventors, the boldest mariners, the greatest colonisers."

Physically, the Phœnicians—the Philistines of the Jewish writers—resembled the kindred races, the Assyrians, Aramæans, and Jews. They figure on the Egyptian monuments as strongly built, with features of a somewhat Aryan type, though less refined and less regular than those of true-bred Aryans, having heavier brows, thicker and more hooked noses, and fuller lips and chins: their skin was rich and dark, and their hair and beard black.

From a very early date Phœnician mariners coasted along the shores of the Mediterranean and Ægean, landing wherever they found the tiny shell-fish from which they extracted the famous dye known to the ancient world as the "Tyrian purple," or wherever they could mine copper or gold. Gradually the ships of Phœnicia sailed farther and farther westwards along the Mediterranean, and ultimately crossed the Atlantic, at least as far as the Æstrimnides (Scilly Isles) and Cornwall, to trade with the natives for tin, without which they could not produce the bronze vessels and ornaments for which their smiths were famous. From the fact that its coins were inscribed with the words "Am-b-canaan" (Mother-city of Canaan), Movers suggests that the earliest of all Phœnician cities was Ramantha, which stood on the site of the later city of Laodicea, just opposite to Cyprus. But, as Sidon was called "the first-born of Canaan," there was perhaps not much difference in the date of their foundation. About the eleventh century B.C., Tsur (Tyre), about twenty miles south of Sidon, which has a more commodious harbour, superseded Sidon as the chief centre of Phœnician commerce. In time, both Sidon and Tyre became the "mother-cities" of others scarcely less important: Sidon founded Utica (Old Town) on the north-west coast of Africa, and Tyre founded, in the ninth century B.C., its "New Town" (Kirjath-Hadeshath), which the Greeks knew as "Karchedon" and the Romans as "Carthago magna." Still later, Carthage[1] had her own colonies all about the Mediterranean, the best known being New Carthage or Carthagena, and Gadeira or Gades (Cadiz). On early Egyptian monuments, Tyre is mentioned as "Tsor," a name almost identical with the Phœnician "Tsur," and the later Pharaohs allowed Phœnicians to settle even at Memphis as their agents for the exportation of "the wares of Egypt" to Asia Minor and Greece. These "wares," according to Herodotus, were ebony, ivory, skins, papyrus, corn, gums, pottery, glass, and gems. The Phœnicians also settled early in Cilicia, on the south coast of Asia Minor: its name "Khalak" (rocky) is of Phœnician origin, according to Professor Rawlinson, and some of the coins of Tarsus, its chief city, are inscribed "Baal Tars" (Lord of Tarsus). Phœnician settlers were most active all about the Ægean, and have left traces of themselves at Caphtor, Crete, Cytherea, Rhodes, Samothrace, Lemnos, Tenedos, and especially in Thasos, where Herodotus says he saw "a whole mountain turned inside out" by the Phœnician miners in their search for gold. Phœnician sailors had a great reputation in Egypt at the time of Necho, who, as Herodotus tells us, sent

[1] Carthage was founded a century earlier than her chief rival, Rome.

three ships manned by Phœnicians with orders to sail down the Red Sea on a voyage of discovery. After three years these ships returned to the Nile, by way of the Mediterranean. Though Herodotus tells the tale, he declines to believe it, for the very reason that, to us, proves its truth. The length of the voyage was due to the fact that the ships were too small to carry sufficient stores; the sailors had therefore to land, sow wheat, and wait to reap the harvest several times during the expedition. They said, on their return, that "in sailing round Africa they had the sun on their right hand: others may believe this, I do not," says Herodotus.

A very interesting glimpse of a Phœnician ship of his time is given us by Xenophon about 400 B.C. He says: "I think that the most perfect arrangement of things I ever saw, was when I went to see a great Phœnician sailing vessel; for I saw the largest amount of naval tackling separately disposed in the smallest stowage possible . . . and I remarked that the things lay in such a way that they did not obstruct one another . . . and were ready to hand . . . when suddenly wanted for use; . . . also I found the captain's assistant so well acquainted with the position of everything, that even at a distance he could tell where everything lay. . . . Moreover, I saw this man, at his leisure, examining and testing everything needed by the vessel at sea. . . ."

Herodotus, born at Halicarnassus in 484 B.C., and therefore speaking of an earlier time, gives a graphic account of the method of barter often adopted by the Phœnicians :—“ When they arrive, they at once unload their wares, and having arranged them in order on the beach, they return to their ships, and raise a great smoke. When they see this smoke, the natives come down to the shore, and laying out to view so much gold as they consider the wares to be worth, they withdraw to a distance. Upon this the Carthaginians come ashore and look. If they think the gold enough they take it, and go their way; if not, they go aboard once more and wait patiently. Then the others approach and add to their gold, till the Carthaginians are content. Neither deals unfairly with the other.” That may have been the rule with the Phœnicians. But Herodotus tells us, in another account of them, that on one occasion they landed on the coast near Argolis, where for five days they traded in the manner already related with the natives. Then, on the sixth day, “ when almost all was sold,” some women went down to the shore,” and among them the daughter of the king, who was (the Persians say, agreeing herein with the Greeks) Io, the daughter of Ianchus. So the women were bargaining, and were standing crowded about the stern of the ship, intent on their purchases; when, suddenly, the Phœnicians, with a general shout, rushed upon them. The greater part made their escape, but some were seized and carried off. Io herself was among the captives. The Phœnicians put the captured women aboard and set sail for Egypt.” There can be no doubt that this kind of thing was not uncommon. It is well known that the Phœnicians were slave-dealers, and rarely missed an opportunity to kidnap any handsome young women or boys, for whom they found a ready sale in Egypt, Assyria, and Babylon.

Pliny tells us that in the fifth century before our era an expedition started westwards from Carthage, under the command of Himilco, to explore the coasts of Europe. After a four months' voyage Himilco reached the Scilly Isles (Æstrimnides)—"rich they are in metals: spirited and industrious are the race which inhabit them; fond are they of trade, and they traverse the boisterous sea, not on barks of pine or oak, but on coracles made of skins sewn together. At a distance of two days' sail from here is the Holy Island, with its abundant emerald pastures."

At the time of the third Punic war, which began 149 B.C., the population of Carthage was estimated at 700,000, and the city with its suburbs was twenty-three miles in circumference. It was ruled by an oligarchy, not unlike that of Venice at a later date, and "was governed," says Cicero, "with wisdom and statesmanship." The senate, partly hereditary, partly elective, was presided over by two chief magistrates called "shophetim," who were chosen for life. Rather than fight Asshur-nazir-pal, in 880 B.C., the Phœnician senate consented to pay him a rich tribute; but when Shalmaneser, in 717 B.C., attempted to subjugate Tyre, he was beaten off by the leagued cities of Phœnicia.

Esarhaddon and Asshurbanipal were, however, both too powerful for them, and the Phœnician cities all paid tribute to Assyria until 630 B.C. The next half-century was perhaps the most flourishing time that Phœnicia ever knew. Writing about this period, Ezekiel exclaims of Tyre: "Thy borders are in the heart of the sea, thy builders have perfected thy beauty. . . . Thou didst enrich the kings of the earth with thy merchandise and thy riches." Speaking of the splendour of the "ships of Tyre," he says: "The oaks of Bashan furnished her oars, the cedars of Lebanon her masts"; and he tells us of "benches of boxwood inlaid with ivory" from "the isles of Chittim," and of the costly sails manufactured in Egypt and in Greece. After a five years' siege Nebuchadnezzar took Tyre and Sidon, and for a time the commerce of Phœnicia was destroyed. But it revived once more under the wise rule of Darius, the Phœnicians contributing a war-fleet of three hundred triremes towards the defence of the empire. The Phœnician fleet, however, was twice beaten by that of the Ionians off Salamis—once in 498 B.C., and again in 485 B.C. During the next century Sidon had become so strong that it attempted to regain complete independence, in consequence of which the city was besieged, when, rather than surrender unconditionally to the Persian conqueror, its inhabitants burned the city, forty thousand of them perishing in the flames. By Alexander's time both Tyre and Sidon had been rebuilt, and though they were willing to acknowledge him as lord paramount, they would not consent to be garrisoned by Macedonian troops. Both cities, in consequence, once more suffered siege, with the result that eight thousand Phœnicians were killed, two thousand taken in arms were crucified, and thirty thousand men, women, and children were sold as slaves. A large number escaped to Carthage. In revenge, the Carthaginians sent an expedition under Hamilcar against the Greek settlements in Sicily, and for the next century the Hellenic culture in that island had to give way to the Semitic. But in 310 B.C. Agathocles took the bold course of invading Africa, and met with such success in thus carrying the war into the country of the enemy that in 146 B.C. the Roman general, Scipio, determined to follow the same course, and so brought the third Punic war to a close by the capture of Carthage itself. The Carthaginians fought with great courage and resource, but, after a heroic resistance, "every building was levelled with the ground, and nearly every survivor sold into slavery." No leader could have been braver, more brilliant or enterprising than Hannibal, the grandson of Hamilcar, who was also one of the best administrators of ancient times; but, in spite of all, the Semitic race was forced at last to yield to the Latin.

Between Assyrians, Aramæans, Jews, and Phœnicians there was no great racial difference. But the Hittites, though mainly Semitic, were differentiated by a strong Turanian element, which was due to the influx into the Syrian plains of hordes of mountaineers from the highlands of Cappadocia. The tendency of thought and culture, however, in all these kindred races was similar, modified, of course, by their special local influences. The Semite is distinguished beyond all other races, says Dr Robertson Smith, "by the extreme prominence he gives to the idea of sex"; and it is worth noting, he says, that "the word 'Baal' in its secondary sense means 'husband,' and is indeed ordinarily used in Arabic in this sense." This, he thinks, accounts for the fact that in all the cities throughout Syria, Asia Minor, and Canaan female deities were specially worshipped. At all times of religious excitement sexual licence was unbounded among the Semites, notably in the Hittite cities of Byblis, Kadesh, and Karkhemish, and in the cities of the Phœnician coast. The original idea of sacrifice among the Semitic races is that of communion; this idea they symbolised by partaking themselves of the victim which they offered to their god. In the earliest record that we have of any form of Arab sacrifice, we find that a live camel was bound on an altar, built of rude stones, round which the worshippers walked, chanting. As the sacrificial chant ceased, the leading worshipper drove his sword into the body of the victim and drank of the warm blood which gushed forth, and then his followers hacked off, with their swords, pieces of the victim's quivering flesh and devoured it raw, the idea being to eat the flesh whilst it was still alive. In Syriac, raw flesh is called "living flesh." As customs became less savage, the warm blood of the victim was poured out on the altar, as the share of the deity, and before eating their share of the communion-feast the worshippers roasted it. As Dr Robertson Smith remarks, "the sacrificial feast was not only an expression of gladness, but a means of driving away care, for it was set forth with every circumstance of gaiety, with garlands, perfumes, music, wine, and meat." To such stimulants the sensuous Semitic temperament responded with an energy unknown to the slower blood of the West: "to the Arab it is an excitement and a delight merely to have flesh to eat." No wonder that in these early times religious excitement often ended in sensuous abandonment, in which, for the moment, sorrow and care were forgotten. Thus it mostly happened that the wailings and lamentations for Tammuz (Adonis) of the Canaanite, and the Jewish ceremonies of atonement, terminated in revelry, if not in orgie. "A religion," says Dr Robertson Smith, "whose ritual culminates in a jovial feast, seeks nothing higher than physical *bien-être.*" Between sensuality and cruelty there is a curiously close connection. This revealed itself sometimes in a ghastly manner in the ancient Semitic worship: the shrines, that in times of prosperity resounded with mirth and sexual revelry, were filled, in times of national adversity, with the wailings of savage egotists, willing to propitiate an offended deity by the cruel sacrifice of their own children. In his *History of the Hebrews* Professor Sayce says that the sacrifice of first-born children "was not confined to the Canaanites. . . . Up to the closing days of the Jewish monarchy, the 'Valley of the Son of Hinnom' was defiled with the smoke of the sacrifices, wherein, as it is euphemistically said, the kings and people of Jerusalem made their children 'to pass through the fire.' . . . The first-born belonged to Yahveh. . . . The religious beliefs and practices of Canaan entered deeply into the soul of Israel," and at the time of Jerub-baal, who was "high-priest among the Israelites and king among his Canaanite subjects," it was in the sanctuary of Shiloh alone that there was no image of the deity.

It is the theory of some of our modern students that the subtle and abstract ideas of religion evolved by the Aryan races are quite unintelligible to the mind of the Semite, and it is suggested that this may be due to the peculiar skull and brain-formation of the Semites, who belong to the "occipital races," *i.e.* races in which the back of the brain is unusually developed. In the occipital races the separate bones forming the skull are firmly united at the age of sixteen, whereas in the Aryan races the skull-bones remain flexible, allowing of brain expansion up to an advanced age. Emil Burnouf says that in Egypt and Palestine, and along the Red Sea coast, "intellectual development is often arrested at the age of ten years." He verified this fact "in all the larger schools of the Mediterranean." At Cairo, he found the young Arab scholars more intelligent than Franks of the same age, but with the older scholars it was exactly the reverse. At Beyrout, where children of many races are taught in the same schools, the Semites, he says, make rapid progress up to eight years of age, after which they learn very slowly; the same fact has been observed in the schools at Alexandria, Smyrna, Aleppo, and Jerusalem. During the construction of the Suez Canal, the French engineers discovered that, when the cleverest Semitic workmen were advanced to the post of overseers, they were unable to understand, and therefore unable to repair, the simplest machinery under their charge:

when the least thing went wrong, they had to appeal to their subordinate European workmen.

Experts account for the strange absence of architectural remains throughout Phœnicia by the supposition that the upper stories of all Phœnician buildings were constructed of cedar-wood. The few stone ruins which remain show that the ground-floor apartments were most solidly built. Among the ruined cities in the deserts of Canaan are found blocks of hewn stone, averaging 3 feet long; very many are 6 feet long, whilst some measure 15 feet, and one block is mentioned, 38 feet 9 inches in length, which is estimated to weigh one hundred tons. Nor have many Phœnician inscriptions been found. The longest and best known is on the tomb of "Esmun Azar, son of Tabnit," who, like his father, is called "King of the two Sidons."

It is to the Phœnicians that Europe owes the system of written characters which, in a modified form, is to-day in use. As we know from the engraved monuments, the early Egyptians used an alphabet, at the time of the second dynasty, in which the twenty-one simple sounds of the language were represented by picture-signs. These signs, or hieroglyphs, became gradually modified into the cursive writing on papyri, which was used in all business transactions. During the period of the so-called "Hyksos kings" in Egypt, the coast of the Nile Delta became so thickly peopled with Phœnician traders and settlers that it became known as "Keft ur," or "Caphtor," or "Greater Phœnicia." Such keen business men as these old Phœnicians were quick to see the advantage of adopting, and adapting to their use, the hieratic writing of Egypt, which they simplified and modified in accordance with some of the signs derived from Babylonia, with which country they carried on also a great trade. Not only the names which the Phœnicians gave to their alphabetical[1] signs, but some of the signs themselves, clearly show that each sign was originally intended to suggest a definite object. Thus, the first sign of the alphabet, which consists of three lines ∀, and is called "aleph" (ox), evidently suggests the head of an ox with its ears and horns. It is, of course, the far-off original of our own sign or letter A. The two simple lines which form the sign 7, called "gimel" (camel), as evidently indicate the long neck and head of this animal.

Although the later Hebrew alphabetical signs are different, the early Hebrew signs for "aleph" and "gimel" are the same as the Phœnician. Indeed, we have it on the authority of Professor Rawlinson, that fifteen of the twenty-two letters used by the Phœnicians were "identical" with those anciently used by the Hebrews. So alike, indeed, were the two languages that he says: "The words most commonly in use, the particles, the pronouns, the forms of the verb, the principal inflexions and the numerals in Phœnician are nearly identical with pure Hebrew." He gives, as instances, such words as "el" (god), "baal" (lord), "malek" (king), "adon" (lord), "ab" (father), "am" (mother), "ben" (son), "bath"

[1] The word "alphabet" is derived from "alpha-beta," the first two letters of the Greek alphabet, which simply mean "aleph-beth," the first two letters of the Phœnician and Hebrew alphabets.

(daughter), "akh" (brother), "ish" (man), "ishar" (woman), "beth" (house), "shemesh" (sun).

On the other hand, Professor Sayce assures us that the Hebrew language is very closely allied to the Assyrian. He says "they are as closely related as two strongly marked English dialects are to each other." The fact is, as has already been said, all the Semitic races are akin. The Assyrian monuments show us how strong was the physical resemblance between Assyrians, Jews, Phœnicians, and the Kheta (or Hittites, as Professor Sayce prefers to call them), and, when we come to analyse the religion of the Aramæans (Syrians or Canaanites), Phœnicians, and Hittites, we find the same striking similarity.

It is suggested that these Semitic nations probably at one time all worshipped one supreme god; but the only proof adduced of this theory is that this deity was invoked by various Semitic races as "Ram" or "Rimmon" (High), "El" (Great), "Eliun" (Supreme), "Moloch" or "Melek" (King), "Baal" (Lord), "Adonai" (Lord), "Bel-Samin" (Lord of Heaven). What we really know is, that one and all of them adored the great Dual Principle in nature, which was manifested to them in the wonderful reproductive forces of moisture and heat, and that they deified these two forces, chiefly under the names of "Ashtoreth" and "Baal." The name "Ashtoreth" appears to have been derived from the older Chaldæan name "Ishtar," and was Hellenised later as "Astarte" in Assyria and in Greece. Later still, the goddess was called

"Aphrodite," and probably was introduced into Greece from Cyprus,[1] and hence was known as the goddess "born of the sea." "Ashtoreth" represented the passive, feminine, productive, or moist principle in nature; she is the personification of essential motherhood; the symbol of voluptuous joy, and of nature's everlasting fecundity. Her chief emblems are sufficiently characteristic of this: they are the fish, with its positively countless eggs, and the pomegranate, with its numerous thirst-allaying seeds. At Ascalon, the dual divinity was worshipped under the names of "Dagon" and "Derketo." "Dag" in Semitic idiom means "fish"; and we find the Nature-goddess (Derketo) represented as a woman down to the waist, and thence downwards as a fish; whilst the Nature-god (Dagon) is portrayed with the head, chest, and feet of a man, and the intermediate parts of a fish, reminding us strongly of "Eâ-an," or "Oannes," the Babylonian deity. There was a great temple of Ashtoreth at Sidon, who was there invoked as "Mother of Life." At the great Hittite city of Karkhemish, she was worshipped as "Atargatis." Recent discoveries of Hittite remains tell us that at Ephesus there was a temple dedicated to "Ishtar," whose worship was no doubt introduced overland by the trade-routes from Babylonia, even before the time when the goddess was worshipped by the Hittites as "Atargatis," and of course long before the Greeks from Ionia settled

[1] Cyprus was called "Iavan" in Hebrew, according to Professor Sayce; other authorities consider "Iavan" to have been synonymous with "Ionian." The Phœnicians called Cyprus "Kittim." The old Phœnician colony of "Kition" was the modern Larnaka.

there and worshipped her under the name of "Artemis." The Lydians were of Hittite origin, and worshipped Ishtar as "Kybele," a name afterwards adopted by the Greeks.[1] The Ephesian "Artemis" is called by some old writers "Dea multimammæ," and is represented with a great number of breasts, suggestive rather of a bunch of grapes than a mass of animal udders. All the extremities of the goddess are black, and her features are of a distinctly negroid type, somewhat like those of the Egyptian Sphinx. Her origin is evidently Kushite or Ethiopian.

Everywhere throughout Asia Minor the Nature-goddess was worshipped as the lover of the youthful "Tammuz"—afterwards Hellenised as "Adonis" (from his Semitic title, "Adonai" (Lord),—who was the personification of the balmy and generative sunshine of spring and earliest summer. At Byblus, where the Nature-goddess was worshipped under the name of Baaltis, and also at Karkhemish, her amours with Tammuz were celebrated and symbolised by the most orgiastic licence among the worshippers. "Baal" (identical with the older Chaldæan "Bel") was the name under which the sun-god was chiefly worshipped in Canaan or Phœnicia, and especially at Tyre. There is at least one inscription extant, in which he is addressed as "Baal-Tsur" (Lord of Tyre). But he was often invoked as "Moloch" (King). At Carthage he was called "Melech-Kirjath" (King of the City), or more popularly "Mel-Karth." No shrine, however,

[1] Professor Sayce identifies the Lydian Cybele and the Greek Astarte and Aphrodite as the same goddess.

was specially dedicated to "Moloch" in Carthage, because the whole city was held to be his temple. Baal represented the active, generative, or male principle in nature-heat, as manifested not only in the stimulating warmth of the sun, but also in the sun's terrible power to scorch and kill. Therefore Baal was worshipped under two aspects, the gentle and the terrible god. He was "Adonai" (Lord), emblem of the genial warmth of spring and autumn, and, as such, was personified as "Tammuz," the beautiful lover of Ishtar, the Nature-goddess, who exhaled moisture under his gentle embraces. It was in his fierce aspect that Baal was worshipped as "Moloch," "the consuming fire" that scorches and kills. To Moloch were sacrificed not only horses and bulls, but even children. Diodorus describes a bronze statue of Moloch, seated, with arms outstretched. The victim was placed in the arms of the god, and from them rolled down, through the open lap of the statue, into the glowing furnace below. Professor Rawlinson surmises that the "Minotaur" of Crete, a monster with a bull's head on a human body, was identical with this Phœnician "Moloch." The hero Theseus, it will be remembered, abolished Moloch-worship in Crete, with its savage sacrificial rites.

Jews are sometimes spoken of as "Hebrews." But, as Professor Sayce, in his *Early History of the Hebrews*, published in 1899, asks, "who are the Hebrews?" No trace of "any such name," he says, can be found in any of the inscriptions of Babylonia, Assyria, or Egypt. In all these texts "the south of

Palestine is called Khar." So that the use of the term in the Jewish Scriptures—the only place where it is mentioned,—he says, "is by no means clear," and adds, "unfortunately the evidence of the Old Testament is by no means clear" either. The more, indeed, our modern experts sift the account, given in the Jewish Scriptures, of the early history of the Jews, the more legendary it proves to be. In the *Encyclopædia Biblica*, published in 1901, Professor Guthe says: "There can be no doubt of the dependence of the Biblical narratives on Canaanitish legends. . . . It is clear that, in constituting these legendary figures its own ancestors, Israel attached to them all that was significant for its own individuality —origin, wanderings, fusions, partings, religion, and cultus." Another authority, Dr G. T. Moore, regards the Pentateuch, or "Five Books," ascribed to Moses, as "a series of interconnected genealogies," which the unknown author has made to serve as "the basis of a systematic chronology." The only incidents which are related in detail in this chronology are those of "the Creation, the Flood, and the covenant with Abraham." Dr Moore points out that the "story of the Flood" has been worked up "from the Babylonian original," and that "the stories of the patriarchs—Abraham, Isaac, Israel, and his sons—belong to the realm of pure legend." This opinion is supported by Professor Wellhausen, who says that "the substance of the Pentateuch is not historical but legendary," and that "the priestly narrator"—whether Ezra or another—"has used all means to dress up the old naïve traditions into a learned history. Sorely against its real character, he forces it into a chronological system, which he carries through without a break from Adam to Joshua." Again, Professor Sayce says: "No one can study the Old Testament in the light of other works of similar kind, without perceiving that it is a compilation, and that its author or authors have made use of a large variety of older materials," these materials being "Babylonian, Canaanitish, Egyptian, and even Edomite records." He too comes to the conclusion that we must reject the whole chronology of the patriarchs and kings, and also the account of the census taken of "the children of Israel," as all involving "hopeless anachronism." He pleads, however, that possibly the story of the wanderings of Abraham "may be founded on fact," but his only reason for thinking so is that the tablets recently discovered at Tel-el-Amarna, in Middle Egypt, show that Semitic tribes were constantly wandering westwards up the valley of the Euphrates before 1400 B.C., and therefore "the route" ascribed to Abraham by the writer of the legend "was well known."

These Tel-el-Amarna tablets prove also, among other things, that, as early at least as 1400 B.C., Jerusalem was already a town of some importance, being at that time "the capital," as Professor Sayce admits, "of a territory which stretched away towards the desert of the south: its name was already Uru-Salim (city of Salim), and the hieroglyphics of Egypt speak of it simply as Shalama, or Salim, omitting the needless 'uru' (city)." Amongst the Tel-el-Amarna tablets are some letters sent to the reigning

Pharaoh by Obed-Tob, king of Uru-Salim. When, therefore, we call to mind that Jerusalem was said to have been built subsequent to the settlement of the "children of Israel" in the "promised land," and that these "children of Israel" are only supposed to have started on their wanderings from Egypt during the reign of the Pharaoh Menepthah, two centuries *after* these tablets of baked clay were sent to the Pharaoh by the king of Jerusalem, we may well agree with Professor Sayce that "the statements in regard to the lapse of time in Egypt" of the descendants of the patriarch Abraham are "contradictory," and that "the geography of the Exodus is an insoluble problem." Even Mount Sinai, the mountain on which the mythical Moses received the engraved tablets of the law, cannot, he says, be located: "Jebel-Musâ can alone claim the support of any tradition"; and when we inquire further, we find that even this "tradition" is no earlier than "the third or fourth century A.D., when Christian hermits first settled in the neighbourhood." Professor Sayce suggests that the name "Sinai" may be derived by the unknown author of Genesis from "Sin," the name of the Babylonian moon-god, as "Nebô," the name of another well-known deity, is also the name of the mountain on which Moses is supposed to have died. The name "Moses," Sayce thinks, is "really the Egyptian 'Messu' (son)."

Speaking of the Flood, the origin of which mythos has come down to us in the series of old Babylonian or Akkadian tablets containing the epic of Gilgamesh, Professor Sayce says that the story "was composed by Sin-liqi-unnini upon an astronomical plan, in twelve books, corresponding to the signs of the zodiac and the months of the year named after them," and he admits that "in certain cases the epic explains what is doubtful or obscure in the Hebrew text" of the story of the Flood, as told in the Book of Genesis; whilst, as he remarks, "the whole conception takes us back to the alluvial plain of Babylon, liable at any time to be inundated." He also alludes to the very suggestive fact that in one of the old Babylonian hymns the rainbow—the biblical sign that Jehovah will not again destroy mankind by a flood—is called "the Bow of the Deluge," whilst in other records it is called "the Bow of Ishtar." Not only is the rainbow the "Bow of Ishtar," but, in the opinion of Professor Sayce, the name of Samson "is derived from Shamash, 'the sun'; . . . his hair, in which his strength lay, reminds us of the face of the sun-god engraved on the platform of the Phœnician temple at Rakleh, on Mount Hermon, where the flaming rays of the sun take the place of human hair, . . . and it cannot be denied that stories relating to him have come from popular tradition. . . . The compilers of the 'Book of Judges' have turned this hero of story, this lover of Philistine women, into a judge of Israel." And again, as regards the story of Joseph the son of Israel, the overseer of Pharaoh, Professor Sayce says that "one of the most characteristic portions of it"—the attempted seduction of the young Israelite by the wife of Potiphar—was probably translated into Hebrew from an Egyptian original, known as the "Tale of the Two Brothers," which was written for Pharaoh Seti II. "by the scribe Enna." Neither is the Jewish Scripture historically reliable as regards the origin of circumcision, of the sabbath, or of the ark of the covenant. Instead of the rite of circumcision having had its origin as a sign of the covenant made between Abraham and Yahveh, in order to differentiate the chosen people from the rest of humanity, as asserted in Genesis, it was, as Professor Sayce himself points out, of "immemorial antiquity" in Egypt, and is practised "among most races and tribes in Africa." Nor is the sabbath-rest an original Jewish institution. In Exodus the Jews are told to rest on the seventh day, in memory of the rest of Yahveh after his six days' creative labour; whereas, in Deuteronomy, the Jews are ordered to rest on the seventh day, in memory of the day when with "a mighty hand" Yahveh brought them out of the land of Egypt. The author of Genesis probably borrowed the idea of the ark of the covenant from Egypt or from Assyria, in both of which countries it was the custom to carry in religious processions arks, which were supposed to be the temporary resting-place of the god. The Egyptian ark was sometimes shaped like a boat. It contained the sacred emblems of life, and was borne aloft on the shoulders of the bearers by long rods passed through rings fastened into the sides of the ark. But even this acknowledged "compilation of Babylonian, Canaanitish, and Egyptian records" has not come down to us in any original form, but, as Professor Sayce says, "has passed through many editions; it is full of interpolations . . . and it probably received its final shape at the hands of Ezra."

The early history of the Jews, therefore, like that of all ancient peoples, is a mere series of hero-legends, so that no reliance can be placed on the biblical stories of Samson, Saul, David, and Solomon. The accounts of Jeroboam and Ahab are perhaps less legendary. We know at least that Ahab is an historical personage, that he was a vassal of Bir-idri, the ruler of Damascus, whom he supported with a contingent of Israelitish troops in his warfare with Salmanassar II., in 854 B.C. Salmanassar mentions also Jehu as being one of his tributaries, in 842 B.C. In 735 B.C., Ahaz of Judah, to save himself from a combined attack of Israel and Damascus, sent presents to Tiglath-Pileser of Assyria, saying: "I am thy son and thy slave; come up and help me." In answer to his appeal the king of Assyria marched to help his new vassal, and in 734 conquered Israel, and in 732 he took Damascus. But ten years afterwards, Hoshea, king of Israel, was reckless enough to refuse tribute, so that Sargon of Assyria marched up to Samaria, and carried away prisoners Hoshea and twenty-seven thousand Israelites, whom he distributed in settlements near Harran on the river Chabur. From this time Israel, as a nation, ceased to exist. But Judah, the vassal of Assyria, remained in Palestine. When Sargon died in 705 B.C., however, Hezekiah of Judæa ventured to ally himself with Egypt and refused to pay the Assyrian tribute. Therefore, in 701 B.C., Sennacherib marched into Judæa and, after sacking forty-six Jewish towns and devastating the country, took Jerusalem. The conqueror spared the city itself, but carried captive two hundred thousand men of Judæa to Assyria. Hezekiah died in 686 B.C., and his son Manasseh in 641 B.C. The son of Manasseh was murdered, and his grandson Josiah, a boy of eight years of age, was placed on the throne of Judah by the priestly party at Jerusalem. In 621 B.C. the priest Hilkiah brought to the young king a book of the Mosaic Law, which he said had been discovered in the temple. There is no scrap of evidence as to the authorship of this book, which is known as the Deuteronomion (Deuteros = "second"; nomos = "law") or the "Second Law," or "Revised Law"; but there can be little doubt that it was a compilation made by the priests in order to keep the power in their own hands. It was originally the Jewish custom for the head of each household to offer sacrifice for the family, but the Book of Deuteronomy, now called the "Fifth Book of Moses," instituted a priesthood which was confined exclusively to the tribe of Levi. From that time, it was held that only in Jerusalem could Yahveh be properly worshipped; consequently national worship was thenceforth practically limited to the three great annual feasts, the Feast of Unleavened Bread, the Feast of Weeks, and the Feast of Tabernacles. The first was held in the spring, when the first-fruits were offered to Yahveh, the second was the harvest-festival, and the third, which took place at the time of vintage, was now declared to be held in memory of the journey through the wilderness, when the children of Israel dwelt in tents.

It was about this time (627 B.C.) that the learned ascetic, Jeremiah, first began the attempt to spiritualise the religion of his compatriots by uttering his "prophecies" in the Temple. By the year 605 B.C. he had committed these utterances to writing, and charged his pupil Baruch once more to read them aloud in the Temple. When Nineveh fell, Jeremiah urged the wisdom of paying tribute to the conqueror of Assyria, but the king refused to listen to his advice. The result was that, in 597, Nebuchadnezzar of Babylon marched up to enforce payment of tribute, appointed Zedekiah his viceroy in Judæa, and carried away captive ten thousand Jews, chiefly, as he tells us, "skilled artificers, smiths, and mighty men of valour." Not long afterwards, Zedekiah foolishly allied himself to the Egyptian Pharaoh, and refused to pay the Babylonian tribute; upon which Nebuchadnezzar besieged Jerusalem, which he took in 586 B.C., and destroyed both Temple and city. After slaughtering all the children of Zedekiah before his eyes, he blinded him and carried him into captivity to Babylonia, together with all but the very poorest Jews. The prophet Jeremiah fled into Egypt, where he died soon afterwards, stoned to death, it is said, by his fanatical fellow-Jews, because he had foreseen and warned them of the destruction of their country. Jeremiah appears to have been the first Jewish teacher who insisted with any real emphasis that Yahveh was the one and only God,[1] and who dared to denounce

[1] Professor Cornill says: "The Arabic gives a concrete explanation of the name 'Yahveh': it means 'the feller, the god of storms, who by his thunderbolt fells and lays low his enemies."

the cruel custom of the sacrifice of children, which the Jews of that period practised exactly in the manner of their fellow-Semites in Canaan and Phœnicia. "They have built," he says, "the high places of Tophet, which is in the valley of the son of Hinnom, to burn their sons and their daughters in the fire." But although Jeremiah preached an only God, we cannot attribute to the Jewish thinkers the origin of the grand conception of an abstract deity. "In the pre-Semitic days of Chaldæa," says Professor Sayce, "a monotheistic school had flourished, which resolved the various deities of the Akkadian belief into manifestations of the one supreme God." There seems, on the other hand, little doubt, as Dr Kuenen suggests, that "the earliest conception of Yahveh among the Jews was that of a sun-god—Baal-samen, the Lord of Heaven." Baal, the supreme Lord, was adored by the Semitic races of Babylonia, Canaan, and Phœnicia under a twofold aspect, as Professor Sayce, among other authorities, points out, viz., "as the kindly deity who gives life to all things," and "as the scorching sun of summer who demanded the sacrifice of the first-born to appease his wrath." The Canaanite epithet for the chief deity—"Baal" (the Lord)—was constantly used by the Jews, because Yahveh, whose chief command was to "increase and multiply and replenish the earth," was identical with Baal in his gentler aspect, as giver of all life; whilst in his fiercer aspect, as destroyer of life—the cruel, scorching heat of midsummer — Baal resembled

Yahveh is therefore the equivalent of Thor the thunderer, Zeus the thunderer, Moloch the slayer, and Apollo the slayer.

Yahveh in his character of the "God of vengeance," who demanded a life for a life, and the first-fruits of all things. The prophet Isaiah speaks of the "slaying of children in the valleys," and the prophet Jeremiah denounces his countrymen "because they have filled this place with the blood of innocents," and because "they built the high places of Baal which are in the valley of the son of Hinnom, to cause their sons and their daughters to pass through the fire unto Moloch." Schopenhauer seems, indeed, justified in his remark that "the real religion of the Jews, as represented and taught in 'Genesis' and in all the 'Historical Books' to the end of 'Chronicles, is the rudest of all religions, because the only one which has no doctrine of immortality at all, nor any trace of it." Professor Wellhausen sums it up thus: "The soil, the fruitful soil, is the object of Jewish religion. Jehovah gives the land and its produce: he receives the best of what it yields, as an expression of thankfulness—the tithes, in recognition of his seigniorial right."

The prophets or seers were earnest thinkers, who lived for the most part the life of ascetics, and who felt themselves to be messengers, inspired by Yahveh to denounce the prevalent mode of worship and to urge men to lead better lives. Amos, who wrote probably in the early part of the eighth century B.C., in his assumed character as Yahveh's messenger, says:—"I hate and despise your feast-days, and I will not smell in your solemn assemblies, though ye offer me burnt-offerings; and your meat-offerings I will not accept. . . . Take thou away from me the noise of thy songs, for I will not hear the melody of thy viols. But let judgment run down as water, and righteousness as a mighty stream. . . . Hate the evil, and love the good. . . . I will cause you to go into captivity beyond Damascus, saith the Lord! . . . Ye that lie upon beds of ivory . . . and eat the lambs out of the flock and the calves out of the midst of the stall; that chant to the sound of the viol . . . that drink wine in bowls and anoint themselves . . . I will turn your feasts into mourning, and all your songs into lamentations!" Hosea, the next prophet, seems to insist rather on the mercy of Yahveh—the father who punishes his children for their good. He cries :—"When Israel was a child I loved him and called him, as my son, out of Egypt. But, the more I called, the more they went from me; they sacrificed unto Baalim and burnt incense to graven images. . . . Of me they will know nothing. So shall the sword abide in their cities, destroy their towers, and devour their strongholds." Isaiah reproaches them with "inflaming yourselves with idols under every green tree." Jeremiah tells them that outward circumcision is useless, and that what Yahveh demands of them is circumcision of the heart. "I the Lord search the heart, I try the reins, even to give every man according to his ways, and according to the fruit of his doings. . . . I will bring evil upon this place . . . because they have filled this place with the blood of innocents; they have built also the high-places of Baal to burn their sons with fire, for burnt-offerings unto Baal."

As a matter of fact we have no really historical

account of the religion of the Jews previous to the period of the Babylonian captivity. The only genuine fragments of early Jewish thought that have come down to us apparently are some short lyrics, the most important of which is known as the "Song of Deborah." It describes how, led by Barak, the children of Israel conquered the Canaanites under the leadership of Sisera, on the Plain of Megiddo. This song is very characteristic of the innate cruelty of the early Semitic race, and glorifies an exceptionally base murder as an act of heroism. It says:—

> "Blessed among women be Jael! . . .
> Water he asked, milk she gave him,
> In a lordly dish she brought forth butter:
> Her hand she put to the tent-pin,
> And her right hand to the workman's hammer,
> And with the hammer she smote Sisera:
> And she shattered his head, and struck and pierced his temple,
> At her feet he bowed, he fell, he lay down,
> At her feet he bowed, he fell;
> Where he bowed, there he lay dead. . . .
> So may all thy enemies perish, O Yahveh!"

And this cruel murder, it must be remembered, was wrought on the fugitive who had sought refuge with her, and after she had entertained him as a guest and had lulled him to sleep.

All trace is lost of the immense number of Israelites who were carried captive into Assyria in 722 B.C. and 701 B.C., and also of the Jews who were carried captive into Babylonia in 597 B.C. and 586 B.C. After this last date the Jews practically ceased to have any national existence. Among the captives taken to Babylon in 597 B.C. was Ezekiel,[1] the son of Buzi. The prophet felt himself to be the missionary of Yahveh to convince his countrymen of sin, and to urge upon them repentance and reform. He imagines the voice of God calling to him:—"If the wicked man sin, and thou givest him no warning to save his life, the same wicked man shall die in his iniquity, but his blood will I require at thy hand. Yet, if thou warn the wicked man, and he turn not from his wickedness nor his wicked way, he shall die in his wickedness, but thou hast delivered thy soul." Urged by this inner voice, Ezekiel strove to reform his countrymen, to arouse in them the spirit of brotherhood, and to encourage them to look forward to the ultimate revival of the kingdom of Judah. The learned Jews took advantage of their residence in Babylon to examine the ancient Babylonian records, and there is no possible doubt that from them they borrowed and adapted many legends and records with which to supplement their own scanty national history. They worked on the idea that, the more venerable and the more splendid they could cause the past history of Israel to appear, the more they should stimulate the desire of their countrymen to revive the glorious past.

The comparative weakness of the Babylonian government after the death of Nebuchadnezzar, in

[1] It is the opinion of Professor H. Troy that the active career of Ezekiel must be placed between 592 and 570 B.C., and that "he may have begun the adaptation of the Babylonian material which is now found in Genesis." The "Visions" of Ezekiel are, he thinks, "the product of careful study and composition."

561 B.C., combined with the success of Cyrus in his wars against Media and Lydia, made the Babylonian Jews anticipate the probability, at no distant date, of a siege of Babylon by the Persian conqueror. In that event there seemed to be a good chance that a change for the better might take place in their condition, and therefore they were prepared to do all they could to aid Cyrus as soon as the time came. We now know that all the latter part of the Book of Isaiah—from the fortieth chapter onwards—was not written by Isaiah, but by an unknown Jewish writer of greater literary and poetic power, who lived at Babylon during the captivity. We find this writer alluding by name to Cyrus: "Who hath raised up the man from the east, in whose footsteps victory follows, hath given the nations before him, and made him rule over kings? Hath given them as dust to his sword, and as the driven stubble to his bow? He pursueth them and passeth on safely, even by ways that his feet have never trodden. . . . I am the Lord God that saith of Cyrus: He is my shepherd and shall perform my pleasure, even saying unto Jerusalem, Thou shalt be built, and to the temple, Thy foundations shall be laid again." And so, with this great hope in his heart of the revival of the city and the nation, the prophet cries: "Comfort ye, comfort ye my people, saith your God; speak ye comfortably to Jerusalem, and cry unto her, that her day of trial is accomplished, and that her iniquity is pardoned. . . . O Jerusalem that bringeth good tidings, lift up thy voice with strength; lift it up, be not afraid; say unto the cities of Judah,

Behold your God! . . . For the mountains shall depart, and the hills be removed, but my kindness shall not depart from thee, neither shall the covenant of my peace be removed, saith the Lord, that hath mercy on thee. O, thou afflicted, tossed with tempests and not comforted, behold, I will set thy stones in fair colours, and lay thy foundations with sapphires. I will make thy pinnacles of rubies, and thy gates of carbuncles, and all thy borders of precious stones!" How characteristically Jewish!

Therefore, when Cyrus besieged Babylon in 538 B.C., the Jews did what they could to help him, and after the taking of the city they no doubt claimed their reward. It was the evident policy of Cyrus to secure a friendly people in Palestine, a country lying so near to Egypt, with which he well knew he would soon be engaged in warfare. Thus the Jews had no difficulty in getting his permission for some thousands of them to migrate from Babylonia to the province of Judæa; and Cyrus, with good political judgment, not only gave them a considerable sum of money to defray the expense of rebuilding their temple, but also restored to them all the sacred vessels that Nebuchadnezzar had brought from Jerusalem, at the time of its destruction. Of this first migration of Babylonian Jews to Judæa all we know is that they started under the leadership of the Persian Sheshbazzar and twelve Jewish officers, amongst whom was Zerubbabel, the grandson of Jehoiachim, and Joshua, the grandson of the priest Seriah. According to Haggai, the corner-stone of the new temple at Jerusalem was laid in 520 B.C., at which epoch we hear for the first time of the office of high-priest. Zerubbabel had returned to Babylon, and in 520 B.C. Darius appointed him viceroy of Judæa. When the new temple was finished, about 515 B.C., the pious Jews of Babylon sent Zerubbabel a golden crown, in the hope that he was the long-desired Messiah who was destined to restore the glory of Israel.

With the object of hurrying forward the restoration of Jerusalem, Darius permitted a further emigration of Jews in 458 B.C., who left Babylonia under the leadership of Ezra, a relative of the high-priest. But matters still progressed slowly, until a Babylonian Jew, named Nehemiah, who held the important post of cup-bearer to the Persian king, was appointed viceroy of Judæa. In 445 Nehemiah summoned a great national assembly at Jerusalem. At this assembly Ezra took an oath of the people to accept the Book of the Law compiled by him, as the future law of the land. Those who refused had to leave Judæa. This "Law" is a cultus which practically separates the Jews from all the rest of their fellow-creatures. It causes the so-called "Chosen People" to look with contempt upon all others, with the natural result that they are themselves distrusted and hated by the rest of mankind. Later, when the Hellenic spirit and the Hellenic culture permeated the greater part of the ancient world, it had little or no effect on the Jews.

We have no reliable records as to the number of Jews who, from first to last, migrated from Babylonia to Judæa. But it is certain that, notwithstanding all the Jews who left, a very large number of Jews, the majority probably, remained in Babylonia, preferring naturally the easier life there to the rougher life in Palestine. We must remember that six or seven generations of Jews had been born in Babylon, and that the longing for the land of their ancestors must have died out amongst all who held lucrative posts under the Babylonian government, and amongst the immense number of merchants who had grown rich on the large commerce which passed through Babylonia from India and the East on the one side and Egypt and the Mediterranean on the other. From very early times, the Jews showed themselves keen traders; commerce had never flourished before as it did under the firm government of Darius, who taxed his provinces strictly according to their wealth, who introduced a common coinage for the whole of his vast empire, and who united all the chief cities by broad high-roads, suitable for the safe passage of trading caravans as well as for the rapid transit of his troops. After Darius had adopted Aramaic, the language of Northern Syria, as the official language for the whole of the Persian empire, trade became easier still; and it is the opinion of Professor Sayce that "this common use of Aramaic explains how it was that the Jews gave up the use of Hebrew." In later times, when Greek had become the universal language of commerce, it was for the benefit of the large Jewish population in Alexandria, who could not understand Hebrew, that Ptolemy had the Temple-copy of the Pentateuch, or Five Books of Moses, which Ezra had compiled, brought from Jerusalem to

Alexandria and translated into Greek. This translation was made by seventy learned Hellenistic Jews, and hence is known to us as the "Septuagint" version. The MS. compiled by Ezra was afterwards sent back to Jerusalem, and perished when the Temple was burnt during the siege of the city by Titus in 70 A.D. The Jewish population in Alexandria about this time numbered one million.

Notwithstanding the departure of Ezra and so many pious Jews to Jerusalem, the chief centre of Jewish culture continued for many centuries to be the Rabbinical college at Nahada, in Babylonia; it was from this college that, about 30 B.C., the famous Rabbi Hillel went to Jerusalem. Professor Deutsch considers that the difference between Zoroastrianism and the religion of the Babylonian Jews, at the time of Ezra, was very slight: "The analogies between the Persian creed of the time and the Judaism of 'the Captives' are so striking, that we may fairly doubt which has most influenced the other. We only see clearly the extraordinary and radical change, which within the space of a few generations came over the exiles, under the influence of the civilisation and religion of Persia." Emil Burnouf also points out how much Zoroastrian teaching is to be found in the Book of Wisdom, in Ecclesiasticus, and in the Septuagint. One of the most striking changes alluded to by Professor Deutsch is the doctrine of the immortality of the soul, about which the Pentateuch gives no hint. The Mosaic teaching is that all punishments and rewards take place on earth, and even up to the time of the destruction of

Jerusalem it was the boast of the Sadducees that they taught the Law as delivered by Moses. It is suggested by Mather that the term "Pharisee" was first applied to those Jews who accepted the Persian theories. Josephus distinctly says that the Pharisees held the doctrine of the transmigration of souls, and that they explained resurrection to mean the birth of the soul into a new body, certainly not the revival of an old body. This doctrine is clearly held by the author of the Book of Wisdom. He says: "It was through being good that I came into an undefiled body." Several Rabbis speak of "cycles of the soul" (Gilgul Nashameth).

The three books of the Jewish Scripture now known to us as "Chronicles," "Ezra," and "Nehemiah" originally constituted one work, which, according to Dr Moore, was compiled at some period "after 300 B.C." by some "unknown author connected with the Temple," to serve as a "History of Jerusalem." It is, says Dr Moore, simply "edifying fiction with an historical background—historical 'Midrash.'" Very soon after Ezra had compiled the written Book of the Law, or "Torah," Jewish Rabbis began to give oral explanations of the text. This oral teaching was known as "Talmud." Successive Rabbis taught their own views of the philosophy and ethics of the Torah, and illustrated them by parables, traditions, and legends not found in the Torah itself. This mass of oral doctrine was handed down from one generation of Rabbis to another, being communicated to their chosen disciples only. But the Jewish colleges in Palestine were suppressed in the fourth century A.D., and those in Babylonia were suppressed during the next century; and then the Rabbis began to commit this hitherto oral teaching to writing. In this way there came to be two distinct versions of the Jewish Talmud, one issued by the Rabbis of Jerusalem, and one, the more voluminous edition of the two, issued by the Babylonian Rabbis. The basis of the whole Talmud is said to be the teaching of the Rabbi Jehuda Hanasi, who died in 219 A.D. The text of the Talmud is written in Hebrew, but all the later commentaries on it were written in Aramæan. We have thus, first of all, Ezra's version of the Mosaic Law, contained in the Pentateuch, or five books attributed originally to Moses: this is called the "Torah." Next, we have the commentary on the Torah, which is called the "Talmud." The text of the Talmud is called the "Mishna," and the commentaries on this text, which are all written in Aramæan, are known as "Gamarah."

A learned Hebrew scholar describes the Talmud as "a literary wilderness"—a tangle of Jewish, Persian, Greek, and Gnostic thought. In his essay on the Talmud, Professor Deutsch points out "the striking parallels of parable, dogma, of proverb and allegory, shown by the Talmudical writings and the Gospels." This is not at all surprising, when we remember the prevalence of Jewish thought at Antioch and Alexandria at the time when the early Christian Church was in process of evolution in those two cosmopolitan centres of thought. How close is the resemblance between Jewish and Christian thought may be seen from the following quotations from the Talmud. It is said that Rabbi Hillel, when challenged to sum up the whole of the teaching of the Jewish law "in so short a time as a man can stand on one foot," replied:—

"Whatever is not pleasant unto thee, do not unto thy fellow-man. This is the substance of the Law and the Prophets: all the rest is commentary thereon. Go and reflect on it!" This saying antedates, by at least half a century, the famous "Love thy neighbour as thyself."

"In every act it is especially the thought which God looks at, and judges. . . .

"It is better to make a short prayer with reflection, than a long prayer without fervour. . . .

"Whosoever does not persecute them that persecute him; whosoever takes an offence in silence; whosoever does good because of love; whosoever is cheerful under his sufferings—these are the friends of God. . . .

"Be thou the cursed, not he who curses. Be thou of them that are persecuted, not of them that persecute. . . .

"Avoid a small sin, lest it lead thee on to a great sin. Follow out a small precept, for it will draw thee close to a great precept. . . .

"Never put thyself in the way of temptation. . . .

"He who can feel ashamed, will not readily do wrong. . . .

"There is a great difference between one who can feel ashamed before his own soul, and one who is only ashamed before his fellow-men. . . .

"When you do wrong, you first make sure that no human eye sees you: show the same fear of God, who sees everywhere, and everything, and at all times. . . .

"Few are they who see their own faults. . . .

"He who hardens his heart with pride softens his brains with the same. . . .

"Trust not thyself, till the day of thy death. . . .

"Truth is heavy, therefore few care to carry it. . . .

"The best preacher is the heart, the best teacher is time, the best book is the world. . . .

"Life is but a loan to a man. . . .

"Silence is the fence round wisdom. . . .

"Say little, and do much. . . .

"Let thy nay be nay, let thy yea be yea. . . .

"Be there no torment to thee from the care of morrow, for thou knowest not what a day may bring forth. . . .

"Its trouble sufficeth for each hour. . . .

"Judge not thy neighbour, so long as thou art not in his place. . . .

"He who suspects the innocent will be punished for his suspicion. . . .

"When the judge sits in judgment on his fellow-man he should feel as though a sword was pointed at his heart." [In cases where the penalty was death, the judge was obliged to fast all day before delivering judgment.]

"Who gains wisdom? He who is willing to learn from all sources. . . .

"Who is the mighty man? He who subdueth his temper. . . .

"Who is rich? He who is content with his lot. . . .

"Who is deserving of honour? He who honoureth mankind. . . .

"Charity is more than sacrifice. . . .

"Food needs to be salted, in order to be preserved: money also needs to be salted to be preserved: wherewith does money need to be salted? With charity. . . .

"It is as good not to give at all, as to give in public, ostentatiously. . . .

"He who has more learning than good deeds is like a tree with many branches, but weak roots; the first great storm will throw it to the ground. . . . The reed bends, but it breaks not, for it grows by the water, and its roots are strong. . . .

"Hospitality is an expression of divine worship. . . .

"Hospitality is as great a virtue as studying the Law. . . .

"A miser is as wicked as an idolater. . . .

"With the measure with which a man measures, men will measure him. . . .

"Whosoever is quick in forgiving, his sins also shall be forgiven him. . . .

"He who curbs his wrath merits forgiveness of his sins. . . .

"When others gather, do thou disperse; when others disperse, do thou gather. . . ."

Rabbi Ishmael taught: "No atom of matter in the whole vast universe is lost; how then can man's soul, which comprises the whole world in one idea, be lost? . . . Death is but transformation. Sin is an obstruction in the heart—an inability to feel and to comprehend all that is noble, true, and great, and to take part in the good."

Rabbi Philo, of Alexandria, said: "They scour their bodies by lustrations and purifications, but to wash off from their souls the passions that pollute their life, they neither desire, nor have a care. They are earnest to flock to the temples in raiment of white, robed in garments without a stain, but they have no shame at bringing to the very shrine a mind that is all stains. . . ."

Examples might be multiplied indefinitely, but more than enough has been quoted above to justify the parallel which Professor Deutsch draws between the Talmudical teaching and that of the early Christian Church.

The following will suffice as an illustration of the way in which the Talmud amplifies the stories of the patriarchs, etc., as related in the Torah. We are told that "Ab-ram, meaning 'Great Father,'" was the grandson of "Nahor, a chief officer of King Nimrod," and that his father, "Therach, was chief officer of Merdon, the son of Nimrod." . . . "On the night of Ab-ram's birth, Therach entertained a number of his friends, includ-the wise men and magicians of Nimrod, the king. They passed the night in revelry and merriment; and when they went forth from the house of their host, morn was dawning. Lifting up their eyes towards heaven, they beheld a large and brilliant star rise before them in the east." . . . "Ab-ram was fifty years old when he left the house of his instructor, Noah, and returned to Therach, his father." Therach "had in his house twelve large images of wood and stone—a separate god for each month of the year." Ab-ram "destroyed these idols before his father's eyes," who therefore "took him before Nimrod," by whom Ab-ram was condemned to be cast into a fiery furnace, the heat from which was so intense that the men who cast Ab-ram into it "were consumed by it"; but "Ab-ram walked about in it, unhurt." When therefore Nimrod ordered him to be released, he seized the first opportunity, and, taking his father Therach and his teacher Noah with him, he fled "from Ur-Chaldee, from the city of Babel, to the land of Charan . . . and pitched his tent in Canaan," where, at the ripe age of "nine hundred and fifty years," Noah eventually died. Damascus was, we are told, at this time already a city of repute, and we also read that the Assyrian king, "Nimrod, lived two hundred and fifteen years, and was then killed by a descendant of Ab-ram, as he had foreseen in a dream." The death of Nimrod is thus described: "Esau happened to see Nimrod when all his attendants save two men had left him. Esau concealed himself, and when Nimrod passed the place where he was hiding . . . he shot Nimrod through the heart. Then, rushing from his concealment, Esau engaged in a deadly struggle with Nimrod's two attendants, and overcame, and killed them both." Hastening home, weary and hungry, after this struggle, Esau met Jacob, to whom he then and there "sold his birth-right." But the

Talmud says: "For money did Jacob purchase these rights, and, after the bargain was concluded, he gave his brother the food he had asked for—bread and pottage of lentils."

Of all the commentators of the Torah, Talmud, and Mishna, the most scholarly was the Spanish Jew, Rabbi Moses ben Maimon, best known under his Greek name of "Maimonides." Maimonides was born in 1135 A.D., at Cordova, and became court-physician, at Cairo, to Saladin. In 1168 he wrote, in Hebrew, a commentary on the Talmud; and twenty years afterwards he wrote, in Arabic, for the instruction of his pupil Joseph ben Jehudad (who had joined him in Cairo, and who in his turn later became physician to the son of Saladin, Ed-Dhahir Ghazi), his most famous work, entitled "The Guide for the Perplexed" (Dalahat al-haïrin). Maimonides tells us that he composed this work "specially for thinkers, who have studied philosophy, and who are bewildered and perplexed, on account of the ambiguous and figurative expressions employed in the holy writings." . . . He says that "the thinker whose studies have brought him into collision with religion will derive benefit from every chapter. . . . God knows that I hesitated very much before writing on the subjects contained in this work: they are topics which, since the time of the Captivity, have not been treated by any of our scholars, so far as we possess their writings."

Maimonides holds the opinion that the story of the creation of the world, as told in Genesis, is "a deep mystery, and, in the words of Solomon, 'far-off and exceeding deep; who can find it out!' It has been treated in metaphors, in order that the uneducated may comprehend it according to the measure of their faculties and the feebleness of their apprehension, while educated persons may take it in a different sense. . . . The literal acceptation of a figure is of no value in itself. . . . Our sages compare the hidden meaning included in the literal sense of a simile to a pearl lost in a dark room which is full of furniture. It is certain that the pearl is in the room, but the man can neither see it, nor know where it lies. It is just as if the pearl were no longer in his possession, for it affords him no benefit whatever until he kindles a light. . . . It is the function of the intellect to discriminate between the true and the false — a distinction which is applicable to all objects of intellectual perception."

Evil, says Maimonides, is but the negative of good, and has its origin only on the material plane. He calls matter "the partition" between humanity and pure intelligence: it is "the thickness of the cloud" which true knowledge has to pierce. Those who have the courage to free themselves from the tyranny of the body may escape most evils. The sciences, he explains, are called "mysteries" (sodeth), are veiled in riddles, and are taught in secret only to "the wise." The "Torah" (Law) is intended "for the instruction of the young, of women, and of the common people," and therefore it is written in language that they can understand. "As regards ideals only such remarks are made" in the Book of the Law "as would lead to a knowledge of their existence, though not to a comprehension of their essence." But, "when a man attains to 'perfection,' and arrives at a knowledge of 'the secrets of the Law,' either through the assistance of a teacher, or by self-instruction, he will have a true knowledge of those things which previously he received in metaphors and similes." But "a wise man will refrain from elucidating to the mass any object that is beyond their comprehension." Maimonides considers that the universe is "one individual being," a series of "spheres," of which the earth is the centre. The sphere of the earth is surrounded successively by the sphere of water, air, fire, and that of "a fifth element," which forms the "outermost sphere." This "fifth element" postulated by Maimonides seems to be identical with the "Akâsa" of Indian philosophy and the primordial "Substance" of ancient Greek thinkers. "All existing things stand in the same relation to the fifth sphere as a part of a thing stands to the whole." The elements may all be "transformed, one into the other," such transformations being primarily due to the eternal activity of the "fifth element." Every "motion in the universe has its origin in the motion of the outermost sphere, in the same way that action in the human body has its origin in the pulsation of the heart." But this parallel of Maimonides' between the body of the universe and the body of man does not altogether hold good; for, the most vital part of the human body is the centre, whereas he says that "all existing life in the universe originates in the outermost sphere (arabhoth)." The universe is controlled by a "certain force," and "without that force, the existence of the sphere would be impossible. That force is God, blessed be His Name! . . . We use the word 'One,' in reference to God, to express that there is nothing similar to Him, but we do not mean to say that an attribute of unity is added to His essence. . . . Our knowledge of God consists in knowing that we are unable truly to comprehend Him." And, having said this, Maimonides castigates the theologians of his time who assume so thorough a knowledge of God—"those foolish persons, extravagant in praise, fluent and prolix in the prayers they compose and in the hymns they make in the desire to approach the Creator. They describe God in attributes which would be an offence if applied to a human being. Treating the Creator as a familiar object, they describe Him and speak of Him in any expressions they think proper; they eloquently continue to praise Him in that manner, and believe that they can thereby influence Him and produce an effect on Him. If they find some phrase suited to their object in the words of the Prophets, they are still more inclined to consider that they are free to make use of such texts, to employ them in their literal sense, to derive new expressions from them, to form from them numerous variations, and to found whole compositions on them."

Speaking of the soul, he says: "The soul and the spirit of man during his life are two different things. . . . Separate from the body, only the soul exists." This theory is especially interesting as showing the progress in Semitic thought, for, in the Pentateuch, there is no allusion to the immortality of the soul. Much of the Pentateuch, says Maimonides, is pure allegory. As such he particularly instances Adam's fall and Jacob's dream. "Adam, Eve, and serpent" are symbols respectively of man's "mind," "body," and "imagination," whilst "Samael" (Satan), mentioned in the Midrash, is man's "animal appetite." There are various copies of the Targum, but he says "we do not possess the Targum in the original of Onkelos." He also reminds his pupil that it is stated in the Talmud and Midrash that "when the Israelites went into exile, not one of them could remember what he had learnt." He defends his own interpretation of the Pentateuch, saying that "these excellent ideas, comprehended only by the greatest philosophers, are to be found scattered in the Midrashim. . . . They are too difficult for the common understanding of the people. . . . Many branches of science relating to the correct solution of these problems were once cultivated by our forefathers, but were, in course of time, neglected, especially in consequence of the tyranny which barbarous nations exercised over us. Besides, speculative studies were not open to all men. . . . Even the traditional Law, as you are well aware, was not originally committed to writing, in conformity with the rule (to which our nation generally adhered), 'Things which I have communicated to you orally you must not communicate in writing to others.' . . . These secrets were orally communicated by a few able men to others who were equally distinguished.

. . . The natural effect of this practice was, that our nation lost the knowledge of those important disciplines. Nothing but a few remarks and allusions are to be found in the Talmud and the Midrashim, like a few kernels enveloped in a quantity of husk."

CHAPTER IV

HINDU THOUGHT

In many parts of India, and nearly always close to oak-trees, are to be seen monuments and monoliths of unhewn stone, which strangely resemble the ancient Celtic remains in Brittany. These were erected by early inhabitants of India who used the stone implements and weapons found near the monuments, and whose burial-mounds contained rough pottery and ornaments of copper and gold. Later than these stone-using races came the Kolarians from Assam and the Dravidians from the North-West. Later still the Aryan tribes descended into India from the Panjab. It is to the Hindu-Aryan race that the world of thought owes the Rig-Veda. This remarkable collection of hymns bears internal evidence of having been composed by a people living amongst rushing streams, forest-clad slopes, and snowy mountains—just such a country, in fact, as the Panjab. The exact meaning of the word "Aryan" is doubtful. Some of our experts translate it "tillers of the soil," others "the noble race." But whatever may be the meaning of their name, the poems show that the Aryans came down into the Indian lowland from a highland region, where the climate must certainly have been colder, because we find that their years are reckoned by their winters. It also seems certain that they lived in houses, with roofs, doors, and windows; that they cultivated barley and raised cattle; that they yoked their oxen to wheeled carts; that they used boats propelled by oars, and also probably ploughs; that they wrought in metal, and spun and wove; and that they fought with spear, sword, and shield as well as with bow and arrow. They respected private property, held the idea of the family in much reverence, and counted beyond a hundred. Thus it is evident that, wherever they came from, the Aryans were a distinctly civilised people when they appeared in the Indian peninsula.

It is to be inferred from the Rig-Veda that the five chief Aryan tribes had neither priests, shrines, nor temples, and that they worshipped only at the household altar, on which they kept the sacred fire ever burning, as the emblem of life. From very early times the subtle minds of the Aryan thinkers delighted in contemplation, and in solving various problems of astronomy, geometry, and mathematics. They invented numerical signs, among others the zero, as well as the decimal system. According to Lassen, there is authentic record of thirteen early Hindu astronomers, and in the fourth century A.D. the Hindu mathematician, Aryabhata, not only discovered that the earth rotates, but calculated the length of the orbits of the nearer planets and even the precession of the equinoxes.

The subtle Hindu mind was, however, too fond of abstraction and symbolism to evolve in the direction of art. It delighted, indeed, in the expression of vastness, but had no true sense of reticence or of proportion, which is so very characteristic of the Greek mind. The Hindu artist insists on excessive elaboration of detail, however discordant. Of this we see a striking example in what may be termed the interminable architecture at Ellora. And again, so little appreciation has the Hindu painter or sculptor for the beautiful harmony of the human form that he never hesitates to make it grotesque by abnormal limbs and appendages. But when the Hindu thinker expresses himself in words, he builds up forms of thought as beautiful as the world has known.

The Rig-Veda,[1] or Vedic Hymns, are, says Max Müller, "probably much older than 1500 B.C." They are "the oldest literary composition we possess of any of the Aryan nations," and "as far back as about the fifth century B.C. every word, every letter, every accent of the Veda had been settled by authority." These hymns consist chiefly of invocations, addressed to deities who personified the great productive and reproductive forces of nature. They were composed at various epochs, and show a progressive evolution of ideas. All the nature-gods are in turn addressed as Supreme God and Creator of the universe, and consequently, taken as a whole, the Rig-Veda may be regarded as the recognition by the early Aryan bards of the presence in the universe of a divine mysterious force. The luminous sky, the source of light, heat, and moisture,

[1] The word "Veda" has its root in "vid" (to know, to perceive); hence the Latin "video."

is personified in the hymns as Dyaus (the Shining One), and is invoked as "Dyaus-Pitar"[1] (the Shining Father). Co-eternal and co-equal with this god is the goddess "Prithivi," who personifies the teeming earth, and who is adored as "Deva-Matar" (Divine Mother). From the union of this Divine Duality spring all the "Devas"[2] (bright gods)—the elementary forces of nature.

But the sky is not always bright: by day it is often clouded, and at night is often absolutely dark. It has, however, one quite permanent attribute—it *covers* the earth. Therefore the old Hindu thinkers called it "Varuna"[3] (Coverer, Enfolder). An old hymn to Varuna says: "He pushed the sky, the bright and glorious, upwards, and stretched the starry sky and earth asunder." This, it will be noticed, is exactly like the action of the god "Seb" of the early Egyptians. "Varuna covers the earth with a robe, with all the creatures thereof." . . . But Varuna not only "measures out the earth and marks her uttermost bounds," he is also witness of all that takes place on earth: nothing is hidden from Varuna. "If one stand, or walk, or hide, the Great Lord sees, as if near: he knows what two whisper together: he who should flee beyond the sky, would not escape Varuna." . . . "Wherever, O Varuna, we men commit an offence before the heavenly host, wherever we break thy law through thoughtlessness, have mercy,

[1] The Greek "Zeus-Pater" and the Latin "Iu-piter" (Father of the Gods).

[2] The word "Deva" has its root in "div" (to shine); hence our English "divine."

[3] The word "Varuna" has its root in "vri" (to cover).

Almighty, have mercy!" In the later hymns of the Rig-Veda we find Varuna invoked in conjunction with the god Mithra, the personification of light. Light is sometimes called "the chariot of Mithra and Varuna," and the sun is spoken of as "the eye of Mithra and Varuna."

The earth was undoubtedly the earliest Deva-Matar or "Divine Mother" of all things. But in the later Vedic hymns, Aditi (the Beyond, the Infinite) is generally addressed as "Deva-Matar," whilst the secondary deities—her "children"—are called Adityas. The most powerful of these Adityas are Indra, Vayu, and Surya. Indra is the storm-god, "the Thunderer," who, hurling his fiery dart, lets free the waters imprisoned in the gloomy clouds. Scarcely second to Indra is the wind-god, Vayu, "he who flies along on airy paths: he never rests: where was he born, from whence came he, the vital breath of all the gods, the earth's great offspring? His rushing sound we hear, his form we never see." The sun-god, Surya, is adored as the "three-stepped" (tri-vikrama), under his threefold aspect, as morning sun, noontide sun, and evening sun. Hymn 121 of the Rig-Veda calls Surya

"The Shining-One, who by his might is king
Of all the breathing, sleeping, waking world.
Where'er, let loose in space, the mighty waters
Have gone, depositing a fruitful seed,
And generating fire, there he arose,
Who is the breath and life of all the gods;
Whose mighty glance looks round the vast expanse
Of watery vapour—source of energy,
Cause of sacrifice—the only God
Above the gods."

Surya, however, is far off from man; he is not always visible, nor is he always to be "found," like Agni, his representative, on earth. It is Agni, therefore, who is more universally worshipped. "Agni is Surya in the morning, Surya is Agni at night," says one of the Vedic hymns. It is probable that Agni is a later development of Mithra, for, like Mithra, he is invoked as the "Friend of man" and the "nearest of the gods." Like Surya, Agni is a triune god—"Agni of the three abodes." He personifies the heat of the sun, the heat of electricity (lightning), and the heat of fire, and is said to be "thrice-born"—viz. in the thunder-cloud, in the water, and in vegetation. In an ancient hymn we read: "When Agni is brought down from the Heavenly Father (Dyaus), he climbs into the sap of plants, to be born again, ever most young." The worshippers of Agni can always "find" the "Holy One" by the simple means of the rapid friction of two pieces of dry wood of the sacred pippala tree (*Ficus religiosa*). The fire kindled from the sacred spark, thus produced, was never used for ordinary purposes; it might not be blown up or blown out by the mouth, but only by a fan; nor might any fuel be put on to it that had not been thoroughly "examined" and found to be pure. Agni was "the Brilliant Guest" in the house, the symbol of God present in the home. At the daily family worship Agni was the "Mediator" rising in the sacred flame to Heaven, the bearer to his Heavenly Father of the aspirations and supplications of the worshippers. Agni is addressed as "the Purifier," the "most intimate Friend and Protector," as "Thou that goest wisely between men and gods." . . . "Come hither, youthful god, to us who call thee, and bring the gods, O son of Strength, towards us!" . . . "Come here, most youthful Messenger." . . . "Agni, between both worlds, O sage, thou passest, as Messenger."

Every student of the Vedic hymns must be struck with the fact that the various deities are so often invoked indifferently, in the same hymn, as symbols of so many various attributes of one great Power, and that they are not differentiated from one another in any essential respect. In short, as one of the old Vedic bards says: "That which is One the wise call many ways: they call It 'Indra,' 'Mithra,' 'Varuna,' 'Agni.'" . . . Another hymn says: "Thou, Agni, art Indra, art Vishnu, art Brahman-aspati. Thou, Agni, art born Varuna, thou becomest Mithra when kindled. In thee, Son of Strength, are all the gods!

"Whatever sin we may have committed, O Indra, let us obtain the safe light of day: let not the long darkness come upon us.

"Preserve us, O Agni, by knowledge from sin, and lift us up for our work and for our life.[1] . . .

"May I, free from sin, propitiate Rudra, so as to attain his felicity, as one who, distressed by heat, finds relief in shade. . . .

"To Indra the heavens and earth bow down. With his thunderbolt he looses the waters. At his might the mountains tremble . . . . Indra contains

[1] This verse from the early Vedic hymns breathes a spirit that the student will at once identify with that in the later teaching of the Vedânta.

all the gods as the felloe of a wheel surrounds the spokes. . . ."

It is said even of "Soma," in the Rig-Veda, that it "generates all the gods, and upholds the world," the exhilarating alcohol distilled from the soma-plant being accepted here evidently as a synonym of "Life."

In his sympathetic study of Oriental thought, and particularly of Indian religious thought, Emil Burnouf says: "The Agni of the Vedic hymns is fire in all the direct and figurative acceptations of the word." Not only does Agni signify the fire of the household altar, but it is an emblem of "the life and thought of men. There is no attentive reader of the Veda, who, if he is sincere, will refuse to recognise the spirituality of the old Aryan idea of Agni." Burnouf points out that the thinkers of ancient India knew perfectly well that heat manifests itself not only as fire, but as electricity and wind: they knew that, were it (Agni) not already imprisoned in the wood, there would be no combustion: they knew that "motion, which puts life into nature, is the result of sun-heat, sun-fire, fire-heat, Agni. They saw that the vital energy of animals is in proportion to their participation of heat." He suggests that the soma-spirit was used as a libation on the altar-flame, because it is "the essence of fire derived from the vegetable world." Thus soma is "a symbol of life," and those who drink this "spirit" feel "a glow of heat which rouses their energy and fires their brain."

The Hindu thinkers arrived at last at the conviction that behird all "the bright gods" was an invisible power of which they knew nothing, and they called this mystery "Tad-ekem" (That-One). It is this Unknown God, that One whom "the wise call many ways," who is the subject of the very remarkable Hymn X. (129) of the Rig-Veda, a hymn which, as Max Müller says, "is important not only by what it says, but by what it presupposes. Whatever date we may ascribe to it, as incorporated in the Rig-Veda, many generations of thinkers must have passed before such questions could have been asked." This Hymn X. says:—

"In the beginning arose the germ of golden light" (Hiranyagarbha), or, as another translator renders it, "an embryo of light, born in the waters," whilst, in another hymn, the beginning of the visible universe is described as the springing of "the existent from the non-existent," or, as we might put it in modern scientific language, from the homogeneous evolved the heterogeneous. "When the great waters were everywhere, enfolding the germ, and generating fire (heat), thence It arose, which is the sole life of the bright gods. . . . There was neither that which is, nor that which is not. There was no sky, nor heaven which is beyond. There was no light[1] between night and day. That-One breathed by Itself breathless. Other than It there has been nothing. That-One was born by the power of heat (tapas). . . . Who knows, who has declared it here, from whence this creation came? The highest Seer, in the highest heaven, he perhaps knows, or, even he knows not?"

Conceiving the idea that life was the manifestation of the mysterious force which they found everywhere

[1] Max Müller translates this, "there was no distinction."

present in nature, the Hindu thinkers called this force "Âtman"—the "Breath of Life." Max Müller tells us that in some places in the Rig-Veda "Âtman" has the meaning of "Breath," whilst in others it must be translated as "the inmost nature of everything, particularly man." The next postulate of the Aryan philosophers was, that the mysterious power known to us as thought was probably also an aspect of this universal Âtman. It was necessary, however, to distinguish between the two aspects of this one force, and therefore these Indian thinkers called the invisible divinity in man "Âtman," and the invisible divinity in nature "Param-Âtman. Later, as they observed how all life and all thought grew, expanded, evolved, they called the one great unfathomable mystery Brahmâ, from the root-word "brih" (to expand, dilate, grow). The term Brahmâ appears to date from the time of the "Upanishads." The word "Upanishad" means "sitting near." It was the term used to signify the esoteric teaching of the Veda communicated by the Hindu sages, "Rishis," or "Gurus" to the disciples who sat around them. We may therefore translate "Upanishads" as "Commentaries."

Brahmâ is described in the Upanishads as "nirguna" (devoid of qualities). We shall perhaps best understand the Hindu idea of this abstract deity if we think of it as meaning "Law." Brahma is called the "Causeless Cause" of the universe, which has "nothing before It, or after, nothing without It, or within": it has its being "where eye cannot penetrate, where speech is baffled, where mind fails: we cannot know It, we cannot grasp It: whom then shall we instruct about It? It is beyond the known, beyond the unknown!"

Simple minds being unable to grasp so abstract a conception, the Brahman teachers, who at this period had already developed into a sort of priesthood, possessing great social power, postulated a personal "Creator" to suit the understanding of the ordinary man. This postulate of later Hindu philosophy is known as "the qualified Brahma." This "Creator" is supposed to be invisible; but men may see the manifestation of his presence and his power in the "Trimurti" or Trinity of those resistless forces known to us as evolution, preservation, and dissolution. Some students of Hindu philosophy consider this Trinity to be composed of Brahma, Vishnu, and Siva. But, since even the "qualified" Brahma is too abstract, too remote a deity to be invoked by men, or to be prayed to and adored, the Trimurti actually worshipped by the mass of people in India consists of Vishnu and a double deity called Rudra-Siva. Vishnu is the "Preserver," whilst Rudra-Siva are the joint agents of the alternate disintegration and reintegration of the visible universe.

The "Rudra" of Brahmanism appears to be a revival of the idea of "Indra," the storm-god of the early Vedic hymns. The root of the name "Rudra" is "rud" (to roar, to howl), and the theory is that all existing beings and things are disintegrated, or annihilated, by the action of Rudra, if not before, then certainly at the end of each Kalpa, or Manvantara, or Cycle-of-manifestation of the universe. After each Kalpa follows a time of rest, after which a new Kalpa begins, and then, by the action of Siva, everything is once more created or reintegrated. Rudra is often represented as "Kala"—Time,—"the destroyer of all things." Siva is also sometimes portrayed as "Time." In this aspect, Siva is seen in the Kailāsa Cave, at Ellora, depicted as a skeleton. Siva is usually shown with three eyes, symbols of time past, time present, and future time; he is also sometimes seen with an hour-glass ("damara"), and with a crescent on his forehead, emblem of the moon, the great measurer of time. Sometimes we see round the neck of Siva a necklace of human skulls, in allusion to the numerous generations or races of men the passing away of which has been witnessed by Siva. Siva is now held, in the estimation of the lower classes of Hindus, to be the "Maha-Deva" (Great God), and his most popular emblem is a simple upright stone, or "Lingham," which is reverenced as the symbol of the generative force of nature. A brazen bull, which is the animal type of reproductive force, decorates indeed the shrine of Siva at Bombay; but the bull-emblem is suggestive only to the unthinking many: to the cultivated Hindu thinker Siva stands simply as the symbol of the renewal of life. Vishnu, "the Preserver," is also "the Mediator" between Siva and Rudra, and is the emblem of the pause between life and death, the interval between integration and disintegration. The name of the god Vishnu is derived from the word "vish" (to pervade), and we find that "the Pervader" is one of the many titles given in the Rig-Veda to the sun-god, Surya. Like Agni, who is the symbol of Surya on earth, Vishnu is the deity who is fabled to be nearest to man, and who is believed actually to incarnate at certain intervals in a human body in order to teach truth to men. Of these legendary incarnations of Vishnu, the best known are the seventh and eighth, in which Vishnu is held to have appeared on earth under the guise of Rama and Krishna.

As Max Müller suggests, it is only in a land where all that is necessary to support life can be had with so little trouble as in India, and where, therefore, the struggle for existence may be said to be reduced to a minimum, that man can easily turn to a life of contemplation. And, as Max Müller shrewdly asks, "What was there to do for those who, in order to escape from the heat of the tropical sun, had taken up their abode in the shade of groves, or in the caves of mountainous valleys, except to meditate on the world in which they found themselves placed, they knew not how or why? There was hardly any political life in ancient India, such as we know it from the Vedas, and, in consequence, neither political strife nor municipal ambition. Neither art nor science existed, as yet, to call forth the energies of this highly-gifted race. . . . Life in a forest was no impossibility in the warm climate of India, and, in the absence of the most ordinary means of communication, what was there to do for the members of the small communities dotted over the country, but to give expression to that wonder at the world which is the beginning of all philosophy?" Then Max Müller goes on to give the old Hindu thinkers a splendid character for honesty. "Hindu philosophers," he says, "never equivocate, or try to hide their opinions, where they are likely to be unpopular. . . . They never try to deceive us as to their principles and the consequence of their theories. If they are idealists, even to the verge of nihilism, they say so, . . . because their reverence for truth is stronger than their reverence for anything else. . . . Whatever we may think of such views of the world as they put forward, there is one thing we cannot help admiring, and that is the straightforwardness and perfect freedom with which they are elaborated."

Amidst the successive phases of Brahman philosophy, the systems of thought which stand out with most clearness are the Samkhya, the Yoga, and the Vedânta. Experts are by no means sure which of the three is the earliest. It is generally thought that, in its origin at least, the Samkhya is the first, although Max Müller suggests that the teaching contained in the Sutras, attributed to Kapila, the chief exponent of the Samkhya philosophy, is probably "a toning down of the extreme monism of the contemporary Adwaita Vedânta."

The meaning of the word "Samkhya" is to distinguish, to weigh, to judge, and therefore it is not surprising to find that the doctrine of Kapila has much in common with that of Gautama, "the Buddha," who lived at an earlier date. Like Gautama, Kapila considers it useless to consider the question of a First Cause. He does not say in so many words that such a conception as Brâhman or Iswara is contrary to reason, but he asserts that he can find no reliable evidence of any such super-natural power in the universe. Kapila therefore starts with the postulate of an eternal coexistent duality, which he calls substance and soul — "prakriti" and "purusha." Kapila rejects the Vedânta theory of the absorption of the many in the one, contending that those passages in the Vedas, which the Vedantist relies upon as proof of the oneness of soul, when studied from the point of view of common sense, only indicate the comprehensiveness of genus. His theory therefore is, not that there is but one purusha, or Âtman—one Soul-of-the-Universe,—but that there are innumerable purushas, or individual souls, all of which souls—divine, human, animal, and even vegetal—are as eternal as the objective universe itself. The universe evolves from prakriti,[1] the primordial substance, which, in its initial state, is homogeneous, undifferentiated, and invisible, and holds within itself, in perfect equipoise, its three constituent "gunas" (qualities or conditions), called sattva, rajas, and tapas. "I am bound to confess," says Max Müller, "that the nature of the three gunas is by no means clear to me, whilst unfortunately to Indian philosophers they seem to be so clear as to require no explanation at all." And he adds: "Indian philosophers are honest in their reasoning, and never use empty words." On the whole, he thinks that the three gunas may be "best explained by the general idea of two opposites, and the middle between them, these being manifested in nature by light, darkness, and mist, and in morals by good, bad, and indifferent."

The word "prakriti" literally means "producer,"

[1] Loosely translated "nature" by some Sanskrit students.

being derived from "kri" (to produce) and "pra" (forth). It is best explained as undifferentiated cosmic substance, containing within itself the potentiality, not only of physical but also of psychical evolution. Prakriti is the Hindu attempt to account for the mysterious intermingling of our unconscious and conscious powers, which prevents us from recognising the true relation of body to mind. Kapila advances the theory that, under the stimulus of purusha, prakriti evolves not only into the objective and material world, but also into the subjective and intelligent world. The starting of the evolutionary process is due, he says, to disturbance of the equipoise in which, during pralaya,[1] the three gunas rest, and which disturbance results in the evolution of Buddhi. Buddhi, says Kapila, is "the most wonderful phase of prakriti." The word has its root in the verb "budh" (to awake), and therefore may be translated as "perception." It is, in fact, the very first phase of being, for to perceive is to be. In the "awakening" of dormant prakriti, "manas" is evolved. Manas may be translated as "mind," and appears to be analogous to the Greek "nous." Purusha is eternal, but manas is only relatively eternal, ending with the manifestation of the universe. Kapila calls manas "the mediator," or intermediary between perception and volition. It is due to the presence of manas that individual action is possible to any kind of entity or being.

The Samkhya theory is that, when once the

[1] Pralaya is the latent condition which the universe assumes in the intervals between its manifestations.

human being has evolved buddhi and manas, it is capable of attracting to itself some purusha (soul) which happens to have reached a stage of upward evolution towards ultimate spirituality which is, as it were, on a level with its own. Thus manas, "the mediator," unites volition, which belongs to purusha, with perception which has been evolved by the human entity. No sooner has this union taken place, than the three "gunas"—sattva, rajas, and tapas—come into action. Kapila takes great pains to make it clear that the gunas are not attributes of the soul itself, but are qualities inherent in matter, and that man's soul is therefore, by its nature, *outside* of, and, if the man so wills, independent of, these "blind forces." The action of the gunas is threefold, and by their influence the soul may be drawn by "sattva" (goodness) upwards towards spirituality, downwards by "tapas" (grossness), or may remain on what we may call the mean level of animal activity and passion ("rajas"). The basic thought is that, unless it is associated with prakriti (matter), purusha, or soul, is quite powerless to *act* in any way, and therefore can evolve neither upwards towards pure spirit, nor downwards towards gross matter. On the other hand, prakriti must remain "in pralaya" (dormant) until it is "awakened" by the impulse of purusha. The united action of purusha and prakriti is picturesquely compared to the progress of a "lame man" (purusha), who is borne along on the shoulders of "a blind man" (prakriti). Kapila distinctly teaches that the whole end and aim of the soul's progress through life is "liberation," that is, liberation from the tyranny of the three gunas. He nowhere suggests the idea of the soul's ultimate annihilation, as some critics imagine. He explains that the phrase, "Neither I am, nor is aught mine," has no other meaning than that the soul, *per se*, experiences neither pain nor pleasure. He, however, does not suggest the nature of the soul's existence after liberation, but contents himself with the idea that the state of the liberated soul is incomprehensible to the human mind.

In the earlier Samkhya philosophy "purusha" is often called "Âtman," the self, and constitutes a theoretical unity. But, all the same, purusha is practically always regarded as multitudinous. The relation to the synthesis of the individual purusha, jivas, egos, or souls is indicated by saying that they are what sparks are to the fire, what drops are to the ocean. Every conceivable phenomenon in the cosmos, from a mountain at one end of the series to a human mind at the other, is looked upon as the result of the ever-renewed union of the active and passive forces of nature. It is this old philosophical idea which we see to-day so very crudely symbolised throughout India by the well-known emblems of the Lingham and Yoni. The Samkhya system of philosophic thought anticipates the postulate of our modern scientists that the world consists of matter and energy, and that all the elements may be mere structural modifications of one primal element, which perhaps is hydrogen. It is just this "primal element" which Kapila calls "prakriti." The Hindu poets speak of prakriti as the "Great Mother of the Universe," or as the "Uncreated Germ." It is, in other words, the passive productive force in nature, which produces the universe when acted upon by the generative impulse, called "purusha." The first result of this joint action of the productive and generative forces is the differentiation of the five "tattvas" or elements, viz. "akâsa" (ether), "vayu" (air), "tejas" (fire), "jala" (water), and "prithivi" (earth). As akâsa is the first differentiation of prakriti, at the starting of the evolutionary process which results in what we know as the manifested universe, so is akâsa the last stage in the reversed process of involution of the universe, before prakriti sinks once more into the latent state, called "pralaya." The Samkhya theory is, that the universe is alternately evolved out of, and then reabsorbed into, the undifferentiated cosmic substance (prakriti) at the unthinkable intervals of 4320 millions of solar years. These postulated alternate cycles of cosmic activity and rest are called "days and nights of Brâhma": "At the approach of 'day' the visible universe issues from the unmanifested: at the approach of 'night' it dissolves in Him who is called the Unmanifested." A "day of Brâhma" is also called a "manvantara." Only during the continuance of the manvantara is the human soul held to exist as an entity. But, on the other hand, the idea that the soul could possibly come to an end before the end of the manvantara during which it was evolved, is to the mind of the Hindu thinker so inconceivable that, as Max Müller points out, the doctrine of the soul's repeated reincarnations ("Samsara") during the manvantara is never called in question. It is taken for granted that every human soul that has any aspiration at all must continue to incarnate, until it has become so spiritualised that it can exist without the need for an earthly body. This is "liberation from the wheel of rebirth," which should be the aim of every wise man. Max Müller remarks that "no philosophy of ancient or modern times realises so completely as the Vedânta and Samkhya what may be called the idea of the soul, as the Phœnix consumed by the fire of thought, and rising from its own ashes, soaring towards regions that are more real than anything that can be called real in this life."

These repeated incarnations of the soul are postulated as being possible by means of an indestructible vehicle called the "linga-sarira,"[1] or subtle body of the soul, which, as Max Müller explains the idea, is "a seminal and potential body, which at death leaves the coarse material body without being itself injured. . . . It forms what we should call our personality . . . and determines by its acquired dispositions the special kind of the successive gross bodies into which it has to enter." In the words of the modern Indian Yogi, "as the body is modified in our everyday life by the action of the thought-forms within, and grows out of them, so, at some period after death, another body grows out of the thought-forms which survive." The bodily likeness of a child to its parents is held to be due to the thought-forms of the parents, at the time when the child is generated and conceived. The similarity of mind between the child and its parent is due to the magnetism which attracts a

[1] The Vedânta calls it the "Sukshma-sarira."

purusha, jiva, ego, or soul, that is ready for rebirth, to parents whose minds are in harmony with itself. The "Bhagavad-Gîta," which gives us the key to the meaning of much of the earlier Hindu philosophy, explains that "no one who acts uprightly goes the evil way," that is, to "tapas"; but "he who has wavered in devotion, after he has attained the region of the just, and has dwelt there unnumbered years, is born again in the house of the good and great, or is born in a family of wise devotees. But a birth like this is hard to obtain. If he goes to dissolution when passion (rajas) prevails, he is born among those who are attached to works. If he departs when darkness (tapas) prevails, he is born in the womb of the stupid." . . . "As a man having cast off his old garments takes others that are new, so the embodied (soul), having cast off old bodies, enters into others that are new."

This ancient Indian theory of the rebirth of the soul is the strictly logical outcome of the great law of cause and effect, which ensures that no soul can possibly escape the effect of the causes started by *itself*. The Indian thinker speaks of this as "Karma," and holds that not only every act but every thought must have a result, and therefore, that whenever a human soul reappears in bodily life, it inevitably finds itself surrounded by the conditions ("uphadis") which it has *itself* brought about. It will be seen, therefore, that the idea of Karma does away with all sense of injustice, and furnishes a logical explanation of the mystery why the lot of any man should be so much worse or better than that of others. The theory is simply that each human soul is born into that kind of body, has that kind of mind, and is surrounded by those material conditions which are in strict accordance with the use, good or bad, made by the soul of the opportunities for progress which have been offered to it in its previous lives. Like "the tree from the seed, the seed from the tree," each soul must reap the harvest it has sown. But it is held that the result need not inevitably follow the cause started in the life immediately previous: on the contrary, the result may, as it were, be held over during several incarnations. Thus we see that the old Indian thinkers anticipated our modern idea of the working of the law of heredity, according to which inherited tendencies are said to pass over several generations, or to "throw back," as it is termed. The difference, however, is, that the Indian theory is, not that a man *has* ancestors, but that each man *is*, as it were, his own ancestor, except perhaps as regards physical peculiarities, which he may derive from his parents. All the Hindu systems teach the twin-theory of "Samsara" and "Karma," and they also all practically agree that all sorrow and suffering are caused by ignorance.

Yoga has been practised in India from very early times. But the system of philosophy taught by Patangali dates only from the second century B.C. Patangali bases his teaching on the Samkhya, but advocates the practice of extreme asceticism, which was certainly not recommended by Kapila. The word Yoga is often translated as "union," *i.e.* union with the divine. But, according to Max Müller, "it does not mean anything but pulling oneself together, exertion, concentration; . . . it is a steadying of the mind." Its ultimate state, he explains, is "pure ecstasy." It was to help his disciples to gain control over the senses, to enable them to ignore both pain and pleasure, that Patangali advised them, during periods of contemplation, to adopt certain strained positions of the body, and to practise systematic restraints of breathing, prescribing eight different methods of regulating the breath. But he intended all this as mere means to an end; the end being complete power of concentrating and abstracting the mind; and he seriously warned his disciples that, if they used such methods for the purpose of developing abnormal powers ("siddis" = perfections), these powers would act as hindrances to the release of the soul from the "wheel of rebirth," to attain which was the end and aim of his philosophy. And this is what has actually happened, for, after the death of the master, Yoga has been practised chiefly in order to develop abnormal will-powers or "astras." These astras (literally "arrows of the will") border on the supernatural. They are enumerated as being: (1) the power of self-nutrition, without partaking of food; (2) the power of restful repose at any moment and under any conditions; (3) the power of making the body invisible, and able to pass through solids; (4) the power of divesting the body of gravity and thus being able to walk on water or float in air; (5) the power of being instantly present anywhere by force of will; (6) the power of holding in subjection and of directing the will of others; (7) the power of obtaining all one desires. This is, no doubt, a startling list of "powers"; but there is evidence that some of them, at least, were possessed by certain well-known Yogins. Our modern practice of hypnotising, by fixing the eyes steadily on one point—if luminous so much the better,—has been adopted from time immemorial by the Yogins of ancient India. We read in the Bhagavad-Gîta of the Yogins who gazed down on the ends of their noses, or who squinted up at the corners of their eyebrows, and also of Yogins who adopted the present practice of "mesmerising" a person by fixedly staring into his eyes. But nothing of this sort was taught by Patangali. On the contrary, all such things were expressly discouraged by him. Reduced to the simplest phrasing, his teaching is, that the soul may emancipate itself from rebirth by pious meditation on the Supreme. He says: "When both mind and the self have acquired the same purity, 'Kaivalya' (aloneness, or aloofness) is reached."

We gain some knowledge of Patangali's teaching from the opening stanzas of the Bhagavad-Gîta epos, which the unknown author tells us was written for the express purpose of reviving the Yoga-teaching of Patangali, then "almost lost by length of time." In the translation of that poem by J. Davies we read:—

"The heart of the man who obeys the roving senses carries his knowledge away, as the wind ships at sea. . . . When one withdraws his senses from sense-objects, as a tortoise draws in his limbs in every part, the knowledge of this man is fixed. . . . He who meets sense-objects with senses free from desire or aversion, and is self-controlled, he, being well-ordered in soul, attains peace. . . . He attains peace in whom all desires enter, as the rivers enter into the ocean, which is ever filled, and ever remains within its bounds. . . . This is the Brâhman-state. He who has attained it, is troubled no more. He who retains it till the hour of death, passes on to Nirvâna in Brâhman. . . . Each one ought to raise himself by himself, and ought not to debase himself; for he is himself the friend and also the foe of himself. . . . Devotion is not for him who eats too much, nor for him who fasts excessively; not for him who is disposed to sleep too much, nor for him who is ever wakeful. . . . The devotion which destroys all pain, is for the man who is moderate in food and in recreation, who uses moderate effort in his actions, is moderate in sleep and in waking.[1] . . . 'As a lamp sheltered from the wind flickers not,' is the accepted simile of the Yogin who is subdued in thought, and is engaged in the devotion of the soul. . . . When thought is wholly at rest and when contemplating himself in himself he is satisfied in himself: when he knows the boundless joy which is beyond the senses, which the mind apprehends, and, fixed therein, never wavers from the truth; when, having obtained it, he thinks no other acquisition is superior to this; let him know that this severance from all trouble is called Yoga. This Yoga must be practised with constancy till thought is repressed. . . . For supreme happiness comes to the Yogin whose heart is at rest,

[1] This is practically his predecessor Gautama's teaching of the excellence and beauty of the "Middle Path."

in whom passion is tranquillised, who is one with Brâhman. . . ."

Every cause must work out its own appropriate results. Therefore the practice of Yoga is intended to avoid any kind of action that can possibly be avoided, and thereby to prevent the starting of new causes, and thus to hasten the time of the soul's release from the wheel of rebirths in a physical body. But Patangali teaches that all the higher knowledge which may be gained through the practice of "Râja-Yoga"—the higher kind of Yoga—is quite useless to him who is not prepared for it by that experience which is only to be obtained in the due performance of the duties of life. Only when a man has been both "householder and father," only when he has fulfilled all his just obligations to society, is he fit to become an initiate of Râja-Yoga. As Max Müller reminds us, the passage through life of a so-called "twice-born" man is divided into four periods, viz.: "(1) the pupil; (2) the married man or householder; (3) the forest-recluse; (4) the ascetic." The last of these, "forgetting all that had once troubled or delighted his heart, drags himself away into the deepest solitude, and falls at last into the arms of his last friend, death."

It is interesting to know that the practice of Yoga prevails in India to-day, very much as it did at the beginning of the Christian era. Writing in 1902, Mr Edward Carpenter tells us that, during his residence in Ceylon, he became acquainted with a typical Yogin. This man was a Brahman, "well versed in law, in statecraft, and grammar, and had a practical knowledge of the world," and Mr Carpenter was in the habit of discussing with him questions of ethics, religion, philosophy, or cosmogony. This Yogin spent most of his time "absorbed in trance-conditions," and yet was able, at any moment, to throw himself energetically into any kind of work. He would talk with Mr Carpenter "for hours together, with great power and concentration of mind." But when the talk ceased, all his interest in the subject ceased, and the Yogin reverted immediately to "the state of interior meditation, which had apparently become his normal condition." He explained to Mr Carpenter that to be able to concentrate the mind, at all times, on what one is doing is "a distinct step in 'gnanam' (knowledge)." Not until the student of Yoga can do this can he advance to the second step, which is "the faculty of effacing thought." To efface thought the Yogin must retire to a place where he is absolutely free from all disturbance, and must keep his body quite motionless—not in an attitude of ease, but "sitting or standing erect with muscles tense." All his power of will must be called into exercise to do this, because it is necessary "to 'destroy' every thought on the instant of its appearance." Naturally the student fails at first to do this; his thought gives place to oblivion, and then to sleep, by which no progress is gained. But, if the Yogin resolutely continues this practice, his power to control his mind gradually increases, "month by month, and year by year, and slowly the student becomes conscious of curious but distinct physiological changes." Then, at last, as the Yogin explained, he finds that thought has gone, and, in its stead, "there streams through his being a vast and illumined consciousness, which surrounds and overflows, so that he is like a pot in water, which has the water within it and without! This, at last, is 'Samadhi'!" Those who can attain to Samadhi have acquired the faculty of separating the soul from the body, and to such, death, when it comes, is no longer an agony. It is evident that this state of Samadhi of the Indian ascetics is identical with the state of trance into which both Plotinus of Alexandria and Paul of Tarsus were able to throw themselves, and that it resembles the "beatific vision" of Augustine, and the "extasis" of Clement.

Two states of Yoga are recognised, the Higher or "Râja Yoga," as practised by the Yogin above mentioned, and the Lower or "Hâtha Yoga," the only object of which is to develop the "siddis," or abnormal powers. The essence of all Yoga is to acquire the power to concentrate the mind and control the will. Europeans use their will-power chiefly to overcome the external world, whereas the Indian Yogin makes use of his will-power to gain mastery over the inner world. To use the words of the Yogin, spoken to Mr Carpenter, "When their thoughts cease to move, the wise perceive within themselves the Absolute Consciousness which is the witness of all things (sarva sakshi). . . . The true quality of the soul is that of space (akâsa), by which it is everywhere *at rest*. But this space within the soul is something far above material space. The whole of material space, including the suns and stars, appears to you then as it were but an atom of soul-space." Mr Carpenter says that the prevailing expression on the face of this Yogin was one of "intense happiness," and that he described his own state of mind as being "joy, always joy!" (Sandosiam, sandosiam, eppotham!).

The Vedânta is, says Max Müller, the only system of philosophy now studied in India. The word Veda means "knowledge"; the word Vedânta means "the end or aim of all knowledge." The aim of the Vedânta system of thought is to help the thinker to rid himself of Avidya (nescience, or ignorance), which causes him to mistake his personality for his real self, by showing him the true relation between subject and object. The Vedânta explains that the subject is the soul or Âtman; it is the self, the ego, the knower; it can neither be seen, heard, nor touched. It is the only reality, and is identical with Brâhman, or Param-Âtman, as the Vedânta often calls this postulate. The object is the not-self, the non-ego—everything, in fact, that is outside the self. Even our bodies and all our physical powers must be considered as belonging to the non-ego, not to the self. The whole teaching of the Vedânta, says Max Müller, "is summed up in the words, 'Brâhman is true, the world is false; the soul is Brâhman and nothing else. . . . He who knows Brâhman *is* Brâhman'; and still more concisely in the well-known phrase: 'Thou art That.'"

But, although in its relation to Brâhman everything is unreal, we may think of the universe as being at least phenomenally real in its relation to the human soul, or Âtman. As Professor Deussen puts it, "the world is nothing more than my representation of it, that is, it is the form in which things appear to me. The world is as real as we are real." The most famous of all the commentators of the Upanishads, Samkara, says: "The whole complex of phenomenal existence is considered as true, so long as the knowledge of Brâhman and the Self of all has not arisen, just as the phantoms of a dream are considered to be true until the sleeper awakens." Samkara teaches that the thinker and his thought, the knower and the known, are all alike illusions; there are not two things which may be called mind in itself, and matter in itself, as it were, but both are mere manifestations of one Absolute Being, of one unknowable entity. Brâhman and the universe being conceived as identical, cause and effect (Kârana and Kârya) must also be considered as being one and the same, because the effect must always be latent in the cause, and must be itself the cause of further effect: as the Vedânta puts it, "they are not other, are not different from each other."

The earlier teachers of the Vedânta aimed at the removal of nescience, or Avidya, from the minds of their disciples. Later teachers insist more on the necessity to get rid of Mâyâ, or illusion. Some commentators speak of Mâyâ as "the creative Mother of the Universe." Starting with the fact that the human consciousness persists unchanged through all the changes of human life, the Vedânta teaches that it is the mind of man alone which creates all the differences of name and form (nama rupa), and which, having done so, foolishly identifies itself with its own creations, and thereby suffers pain and joy. The Katha Upanishad says: "The Knowing Self is not born, it dies not. . . . The wise, who knows the self, as bodiless within the bodies, as unchanging among changing things, as great, and present everywhere, he never grieves. But he who has not turned away from his wickedness, who is not subdued and at peace, whose mind is not at rest, he can never obtain the self (even) by knowledge." Even this wise man, however, it seems, can only fully realise the truth that the universe is Mâyâ, or illusion, when he happens to be in a peculiar phase of consciousness known as "Moksha," which is the state of ecstatic trance, during which the soul feels itself for the time to be a part of the Divine Unity.

All this, however, belongs to the esoteric doctrine of the Vedânta. Samkara in his exoteric teaching postulated a creator of the phenomenal universe whom he called "Iswara" (the Lord). As a Vedantist of modern India, the Swami Abhedanada, says in his English essay on "The Ideal of the Vedânta," written in 1898, "the Vedânta declares that there is no logical evidence of any Iswara." Like all else, Iswara is Mâyâ—a mere abstraction—which it is "convenient" to speak of as the Universal Soul, or the soul of nature. "We have made ourselves," says Abhedanada, "slaves of delusion, slaves of passion, slaves of desire"; therefore the ideal aimed at by the Vedânta-teaching is to free our minds from the "bondage of delusion," caused by our ignorance of the truth. "The truth is one: it cannot be many!

It is the unchangeable reality of the universe. . . . Whether we call that unchangeable reality 'Iswara,' or 'the Reality of the universe,' or 'Âtman,' our real nature, the difference is one of name only. Because they look at it from the outside, the dualists call that truth 'Iswara': those who look at it from the inside, call it 'Âtman,' or 'Self,' or 'Reality within us.' . . . Knowledge of the truth means knowledge of the underlying unity of existence, . . . the oneness of the reality within us with the reality of the universe." Each human soul must in the course of "ages" attain by natural "process of evolution" to the ideal state of "Moksha." But "let us shorten the time," says the Swami, "by trying our best to attain freedom and perfection in this life! . . . The very moment we realise this Âtman, that very moment we become unselfish, we become conscious how great and majestic we are. Then we know that all the powers of the universe have proceeded from the infinite source of powers within each individual soul. . . . Then we shall be able to reform the social, political, and religious evils that exist to-day; then will the kingdom of heaven manifest here, for our real nature is divine." We must admit the grandeur of this Indian ideal.

The idea of Brâhman is scarcely less difficult to understand than the idea of Mâyâ. Stated in the fewest possible words, Brâhman is anything and everything that contains in itself the possibility of growth, development, evolution, the root of the word being "bri," which means "to expand, to dilate, to grow." Brâhman is therefore to be understood as the eternally evolving universe of mind and matter, "the One," the "Divine Monad." Space may seem to be, as it were, enclosed in separate rooms or vessels, but is nevertheless all one; and in the same way all soul is one, although to us there seems to be a separate soul in every bodily form. Brâhman is therefore the "Universal Soul"—the synthesis of all souls, animal, human, and superhuman. In its aspect of synthesis of all being—material or spiritual—Brâhman is spoken of as the "conditioned" or "qualified," or "Saguna-Brâhman," and is adored as "Iswara" (Lord) by all Vedantists who feel the necessity for some object of worship. But, beyond "Iswara," who personifies the visible universe of matter, and the invisible universe of mind, the Vedânta philosophy postulates a still more metaphysical abstraction which it calls the unqualified, unconditioned, and absolute Brâhma, or "Nirguna-Brâhman." This is the Causeless Cause of all being. It is possible, as the Hindu philosophers say, to apprehend at least the concept of this invisible and changeless "Saguna-Brâhman," because it is, as it were, reflected to our minds in the physical and psychical phenomena which make up the universe, just as sunlight is reflected to the eye in water. But to imagine the "Nirguna-Brâhman" is beyond the power of thought.

The Mundaka Upanishad says of Iswara, the conditioned Brâhman: "As the flowing rivers come to their end in the sea, losing name and form, so, liberated from name and form, proceed the the wise to the Divine Soul." The Brihad Upanishad says of the conditioned or Saguna-Brâhman: "It is not apprehended by the eye, nor by devotion, nor by rites; but he, whose mind is purified by the light of knowledge, beholds the undivided One . . . inconceivable by thought, more distant than all distant things, and also here dwelling in the heart of him who can behold. . . ." Max Müller is of opinion that "Brâhman, the ultimate reality, is but another name for what European philosophers have called "the ultimate," "the unknowable." But this is not quite the case; for, when we compare the Eastern and Western ideas, we find that, whilst life is not postulated as inherent in the "unknowable" of European philosophers, the Indian postulate of "Param-âtman," or of "Brâhman"—as it is indifferently called—is a synonym for life itself. The Brihad Upanishad says: "Life is the immortal One, names and forms conceal this. Life is the preserver of all forms; by Life the universe is sustained. . . . It is the creator, and all that moves and breathes and sleeps has its origin in It; It is their goal. . . . Life is the soul of the whole; It is all the gods." The Vedantic theory is that psychic life, or Âtman, inheres in the most minute molecule of matter, and that it is only by assuming the whole universe of matter and mind to constitute one life, that it is possible to explain that strange power which is certainly possessed by some Indian Yogins of to-day, the power, namely, of being conscious, when in the state of self-induced hypnotic trance, of events taking place at a distance.

Quite one of the most thoughtful and intelligible of the modern Hindu commentators on the Vedânta-philosophy is the Swami Vivekananda, who was the Vedantist delegate at the Parliament of Religions held at Chicago during the time of the Great Exhibition. He is a high-caste Brahman and a disciple of the Hindu saint, or "Sannyasin," Rama Krishna, who died in 1886. Max Müller says: "From what I have seen and read of Vivekananda and his colleagues, they seem to me bent on doing good work. I wish them all the success they deserve by their unselfish devotion and their high ideals." In his definition of Brâhman, or Iswara, as conceived by the Vedânta, Vivekananda says:—"The one appears in various forms, as body, mind, and soul—as many, but really there is only one. . . . The realist looks at the phenomenon only, the idealist tries to look at the noumenon. . . . For the genuine idealist who has truly arrived at the power of perception, where he can get away from changes, for him the changeful universe has vanished, and he has the right to say that it is all delusion—there was no change; whilst the realist, who looks only at the changeful, has a right to say that this is all real. . . . The impersonal is a much higher generalisation than the personal. The Infinite can only be impersonal; the personal is only limited. . . . If we think of the individual as separate from everything else in the universe, it cannot stand a moment, such a thing never existed. . . . To understand the personal, we have to refer always to the Impersonal, the particular must be referred to the general. . . . The Impersonal is the Truth, the Self of man, but the personalised manifestation (John Smith) is not referred to as that

Truth." . . . "The idea of the Impersonal, . . . and that nature is the evolution of the Impersonal, is the nearest we can get to any truth that is demonstrable. . . . The only argument in favour of the partial conception of a personal God, is that, as yet, it is necessary for many. . . . The clear light of truth very few minds can bear, much less work upon. It is necessary, therefore, that this comfortable religion (belief in Iswara or God) should exist; it helps many souls, in time, to better."

As Max Müller says: "How the change from the real to the phenomenal came about, Vedantists can tell us as little as we can tell them. They simply point to the fact that it has come about, that it is there, and that it can be nothing but phenomenal to us, but that the phenomenal could not even seem to be without the real behind it." When they say that the universe is our own mental creation, and mere Mâyâ, Vedantists do not mean that it is illusion to ordinary minds, because the facts of seeing, hearing, touching, and smelling cannot be denied. But they mean that the universe is *relative to*, not independent of, our minds. The normal mind perceives it as a material world, the spiritualised mind might perceive it as "heaven," whilst another kind of mind might consider it "hell." The universe cannot be called non-existent, but it depends entirely on the mind that perceives it. Vivekananda says:—"We know nothing about this universe, and yet we cannot rightly say we know nothing. Everything we see or do may be a dream. . . . This standing between knowledge and ignorance, this mystic twilight, this mingling of truth and falsehood, of seeming and reality, is the fate of all of us. Matter, spirit, mind—give things any name you please, we cannot say they are, we cannot say they are not. This eternal play of light and darkness, this is Mâyâ. Stretch your ideas as far as you can, make them higher and higher, call it 'Infinite,' or any other name you choose; every idea is within this Mâyâ, everything that calls up an idea in the mind, everything that is bound by the laws of time, space, and causation, is within Mâyâ."

The "One Life" of the universe is called "Prana," when considered from the physical point of view, and "Âtman," when considered from the psychical point of view. Prana (life) inheres in the one element (Akâsa) from which differentiate all the elementary forces of the universe. The spark of individual physical life, inherent in every atom of the universe, is called "Jiva," whilst the spark of psychic life inherent in every human being is called "Jiv-Âtman," a term which we may translate as "soul." Jiv-Âtman is considered to be merely a very highly evolved state of Prana—the One Life. It is interesting to note that a theory very suggestive of the Vedantic theory of Mâyâ is advanced by some of our modern physicists, who tell us that all the metamorphoses of form, all the correlations of force are more or less illusory. We are assured that our bodies, seemingly so solid, and all our surroundings, stationary and massive as some of them appear to be, are mere aggregations of molecules, which are vibrating with inconceivable rapidity. We get an idea of the marvellous rapidity of this molecular vibration from the estimate of our experts that the average number of undulations *per second* of the "luminiferous ether" in the propagation of light is nearly six hundred billions, and also from their demonstration that there are nearly sixty thousand undulations of the "extreme violet rays" *in one inch.* Waves of light and waves of sound are, in fact, so unthinkably rapid that they must ever remain imperceptible to our senses. Our modern theory of atoms was anticipated in India, in the fifth century B.C., by Kanada, who, in the Vaiseshika Sutras, says that the homogeneous Akâsa is composed of Anus (atoms) so small that six of them are not equal in size to the mote in a sunbeam. When, at the dawn of a cycle of manifestation, motion begins amongst these atoms, they first unite in couples, and, as the evolutionary process continues, these double atoms cohere in gradually increasing groups until forms are produced.

Another suggestion of our Western thinkers is that differentiation may have commenced by the whirling motion of innumerable minute vortices or centres of motion in the ether. But how these vortices were set in motion is not suggested. As yet, no bridge has been found to span the gulf between organic and inorganic: the appearance of the first germ of life is, so far, unaccounted for. The Vedânta avoids this immense difficulty, by boldly asserting that life is latent everywhere, even in what we call inorganic substance. There is no such thing as "dead matter," says the Vedantist: the whole universe is one life, is one thought, is Brâhman.

Buddhism was the consequence of Gautama's desire to simplify and popularise the teaching of the Vedas. Buddhism was from the first a missionary religion. More than three centuries B.C., the followers of the Buddha wandered far and wide "preaching universal brotherhood." But it is only in recent years that Vedantism, the latest phase of Brahmanism, has been taught out of India. The Hindu saint, Rama Krishna, who died in 1886 A.D., "was well known in India," says Max Müller, "as a Mahatman," and he explains that "Mahatmans know, by long practice, how to put themselves into a real trance, and thus make people believe that they have been outside their body and have received inspiration from a divine source."[1] A well-known disciple of Rama Krishna says: "Sri Rama Krishna attained great Yoga-powers, such as thought-reading, predicting future events, seeing things at a distance, healing disease by simply willing." As Max Müller explains, "men of the class of Rama Krishna are addicted to devotion or love (bhakti) rather than knowledge or pure philosophy (gnâna). They speak of Krishna (the supposed incarnation of Vishnu) rather than of Brahmân." The modern Hindu teachers themselves put the matter thus: "The sages try to reach Brâhman by wisdom (gnâna), the yogins try to reach Param-Âtman through contemplation (yoga), but all men

[1] Paul of Tarsus could pass at will into this state of ecstasy or trance. He speaks of it as being in "the Third Heaven," and says that when in this state he heard "unspeakable words." Speaking to the Corinthians, he says that he did not know if the divine revelations came to him when he was in his body or outside it: "whether in the body, or out of the body, I cannot tell: God knoweth."

may reach Krishna, the Bhagavan (Lord) by devotion (bhakti)." Rama Krishna, speaking of Mâyâ, says that it is "attachment to one's own self, family, sect, or country." His teaching appears to have been very broad. His disciples quote many of his sayings, such as: "Different creeds are but different paths to reach Iswara." . . . "As from the same gold various ornaments are made, having different forms and names, so Iswara is worshipped in different countries and ages, and has different forms and names." . . . "Iswara is in all men, but all men are not in Iswara. That is why they suffer." In a series of lectures on the Vedânta, delivered in his own racy English, in London, a few years ago, the best known of Rama Krishna's disciples says: "We may look upon the Bhagavad-Gîtâ as the last of the Upanishads. Every verse has been collected from some portion of the Upanishads." He calls it "the best commentary on the Vedânta philosophy," and says that "the doctrine which stands out luminously in every page of the Gîtâ is intense activity, but in the midst of calmness. . . . This idea is called the secret of work. . . . The less passion there is, the better we work; the calmer we are, the more work we do. . . . The man who gives way to anger, or hatred, or any other passion, only breaks himself to pieces. It is the calm, forgiving, well-balanced mind that does most work. . . . Vedânta preaches to men to have faith in themselves, first of all. . . . We are fools to cry out that we are weak and impure. . . . The Vedânta recognises no sin: it recognises error. The greatest error is when you say you are weak, and a sinner, and a miserable creature. Do not say you cannot do this or that, because every time you even think such things, you rivet one more link in the chain that holds you down, you send a bad thought out into the world. . . . No man becomes purer: it is more or less of manifestation, the veil goes away and the native purity of the soul manifests itself. . . . The difference between weakness and strength, between vice and virtue, between life and death, is one of degree only, because *oneness* is the secret of everything. . . . The knowledge of the oneness of the universe is eternal bliss. . . . The Vedânta does not really denounce the world, it teaches the deification of the world. We have to give up the world, as we seem to know it, and to acknowledge what it really is—Iswara: we have to see God in everything. . . . There is a use in evil: it is a great teacher. Every one of our errors teaches us a lesson. We are the resultant of all we have done, all we have thought. . . . The highest temple of worship, says the Vedânta, is the human soul. Neither forest, nor cave, nor holy Benares gives clearer vision. The same state goes with the man everywhere, because man makes his own world. . . . The divine nature in man has to be called out, and it will work itself out. Fire exists in flint, or in two pieces of dry wood; but friction or steel is necessary to call that fire out; so this fire, the natural freedom and purity in the very nature of every soul. . . . To think that we are bound, is to hypnotise ourselves. As soon as we say, 'I am bound,' 'I am weak,' 'I am helpless,' woe to us! We become miserable because we are weak: we commit crime because we are weak: we suffer because we are weak. . . . Nothing makes us work so well, at our best and highest, as when *all responsibility* is thrown upon *ourselves*, when we have nobody to lay any blame on, or to grope towards—neither devil nor a personal god. I am responsible for my fate. I am the bringer of good or evil to myself. I am existence, knowledge, Bliss Absolute. This, says the Vedânta, is the only prayer, this is the only way to reach the goal. . . . It is through the heart that Iswara is seen, not through the intellect, but through feeling intensified, deified, till it feels the oneness in everything, till it feels God in itself and others. . . . Feel like Buddha, and you will be a Buddha."

Buddhism is a protest against the extreme subtlety of Brahman thought. Its leading doctrine is that the solution of the mystery of sorrow and the way to attain peace is in all things to follow "the Middle Path" of temperance and virtue. The origin of the teaching is ascribed to Gautama, called "the Buddha," or "Enlightened One," who is said to have died at Kusinagara, a town about eighty miles distant from Benares, about 380 B.C., at which time it is certain that many Buddhist missions were active in Western Asia. We hear of these missions from Megasthenes, who was sent by Seleucus Nicator as Greek ambassador to Kandragupta, the rajah of Maghadda, the warrior who drove the Macedonians out of India. Megasthenes speaks of these Buddhists as "the Hindu Gymnosophists," and says that "they live in simple style, and lie on beds of rushes and skins. They abstain from animal food and from sexual pleasures, and spend their time in listening to serious discourse, and in imparting knowledge to such as will listen to them."

The grandson of Kandragupta, named Piyadasi, who acquired the title of "the Kind-hearted," and who is better known to us under his Pâli name, Asoka, was an enthusiastic Buddhist, and caused the Buddhist precepts to be inscribed, in various Prākrit dialects, on stone-pillars and on rock-tablets in all parts of his dominions. The stone-pillars have been found at Delhi and Allahabad, and the rock-tablets near Peshaur, at Girnar in Guzerat, at Dhauli in Orissa, and at Babra on the road south-west of Delhi. In these inscriptions, which have lately been translated, we find that Asoka enjoins his subjects to be just, virtuous, and generous, to be obedient to parents, kind to children, to be charitable to all men and merciful to all animals. "There is no higher duty," says Asoka, "than to work for the good of the whole world." We also find, from these inscriptions, that this benevolent Buddhist rajah caused wells to be sunk wherever they were wanted, that he erected hospitals not only for men, but also for animals, that he planted trees to shade the highways, and cultivated gardens of medicinal plants. We are able to fix within a few years the exact date of Asoka's reign, because his inscriptions record the sending by him of embassies to four different Greek rulers.

It was about 250 B.C. that a council of the chief Buddhist teachers assembled at Patna, under the presidency of Asoka, to decide on the authenticity of the numerous doctrines ascribed to the Buddha. The collection (Pitaka) then chosen has been held by Buddhists ever since to be the actual teaching of the Buddha, handed down by his earliest disciples in the very words of "the Holy One." Not long after this council at Patna, no less than nine missions left India to preach the gospel abroad. At this time Asoka's own son, Mahinda, had been already for twelve years a member of the order of mendicants ("Sangha") which the Master had established during his lifetime, and he was therefore sent by Asoka to convey Buddhist doctrine to his friend Tissa, the ruler of Ceylon. Tissa, we know, reigned in Ceylon from 250 B.C. to 230 B.C.

The most devout Buddhists always seem to have led the life of solitary forest-recluses. But the majority of Buddhists simply belonged to the "Sangha"; that is to say, they lived together in brotherhoods, in forest-groves or in gardens, given to them by wealthy friends and sympathisers. As these brotherhoods became larger, permanent residences were built for the various Sangha, which were frequently endowed with a fixed income. Thus, in time, many of these Buddhist monasteries became wealthy. But at no time do these early Buddhist monks appear to have had any kind of church or any kind of ritual. The only practice that was even suggestive of ritual was the placing of flowers before the various statues erected to the memory of "the Holy One." The Buddhist doctrine is that the only true sacrifice is the sacrifice of self. Without any outside help, without the aid of any authority, every man must evolve his own character: he must follow with fortitude the "Middle Path," that narrow "Way" which avoids on the one side the degrading self-indulgence of the sensualist, and on the other the silly austerities of the ascetic. All the sorrow and suffering in life comes from selfishness. The thirst (tanha) for sensuous enjoyment at the expense of others produces that feeling of separation which exists between man and man. Quench this thirst, keep the self in complete subjection, and all will be well. The Buddhist teaching is summarised in the Four Noble Truths. These are: (1) suffering; (2) the cause of suffering; (3) cessation from suffering; (4) the Path which leads to the evolution of man's higher nature.

Applicants for admission to the Sangha or Brotherhood had to pass through a very simple ceremony of initiation, which Professor Rhys Davids thinks was identical with that used in Ceylon to-day. This consists merely in publicly repeating the Five Commandments (Pancha-sila, or Pan-sil). These commandments are held to have been handed down in the very words of the Master. They run thus:—

"Now, I will tell you the life which a householder should lead. . . . Such duties as are peculiar to the mendicant cannot be fulfilled by one who has a family.

1. "Let him not destroy, or cause to be destroyed, any life at all, or sanction the acts of those who do so. Let him refrain even from hurting any creature, both those that are strong, and those that tremble in the world.

2. "A disciple should refrain from stealing anything at any place, should not cause another to steal anything, should not consent to the acts of those who steal anything, should avoid every kind of theft.

3. "A wise man should avoid unchastity as if it were a burning pit of live coal. One who is not able to live in a state of celibacy should not commit adultery.

4. "When one is come to any royal assembly or gathering [*i.e.* any official inquiry] he should not tell lies, or consent to the acts of those who tell lies. He should avoid every kind of untruth.

5. "The householder who delights in the law should not indulge in intoxicating drinks, should not cause others to drink, should not sanction the acts of those that drink, knowing that it results in insanity. The ignorant commit sins in consequence of drunkenness . . . though it is pleasing to the ignorant."

The Buddhist philosophy teaches the actual existence of the material world as the home of conscious beings. We know that both the universe and all in it evolves, but we can never know either the beginning or the end of this eternal evolution. Everything passes away—men's bodies, men's souls, men's thoughts; all that remains is "Karma," the changeless law of cause and effect. Although Buddhism rejects the Brahmanical theory of a metaphysical ego, or "Âtman," which persists from one incarnation to another, it does not deny the existence of the soul in man. But it explains that what, for convenience, it calls the soul, or "the Self," far from being a monad, or simple unit, is neither more nor less than the aggregate or sum-total of the man's sensations, desires, and aspirations. We might say that the teaching of Buddhism is not that man *has* ideas, but that man *is* ideas. The theory is that the physical and psychical being of man consists of a number of "soul-structures," or, in other words, of physical and psychical tendencies and formative faculties which persist through a series of incarnations in accordance with the law of cause and effect, or Karma. Each "Self" or soul is considered to be the logical, just, and inevitable result of its own Karma; it is the effect of a long chain of antecedent causes—the impulses, motives, aspirations, and desires which have been the motive powers of the Self during a series of lives in a human body. It will be seen, therefore, that, although Buddhist philosophy rejects the Brahmanical idea of a persistent metaphysical ego, it teaches the theory that those thoughts, aims, and desires which are especially characteristic in any one incarnation have the tendency to reappear in another. Therefore we may say that the Buddhist holds that the same *type* of soul reincarnates, whilst the Vedantist imagines that it is the identical individual soul.

Buddhist teachers illustrate the idea of the rebirth of the Samkaras by three favourite similes. The Self, they say, is reborn as the mango is reborn from its own seed, as one flame is lighted from another, and as knowledge is passed from mind to mind. The Samkaras, moreover, whilst incarnated in a human body, appear as an individuality, so that, during his lifetime, a man's mind, character, name, and form must be considered as realities, and the man must strive his utmost to strengthen his character by self-discipline and self-culture. The teaching is: "All that we are is the result of what we have thought: it is founded on our thoughts, it is made up of our thoughts. . . . By oneself evil is done: by oneself one suffers. Purity and impurity belong to oneself. No one can purify another." The wise man gets rid of the illusion of the self, because selfishness is the source of all those evils from which he desires emancipation. It is "trishna," or "tanha," as it is called in Pali, the thirst, or yearning, or grasping after physical sensations and physical expression, which impels the Samkaras to incarnate in one body after another. The Buddhist thinker postulates five classes of Samkaras, viz.: (1) bodily qualities, (2) sense-perceptions, (3) mental tendencies, (4) abstractions, (5) spiritual faculties. All these manifest in a body and amidst those conditions which are more or less in harmony with them. The teaching warns us against yielding to trishna, this keen longing for physical sensation. "The man whom this contemptible thirst, this poison in the world, overcomes, that man's sorrows grow like the birana weed when it is spreading. He who overcomes this contemptible thirst, difficult to be conquered in this world, from him sufferings fall off, like water from a lotus-leaf." When once a man has quenched all longing for physical enjoyment, the impulse towards reincarnation subsides, just as a flame ceases to burn, or live, when the oil in the lamp is exhausted: "the wise are extinguished like this lamp." A man who has become so completely spiritualised, that life in a body is no longer necessary, is said to have attained to the state of "Nirvâna." Lust, hatred, and delusion are called "the three fires," the extinction of which is the state of the "Arhat," the state of "Nirvâna." As the literal meaning of the word Nirvâna is extinction, it has caused some Orientalists to suppose that the word is synonymous with "annihilation." But Nirvâna really means the higher life of the man who has risen above himself. It means the extinction of the illusion of self, and the consequent annihilation of selfishness. It is the state of complete enlightenment, of perfect goodness, and of perfect peace. Gautama compares it to "a city of peace," and to "an island which no flood can overwhelm." Professor Rhys Davids proposes to translate it "holiness," whilst Bunsen's translation is "inward peace." It is identical with the beatific vision of the Christian saints. "Tranquil is the mind, tranquil the words and the deeds of him who is thus tranquillised and made free by wisdom." . . . "Like a lake, unruffled; for such there are no more births."

The goal of Nirvâna cannot be reached in one incarnation; but, by right thinking and right doing, progress may be made along the "noble eight-fold path" which leads upward and onward. The "eight steps" of this path are defined as (1) right views, (2) right aims, (3) right words, (4) right conduct, (5) right mode of livelihood, (6) right exertion, (7) right-mindfulness, (8) right meditation. "I teach Siha," says Gautama in the Dhammapada,[1] "the not doing of

[1] "The Dhammapada," says Professor Rhys David, "is a collection of verses culled from other Buddhist scriptures, and purport to be the real words spoken by Gautama."

such actions as are unrighteous, either by deed, or word, or thought: I teach the not bringing about of the manifold conditions which are evil and not good: I teach Siha, the doing of such actions as are righteous. . . . I proclaim the annihilation of lust, of ill-will, of illusion."

Buddhism, as generally practised to-day, is at least as unlike the teaching ascribed to Gautama, as the popular Christianity of the twentieth century is unlike the simple rule of life laid down in the "Sermon on the Mount." The present "Māhayāna" school of Buddhism, as we find it in Tibet, China, and Japan, veils the simple beauty of the gospel attributed to the Buddha under a rank growth of superstition. The following extracts from the Dhammapada will, however, give an idea of Buddhist ethics four centuries B.C.:—

"One day of endeavour is better than a hundred years of sloth. . . .

"Attack vigorously what is to be done. A careless man scatters only more widely the dust of his passions. . . .

"He who rouses not himself when it is time to rise, who, though young and strong, is full of sloth, whose will and thought are weak, that lazy and idle man will never find the way of knowledge. . . .

"Earnestness is the path of immortality: thoughtlessness is the path of death. Those who are in earnest die not; those who are thoughtless are as if already dead. . . .

"As a plant sheds its withered flowers, so a man should shed passions and hate. . . .

"Think not lightly of evil: drop by drop the jar is filled. Think not lightly of good: the wise is filled with purity, gathering it drop by drop. . . .

"Among men who are greedy, let us dwell free from greed. Let us live happily, not hating those who hate us. . . .

"Let a man overcome anger by kindness, evil by good. Let him conquer the stingy by a gift, the liar by truth. . . .

"What is the use of platted hair, O fool! what of a garment of skins? Your low yearnings are within, and the outside ye make clean! . . .

"Never in this world does hatred cease by hatred. Hatred ceases by love. This is always its nature. . . .

"As rain breaks in upon an ill-thatched hut, so passion breaks in upon an untrained mind. . . .

"As long as sin bears no fruit, the fool thinks it honey. But when the sin ripens, then indeed he goes down into sorrow.

"Let a man cultivate good-will without measure towards the whole world, above, below, around, unstinted, unmixed with any feeling of differing or opposing interests. Let a man remain steadfast in this state of mind all the while he is awake, whether he is standing, walking, sitting, or lying down. This state of mind is the best in the world. . . .

"It is good to tame the mind, difficult to hold in, and flighty, rushing where it wills. A tamed mind is the bringer of bliss. . . .

"One may conquer a thousand men in battle, but he who conquers himself alone is the greatest victor. He who holds back rising anger, as one might a rolling chariot, him indeed I call a driver: others only hold the reins."

The subject of the "Bhagavad-Gîtâ," or "Blessed Path," which is but a section of the great Maha-Bhârata epic, is the fight between the rival clans of the Pandavas and Kauravas for the possession of the city of Hastinapura. But this subject only serves the unknown author of the poem as the medium of teaching an eclectic system of philosophy and ethics, which, as he tells us in the text, is based on the Yoga-system of Patangali, "already lost through length of time." We find in this poem not only the teaching of Patangali, but also the best ideas of the Samkhya and Vedânta systems. Indeed, the Bhagavad-Gîtâ may be described as a summary of the noblest thoughts in Hindu philosophy and ethics, which are woven round the central idea of Krishna, "the Holy One," the incarnation of Vishnu, in whose mouth the poet puts the teaching. The author, whoever he may be, uses the word "Mâyâ" in a sense that is unusual. For instance, the universe is called Mâyâ, not because it has no real existence, as the Vedânta teaches, but because it hides from man the presence of Iswara (the Lord), and deludes him with the idea that nothing exists which is not perceptible to his senses. Thus Krishna is made to say: "I am not manifest to all. Being wrapped in my mystic mâyâ, this deluded world cannot recognise me, the unborn, the eternal." And again Krishna says: "I am manifested by my own mâyâ; as often as there is a decline of virtue and an insurrection of vice and injustice in the world, I make myself known. Thus

I appear, from age to age, for the preservation of the just, the destruction of evil-doers, and the establishment of virtue."

Although many commentators attribute to the Bhagavad - Gîtâ a much earlier date, Professor Lassen's estimate that it was written about 250 A.D. is provisionally accepted as probably correct. Therefore some theologians jump to the conclusion that the old Indian Krishna-mythos itself must have been borrowed from the story of the life of Christ. The exhaustive study, however, of the various early Hindu traditions of the successive incarnations of Vishnu, leaves no doubt whatever that the legend of Krishna is of Indian origin. Lassen quotes the Greek writer Megasthenes, who lived in the third century B.C., and who, in 315 B.C., was actually Greek ambassador at the court of the Indian prince, Chandragupta, who identifies Krishna as "the Indian Hercules," who was worshipped at Mathura, the legendary birthplace of Krishna, and of whom Megasthenes relates the legend that "he traversed the whole earth and sea to purify them from evil." Like Krishna, both Râmâ and Buddha were held to be incarnations of the divinity; though Râmâ, the seventh "avatara" of Vishnu, who is the hero of the great Ramayana epos, was not supposed to have been so complete an incarnation of Vishnu as the other two. Râmâ, in fact, is the *Ideal Man* of the Hindus. He is the type of all phases of life. Râmâ passes through all the "steps" of student, warrior, husband, father, up to that of recluse. His are all the deepest joys of life; his too are all life's sorrows and injustice ; but by means of these Râmâ develops a heroic self-sacrifice and a high-minded forgiveness of injuries. He is said to "overcome mankind by fidelity, Brahmans by generosity, preceptors by diligent attention to study, and all enemies by sword and bow." He is the poetic embodiment of the Hindu idea of what a son, brother, husband, king, hero, and saint should be ; and after delivering his fellow-men from all kinds of moral evil, he ascends at last to heaven from the banks of the Saraya. The legend is that, as Râmâ steps into the sacred river, a voice calls to him from the sky : "Approach, O Vishnu ! enter thine own body, the eternal Akâsa !" In the Maha-Bhârata epic Krishna is made to say : "Know that Righteousness (Dharma) is my first-born, beloved Son, whose nature it is to have compassion on all creatures. In his character I exist among men, both present and past, in different forms and disguises. . . . I, the unfailing, build up the bulwark of right, as the ages pass, assuming various divine births to promote the good of all creatures."

But the teaching ascribed to Krishna in the Bhagavad-Gîtâ section of the great Maha-Bhârata epos is more subtle than that ascribed to Râmâ. For instance, Krishna is supposed to say :—"Know that the splendour which is seated in the sun and illumines the whole universe is from me. Entering into the earth, I sustain all things by my vital force, and becoming a savoury juice (soma) I nourish all vegetation. . . . I become fire (heat) and enter into the bodies of all that breathe, and, being united with the inward and outward breath, I cook (digest) the four kinds of food." [These four kinds of food are such as are "broken by the teeth, licked by the tongue, sucked by the lips, or drunk."]. . . . "I am the beginning and the middle and the end of all existing things. . . . See my royal mystery! My spirit, which is the source of all, supports all things, but dwells not in them. . . . As the mighty wind moves everywhere, but is ever contained within the Akâsa, know that thus all beings are contained in me.

"At the end of a Kalpa,[1] all things go into my material nature; at the beginning of a Kalpa I send them forth again. . . .

"Know that I am the soul in all forms of matter. . . .

"Know that Prâkriti and Purusha are both without beginning. Know too that variations and modes spring from Prâkriti. When any existence whatever, animate or inanimate, is produced, know, O son of Bhârata! that it exists by this union of Prâkriti and Purusha.

"He who sees that works are wrought in every case by Prâkriti, and therefore that Purusha is *not an agent*, sees indeed. As the Akâsa that pervades all things is not stained, through its subtlety, so Purusha (soul), everywhere seated in bodies, is not stained.

"As one sun illumines all this world, so Purusha illumines the whole of matter, O son of Bhârata!"

A fair idea of the ethical teaching of the poem is given by the following extracts:—

"The gift of alms, made, saying 'This must be given,' to one who cannot return it, in a proper place

[1] A "Kalpa" is another name for a "Manvantara," or a "Day of Brâhma," a cycle of manifestation of the universe.

and time, and to a worthy object, is called 'good' (sattva).

"But that given for the sake of return, or on account of gain hereafter, or given reluctantly, that is regarded as 'passion-born' (rajas).

"The gift given ungraciously, or with disdain, or at an improper place and time, or to unworthy objects, is called 'dark' (tapas). . . .

"He who is the same to friend and foe, and also in honour and dishonour; who is the same in cold or heat, in pleasure and pain, to whom praise and blame are equal, who is silent, content with every fortune, steadfast in mind . . . that man is dear to me. . . .

"No man may abandon his natural work, . . . for every enterprise is surrounded by evil as fire by smoke. . . .

"Abstention from work of obligation is not fitting. The 'renunciation' of him who does a work of obligation, saying 'This must be done,' Arjuna! renouncing attachment and fruit, is deemed to be 'good' (sattva). It is not possible for one who is embodied to abstain from work absolutely, but he who has abandoned the fruit of work is regarded as a 'renouncer.' . . .

"But the action which is done by one who seeks to gain his desires, or from self-conceit . . . is of 'passion' (rajas). . . .

"The devout man, when he has renounced the fruit of works, obtains eternal peace. . . .

"He, whose every effort is free from the impulse of desire, whose work has been burnt up by the fire of knowledge, is called by the wise a 'pandita' (learned man). . . .

"Contented with whatever he may receive, unaffected by the pairs-of-opposites (pleasure and pain, etc.), free from envy, the same in good and evil fortune, he through works is not 'bound.'" [In other words, he produces no new "Karma" that must be worked out in future incarnations.]

"As the kindled fire reduces all fuel to ashes, Arjuna! so the fire of knowledge reduces all works to ashes. For no purifier is found on earth equal to knowledge. One who is perfect in devotion (to knowledge) finds it, in course of time, in himself; . . . when he has obtained it, he reaches without delay Nirvâna. . . .

"Love and hatred are seated in the subjects of the senses. Let none come under the power of these two, for they are his foes. . . .

"As a flame is covered by smoke and a mirror by rust, as a fœtus is enveloped by the womb, so the world is enveloped by desire.

"Knowledge is enveloped by this, which is the eternal foe of the wise. It takes forms at will, and is an insatiable flame. . . .

"Men say that the senses are great. The heart is greater than the senses; the mind is greater than the heart, but this is greater than the mind. Knowing then that this is greater than the mind, strengthen thyself by thyself, and slay this foe, which takes forms at will, and is hard to meet. . . .

"Devotion is not for him who eats too much, nor for him who fasts excessively; nor for him who is disposed to sleep too much, nor for him who is ever wakeful, Arjuna! . . .

"The devotion which destroys all pain is for the man who is moderate in food and in recreation, who uses moderate efforts in his actions, is moderate in sleep and in waking.

"When he fixes his well-controlled thoughts on himself alone, and is indifferent to every object of desire, then he is called 'yukta' (devoted).

"'As a lamp sheltered from the wind flickers not' is the wonted simile of the Yogin who is subdued in thought . . . when thought is wholly at rest . . . when he knows the boundless joy which is beyond the senses, which the mind apprehends, and, fixed therein, never wavers from the truth . . . when, abiding therein, he is not moved by deep affliction, let him know that this severance from all trouble is 'Yoga.'"

"Supreme happiness comes to the Yogin whose heart is at rest, in whom passion is tranquillised, who is one with Brahmân. . . .

"He who sees me everywhere, and everything in me, him I forsake not, and he forsakes not me. . . .

"The Yogin who strives with energy, who is purified from sin, and perfected by many births, goes at length on the highest way.

"The Yogin is superior to the ascetics: he is deemed to be superior even to the men of knowledge: he is also superior to the doer of works. Be thou a Yogin, Arjuna!"

Krishna concludes his whole teaching to the Prince Arjuna thus:—

"Thus a doctrine more mysterious than any mystery has been declared to thee, by me. Having meditated fully thereon, *do as thou wilt!*"

CHAPTER V

CHINESE THOUGHT

ALTHOUGH, as we now know, there were thinkers in China at the time when Britain was still in a state of barbarism, it is but lately that we have come into our heritage of Chinese thought. It cannot therefore be said in any way to have influenced our thinking as have undoubtedly the thoughts which have gradually filtered to us from India and the nearer East. All that we know of early Chinese thought is contained in three sets of books, known as the Shû, the Shih, and the Yi. In the year 202 B.C., these ancient writings were declared to be "classic" (King), or canonical, and since then they are alluded to as Shû-King, Shih-King, and Yi-King. In his translation of the Shih-King, published in 1879, Mr James Legge, from whom I have borrowed my quotations, says that it was "current in China before the time of Confucius, arranged very much as we have it now." Confucius had the greatest admiration for the Shih-King, which he earnestly recommended to the study of all his disciples. The work is a collection of native poetry, called the Minor and

Major Odes, due to "the Master of Music," a high court official who accompanied the sovereign in the tour of inspection which he made every five years throughout his realm. The Shû-King is the record of the doings and sayings of some of the early rulers of China. The Yi-King, or "Book of Changes," dates from the time of the Emperor Wan, who was born in 1231 B.C. It contains eight "trigrams," ascribed to Fu-hei, who lived about 3400 B.C., and from which sixty-four "hexograms" are obtained, which are explained in the text by the Emperor Wan and his son, the Duke of Kau. A study of the Yi was considered by Confucius as a help to the development of the character. Mr Legge tells us that this book was "connected with divination, which we know from the Shû entered largely into the religion of ancient China."

Of the three books only the last, the Yi-King, has apparently come down to us entire. The other two more important books were ordered to be destroyed in 213 B.C. by the ruler of Khin, who at that date proclaimed himself "Ti," or emperor, of all the feudal states. His object was to get rid of the records of earlier rulers whose ideas, maxims, and methods of government were so condemnatory of his own life and tyrannical system of rule. In spite of his proclamation that anyone found in possession of a copy of either the Shû-King or the Shih-King should be put to death, many scholars took the risk of hiding their copies, instead of burning them, as ordered to do, so that, at the death of the despot in 210 B.C., these copies again emerged from their hiding-places. The Emperor Wan, who reigned from 179 to 155 B.C., not only secured all the copies he could of these famous texts for the imperial library, but he took the further precaution to have them engraved on tablets of stone. His copies are known as "the Shû of the modern text." Hidden copies of the Shih-King were recovered from the districts of Lu, Khi, and Han, and these different versions were afterwards known as the Shih of Lu, the Shih of Khi, and the Shih of Han. A commentary on one of these versions by Han-Ying, a scholar of great repute in the reign of the Emperor Wan, "remains entire, or nearly so, at the present day," according to Mr Legge.

The Shih-King gives us indeed much information about the political, social, and moral tendencies in China, but it shows us little or nothing of the religion of ancient China, beyond the fact that ancestor-worship was a universal custom. The only term used in the Shû or Shih to express any kind of Supreme Power is the word "Thien," which Chinese scholars translate "Heaven." Mr James Legge, indeed, translates Ti as "God," and derives it from ⊥ or ⸳̲ (Shang), which means "Above." Thus Heaven is called "Shang-Ti," and the "Son of Heaven," the title given to the ruling sovereign, is called "Ti." But Mr Legge admits that, in China, "Ti never became a proper name like the Zeus of the Greeks." It appears, therefore, as if Chinese thought never imagined or postulated any divine personality above that of the emperor, the "Son of Heaven" The emperor was supposed to be watched over by the spirits of his ancestors, to whom he made sacrifices four times in the year, at the spring equinox, summer solstice, autumn equinox, and winter solstice. We learn from the Shih that these sacrifices were accompanied with much ceremony, and that all those who took part in them prepared themselves by fasting and purification. The sacrifice took place in the ancestral temple, and was attended by as many descendants as possible of former dynasties, and by all the feudal princes of the empire. It began with music and incense and the pouring out of "libations of fragrant spirits" from "jade cups" by the princes of the reigning royal family. Then the emperor himself cut the throat of "a red bull," the fat being burnt with southernwood as incense to attract the departed spirits to "hover between heaven and earth." Then came dancers: "the dancers move with their flutes," and "the sound goes forth filling the region of the air," and "all round the fragrance is diffused"; and all this is done "to please the meritorious ancestors." Other animals, besides the red bull, are now sacrificed, and their flesh is then "roasted or broiled," and the ceremony ends with a banquet in the ancestral temple and complimentary toasts proposed and drunk by both emperor and guests. At these ceremonies the departed ancestors of the sovereign are personated by their living descendants according to a strict rule of etiquette.

Besides these quarterly sacrifices to his ancestors, the king or emperor also performed the ceremony of turning the first furrow, when he offered prayers to "Heaven" for an abundant harvest. At this ceremony the people sang the ode: "... They sow their various kinds of grain, each seed containing in it the germ of life. In unbroken lines rise the blades, and, well nourished, the stalks grow long. Luxuriant looks the young grain, and the weeders go among it in multitudes. Then come the reapers in crowds, and the grain is piled up in the fields. Myriads, and hundreds of thousands, and millions of stacks! ... Fragrant is their aroma, enhancing the glory of the state. ... It is not only here that there is this abundance; it is not only now that there is such a time; from of old it has been thus. ... Yonder shall be young grain unreaped, and here some bundles ungathered; yonder shall be handfuls left on the ground, and here ears untouched for the benefit of the widow."

According to the record of the Li-ki, the king or emperor also superintended the commencement of the fishing season, in the third winter month, and partook of the first-caught fish, after presenting it as an offering in his ancestral temple. The same ceremony was performed at the beginning of the sturgeon-fishery in the third month of spring.

It was presumably during one of these sacrifices that the king's officers and guests sang his praises in the following ode:—"Heaven protects and establishes thee with the greatest security; makes thee entirely virtuous that thou mayest enjoy every happiness; grants thee much increase, so that thou hast all in abundance. Heaven protects and establishes thee, so that in all thou dost prosper. Like the high hills and the mountain-masses, like the topmost ridges and the greatest bulks, like the stream ever coming on, such is thine increase. With happy auspices and purifications thou bringest the offerings and dost filially present them in spring, summer, autumn, and winter. . . . Like the moon advancing to the full, like the sun ascending the heavens, like the everlasting southern hills, never waning, never falling, like the luxuriance of the fir and the cypress—may such be thy succeeding line!"

The Khi Yüeh ode tells us that during the winter ice was collected and stored in ice-houses by the high ministers and heads of clans for public use in the summer; and that the first block of ice taken from the ice-houses was dedicated in the principal hall of the ancestral temple to "the Ruler of Cold, the Spirit of Ice."

One of the most striking of the many odes contained in the Shih-King is one addressed by the Duke Wu of Wei to himself, much after the fashion of Marcus Aurelius. Wu says: "Outward demeanour cautious and grave is an indication of the inward virtue. People have the saying, 'There is no wise man who is not also stupid.' The stupidity of the ordinary man is determined by his natural defects; the stupidity of the wise man is by his doing violence to his proper character. . . . Do not speak lightly; your words are your own. Do not say, 'This is of little importance; no one can hold my tongue for me.' Words are not to be cast away. Every word finds its answer; every good deed has its recompense. . . . Looked at in friendly intercourse with superior men, you make your countenance harmonious and mild, anxious not to do anything wrong. Looked at in your chamber, you ought to be equally free from shame before the light which shines in. Do not say, 'This place is not public, no one can see me here': the approaches of the spiritual beings cannot be calculated beforehand, but the more should they not be slighted."

The whole of the collection of Major and Minor and Religious Odes contained in the Shih amounts to 305 pieces, the earliest dating from the beginning of the Shang dynasty, in 1766 B.C., to the end of the Kau dynasty, in 586 B.C.

The Shû consists of a collection of historical records of some of the ancient kings, which are arranged in five books. Book I. is called the Book of Thang, the dynastic name of the Emperor Yao, 2357 B.C. Book II. is the Book of the Counsels of the Great Yü, 2205 B.C. Book III. is called the Book of Hsia, the name of the dynasty founded by Yü, 2205–1767 B.C. Book IV. is called the Book of Shang, the dynasty founded by Thang, 1766–1460 B.C. Book V. is called the Book of Kau, the dynastic name of Wu, who reigned from 651 to 619 B.C.

The Emperor Yao (2357 B.C.) is said in the Shû to have "united and harmonised the myriad states: and so the black-haired people were transformed. The result was concord." His astronomers were commanded "to calculate and delineate the movements and appearances of the sun, the moon, the stars, and the zodiacal spaces."[1] Yao declares

[1] Mr James Legge says that "there is no chronological difficulty in the way of our accepting the documents of the Shû as being possessed of the antiquity ascribed to them."

officially that "a round year consists of three hundred sixty and six days," and says to his astronomers, "Do you by means of the intercalary month fix the four seasons and complete the year." The Emperor Yu (or Shun), we are told in the Shû, "carefully set forth the beauty of the five cardinal duties"; also, that "he made uniform the standard tubes with the measures of length and of capacity, and the steel-yards." This emperor also "exhibited to the people the statutory punishments, enacting banishment as a mitigation of the five great inflictions." These five great inflictions were: (1) branding on the forehead, (2) cutting off the nose, (3) cutting off the feet, (4) castration, (5) death. "The whip" was ordered to be used in the magistrates' courts, the stick to be used in schools, and money to be received for "re-deemable offences." "Let compassion," said Yu, "rule in punishment." Every five years he made a tour of inspection through all the twelve provinces of the empire. In appointing his Minister of Music, he says: "Khwei, I appoint you to be Director of Music, and to teach our sons, so that the straight-forward shall be mild, the gentle dignified, the strong not tyrannical, and the impetuous not arrogant. Poetry is the expression of earnest thought, singing is the prolonged utterance of that expression. . . ." He appoints a "General Regulator," a "Minister of Agriculture," a "Minister of Communications," a "Minister of Works," a "Forester," a "Director of Music," and an "Arranger of Religious Ceremonies." And charging them all to do their duty, he adds: "My ministers constitute my legs and arms, my ears and eyes. I wish to help and support my people. You give effect to my wishes. . . . The virtue of the ruler is seen in good government, and that government is the nourishing of the people."

In recording the measures he took to remedy the destruction caused by a great inundation of the "Yellow River," Yu says: "The waters of the Hang and Wei were brought to their proper channels, and Ta-lü was made capable of cultivation. . . . The nine branches of the Ho were made to keep their proper channels. Lei-hsia was made a marsh, in which the waters of the Yung and the Zü were united. The mulberry-grounds were made fit for the silk-worms, and then the people came down from the heights and occupied the grounds. . . . The wild people of Lai were taught tillage and pasturage, and brought in their baskets the silk from the mountain mulberry-tree. . . . The grounds along the waters were everywhere made habitable; the hills were cleared of their superfluous wood, . . . the sources of the rivers were cleared, the marshes were all banked, and access to the capital was secured for all within the four seas."

In the record of the "Announcement to his People," published by the Emperor Thang (1766 B.C.), we read in the Shû: "When the virtue of a ruler is daily being renewed, he is cherished throughout the myriad regions; when his mind is full only of himself, he is abandoned by the nine branches of his kindred. Exert yourself, O king, to make your virtue still more illustrious, and set up before the people the standard of the Mean. Order your affairs by righteousness; order your heart by propriety: so shall you transmit a grand example to posterity. I have heard the saying, 'He who finds instructors for himself comes to the supreme dominion; he who says that others are not equal to himself comes to ruin. He who likes to put questions becomes enlarged; he who uses only his own views becomes smaller.' Oh! he who would take care of the end must be attentive to the beginning. . . ."

Thang's grandson, Thai Kia, succeeded him in 1753 B.C., and on the occasion of his ascending the throne his guardian, the sage I Yin, delivers to him these "Instructions":—

"Oh! the former king began with careful attention to the bonds which hold men together. He listened to expostulation, and did not seek to resist it: he conformed to the wisdom of the ancients: occupying the highest position, he displayed intelligence; occupying an inferior position, he displayed loyalty; he allowed the good qualities of the men whom he employed, and did not seek that they should have every talent. In the government of himself he seemed to think that he could never sufficiently attain. . . . Do you but be virtuous, be it in small things or in large, and the myriad regions will have cause for rejoicing." When, after a short course of dissipation, the young king came once more to his better self, he wrote to the sage, asking again for his guidance; and I Yin replies:—"Oh! Heaven has no partial affection. . . . A place of difficulty is the Heaven-conferred seat. . . . Your course must be as when, in ascending high, you begin from where it is low, and when, in travelling far, you begin from where it is near. Do not slight the occupations of your people, think of their difficulties. Do not yield to a feeling of repose on your throne, think of its perils. Oh! what attainment can be made without anxious thought, what achievement can be made without anxious effort? Let the One man be greatly good, and the myriad regions will be rectified by him. . . ." And, shortly before his death in 1713 B.C., the sage gave to the young king his last "Instructions":—"He said, 'Oh! it is difficult to rely upon Heaven, its appointments are not constant. But, if the sovereign see to it that his virtue be constant, he will preserve his throne. . . . Where the sovereign's virtue is pure, his enterprises are all fortunate; where his virtue is wavering and uncertain, his enterprises are all unfortunate. Good and evil do not wrongly befall men, but Heaven sends misery or happiness according to their conduct. . . . There is no invariable model of virtue—a supreme regard to what is good gives the model of it. . . . Do not think yourself so big as to deem others little. If ordinary men and women do not find the opportunity to give full development to their ability, the people's lord will be without the proper aid to complete his merit.'"

Three hundred years after the time of the sage I Yin, another sage, named Yüeh, was appointed by Pau Kang (1401–1374 B.C.) to the post of Chief Minister. The Shû says: "The king raised and made Yüeh his prime minister, keeping him at his side. He charged him, saying, 'Morning and evening present your instructions to aid my virtue. Suppose me a weapon of steel, I will use you for a whetstone; suppose me crossing a great stream, I will use you for a boat with its oars; suppose me in a year of great drought, I will use you as a copious rain. Open your mind, and enrich my mind.'" The sage accepted the high office, saying: "Wood by the use of the line is made straight, and the sovereign who follows reproof is made wise. When the sovereign can make himself wise, his good government and bad depend on the various officers. Offices should not be given to men because they are favourites, but only to men of ability: dignities should not be conferred on men of evil practices, but only on men of worth. . . . Anxious thought about what will be best should precede your movements, which also should be taken at the proper time for them. Indulging the consciousness of being good is the way to lose that goodness; being vain of one's ability is the way to lose the merit it might produce. . . . Do not be ashamed of mistakes and go on to make them crimes. . . ."

According to Mr Legge, the records of King Wu and his descendants, of which twenty documents are contained in the books of Kau, are considered by all Chinese students to be "of undisputed genuineness." King Wu, whose dynastic name was Kau, after putting an end to the corrupt and tyrannical government of Shan, king of Shang, in 1122 B.C., adopts as his own system of government "the Great Plan" which was communicated to him by the Count of Khi, who had been grand master to Shan, and who based his scheme of government on an ancient record "from the times of Hsia and Yü." "The Great Plan" consists of nine sections. The fifth sets forth the duty of the ruler himself. He is exhorted to "establish in himself the highest degree and pattern of excellence. . . . Do not let him oppress the friendless and childless, nor let him fear the high and distinguished. When men in office have ability and administrative power, let them be made still more to cultivate their conduct, and the prosperity of the country will be promoted." The three "royal virtues" are declared to be "straightforwardness, strong rule, and mild rule," and the king is urged, "without deflection, without unevenness," to "pursue the royal way."

At the death of King Wu, his son Sung, who afterwards gained for himself the name of Khang ("the Completer"), was only thirteen years of age, and therefore for some years his uncle, the Duke of Kau, acted as regent. It was during this time that "the Announcement about Drunkenness" was published. "King Wan," says the Announcement, "admonished and instructed the young nobles who were charged with office, or in any employment, that they should not ordinarily use spirits; and throughout all the states he required that such should drink spirits only on occasion of sacrifices, and that then virtue should preside, so that there should be no drunkenness. . . . He said, 'Let my people teach their young men that they are to love only the productions of the soil, for so will their hearts be good. . . . Hearken ye, all my noble chiefs:—when ye have largely done your duty, in ministering to your aged and serving your ruler, ye may eat and drink freely and to satiety.' . . . The king said, 'O Fang, . . . if you are informed that there are companies that drink together, do not fail to apprehend them all, and send them here to Kau, where I may put them to death. As to the ministers and officers of Yin, who were led to it, and became addicted to drink, it is not necessary to put them to death at once: let them be taught for a time: if they follow these lessons of mine, I will give them bright distinction. If they disregard my lessons, then I, the One man, will show them no pity. As they cannot change their ways, they shall be classed with those who are to be put to death.'"

In another Instruction to the young king, the Duke of Kau advises him to emulate the methods of government of his predecessors, Wan and Thang. Wan, he says, "was moderate in excursions and hunting," and "would only receive the correct amount of contributions"; whilst "Thang, 'the successful,' grandly administered the bright ordinances of Heaven. . . . The people in the cities of Shang were thereby all brought to harmony, and those in the four quarters of the kingdom were brought greatly under the influence of the virtue thus displayed. . . . Oh, young son, the king! from this time forth be it ours to establish the government, appointing the high officers, the officers of the laws and the pastors; be it ours clearly to know what courses are natural to these men, and then fully to employ them in the government that they may aid us in the management of the people, . . . and let us never allow others to come between us and them. . . . From this time forth, in establishing the government, make no use of artful-tongued men. . . . Have well arranged your military accoutrements and weapons, so that you may go forth beyond the steps of Yü and traverse all under the sky, even to beyond the seas, everywhere meeting submission. . . ."

Later in his career, King Khang, when appointing Kün-Khan ruler of the Eastern Border, says to him: "You are the wind, the inferior people are the grass. In resolving the plans of your government, never hesitate to acknowledge the difficulty of the subject. Some things have to be abolished, and some new things to be enacted. Going out and coming in, seek the judgment of your people about them, and when there is a general agreement, exert your own powers of reflection. . . . Do not make use of your powers to exercise oppression; do not make use of the laws to practise extortion. Be gentle, but with strictness of rule. Promote harmony by the display of an easy forbearance. . . . Those who are disobedient to your government and uninfluenced by your instructions you will punish, remembering that the end of punishment is to make an end of punishing." King Kang died in 1079 B.C. His great-grandson, Mu, reigned from 1001 B.C. to 947 B.C., and in the "Instruction" which he gives to Kün-ya, his minister of education, he says: "Oh! Kün-ya, your grandfather and your father, one after another, laboured with a true loyalty and honesty in the service of the royal house, accomplishing a merit that was recorded on the grand banner. I now give you charge to assist me. Be as my limbs to me, as my heart and backbone. . . . Diffuse widely the knowledge of the five invariable relations of society, and reverently seek to produce a harmonious observance of the duties belonging to them among the people. If you are correct in your own person, none will dare to be but correct. The minds of the people cannot attain to the right mean; they must be guided by your attaining to it. . . . Think of their hardships, in order to seek to promote their ease, and the people will be tranquil." Mu lived to be a very old man, and, late in his reign, he issued a charge regarding punishments to the princes of the royal house. We read in the Shû: "The king said, 'Oh! lay it to heart, my uncles and all ye, my brethren and cousins, my sons and my grandsons. . . . Heaven, in its wish to regulate the people, allows us for a day to make use of punishments. . . . Reverently apportion the five punishments, so as to fully exhibit the three virtues; then shall I, the One man, enjoy felicity, the people will look to you as their sure dependence, the repose of the state will be perpetual. . . . In settling the five cases of error there are evils to be guarded against: being warped by the influence of power, or by private grudge, or by female solicitation, or by bribes. . . . Do you carefully examine, and prove yourselves equal to every difficulty. When there are doubts as to the infliction of any of the five punishments, that infliction should be forborne. When there are doubts as to the infliction of any of the five fines, it should be forborne. . . . When you have examined, and many things are clear, yet form a judgment by studying the appearance of the parties. . . . When the crime should incur one of the higher punishments, but there are mitigating circumstances, apply it to the next lower: when it should incur one of the lower punishments, but there are aggravating circumstances, apply it to the next higher. The light and heavy fines are to be applied in the same way by the balance of circumstances. . . .' "

The above extracts from Mr James Legge's translation of the "Shu" and the "Shih" give us a clear notion of the drift of educated Chinese thought between 2357 B.C. and 265 B.C.

Three religions are recognised to-day in China, viz. Taoism, Confucianism, and Buddhism. The last was introduced from Ceylon during the third century B.C., but did not become one of the state-religions till the first century of our era, when copies of the Buddhist scriptures were officially received in China. Taoism is said to date back to the twenty-sixth century B.C., the time of Hwang-Ti. "Tâo," according to Mr James Legge, may be translated either as "the Way," or "the Word," or "Reason"; but each rendering, he says, leaves out something of the exact meaning of the word. The most famous teacher of Taoism was Li Tan, generally called "Lao-Tsze," or "the old teacher," who is said to have been born in 604 B.C. at Loyang on the Hoang-ho, in the province of Tsu, the present Honan, which at that period was a great centre of Chinese culture. Lao-Tsze died in 516 B.C. The best part of Lac-Tszc's life was spent as "registrar of foreign decrees" at Loyang. Then, at the age of sixty-five, he retired from public office to lead a life of meditation. The

Tao-teh King, or "Classic of Tao and Virtue," remains our only record of his doctrine.

From the Tao-teh King we gather that Tao is to be considered as the Supreme Power throughout the universe. Tao is the cause and effect of all that is, and yet, in itself, is No-Thing. We learn that, before ever heaven and earth came into being, Tao existed omnipresent and omnipotent in every molecule of matter. Being devoid of all attributes, Tao cannot be defined otherwise than as "the Way," the Eternal Path, along which the whole universe must move. Nevertheless, to those who can rise above desire, to those who are absolutely pure in thought and deed, Tao reveals itself. He who "walks in the Way" becomes at length "one with Tao." The true follower of "the Way" neither loves life nor fears death: his only desire is to be in harmony with Tao, to whom at last, like everything else, he must return. Says Lao-Tsze: "He who is self-displaying does not shine: he who is self-approving is not held in esteem: he who is self-praising has no merit: he who is self-exalting does not stand high."

A later teacher of Taoism, named Chwang-Tsze, recommends his disciples to cultivate the power of throwing themselves into the state of ecstatic trance, because Tao, he says, can be reached only in silence and darkness, and because the external world must be entirely excluded when searching for Tao. But Lao-Tsze does not appear to have entertained any such idea of self-hypnotism.

The most famous of all the teachers of China was Kung-fu-Tsze, better known to us under his Latinised name, Confucius. He was born in 550 B.C., in the province of Lu, the present Shantung, of which at the time his father was military governor; his mother belonged to the noble family of Yen. After receiving a careful education, Confucius successively filled the offices of collector of revenue and chief magistrate of the city of Chung-tu, and, at the age of fifty, was appointed chief minister of the province of Lu. His administration was firm and wise, and during his five years of office he introduced many reforms. But his fearless and impartial justice made him many powerful enemies, against whom the ruling prince was too weak to support him. Confucius therefore resigned his post and devoted himself to public reform by means of teaching. He travelled widely throughout China, and is said to have trained no less than six hundred pupils, of whom seventy-two are known by name. At his death, in 478 B.C., he was buried with great ceremony, and, as a tribute to his memory, all his lineal descendants are accorded the rank of mandarin, and are exempt from all taxation. Confucianism and Buddhism were both officially recognised as state religions in the year 60 B.C.

Confucius was no self-torturing ascetic, no mere dreamer of impossible piety. He was, on the contrary, a keen hunter, a gymnast and charioteer, and taught his disciples that character and conduct were developed by everything that demanded the exercise of their courage, decision, and skill. He is also said to have had considerable knowledge of music and poetry. Confucius appears to have had little taste for abstract speculation, and to have had no idea of founding a religion of any sort. He taught men that simplicity and purity of life can alone lead to happiness, and that honesty is the best policy. He differed entirely from his predecessor, Lao, who taught the doctrine that all injury should be met with kindness. Kindness, said Confucius, must indeed always be repaid with kindness; but, for the sake of society, all injury must be met with justice, however much a man may be inclined to forgive injury done to himself. He condemned capital punishment, however, because he held that crime is mostly the result of stupidity, and of ignorance of its consequences. The only way to prevent crime, he said, was to educate the people.

A favourite theory of Confucius is that whoever sees what is right will, sooner or later, have the courage to do it. Confucius accepts the ancient Chinese postulate of an unknown principle, called Thien (Heaven), which pervades the universe, but considers all inquiry into its nature to be useless. The great secret, he says, is for a man to get true knowledge of himself, to brighten his intelligence, which is dulled by desire, and to do his best to become "a perfect man." "Wash thyself daily," he says, and seek in your own heart for the rule of life and conduct. Only the perfect man is really brave, because he is for ever conquering himself; and if he finds he has done any wrong to anyone, he is not at rest until he has repaired it. The perfect man confesses his ignorance of things he does not understand, so that he may not mislead others who know less than himself. "The perfect man ought to behave himself towards his friends, as he desires that his friends should bear themselves towards him." Justice and duty in small things as in great is the aim of the "perfect man." The foolish man always "swerves from the Path," and does either too little or too much. Confucius is always insisting, as the Buddha insisted after him, on the beauty and excellence of the Middle Path, which Confucius called "the Perpetual Mean." He explains "the Five Cardinal Virtues" as (1) humanity, (2) justice, (3) rectitude, (4) sincerity, (5) conformity to established customs.

The first six chapters of the "Hsiao-King" (Classic of Filial Piety) are considered to be the authentic teaching of Confucius. The text was written down by the pupils of Zang-Tsze from their recollection of their master's account of conversations between himself and Confucius. The Hsiao-King, of which Liu-Hin records that two original copies exist in the Imperial Library, was always a favourite study of Chinese emperors after the time of Confucius; "many of them" says Mr Legge, "have published commentaries on it." The following extracts give an idea of the teaching contained in the Hsiao-King:—

"The Master said: 'Now, filial piety is the root of all virtue, the stem out of which grows all moral teaching. . . . When we have established our character by the practice of the filial course, so as to make our name famous in future ages, and thereby glorify our parents, —this is the end of filial piety It commences with the service of the parents; it proceeds to the service of the ruler; it is completed in the character. . . .

He who loves his parents, will not dare being hated by any man. . . . The lessons of his virtue will affect all people, and he becomes a pattern to all within the four seas. . . . Their actions may fill all under Heaven, and no dissatisfaction or dislike will be awakened by them. . . . As they serve their fathers, so they serve their mothers, and they love them equally. As they serve their fathers, so they serve their mothers, and they reverence them equally. Hence love is what is chiefly rendered to the mother, and reverence is what is chiefly rendered to the ruler, while both these things are given to the father. . . .'

"The Master said: 'Of all natures produced by Heaven and Earth man is the noblest. Of all the actions of man there is none greater than filial piety. . . . Now, the feeling of affection grows up at the parents' knees, and as the duty of nourishing these parents is exercised, the affection daily merges in awe. The sages proceeded from awe to teach reverence, and from affection to teach love. The teachings of the sages, without being severe, were successful, and their government, without being rigorous, was effective. What they proceeded from was the root of filial piety, implanted by Heaven. . . . He who serves his parents will, in a high situation, be free from pride, in a low situation, will be free from insubordination, and, among his equals, will not be quarrelsome. In a high situation, pride leads to ruin. In a low situation, insubordination leads to punishment. Among equals, quarrelsomeness leads to the wielding of weapons.'

"The Master said: 'For teaching the people to be

affectionate and loving there is nothing better than filial piety; for teaching them propriety and submissiveness there is nothing better than fraternal duty; for changing their manners, and altering their customs, there is nothing better than music.'"

The following are among the many maxims attributed to Confucius. Even if they were not sayings uttered by this teacher, they are at least interesting illustrations of Chinese thought:—

"The wise man blushes at his faults, but is not ashamed to amend them.

"The wise man seeks the cause of his defects in himself, but the fool, avoiding himself, seeks it in all others besides himself.

"The good man sins sometimes; weakness is natural to him. But he ought to watch so diligently over himself, that he may never fall twice into the same sin.

"Remember always that thou art a man, that human nature is weak, and that thou mayest easily fall—and thou shalt never fall.

"But if, happening to forget what thou art, thou chancest to fall, be not discouraged: remember, that thou mayest rise again: remember, that it is in thy power to break the bands which join thee to thy offence, and to subdue the obstacles which hinder thee from walking in the path of virtue.

"Innocence is not virtue. Most of the great ones have fallen therefrom. But, if thou askest what must be done to be virtuous, I answer that it is necessary to conquer thyself. . . . The victory is difficult, but not impossible, for to conquer thyself is to do what is agreeable to reason."

CHAPTER VI

ARYAN THOUGHT

EVEN now, it is by no means certain who the Aryans are, or whence they came. Grimm, Schlegel, Lassen, Max Müller, Schleicher, and Sayce all maintained, not so very long ago, that successive "swarms" of Aryans came into the Panjab from Bactria, and thence descended into Southern India; whilst other "swarms" passed into Persia, and from Persia found their way gradually into Europe. Professor Sayce has apparently now given up the theory of the Bactrian origin of the Aryans, in favour of the European; but, to the end of his life, Professor Max Müller maintained that "the cradle of the Aryans" was "somewhere in Asia."

The ancient kings of Persia boasted of their Aryan descent. Persian tradition located the original home of the race, which they called "Airyana-vaeja," in the district south of the Caspian. But, as Professor Rhys Davids points out, there is no evidence at all of any Aryan settlement in India "before the close of the sixth century B.C."

The most recent theory altogether denies the

existence of any united Aryan race, from which the Caucasian races are descended. It is convenient to speak of the Aryan language, but it is impossible to trace any blood-relationship between the different peoples—now comprising half of the whole population of the globe—who use some variation of Aryan speech. We have, indeed, no evidence where the language was first spoken; but it seems certain that it was not east of the Caspian Sea, simply because there are no common Aryan names for such well-known animals, native of the East, as lion, tiger, and camel. On the other hand, the words "sheep," "dog," and "cow" may all be traced back to Aryan roots. This fact shows that, wherever they lived, the early Aryans were a pastoral people. The general name for "cattle," in Sanskrit, Zend, Lithuanian, Latin, and German, is derived from the root "pak," which means something that is "tied up." From "pak" comes the Sanskrit "pacu," the Zend "pasu," the Lithuanian "pekus," the Latin "pecus," and the German "vieh."

In 1871, Cuno conceived the idea that the great plain which stretches across the north of Germany and France, and extends from the Ural Mountains to the Atlantic Ocean, and which is so suitable for a great pastoral people, may have been the original home of the Aryans. The suggestion of Cuno is supported by the fact that, at the dawn of the historical period, this region was undoubtedly occupied by the Aryan-speaking Celts, Teutons, Slavs, and Lithuanians. In 1873, Spiegel said that "the cradle of the Aryan race" must certainly be "somewhere between the 45th and 60th parallels of northern latitude," because only men born in a temperate climate would possess the vigour and energy necessary to make them successful colonists. The steppes of Central Asia, west of the Caspian Sea, have also been suggested as a likely place of origin for a pastoral and nomadic race, such as the Aryan. This region is, in fact, the actual home of the Turko-Tartáric race, a race which gives us a fair idea of what the Aryans were probably like in their first nomadic state. Cuno's theory of the European origin of the Aryans is strengthened by the fact, first pointed out in 1883 by Schrader, that the Teutonic, Latin, and Greek races have all practically the same name for the beech-tree. This tree has never been found growing east of a line drawn from Königsberg to the Crimea, from which we may infer that the origin of the language spoken by the Aryan Teutons, Latins, and Greeks must be sought for west of this imaginary line.

Several thousand years would be necessary to differentiate the early Aryan dialects into those characteristic languages which have evolved out of them: therefore it is possible that, during that time, the more adventurous Aryan tribes may have crossed the mountains of Central Europe and may have settled in Italy and Greece. Here, perhaps, many of them remained, whilst the more adventurous pushed on, eastwards, into Persia and India. When carefully compared, the different Aryan languages appear, indeed, to be linked in a chain of gradual evolution. We find that the languages which are geographically nearest to one another always have the greatest number of words and structural forms in common. Dr Isaac Taylor considers the "Celto-Slavic" peoples to be the most typical representatives of the early Aryan race, and suggests that their language may have evolved out of a language of the "Ural-Altai class."

The theory of the European origin of the Aryan races is further supported by the pile-dwellings which many of them erected in various parts of the continent during the later Stone Age, when the climate was practically the same as it is now. M. Morlet estimates that the oldest of these pile-dwellings known to us were built seven thousand years ago. A Dacian pile-dwelling is represented on Trajan's column, at Rome, and Herodotus tells us of a Thracian pile-dwelling at Lake Prasias. In the pile-dwellings discovered at the Feder-See, in Wurtemberg, at the Starnberger-See, in Bavaria, and at Lake Fimon, near Vincenza, were found charred wheat and the mealing-stones to grind it, also bones of the ox, stag, sheep, and dog. In the pile-dwelling near Vincenza stores of nuts were found, some of them already roasted for food. In the lake-dwellings in Switzerland, which date also from the later Stone Age, were found ornaments of amber, jade, and coral, which, as M. Joly points out, prove that the race which inhabited these pile-dwellings must have had trade-intercourse with the Baltic for their amber, with the Mediterranean for their coral, and with the East for their jade. Weapons of copper and bronze were also found in most of the pile-dwellings, and we are led to infer that bronze was introduced from the Mediterranean, because the farther we go north, in Italy and Switzerland, the more implements we find of stone, and the fewer of bronze. Anthropology and craniology also lend their evidence to support the theory of the European origin of the Aryan races. Our experts are now able to classify with exactness the large number of prehistoric skulls and skeletons which have been brought to light, and, from their study of these, have come to the conclusion that, from time immemorial, most Aryan races have persisted more or less in the same districts. It is noteworthy that the skulls found in the round barrows of the Celts of Britain—the men who erected the stone temples at Stonehenge and Avebury—resemble the skulls of the Celts of Belgium and Denmark, and the skulls of the Swiss Celts found at Sion, in the Rhone valley. Skulls found in prehistoric graves in the east of Switzerland are considered by Huxley to "belong with South-Germans, Slavs, and Finns to one great race, which has extended across Europe, from Britain to Sarmatia, and we know not how much farther to the east and south." Thus we see that all the latest theories of science point to the conclusion that the Aryans, or Eranians, whom history first mentions as inhabiting Media and Persia, are far more likely to have sprung from races which once dwelt on the great plain of the Danube, than from races which lived in Bactria, or wandered among the wind-swept deserts of the Pamir plateau.

The country of the Madai, or Medes, was the lofty table-land which lies on an average 3000 feet above the Mediterranean, and is situated north and east of the Zagros range. These mountains slope down steeply to the valley of the Tigris, enclosing the two great salt-water lakes, Van and Urumiyeh, the one 5400, the other 4200 feet above the sea-level. The early Babylonians called the country Auzan; the later Assyrians spoke of it simply as the land of the Madai. The country is on the whole unproductive, but the herbage in the fertile glens among the mountains is particularly good, so that, from very early times, Media was famous for its excellent breed of horses, which resembled the Turkoman breed of to-day. The Assyrian kings tell us in their records that the Madai paid them tribute in horses, and we know also that the Persian kings, after their conquest of the Medes, fixed their annual tribute at three thousand horses. Diodorus Siculus says that, at one time, the pastures of Bagistan fed no less than one hundred and sixty thousand horses.

The early home of the Barsua or Parsua (who are mentioned in 836 B.C. in the inscriptions of Shalmaneser II. of Assyria in conjunction with the Madai) lies still farther to the east and south, behind the continuation of the Zagros range. The Greeks called the country Persis, and it is probably identical with the modern Persian province of Farsistan. In his description of this district as it is to-day, Fraser says that it is "in places richly fertile, picturesque and romantic beyond imagination, with lovely wooded dells, green mountain-sides, and broad plains, suitable for the production of almost any crops. Yet it has, on the whole, a predominant character of barrenness." It may be summed up as a "great mountain-chain pierced by extraordinary gorges," which makes it a country eminently "easy of defence." Very little is known of either Medes or Persians till late in the seventh century B.C., at which time, under the leadership of Kyaxares, the son of Phaortes, the Madai, in alliance with the rebel viceroy of Babylon, besieged and took Nineveh. Both Medes and Persians first appear on the horizon of history as hardy mountaineers, vigorous races, fit to conquer and to rule. Like their neighbours, the Scythians, their favourite weapon was a short bow with arrows a yard long. Both Medes and Persians were splendid horsemen, who could take aim and shoot whilst galloping, and both were formidable foes. The Medes, after their conquest of Nineveh, adopted the flowing robes and the luxury of the Assyrians, eating rich foods and drinking wine to excess, so that, a century later, the race had so degenerated as to be easily subjugated by the hardy Persians from the eastern highlands.

Greek historians describe the ancient Persians, who, we must remember, were not only their rivals but also their conquerors, as keen-witted, energetic and brave, and, above all, truthful. "In boldness and in warlike spirit," says Herodotus, "the Persians are not at all behind the Greeks. . . . To buy and sell wares in the market, to chaffer and haggle over prices, is distasteful to them." We hear from Xenophon and from Strabo how carefully the Persian lads of the ruling class were trained. From the age of seven they had to undergo the discipline of soldiers: to rise at dawn, to learn to ride, to leap from their horses at the gallop, to shoot an arrow, to throw a javelin, and never to tell a lie. As they grew older, they had to endure extreme cold and heat without a murmur, to sleep in the open air, and to take food but once in four-and-twenty hours. When the Persians conquered the Medes, the richest among them were frugal and sober, eating only barley-cakes and wheaten-bread and simply roasted meat, and drinking only water. But, in later times, they too, like the Medes, became excessively self-indulgent and luxurious in their mode of living.

In physique the Medes and Persians were scarcely distinguishable races. Compared with the Semitic races, they were tall and graceful, and were distinguished by a high and straight forehead, and a well-formed nose, sometimes aquiline, but oftener on a line with the forehead; the chin was firm and rounded; the beard curly; the hair curly and abundant. Xenophon speaks in admiration of the stature and beauty of the Median women, whilst Plutarch gives equal praise to the women of Persia.

Our first important record of Aryan, Eranian, or Persian thought is to be found carved on the precipitous surface of the great rock of Behistûn. This inscription dates from about 520 B.C., and describes the struggle for supremacy between "Gaumata," the chief Magus of the period, and "Darayâvush, son of Vishtâspa," better known to us under his Hellenised name, "Dareios." The king says that "Gaumata, a Magian, lied to the state," and "the whole state became rebellious." . . . "There was not a man, neither Persian nor Mede, nor any one of our family (the Akhœmenian), who could dispossess that Gaumata. . . . The people feared him exceedingly. . . . Then I prayed to Ahura-Mazda; Ahura-Mazda brought help to me. On the tenth day of the month Bagayadish (March–April), then it was that I, with my faithful men, slew that Gaumata, the Magian, and the men who were his chief followers." . . . "The empire, which had been taken away from our family, that I recovered. I established the state in its place, both Persia and Media and the other provinces. . . . By the grace of Ahura-Mazda I did this. . . ." On his tomb Dareios also carved the inscription: "A great god is Ahura-Mazda; he has created this earth, he has created yonder heaven, he has created man, and all pleasant things for man, he has made Darayâvush king, the only king of many. That which I have done, I have all done through the grace of Ahura-Mazda." The first thing that Dareios did, after his victory over Gaumata, was to restore the simple style of the worship which had long ago been established by the sage, Zoroaster, and which the Magi, for some time previously, had corrupted. Then "the Great King" set himself the task of reorganising his vast empire, and gave to the ancient world the first example of a fairly just ruler. To judge by his inscriptions, the thing he most hated was "a lie." The whole Persian Empire was divided into twenty provinces; each province was surveyed and taxed according to its resources. A fixed land-tax was collected, in gold and silver, from each province, and a tribute, in kind, of its chief product; besides which, dues were collected by the state from mines, forests, fisheries, and irrigation. In this way, the annual state-income, according to the present value of money, is estimated to have reached two hundred and sixty millions sterling. In order to promote trade, and at the same time to keep a firm grip on his distant provinces, Dareios spared neither time, labour, nor expense in making broad roads in all directions from Susa, the capital, to the distant frontiers of the empire. Many of these "Highways of the Great King" may still be traced, and on all of them, at regular intervals of fourteen miles—the recognised distance which a good horse can cover at a hand-gallop,—he established post stations, where relays of horses were kept saddled, day and night, in immediate readiness for the king or his couriers. The great satraps were almost autocrats in their respective provinces, but none of them knew when Dareios would suddenly arrive on a surprise-visit of inspection; and woe to that satrap whose province the king found to be ill-governed!

That we have so few architectural records of this great Persian Empire is due to the fact that both Medes and Persians built mostly of wood, no doubt tempted to do so by the magnificent forests of cedar and cypress which clothe the slopes of the Zagros Mountains. We know from Herodotus that the Persian palaces were constructed of these woods, the inner walls of the chief apartments being overlaid with plates of hammered gold or silver, and the timber roofs also being frequently covered with silver plates.

But, if few material records exist to-day of this powerful Aryan race, they have left us a very remarkable collection of their national hymns. These are known as the Vedic Hymns, or "Rig-Veda," and from them we gain our knowledge, not only of Persian Mazdeism, but also of Hindu Brahmanism. These two kindred religions, Mazdeism and Brahmanism, had their origin in nature-worship. Light, heat, moisture, fire, wind, and rain were adored as powers of good; whilst darkness, drought, storm, and pestilence were cursed as powers of evil. The Turanians on the Persian borderland were also worshippers of nature, but the difference between them and the nobler Aryans was great. The one object of the Turanian worship was to propitiate the evil powers. This the Aryans scorned to do, relying entirely on the beneficent powers for prosperity and safety. We learn from the "Gathas" (hymns) that the luminous sky, personified in the earlier Vedic hymns under the name of "Dyaus," and in the later hymns under the name of "Varuna," was the chief object of Aryan adoration. The places of worship of the early Persians were simple circles of stones, in the centre of which they kindled the sacred fire. They had neither temples nor statues, holding it to be unworthy of the deity to be symbolised by any definite form, or to be worshipped in any confined space. The whole universe was his temple, and the universal element of fire his only suggestive symbol. Herodotus says: "They have no images of the gods, no temples or altars, and consider the use of them a sign of folly. Their wont is, however, to ascend the summit of the loftiest mountains and there to offer sacrifice to Zeus (Dyaus), which is the name they give to the whole circuit of the firmament. They likewise offer to the sun and moon, to the earth, to fire, to water, and to the winds. These are the only gods whose worship has come down to them from ancient times." Varuna, or Dyaus, is called "the all-knowing," because the sky looks down upon the whole earth; the sun is addressed as "the eye of Varuna," and the lightning as "the son of Varuna." The Persian name for lightning was "Athar-van" (he who has fire), and in the hymns a prominent part is attributed to "Athar-van" in the eternal warfare waged by the powers of light and life against the powers of darkness and drought. The demons of drought try to hide the life-giving rain within their gloomy "towers," but these are pierced by the fiery shafts of "Athar-van," and they are forced to yield up their concealed treasure. Another old Aryan fancy compares the "fleecy" clouds of summer—the kind of sky which the French so aptly call "un ciel moutonné"—to a wandering herd of kine, and speak of the gently-dropping rain as "the milking of the heavenly cows"; whilst the drought-demons are execrated as "cow-stealers," who shut up their booty in their gloomy strongholds, from which they have to be released by "Indra" and "Vayu," the gods of storm and wind. Indra and Vayu are the Hindu names for the storm-god and wind-god, but the old Eranian name for the storm-god is Tishtraya. Long is the conflict between Tishtraya and Apaosha, the drought-fiend; but Apaosha is vanquished at last by Tishtraya[1] in the form of a white horse.

The religion of those Aryan tribes who wandered into the plains and forests of India was characterised later by great imagination and extreme subtlety of abstract thought. But the faith of the Aryan tribes who remained among the mountains of Persia became perhaps the purest and simplest that was held by any thinkers of the ancient world. For, behind the sky-gods, these old Eranian sages imagined an unknown and unknowable abstract divinity whom they spoke of as Ahura-Mazda, literally "Lord of all Knowledge." The luminous sky was the mere vehicle of his manifestation to men, "the garment of heavenly substance which Mazda puts on," "the most beauteous body of Ahura"—"We worship his most beauteous body." This unseen God was afterwards spoken of as "Spenta-mainyu" (the Good Spirit), and was regarded as being the aggregate or sum-total of the good qualities attributed to all the beneficent spirits of nature. Later still, when sacerdotalism complicated the simplicity of thought, the six chief attributes of the Good Spirit were called "the six ministering spirits of Spenta-mainyu," and were worshipped as individual spirits under the names of (1) the Good Mind, (2) the Highest Truth, (3) Sovereignty, (4) Piety, (5) Health, and (6) Immortality. Finally, the six spirits and Spenta-mainyu — the synthesis of them all — were adored as "the seven Amshaspends," a name which

[1] Some authorities identify Tishtraya with the "Dog-star," Sirius, who is said to preside over the "dog-days," when the drought-fiend is most powerful.

survives in the "Amsha-Spanos" of the modern Parsis. But, from numerous passages in the sacred writings, it is evident that "these luminous ones," as they are called, "who are all seven of one speech, who are all seven of one deed," were still sometimes considered as together forming one supreme deity. "We worship Ahura-Mazda, the Master of Purity: we worship the Amesha-Spentas, the possessors of good, the givers of good: we worship the whole creation of the true Spirit, both the spiritual and the terrestrial, all that supports the welfare of the good creation. . . . We praise all good thoughts, all good words, all good deeds which are or shall be, and we likewise keep clean and pure all that is good. O Ahura Mazda, thou happy being! We strive to think, to speak, to do that which is best fitted to the two lives" (*i.e.* life of body and spirit).

The most interesting personality connected with Aryan thought is that of the legendary sage "Zarathustra," who is better known to us under his Greek name, "Zoroaster." There is a very remarkable discrepancy in the time at which he is said to have lived; but this may be explained by the theory that "Zarathustra" was possibly a generic name borne by a long succession of teachers, the dates of whose birth and death are unknown. There is, however, no doubt that there was at some time an early Aryan teacher spoken of as Zarathustra, who devoted his life to purify the religion of his time, and so endeavour to lead his countrymen back to the simplicity of the ancient faith. This teacher, say the "Gathas" (hymns), was born "by a great water, in a wooded mountain-country," and spent long periods of solitary meditation "on the mountain of holy communings,"—like Moses of the later Jewish scriptures,—from which, at last, he came down among his fellow-men, to communicate to them the thoughts spoken to his soul by "the Voice of Ahura-Mazda." The Persian "Ahura" is pronounced "Asura" in Hindu. In the later hymns of the Rig-Veda, composed in India, the word "asura" is used to signify "evil-spirits," whilst the word "deava" is used to signify "good spirits." But the Eranians used the word "Ahura" as the name of "the Good Spirit," and the word "deava" to signify "devils." This change in the meaning of these words probably took place about 1500 B.C., and, as Eranian tradition ascribes the composition—though it was perhaps only the collection—of the "Gathas" (hymns) to the immediate disciples of Zarathustra, it is likely that the sage was living before 1500 B.C. Zarathustra teaches a very simple dualism, which may have been the original of the later Jewish dualism of Jehovah and Satan. He accounts for the presence in the world of good and evil by postulating two spirits, Ahura-Mazda (the Spenta-mainyu, or spirit of light) and his eternal foe, Angrô-mainyu (the dark spirit). The idea of these "eternal opposites" is the very essence of Mazdeism. Without the idea of darkness, cold, disease, and death, how can man conceive the idea of light, warmth, health, and life? or, without the idea of goodness and truth, how is it possible to conceive the idea of lying and deceit? So Zarathustra tells his disciples that the source of good and evil is in their own hearts, and he insists that "good" is good only if thought, word, and deed all combine to make it so. The life of man, he says, must be a never-ending strife against all that is evil. The highest privilege of man is, that he can choose on which side he will range himself in the eternal struggle. All men must make their choice, he says: "each man for himself," all must fight, either for "the spirit which is all Life," or for "the spirit which is all Death," and, having chosen, all must accept the consequences of their choice.

Good and evil, as explained by Zarathustra, are synonymous with "real" and "unreal": the bad mind is literally the "nought-mind." "Surely, surely," he says, "the sovereignty will be given to those who have aided Truth to vanquish Lie (Druj). . . . Therefore will we belong to those who are to lead this life in time on to perfection. Grant us then, O Mazda, that we may be enlightened, whose mind as yet judges falsely. For then, the blow of destruction shall fall upon the liar, while those who keep the good teaching will assemble in the fair abode of Mazda. If, O men, ye lay to heart these laws, which Mazda instituted, it will go well with you." Zarathustra taught that all souls are eternal, and enjoy a conscious existence after death. They must, however, after a period of rest from earth-life, renew their existence, periodically, in a physical body, until, by the efficacy of good thoughts and good deeds, the spiritual evolution of the soul is complete. We read (Yesht xxii.) that, during the three first nights after his death, the soul of a good man, which has already quitted his body, lingers near his head, and that he "tastes in those nights as much delight as the whole living world can taste." At the dawn of the fourth day after death comes "a scent-laden wind," and "then, at the head of the Chinvat bridge, the holy bridge, made by Mazda, comes the well-shapen, strong, and tall-formed maiden. . . . And the soul of the faithful one addresses her, asking, 'What maid art thou, who art the fairest I have ever seen?' And she answers him: 'O thou youth of good thought, good words, good deeds, I am thine own conscience.'"

The people of Erân, at the epoch ascribed to Zarathustra, were certainly not fire-worshippers, although they reverenced "the fire of Ahura-Mazda" as the purest visible symbol of the unseen God. Every householder in those days was priest of his own home and hearth, and thrice every night it was his duty to tend the symbolical fire burning on the household altar. This fire was fed with small pieces of sandal-wood, "fragrant wood, well examined by the light of day and well cleansed," so that no sort of impurity should pollute the sacred flame. At Bombay, to-day, this time-honoured custom of tending the holy fire of Mazda is kept up by all strict Parsis—the modern representatives of the ancient people of Erân. It seems to have been the practice of the priests, before the Zoroastrian reformation, to stimulate themselves by drinking the potent alcoholic liquor which they distilled from the Haoma plant, but which should only be poured, as a libation, upon the holy fire. "When, O Mazda," cries Zarathustra, "shall appear the men of perfect mind, and when shall they drive away the polluted, drunken joy whereby the Karpans with angry zeal would crush us!" But, in a modified form, the drinking of the Haoma liquor, so strongly condemned by the sage, became, in later Mazdean times, an act of ritualistic worship. A cup of the sacred Haoma juice was held up by the priest before the holy fire, was "shown to the fire," and then drunk by him. In the same way, wheaten cakes were consecrated, and presented as offerings to the symbol of Mazda, before being eaten by the priest, exactly as the Catholic priest of later times elevates the bread and wine at the celebration of the Eucharist.

But the fire-worship, wrongly attributed to the ancient Persians, was no doubt practised by those Turanian tribes which settled in Media, south and east of Lake Van. This wild mountain-region was called by the Eranians, on account of its frequent naphtha-springs, "the Realm of Fire." The Greeks called the district "Atro-patene," and even to-day, it is said that a few "Gebers," or fire-worshippers, live near the ruined fire-towers of their Turanian ancestors, and that the naphtha-flames may still be seen glimmering on the crumbling summits of these towers, fed by the ancient pipes which connect the ever-burning flame with the subterranean naphtha-springs. It is significant that in early Zoroastrian times the priest was called "Master of Wisdom" and "Messenger of the Law," whereas, in later degenerate times, he was called "Keeper of the Fire."

The Persian Book of the Law is usually spoken of as the "Avesta-u-Zend" (Law and Commentary).

According to tradition, it was originally written on twenty ox-hides, which were unfortunately burnt during the great fire which destroyed the palace at Persepolis during the visit of Alexander of Macedonia, 330 B.C. It is on record that, shortly before the fire, Hermippos, a Greek savant in the suite of Alexander, had made a complete catalogue of all the sacred writings, and that, not long after the fire, the whole "Avesta-u-Zend" was written down by a council of Persian magi, who claimed to know the entire text by heart. To us moderns this seems an impossibility; but our Orientalists assure us that the power of memory developed among the old Aryan priests and sages by the systematic training of the memory from their earliest youth was so extraordinary that such a feat is quite possible. At all events, such is the source from whence we derive the text of the Persian "Avesta-u-Zend." The last recension of this text was made about 325 A.D., during the reign of Shapur II., of the Sassanian dynasty.

CHAPTER VII

GREEK THOUGHT

UNTIL the recent discoveries at Knossos, in Crete, which have revealed a civilisation earlier than that brought to light by Schliemann on the sites of Mycenæ, Tiryns, and Troy, our acquaintance with the records of Greek life and thought began with the so-called Homeric poems. The far-off origin of the civilisation of Greece remains still as hidden as that of Babylonia or Egypt. From the many objects of Egyptian manufacture, however, which have been found from time to time in Crete, we had already known that the island had had commercial intercourse with Egypt as long ago as 1500 B.C. But the fragments of Egyptian vases, which are among the late discoveries of Mr Evans at Knossos, are considered by experts to belong to a period a thousand years earlier still. A number of enamelled plaques, belonging to a large mosaic, also found there, although probably of native manufacture, are distinctly Egyptian in character; whilst a small golden vase lately found at Knossos, as well as ornamental sprays of gold wire and beaten gold, forcibly resemble the goldsmiths' work which Schliemann brought from Mycenæ. By his discoveries Schliemann has shown us that the civilisation at Mycenæ, Ilios, and Tiryns was semi-Asiatic, and this description applies also to the character of all similar relics and records found in Cos, Crete, Rhodes, and numerous other sites all over the Ægean.

It is to the age which, for want of a better name, is called Mycenæan that the Homeric poems belong. In their present form these poems consist of the *Iliad* and the *Odyssey*, but there seems little doubt that these two epics have been evolved from a number of ancient sagas, legends, and ballads which were never committed to writing in any connected sequence until long after the hardy Dorian race had become paramount in Peloponnesus. The *Iliad* relates the story of the siege of Troy or Ilios, a coast town in Asia Minor; whilst the *Odyssey* records the adventures of Ulysses, one of the chief heroes of the siege, on his voyage back to his island-home in rocky Ithaca. Greece consisted, long after the time at which this siege probably took place, of a number of small independent states, that were for ever fighting with each other. Athens fought with Megara and Eleusis, Mycenæ fought with Orchemenos, Argos fought with Mycenæ, and also with Tiryns and Sparta. But though war was the chronic state, there were at times short intervals of peace, when minstrels and rhapsodists wandered from one city to another, singing and reciting the songs and sagas that are now known as "Homeric"; and it may perhaps be assumed that the common sympathy with these heroic legends helped, not a little, in the ultimate fusion of these independent states. At any rate, Peisistratos of Athens, at that time ruling as the "tyrannos," or viceroy of the Persian king, first of all collected these poems, between 560 and and 527 B.C., and founded the first library in Greece. The version of the Homeric poems which has come down to us, however, is the recension made by three poets, Zenodotus of Ephesus, Aristophanes of Byzantium, and Aristarchus of Samothrace, who lived about 300 B.C., at Alexandria. These poems, as we know, are attributed to a writer called "Homeros," whose birthplace is claimed not only by Chios and Smyrna, but also by five other different cities. But what we do *not* know is that such a person as Homeros ever lived in the flesh, because it seems that the only scrap of evidence that Homer was a reality is, that Simonides of Amorgos (664 B.C.) mentions that the author of the oft-quoted simile which compares man's life to "the passing of leaves," was "a man of Chios." We may, however, in any case, assume that some unknown poet, whose name possibly *was* "Homeros," *did* collect and collate a number of ancient songs and legends, and that by him, or possibly by other writers, they were remodelled into what we now know as the *Iliad* and *Odyssey*. The internal evidence of these two poems themselves reveals the fact that most of the poetic similes, which are such interesting features of the poems, clearly date from a period long after the time when Homer is supposed to have lived.

But, if the origin of the Homeric poems remains

doubtful, the siege of Troy seems to have been a fact, since Schliemann found "masses of vitrified bricks and calcined beams" on the site of the ancient city. This proves at least that Troy was destroyed by fire, and why not by the Greeks? "In some places," says Schliemann, "the fire had been so fierce as to transform great portions of brick walls into spongy, vitreous substance." The situation of Troy made it so handy a centre for piratical expeditions all over the Ægean Sea, that it has been surmised that the story of the carrying off of Helen, the wife of Menelaus, from Argos to Troy, by Paris, the son of Priam, may be nothing more than a poetic legend of some Trojan expedition so unusually daring that the Achaians and Ionians felt it necessary to combine to crush such a dangerous neighbour. We know, as a fact, that, lower down the coast of Asia Minor, the Cretans certainly formed a league to suppress Carian corsairs.

The *Iliad* begins with the description of the gathering of the Greek warriors under the leadership of Agamemnon, "king of Mykene, rich in gold," who assembled in their ships, some of which, we are told, carried a hundred men, from Argos, Mycenæ, Corinth, Athens, Lacedæmon, Ithaca, Crete, Rhodes, Salamis, Bœotia, Phokia, Lokria, and Eubœa; in fact, all Greece seems to have combined to take vengeance on the piratical, "horse-taming men of Ilios." Nine years later, we find the Greek host encamped on the Asiatic shore of the Hellespont, in sight of Troy, in "huts solidly built and well provisioned." But the Greek camp is ravaged by pestilence, which is said to be sent by Apollo as a punishment for the abduction from his temple at Thebes of his young priestess, the maiden Chryseis, who has been allotted to Achilles. Therefore Achilles has been ordered by Agamemnon to give up Chryseis, and, having done so, Achilles sulks in his quarters with his "Myrmidons" and declines to fight. The siege goes on with varying success from day to day, and great are the deeds of valour performed by the heroes. The first onslaught of the Greeks is thus described: "As when on the echoing beach the sea-wave lifteth up itself in close array before the driving of the west wind, . . . even so, in close array, moved the battalions of Danaans without pause to the battle. Each captain gave his men the word, and the rest went silently." But the Trojans "had not like speech nor one language, being brought from many lands," so that "the clamour of the Trojans through the wide host" resembled the bleating of "sheep without number." Then, the rival hosts meet in the clash and clang of battle, and, "as two winter torrents flow down from the mountains to join their furious floods within the deep ravine, and the shepherd heareth the roaring afar off among the hills, even so from the joining of battle came there forth shouting and travail." At first the Trojans give way, and Agamemnon cheers on his Achaians: "My friends, quit you like men, and take heart of courage, and shun dishonour in one another's eyes amid the stress of battle: of men that shun dishonour more are saved than slain, but for them that flee is neither glory found nor safety."

The gods favour different sides. Apollo, Ares, Aphrodite, and Artemis cheer on the Trojans; whilst

Poseidon, Athene, Hera, and Hermes side with the Greeks. Nor can the gods themselves long keep out of the fray: one amusing encounter at least takes place between Ares and Athene, who sends the vanquished war-god bellowing away. On one occasion Diomedes, the Argive chieftain, meets a young Trojan, named Glaucos, who seems to him to be a god in mortal guise, and so asks him who he is. Then Glaucos replies, in the oft-quoted words that are attributed to the "man of Chios": "Why inquirest thou of my generation? Even as are the generations of leaves, such likewise are those of men: the leaves that the wind scattereth on the earth, and the forest buddeth and putteth forth more again when the season of spring is at hand; so of the generation of men, one putteth forth and another ceaseth."

After varying success on both sides, the Trojans, under the leadership of Priam's eldest son, "horse-taming Hector," beat back the Greeks, and by the help of Phœbus Apollo shut them up in their fortified camp, before which the victors bivouac. "A thousand fires burned upon the plain, and by the side of each sate fifty warriors in the gleam of blazing fire. And the horses champed white barley and spelt, and, standing by their chariots, waited for the dawn. Thus kept the Trojans watch." Agamemnon is indeed sufficiently hard-pressed to call together his captains and suggest raising the siege. But brave Diomedes cries: "Sir, deemest thou that the Achaians are thus indeed cowards and weaklings, as thou sayest? But, and if thine own heart be set on going, go thy way: the way is before thee, and thy ships stand beside the sea, even the great multitude that followed thee from Mykene. But all the other flowing-haired Achaians will tarry here until we waste Troy." Then Agamemnon tries his best to persuade Achilles to fight, but in vain. And presently Apollo aids the Trojans, by turning the swollen torrents of the two streams, Simoeis and Skamandros, from their natural beds against the dyke which protects the Greek encampment, so that it fills up the deep fosse, allowing the passage of the Trojan war-chariots. But Poseidon inspires the Achaians with fresh courage, as they rally round Odysseus "dear to Zeus" and "stout Aias." And now, "as when a brimming river cometh down upon the plain in winter-flood from the hills," the heroes and their followers charge the Trojans, who flee before them, although the valiant Hector, "lion-like raging in his strength," urges them to turn and "once more cross the dyke" and capture the Greek ships, "drawn up on the shore of the grey sea." Then Agamemnon again suggests that the Greek host should sail back home under cover of the darkness, "for there is no shame in fleeing from ruin, even in the night." But Odysseus will listen to no such craven counsel: "Be silent, lest some of the Achaians hear this word, that no man should so much as suffer to pass through his mouth, none that understandeth in his heart to speak fit counsel, none that is a sceptred king." But, rallied at last by Hector, the Trojans once more advance, driving back the Greeks to their ships. Then Achilles decides to join in the fight. So, on the morrow, "when morning, saffron-robed, arose from the streams of ocean, to bring light to gods and men . . . thick from the ships streamed forth bright-glittering helms and bossy shields, strong-plaited cuirasses, and ashen spears, and the sheen thereof went up to heaven, and all the earth laughed in the flash of bronze."

The crisis of the siege being come, both gods and goddesses gather together to watch the fight, and even join in it themselves. Achilles drives the Trojans back, and as Hector, whose "whole-hoofed horses trampled corpses and shields together, and with blood all the axel-tree below was sprinkled, . . ." is flying from him, Achilles pierces him with his spear. Then after "binding the feet of the slain Hector to the tail of his chariot," the Greek hero drives back to camp, dragging the body of his foe. But Apollo miraculously prevents any "defacement" of the slain Hector, and Zeus sends the goddess Thetis, the mother of Achilles, to urge her son to give back the body to Hector's father, Priam. So Priam goes to "the lofty hut of the son of Peleus" (and Thetis), which the Myrmidons made for their king." And when Achilles saw him, "he sprang from his seat and raised the old man by the hand," saying, "Come thou, sit thee down, and we will let our sorrows lie quiet in our hearts for all our pain, for no avail cometh from chill lament. This is the lot the gods have spun for miserable men, that they should live in pain, yet themselves are sorrowless." Priam puts Hector's body on his mule-carriage and takes it back to Troy. And when Helen, the wife of Menelaus of Argos, sees the body of the dead hero, she cries: "Hector, of all my brethren of Troy, far dearest to my heart!

Truly, my lord is god-like Alexandros, who brought me to Troy: would I had died ere then! For this is now the twentieth year since I went thence, and am gone from my own native land, but never yet heard I evil or despiteful word from thee. . . ."

From the *Iliad* we gain some insight into early Greek thought and customs, though we can ascribe them to no definite date, whilst even the few picturesque passages quoted in this slight sketch of the great epic show sufficiently how much the old ballads and legends must have been worked upon previous to the version which has been given to us by the three Alexandrian poets. We gather from the *Iliad* that the sun-god, "Phœbus-Apollo," was chiefly worshipped in Asia Minor, whilst the favourite deity of the Greeks of the Ægean was "Pallas-Athene"; and from the graphic description of a sacrifice to Zeus, performed in the Greek camp, we learn that the Hellenic rites were not very unlike those with which the Jews worshipped Yahveh. "When they had prayed and sprinkled the barley-meal, they drew back the bull's head, and cut his throat, and flayed him, and cut slices from the thighs, and wrapped them in fat, making a double fold, and laid raw collops thereon; and these they burnt on cleft wood, and spitted the vitals, and held them over Hephaistos' flame. Now, when the thighs were burnt, and they had tasted the vitals, then they sliced all the rest, and pierced it through with spits, and roasted it carefully . . . and feasted and drank." Thus it seems that libations of wine and sprinkling of barley-meal were offered to Zeus, but that, after that, the

Greek, like the Hebrew god, received as his share of the "burnt offering" only the tough thighs and fat, whilst all the best parts of the animal sacrificed were carefully cooked and eaten by the worshippers, who washed down their feast with "crowned" or brimming bowls of wine. Similarly, we are told that, in a sacrifice to Apollo, his worshippers first wash their hands, then sprinkle the customary barley-meal before the god, then slay, skin, and cut up the lambs and "unblemished goats," burning the tough parts in honour of Apollo, but "carefully roasting the tender parts," which they eat "with five-pronged forks," and "crown the bowls with wine."

We get from the *Iliad* also a glimpse of the nature of the athletic sports so characteristic of the Greeks. The particular sports described in the poems were "arranged by Achilles" in honour of his friend, the hero Patroklos, slain by Hector, and consisted of a chariot-race, a wrestling-match, and a running-race. The last was won by Odysseus of Ithaca, who also succeeded, after a great struggle in the wrestling-match, in throwing his opponent, the mighty Aias: "and the folk gazed and marvelled. Then, in his turn, much-enduring, noble Odysseus tried to lift and move him a little from the ground, but lifted him not; so, he crooked his knee within the other's, and both fell to the ground nigh to each other," so that "Achilles adjudged a prize to each." The chariot-race is described with great spirit. The veteran Nestor gives some excellent advice, before starting, to his son Antilochos, who is one of the five competitors, telling him to be careful to keep his horses well in hand and to drive them close up to the stone pillar which marks the turning-point of the course: "Do thou drive close, and bear thy horses and chariot hard thereon, and lean thy body on the well-knit car, slightly to their left, and call upon the off-horse with voice and lash, and give him rein from thy hand; but let the near-horse hug the post, so that the nave of the well-wrought wheel seem to graze it—yet beware of touching the stone, lest thou wound the horses and break the chariot; . . . for, if at the turning-post thou drive past the rest, there is none that shall overtake thee from behind." Antilochos, however, does not win, in spite of all the good advice of the crafty Nestor. It is amusing to read that Aias and Idomeneus, the Cretan chieftain, are disputing as to which of them first passed the winning-post, when Idomeneus cries: "Come, let us wager a tripod or a cauldron, and make Agamemnon, Atreus' son, our umpire!"

We gather from the *Iliad*, too, that these joyous warriors of the Homeric age were always striving to show, in games or war, who was the best man among them, who was king of men, as Zeus was king of gods. They were less thinkers than doers. The aim of the Greek, at this epoch, was to enjoy life to the full. He saw indeed that mysterious forces were active everywhere in nature and in himself, but he felt his inability to solve the riddle of the before and the hereafter, and so he set it aside by the simple process of assuming that nature's inscrutable powers must be beings of ideal beauty, with all the passions of humanity. Thus, Zeus was fabled to be the ruler of "High Heaven" (the summer half of the zodiac), of Olympus, the mountain of the gods, and was therefore the personification of the power of the luminous sky, lord of the rain- and thunder-cloud, and father of the gods; whilst Poseidon, his brother, personified the power of the ocean, and Phœbus-Apollo the power of the sun. Apollo, in later times, was looked upon more particularly as the personification of the power of art, as his sister, Pallas-Athene, was of the power of knowledge in general. The goddess Aphrodite always symbolised the power of material beauty and sexual love.

One of the lesser, but nevertheless one of the most suggestive, of the gods of Greece was Dionysos, worshipped, at least at first, chiefly in Thrace and Bœotia. He was often invoked under the name of Iacchos, and probably in earlier times was only a wine-god, the poetical personation of the culture of the vine. But, in later times, Dionysos became the emblem of life and growth throughout both the vegetable and animal worlds; he was the idealisation of the flowing sap; he was the divine impulse of genius; he was the spirit of enthusiasm and of ecstasy; and for ecstasy, what more suggestive emblem than wine!

The fundamental idea represented by all the Greek mysteries, whether of Dionysos, who was always associated with Demeter, the corn-goddess — the Ceres of the Romans,—or Iacchos, or of Orpheus, was the mystery of the life, growth, and death of vegetation year by year, and the still greater mystery of the life, growth, and death of humanity; and therefore we find that, in all these ancient mysteries, the solemn partaking of bread and wine was one of the most secret and sacred of the rites. There is no doubt that the true orphic life, the "bios orphicos," was more or less ascetic, although in later times, especially after the Asiatic victories of Alexander of Macedon, the celebrations degenerated, so that, instead of the states of spiritual exaltation and ecstasy produced by ascetic practices, the celebrants of the orgies threw themselves into states of enthusiasm and frenzy by means of intoxication produced by wine. It is probable that the later mysteries of Orpheus, the legendary favourite of Apollo, were instituted by the more cultured Hellenes as a protest against these dissolute orgies. From Apollo, Orpheus was fabled to have received the golden lyre, exhibited in the temple at Lesbos, the first city in Greece where lyric music was cultivated.

Dionysos symbolised the power of sense, but Orpheus symbolised the power of mind. An old legend relates how Zagreus, the mystic name for Dionysos, was torn to pieces by the Titans, who symbolised the human passions. Another Greek mythos tells us how Orpheus was torn to pieces, in Thrace, by the frenzied female followers of Iacchos, symbols of the sexual passions. It will be remembered how, in an early Egyptian cult, Osiris was fabled to have been torn in pieces by Set, and that the worship of Osiris was always associated with that of Isis, the corn-goddess. Orpheus is represented by the Greek poets to have visited Egypt, and we have historical evidence of the constant intercourse between Greece and the Nile Delta from the time of Necho onwards. It is said that the culture of wheat and barley was introduced into Greece from Egypt, and it is certain that, as late as 250 B.C., Isis was worshipped by the Greek colony at Cyrene. Herodotus held that Osiris and Dionysos were synonymous, and this opinion is supported by the discovery made in quite recent times, in Orphic tombs in Greece, of a number of plates of beaten gold, on which are engraved directions for the guidance of the departed spirit during his journey through the underworld. This fact shows us that, at one time, in Greece the same idea prevailed as that which prompted the friends of the deceased to enclose mystic passages from the Book of the Dead in the sarcophagi of Egyptian mummies.

The earlier mysteries, sacred to Dionysos, the wine-god, and Demeter, the corn-goddess, or to Persephone, the daughter of Demeter, and goddess of vegetation generally, were celebrated chiefly in agricultural districts; whilst the later mysteries of Orpheus were confined to the more cultured classes in the towns. The Orphic celebration took place at Eleusis, near Athens, in spring and autumn. The "Lesser Mysteries" were held during the time of blossom, the "Greater Mysteries" during the time of fruit, in the month Bedromion (August–September). The oath of silence as to all that should be revealed to them was administered to neophytes during the spring celebration, and, after a six months' probation, they were advanced to the first stage of initiation as "mystes" during the autumn celebration. After a further probation of twelve months, the "mystes" passed on to the complete initiation of "epoptes," or seer. The celebration of the Greater Mysteries began, at Athens, by the purgation or baptism of the "mystes" in the sea, after which all the celebrants walked in procession along the sacred way to Eleusis. Here, in the crypt beneath the temple, the mystes received, during the following night, and only after many trials of their fortitude, the full initiation into the mysteries, and were shown the Apopteia, or sacred symbols of life. These symbols the initiate took from the chest (kista), and, after contemplation, placed them in the basket. The oath of secrecy makes it difficult to say exactly what these symbols were; but prominent among them, according to Callimachus, the chief librarian of the library at Alexandria, who died about 240 B.C., were a golden serpent, a golden egg, and a golden phallus, all well-known emblems of the renewal of life in the physical world, and inferentially also in the spiritual world. No explanation of the meaning of the sacred symbols was given to the initiates; each man had to discover their signification for himself. Naturally, therefore, the meaning varied according as the mind of each epopt was spiritual or sensuous. "Blessed is he," says Pindar, "who has beheld the mysteries, descending into the underworld: he knows the aim, he knows the origin of life." Plato says, in the *Phœdo*: "Those who instituted the mysteries for us appear to have intimated that whoever shall arrive in Hades unpurified and not initiated shall lie in mud, but he who arrives there purified and initiated shall dwell with the gods." Clement of Alexandria, who was ordained presbyter of the early Christian Church about 190 A.D., puts his own interpretation on them, and appears to have been conscious only of what Plato significantly terms "mud." In his exhortation to the heathen, Clement says: "What are these mystic chests? I must expose their sacred things, and divulge things not fit for speech. Are they not sesame-cakes and pyramidal cakes and globular and flat cakes, embossed all over, and lumps of salt, and a serpent, symbol of Dionysus Bassareus? And, besides these, are there not pomegranates and branches and rods and ivy-leaves? and, besides, round cakes and poppy-seeds? And further there are the unmentionable symbols of Themis,[1] marjoram, a lamp, a sword, a woman's comb, which is a euphemism and mystic expression for a woman's secret parts." Apuleius, the writer of the beautiful allegory of Eros and Psyche, tells us that he was himself an initiate of the mysteries, and makes Psyche pray thus to Demeter: "I beseech thee by thy fruit-bearing right hand, by the joyful ceremonies of harvest, by the occult rites of thy cistæ . . . and by the arcana which Eleusis, the Attic sanctuary, conceals in profound silence, relieve the sorrows of thy wretched suppliant, Psyche!"

During the autumn celebrations, at Eleusis, the initiates performed a kind of pantomime, or miracle-play, accompanied by chorus-singing. This panto-

[1] On coins this goddess is represented with a cornucopia and a pair of scales.

mime represented the descent of the disconsolate Demeter into Hades, in search of her lost daughter, Persephone, and their happy return to the world of light and life. The celebration was begun fasting, but the resurrection of the goddess of vegetation was symbolised by the partaking by the celebrants of the life-giving elements of bread and wine. This sacramental feast was held mystically to strengthen the souls of the worshippers and to be typical of the joys of immortality. Proclus tells us of the dirges chanted at Eleusis during the celebration of the descent of Persephone into Hades, and of the joyous hymns which celebrated the subsequent return of the goddess to the upper world. There seems little or no doubt that from the dramatic representations and choruses of the mysteries the Greek drama was gradually evolved.

Like Plato, Sophocles speaks of the elevating tendency of the mysteries, of which, among other famous men, the Emperor Marcus Aurelius was afterwards an initiate. Sophocles teaches that every act of our lives has its own unerring result. He makes Œdipus suffer the necessary consequence of his unconscious crimes; but, having suffered in this life, death brings him no further punishment. In the words of that sympathetic student of Plato, Thomas Taylor, "the ultimate design of the mysteries, according to Plato, was to lead us back to the principles from which we descended, that is, to a perfect enjoyment of intellectual good.' We can trace this educational idea also in the *Odyssey*, which, unlike the *Iliad*, is considered by Grote to have been a connected poem from the very first. Thomas Taylor has translated a very suggestive critical analysis of the *Odyssey* which was written by Proclus, the great exponent of Platonism, in the fifth century of our era. The adventures of Ulysses and his companions after the fall of Troy, which are the subject of the *Odyssey*, must be understood, says Proclus, as an allegory of the upward striving of the human soul, as the contest between the lower and higher nature of man, who "passes in a regular manner over the dark and stormy sea of generation, and thus arrives, at length, at the region where tempests are unknown."

The poet tells us how the storm-driven Ulysses lands first on the island of the lotus-eaters, where Circe fascinates the warrior by "the allurements of delight," so that, soothed by languorous dreams, he forgets, for a time, both home and duty. But, at length, Reason, personified by Mercury, compels him once more to start on his difficult voyage. Escaping next the soft enchantment of the Sirens, "whose song is death, and makes destruction please," and passing safely through the dangerous whirlpools between Scylla and Charybdis, "by which two rocks the poet seems to signify the affections compressing human life on both sides," Ulysses and his comrades land on the isle of Calypso. Here again the hero lingers long, delighting in the love of the goddess, which Proclus thinks is intended "occultly to signify phantasy," until once more Mercury comes to the aid of Ulysses, and enables the hero to regain "the lost kingdom of his soul." The critical moment when the goddess reluctantly consents to let her lover go, is dramatically indicated by Ulysses seating himself "on the throne where Mercury had sat." Then the poet draws a vivid contrast between the soft, seductive twilight of Calypso's cavern, and the brilliance of the palace of Antinous, to which Ulysses comes next. In this illumined hall the wanderer relates at length the story of his adventures. It is the allegory of the man who has attained wisdom reviewing the errors of his stormy youth. And now, having proved the unsatisfying nature of sensuous delights, Ulysses is at last ready to listen to the teaching of Minerva, and determines to attain to perfect self-control by abstracting his mind "from all that concerns the senses." He therefore renounces all worldly possessions, assumes the garb of a beggar, and so finally regains "his long-deserted palace, or the occult recesses of his soul," where he is restored to his wife Penelope, "the image of intellectual purity."

According to Theon of Smyrna, a mathematician who lived in the first century of our era, the mysteries of Dionysos were similar to those of Orpheus, the ritual including purification by bathing or baptism (katharsis), initiation or seeing (epopteia). Peisistratos, the Persian tyrannos, encouraged the mysteries, so that during his term of office they were celebrated with much pomp. Gradually Dionysos became more and more idealised, and was worshipped as the suffering god, the twice-born, the saviour of humanity.

Somewhere between 520 B.C. and 485 B.C., the Orphic poems were collected and arranged by

Onomacritus, an Athenian poet and student of early Greek religious poetry. One of these Orphic poems runs:—"Zeus was the first, Zeus of the bright lightning-flash shall be the last of things. . . . Zeus is the foundation both of earth and starry heaven. Zeus is male, Zeus is divine feminine. Zeus the breath of all things: Zeus the rushing irresistible fire: Zeus the great fountain of the deep. . . . He of the bright thunder-bolt, after hiding all within him, brought them forth again from his sacred bosom to the gladsome day, doing ever wondrously. None saw the First-Born except holy Night alone!"

The Eleusinian mysteries, in later times, taught the mystic unity of all the gods, all being but so many manifestations of Zeus, first and last of gods. One of the Orphic hymns says: "He is the One self-proceeding, and from him all things proceed, and in them he himself exerts his activity: no mortal beholds him, but he beholds all." "There is one royal body in which all things are enwombed, Fire and Water, Earth, Æther, Night and Day, and Counsel, the first producer and delightful Love. All these are contained in the great body of Zeus."

The poet Æschylus, who died in 456 B.C., was an initiate of the mysteries, and it is to this fact that Aristophanes chiefly attributes the inspiration of his tragedies. In his *Agamemnon* Æschylus suggestively says: "Zeus, who prepared for men the path of wisdom, binding fast knowledge and suffering."

But the Greek thinkers in the colonies scattered all along the Ionian shore and along the Mediterranean coast of South Italy began, during the fifth century

B.C., to lose their interest in speculations about the gods, in their attempt to solve the more attractive mystery of the origin of the physical universe. What, they asked, is the "Archê," what the primal element, what the first force that moves the world? As far as we know, the earliest Greek thinker who endeavoured to answer this question was Thales of Miletus, in Asia Minor, where he was born in 636 B.C. At this time, Necho was the reigning Pharaoh in Egypt, and it was part of his policy to encourage intercourse with Greece. Thales is said to have spent some time in the Nile Delta, and to have brought back to Ionia a knowledge of geometry. This science was familiar to the Egyptians of the Delta, because it was necessary constantly to remeasure the land, on account of the annual inundations, which swept away old boundaries, and each year deposited new tracts of alluvium. Thales saw that, without moisture, there could be no life, and came, therefore, to the conclusion that the primal element of the Kosmos must have been water or moisture. It seems just possible that he may have been acquainted with the postulate of "the Great Deep," or "Heavenly Ocean," of the earlier Babylonian thinkers. But, however this may be, this postulate of his is all that we know of his teaching about the physical universe. His ethical teaching shows Thales as a healthy- and high-minded man. Among many other things, for instance, he says:—

"Be not enriched in an ill way. . . .

"Be not idle, even though rich. . . .

"If you rule, rule yourself. . . ."

But there was good ethical thinking on the mainland of Greece, even before the time of Thales. Hesiod of Bœotia, in his *Works and Days*, quotes many proverbs current about half a century earlier, amongst them:—

"A neighbour is a good thing. Help your neighbour and he will help you. A neighbour matters more than a kinsman. . . .

"Hard work is no shame: the shame is idleness. . . .

"The man who wrongs another harms himself. . . .

"Take fair measure, and give a little overmeasure. . . .

"Give is a good lass, but Snatch is a bad lass. . . .

"Give willingly: a willing gift is a pleasure. . . .

"Fools grasp at pelf, knowing not that half is better than the whole, nor how much comfort there is in a dinner of herbs. . . .

"He who follows the right thought of another is good; but he who neither thinks aright nor follows the thought of another is worth nothing. . . ."

In his work *On Nature*, Anaximander of Miletus, a pupil of Thales, who lived in the first half of the sixth century B.C., reveals himself to us as the first evolutionist. He advances the theory that from the primordial unity of the atmosphere proceed the pairs of opposites, moist and dry, and warm and cold. By the action of these opposites, innumerable worlds, which he calls Theoi (gods), evolve; after running their course, these Theoi disintegrate and disappear. Anaximander hazards the surmise that the warm-blooded animals evolve by gradual differentiation from the cold-blooded fish. Individuals and species, he says, are for ever changing and for ever evolving; but the divine "apeiron," the primordial substance of the universe, from which proceed all things, is both uncreated and indestructible.

A pupil of Anaximander, who died about 500 B.C., Xenophanes of Colophon, near Ephesus, settled at Elea, near Pæstum, in Italy, where he founded a distinct school of thought. He tells us a little more of Anaximander's theory of the atmosphere. The "Archê," he says, is ever in motion, and manifests itself in a threefold form, namely, as vapour, as breath, and as spirit ("aer, pneuma, psyche"). The fragments of the "elegies" of Xenophanes, and of his great work *On Nature*, show us that his teaching was pantheistic. He smiles good-naturedly at the gods of Greece, made in the image of their makers. If gods could be conceived by oxen or lions, no doubt, he suggests, they would appear in the forms of lions and oxen, just as the Greek gods assume the forms of men and women. For his part, Xenophanes can imagine but "one God, most high; he is not man-like; he has no parts of body or mind; but, all of him sees, hears, and thinks." This God is "the All," "the One," the Kosmos.

One of the chief influences in Greek thought five centuries before our era apparently was Pythagoreanism. This teaching is popularly ascribed to Pythagoras, who may, however, only have been a personification of it, like so many legendary teachers. It is worthy of note that, though he speaks of Pythagoreanism, Plato never once mentions the name of

Pythagoras, and that nothing is known either of his birth or death. It is said that Pythagoras was born in the island of Samos, that after long years of travel, during which he visited Egypt, Persia, and India, he settled at Crotona, a Greek city founded about 700 B.C., on the south-east coast of Italy, where he founded a mystic brotherhood, and disappeared during a popular insurrection, when many of the Pythagoreans assembled in the temple of Apollo were slain. What seems certain is that at that period Crotona and the neighbouring cities of Sybaris and Tarentum were noted for their extravagant and dissolute luxury, and that Crotona especially was famous for its music and its gymnasts, amongst whom was Milo, the finest athlete in all Greece; and that some teacher, who may have been Pythagoras, attracted the attention of the aristocrats of Crotona and exercised over them an influence similar to that which in later times Savonarola exerted at Florence. This influence was sufficiently great to induce some three hundred of these aristocrats of Crotona to renounce luxurious living and to form themselves into a mystic brotherhood for the study of philosophy and ethics, under the ægis of Apollo, whom they recognised as the symbol of "Light," not only physical but mental. Similar brotherhoods were formed gradually in some of the neighbouring cities, and even in Sicily.

The Pythagorean training laid great stress on physical and musical culture, and it is said that Pythagoras first made the discovery that "the notes of the lyre are proportionate to the length of the strings." The whole aim of Pythagorean teaching was the development of self-possession and self-reliance, in the widest sense of the term. Temperance in all things was strictly enforced—"the middle way"—and even asceticism was not discouraged, whilst self-examination was held to be a duty. The ethics of Pythagoreanism are indicated by such sayings as the following, which the Pythagoreans attributed to their master:—

"Be aware that no false pretence is long hidden. . . . No one is free who is not master of himself. . . . It is more grievous to be the slave of passion than of tyrants. . . . Do great things, without making promises of great things. . . . Esteem that to be above all things good, which in being communicated to another will be rather increased to yourself. . . . Hold those to be your true friends who benefit your soul rather than your body. . . . It is better to argue more with yourself than with your neighbours. . . . Deem that to be fine training by which you are enabled to bear the boorishness of the ignorant."

Pythagorean cosmogony maintained the theory that the universe is a "sphere" (sphaira) which floats in an infinite "void." The void first agitates the sphere and then penetrates it, thereby starting the process of evolution, much in the same way as all things are set going by "the Eternal Breath" in the Indian theory. The result of the impulse thus given by the "void" is to disintegrate the homogeneous mass of the "sphere" into an infinite multitude of infinitesimal particles. Then reaction sets in, causing these particles to combine in accordance with their inherent geometric affinities, whereby they differentiate into the four elements, fire, air, water, and earth. The primary of the four elements is Fire, which is the symbol of the "Divine Essence," whose focus is in "the Central Sun," around which the whole universe revolves. The Pythagorean idea is that everything in the universe is the result of some kind of motion. Motion is mathematically explained something in this way: The point, in moving, creates the line; the line, in moving, creates the plane, or superficies; the plane by its motion produces the cube, or solid body. When once an animal body has been formed, it has its own special evolutionary movements, which create, one after another, sensation, perception, and ultimately intelligence. The mainspring of the whole universe is said to be the "World-Soul," which is sometimes spoken of as the "Harmony of the Kosmos." Of this World-Soul each human soul is supposed to be a constituent particle, "a spark of the Divine Fire," whose immortality it therefore shares.

It will be seen that many of the Pythagorean ideas are distinctly Indian. For instance, it is held that the same Divine Spark animates one human body after another, and that the circumstances among which the soul, or Divine Spark, finds itself during each of its various incarnations are in strict accordance with the state of its spiritual evolution at the time. One of the most characteristic of the Pythagorean ideas is that of "Number," which is supposed to be the chief factor in the evolution of the universe. The World-Soul and the harmony of the Kosmos being one and the same, we may perhaps interpret

Number as being proportion, relation, harmony. Walter Pater, speaking of the Pythagorean philosophy, says: "Kosmos, order, reasonable, delightful order . . . became very dear to the Greek soul. . . . Apollo, the Dorian god, was its visible consecration. It was what, under his blessing, art superinduced upon the rough stone, the yielding clay, the jarring metallic strings, the common speech of every day. Philosophy in its turn, with enlarging purpose, could project a similar light of intelligence on the unmeaning world around us."

Indian theories seem, indeed, to have been quite familiar to several Greek thinkers about this time—to Parmenides of Elea and to Heraclitus of Ephesus especially, both of whom were highly esteemed by Plato as philosophical thinkers. Parmenides was a follower of Xenophanes, if not actually his pupil. He left Elea late in life, and went to Athens about 450 B.C., where Socrates was, at that time, a young man. He is known to us chiefly by his great metaphysical poem, *On Nature*, of which fragments only have been preserved. Enough, however, has come down to us to show that Parmenides followed lines of thought distinctly Indian. He postulates an Eternal "Being," which he defines as self-existent "substance"—continuous, indivisible, indestructible, and imperceptible to the human senses, arguing that the phenomena of nature are unreal. There can be, says Parmenides, neither "Void" nor "Becoming," because there can be no transition from "Non-Being" to "Being."

Heraclitus of Ephesus, who was teaching there

about 513 B.C., is said to have been, like Pythagoras, a great traveller in his early life. His fellow-citizens of Ephesus elected him to the chief magistracy, but he preferred to live the life of a recluse. He has left us a philosophical treatise *On Physics*, in which he maintains the theory that the great principle of the universe is change: everything is for ever in a state of flux or flow, nothing remains still or stationary. He illustrates his meaning by the picturesque saying, so often quoted, that "no man can step twice into *the same* stream," because the water is for ever changing, for ever passing by, and flowing farther away from him. He also graphically compares this eternal state of unrest to a flame. As the great agent of change in the universe, Heraclitus postulates an ethereal fluid, a "plastic fire," as he terms it, which is "self-kindled" and "self-extinguished." Sometimes he speaks of this ethereal fluid as "pur" (burning), sometimes as "psyche" (soul, or warm breath). He seems, indeed, to have been on the verge of the discovery of the hypothetic "ether" of our modern scientists, or of the discovery perhaps of electricity. From this "plastic fire" all things, he says, evolve, and to it all things are ever striving to return—an idea very like that of some modern physicists, who suggest that all organic life may possibly be transformation of solar heat. The theory of Heraclitus appears to be that from "cosmic fire" (pur) vapour is evolved, which by condensation produces water, which, again, by evaporation produces earth. Thus, are the "elements" evolved: and then, by a reversion of the process, each element is successively retransformed, through the various stages, back again to "cosmic fire." The Kosmos, says Heraclitus, was created by no god: it always was, and is, and will be, an everlasting fire alternately kindled and quenched. Primordial "cosmic substance" is indeed indestructible, but all things evolved from it must come to an end, each time it reverts to the initial stage of "plastic fire." This, it will be seen, is nothing more or less than the Indian theory.

The alternate evolution and involution is called by Heraclitus "the way up" and "the way down." It is this strife of opposites, as the Indian thinkers call it, this "struggle for existence," as our modern physicists phrase it, which Heraclitus postulates as the initial cause of all life—vegetable, animal, and intellectual. Pater sums up the teaching of Heraclitus thus: "Perpetual motion, alike in things, and in men's thoughts about them. . . . The principle of disintegration is inherent in the primary elements of matter and of soul alike. . . . All things give way, nothing remaineth!"

Professor Rendall puts the point of view taken by Heraclitus thus: "'Being' was always 'Becoming,' not a *state*, but a *process*, not rest, but motion, and its true image was the flame. This 'plastic fire' operates in man as a kindling movement of inherent life, an inhaling and exhaling heat, or breath, or spirit, which at once conducts and reveals the processes of life."

The theory of Heraclitus that the "elements" can be transmuted into one another is opposed by Empedocles, who flourished about the middle of the fifth century B.C., at the Dorian city of Acragas, or Agrigentum, on the south-west coast of Sicily. According to his theory, the series of phenomena which we call the universe are due to the alternate action, during recurrent cycles of time, of two great forces—the forces of attraction and repulsion (which he poetically calls "concord" and "discord"), upon the "roots of things"—his name for "elements." When, during long ages of time, "concord," or "love," or, as we should say, centripetal force, has united all things into a "Kosmos," "discord," or "strife," or centrifugal force, begins its action of disintegration, until the universe reverts to the state of "chaos." Then another cycle of manifestation, or reintegration, begins, and so on, *ad infinitum*.

The human soul is equally composed of elements, each element of the physical universe having its corresponding soul-element, which alone is able to perceive it, the two being by nature akin. The soul, says Empedocles, is detached from the "sphaira" or sphere of the universal soul by "discord," but must ultimately be reabsorbed into it, by the action of "love," just as the Indian theory is that the spiritualised soul is at last absorbed into Nirvâna. There is no doubt that Empedocles accepted the Pythagorean theory of soul-transmigration. He says: "Human birth is one of a *series* of transmigrations, which are the punishment of some original sin. . . . When one of the Blessed has incurred blood-guiltiness, he must wander thirty thousand years away from blessedness, passing through all forms of mortal life. . . . So now, I am a wanderer and banished from heaven, a victim of the principle of 'strife.' . . . Oh, from what a place of pride I fell, to move among mankind!"

Anaxagoras, born about 500 B.C., at the Ionian city of Clazomenæ, and who about 460 B.C. was living at Athens, advanced the theory that all the phenomena of nature are due to the union or the separation of an infinite but yet fixed number of minute and indestructible "spermata" (germs). Everything is caused by the manner in which these "spermata" are grouped together. The break-up or dissolution of the germ-combinations is "death," after which, the germs are ready immediately to enter into fresh combinations. By their nature, the "spermata" are senseless and inert, and, in order to set them in motion, to give them the proper impulse to combine, an intelligent elementary force is needed: this force Anaxagoras postulates as "nous," and defines as "thinnest of all things." The subtle force of "nous" permeates the motionless chaos of spermata, and starts a whirling movement ("dinos") within the mass. The initial whirling movement develops in due time into more complex motions, which have appropriate results. Anaxagoras points to the rotation of the heavens as a proof that the first whirling motion still persists. "Nous" animates every part of the universe: plants, animals, and man are all animated by "nous," the only difference being that the more complex and delicate structure of the human brain enables the animation of man to be more complete than that of any other living thing. Anaxagoras was probably the first physicist who asserted that the stars and the moon are solid bodies, and that the moon is opaque, deriving its luminous appearance by reflection from the sun. Theories so "impious" shocked the orthodox Athenian crowd so greatly, that it was all that his friends, Pericles and Euripides, could do to save Anaxagoras from being condemned to death. He was ultimately allowed to pay a fine of five talents, and was banished from Athens. He went to Lampsacus, on the eastern shore of the Hellespont, where he died in 428 B.C. Euripides quotes a very characteristic saying by him: "Who can tell, now, whether to live may not properly be to die, and whether that which men call to die may not, in truth, be but the entrance into real life?"

The germ-theory of Anaxagoras leads up to the atomic theory of Democritus, a materialistic philosopher, born about 460 B.C., at Abdera, an Ionian settlement in Thrace. Like Pythagoras and Heraclitus, Democritus has the reputation of having been a great traveller, especially in Eastern lands, during his early manhood. He lived to a very advanced age, not dying till 361 B.C. Democritus held the theory that an infinite number of worlds revolve in space, all of which, physically speaking, are but aggregations of infinitesimal atoms, and that these atoms are drawn together, not through the intervention of any "demiurgos," but by strictly natural means. The atoms differ, indeed, in shape and size, but the chemical composition of all the atoms is identical, so that they cannot attract or repel each other, according to the theory of Empedocles. To account for the initial movement of his chaos of infinitesimal atoms, Democritus postulates no outside influence, like the "nous" imagined by Anaxagoras; but he describes the atoms as being "self-moving," as having a vitality within themselves which starts a gyratory or whirling motion in the mass. The atoms, as they whirl, gradually sort or arrange themselves, according to their respective shapes and sizes—in a way, perhaps, similar to that by which the large and small pebbles and sand-particles are sorted and aggregated on the shore by the action of the waves. Democritus imagines the "lightest" atoms to be forced upwards, where they combine to form the atmosphere. But the "finest and smoothest" atoms, and therefore the "liveliest" of all atoms, are called "soul-atoms." These soul-atoms are said to permeate the entire human body, but to be most numerous in the sense-organs. No individual atom is considered by Democritus to be sensitive, but, when aggregated together in large number, the soul-atoms evolve the faculty of sensation and perception. By what process, however, the evolution takes place, we are not told. Sensation, says Democritus, is the only conceivable source of knowledge, and to it every form and quality of thought may be traced back. He considers the self-consciousness of man to be due to the presence of the soul-atoms in the human body. During sleep, these atoms partially escape from the body; death is caused by their complete escape, and with their departure consciousness ceases. It is noteworthy that the theory of atoms advanced by Kanada, who flourished in India in the fifth century B.C., was not unlike that of Democritus. The atoms ("anus") postulated by

Kanada are so infinitesimal that six of them are "smaller than the mote in a sunbeam." The "anus" unite first in couples, and then these double atoms aggregate to produce forms. Like the other great Hellenic thinkers, Democritus not only interested himself in physics, but also in ethics. Amongst his ethical sayings which have come down to us we find :—

"The whole world is the fatherland of a noble soul. . . .

"Magnanimity is the gentle tolerance of fault or failure. . . .

"A charitable man is he who looks not for return, but deliberately purposes to do well. . . .

"I count him who loves no man as loved by none. . . .

"If you can do good, delay not; but give, knowing that no state of things is permanent. . . .

"It is good not only to abstain from wrong; but not to will to do it. . . .

"He that inflicts wrong is more ill-starred than he who suffers wrong. . . ."

The first, however, of Greek thinkers who aimed above all at ethical teaching was Socrates, the son of a stone-mason of Alopeka, near Athens, where he was born in 468 B.C. Aristotle calls him the founder of the science of ethics. There is no record that Socrates ever practised his father's craft, if he ever learnt it. He is said to have inherited a small patrimony, but to have been always without money: nor would he accept any payment for his teaching, as the Sophists of the period were accustomed to do. He said that he could teach only that he himself knew nothing; all he could do was to help others to teach themselves. We learn from his pupils, Xenophon and Plato, that Socrates was a man of strong passions, but that he had them so under control that he was remarkable for his great temperance in all things: nothing, it is said, could disturb his cheerfulness or his good humour.

Convinced that the human mind cannot penetrate the mystery of the beginning of things, Socrates spent no time in philosophical or metaphysical speculations. What a man can learn, he said, is something about himself: a wise man should know not only what the good is, but also how he can follow the good. The first step, therefore, is to show the average man that he knows nothing; the next is to help him to find the good himself. This Socrates aimed at doing by discussing all kinds of ethical questions with anyone who would talk with him. Xenophon praises the good sense and practical wisdom of Socrates, and says that he was never tired of discussing and defining such things as good and evil, justice and injustice, wisdom and folly, courage and cowardice. We hear of the sage going about everywhere in his native Athens—in the streets, in the public assemblies, in the workshops of artisans, in the studios of artists, and in the banquet halls of aristocrats: everywhere he is the same simple, straightforward, strenuous man, frankly arguing any question that turns up, and always doing his best to help his fellow-citizens to think for themselves. A life without criticism, he said, is worthless.

The method adopted by Socrates was the same whether he was talking with a workman, an artist, a man of the world, a politician, or a philosopher. He always started from the point of view of his companion, and agreed with him as far as he could. Then he began to question him. After a while, it generally happened that he got his companion to admit that he really knew little or nothing about the subject in debate, and then Socrates, by means of further skilful questioning and subtle suggestion, helped the man to discover the truth for himself. The whole end and aim of the teaching of Socrates is to aid men to think for themselves, and thus to become more valuable and useful citizens of the state. Everyone, he maintained, must decide for himself his own course of life, because no man can be truly moral unless he clearly knows what he is doing, and why he does it. Socrates counsels no resistance to the established authority of the state, but he does his best to urge men to forsake the bondage of habit and custom for freedom of thought. He maintained that, as soon as a man attains to a knowledge of the good, it must inevitably lead him, sooner or later, to good actions, simply because vice is due either to stupidity, to ignorance, or to folly. Therefore, beauty and goodness, once perceived, must draw all men to them.

It is perhaps not surprising that this bold teaching, setting reason above authority, should have alarmed the timid conservatives of Athens. At any rate, in the year 399 B.C., when Socrates was seventy years of age, he was condemned to death by a majority of five votes in an assembly of five hundred voters of his fellow-citizens, on the charge of corrupting the youth of Athens by his teaching, and of "bringing new gods to Athens." The latter charge was founded on the assertion of Socrates that he was always attended by a "Divine Voice." We might perhaps assume this inner voice to be what we should now call conscience, except that Socrates does not say that this voice ever prompted him to good action, or restrained him from bad. The friends of the sage implored him to address the judges in his own defence; but Socrates proudly said that his whole life was his sufficient defence, and when called upon by the judges to speak, he addressed the assembly in praise only of truth and justice. Before drinking the poison-cup the master held a last discourse in the prison with his favourite pupils and friends, and, in answer to their questions, declines to express any definite opinion whether there is or is not any future life for man. All he says is that, for his part, he awaits either immortality or annihilation with a mind equally untroubled and at rest.

To most men the death of Socrates seems very like legal murder. But Walter Pater seems to condone the verdict. "Those young Athenians," says Pater, "whom Socrates was thought to have corrupted of set purpose, he not only admired, but really loved and understood, and longed to do them good. Only, the very thoroughness of the self-knowledge he promoted had in it something sacramental, so to speak: if it did not do them good, it could not leave them just as they were." Professor

Campbell finely says of this tragedy: "Socrates did not die for a negation, but for an ideal of justice and a standard of goodness to which the world was still a stranger, an absolute truth which, if discovered, would afford the only sure basis of human life and conduct." Socrates was indeed in the highest sense the apostle of freedom of thought. He upheld the right of every man to live the higher life as he sees it. But Socrates based his teaching on the assumption that every man is able and willing to control himself, ignoring the sad fact that it is the few only who do so. This, however, was apparent to his favourite pupil, Plato. Like his beloved master, Plato hopes that when once a man has grasped "the idea of the good," he will be able to look from a higher point of view on the unrealities of life. But Plato sees, as Socrates seems not to have seen, how full of danger is the transition-period, before the youth has passed through doubt and reached the calm of æsthetic culture. Therefore we find Plato, in his latest writings at least, advocating the firm restriction by the state of the private rights of the citizens, and the subordination of the good of the individual to the good of the "Republic."

Socrates was a man of the people, but Plato was a typical aristocrat. Born in 427 B.C. at Athens, he claimed direct descent from Codrus, the last of the Attic kings, who, during the Dorian invasion, six hundred years earlier, had given his life for his country. On his mother's side, Plato was a lineal descendant of Solon. When, at the age of twenty, he first came under the influence of Socrates, Plato was a keen gymnast, a musician, an able writer, and already a student of philosophy. The death of his master, nineteen years later, affected him so greatly that most of his earlier writings sprang from his resolve to show the Greek world the value of the great teacher who had been done to death at Athens. In the *Apology*, Plato indicates the nature of the defence which Socrates might have made at his trial. In the *Crito*, he tells how Socrates refused to evade the law of his country by escaping from prison, as his old friend Crito had planned. In the *Euthyphro*, he shows that, whilst his judges condemned Socrates for impiety, they did not themselves know what impiety meant. In the *Phædrus*, Plato records the discussion between Socrates and his intimate friends on the idea of the immortality of the soul, during the last hours of his life, before he drank the poison-cup. Socrates himself never wrote anything down, and therefore Plato felt it to be his duty to let men know the ideas of his master on various subjects. His method was to sum up the teaching of Socrates in a series of dialogues, in which he makes Socrates the chief speaker.

In this way Plato discoursed on all kinds of subjects —social, ethical, political, scientific, and philosophical, handing down to us much of the teaching of his master, and revealing to us much of his own thought, but never committing himself to any exact system of philosophy. Though he seems to share the conviction of Socrates, that nothing definite can be known about the origin of the universe, Plato apparently accepts from Heraclitus the theory of its evolution and its eternal change. But he is chiefly interested in the problem of the human soul and in the life of man, from both the ethical and metaphysical point of view. Most Greek thinkers, before Plato, held that the primordial substance of the universe is indestructible, and therefore everlasting, but that the immortality of the soul is relative only, and must cease when the particles of cosmic substance, of which it is composed, disintegrate, at the close of each cosmic cycle. But this idea was discordant to Plato, who held that the soul must be absolutely immortal, because so many ideas conceivable by the mind are of too spiritual a character to be derived merely from the perception of the physical senses. Soul and life, he suggests, are synonymous, and therefore he frankly accepts the inference that all that lives must have a soul of some sort, and postulates a dual soul, viz., a lower or animal soul, and a higher or spiritual soul. The lower soul is common to both man and brute, but the higher soul is man's attribute only. Every soul is held by Plato to be immortal, "for," says Plato, "what is ever in motion is immortal." The soul, he argues, can at no time "come into being," because it is a "principle," and "that which comes into being must have a beginning, or principle from which it comes." Things whose "principle of motion" is outside themselves cannot be held to have soul, but everything which is self-moved or self-determined by the principle of motion within itself must be possessed of soul. In the *Phædrus*, Plato gives us an allegory which represents the soul as a charioteer in a chariot drawn by two horses. These horses are its animal and spiritual tendencies; the one plunges upwards, the other downwards. But a skilful charioteer can so control his horses that the upward course is maintained. The higher nature of the human soul is shown "in her love of wisdom and in her yearning for the divine, to which she is akin." But souls deteriorate; and, in the *Republic*, Plato says that, "in order to see the soul as she really is, not as we now behold her, marred by communion with the body, we must contemplate her with the eye of reason, in her original purity: for, as she is now, she is like the sea-god, Glaucon, whose original can hardly be discerned in age, because his natural members are broken off, crushed and damaged by the waves, and incrustations have grown over them of seaweed and shells and stones, so that he is more like a monster than his natural form." In the *Meno*, Plato says "the soul is immortal, and at one time has an end, which is termed dying, and at another time is born again, but is never destroyed." His theory is, that if, at the time of a man's death, his soul is "pure, and draws after her no bodily taint, having never been voluntarily connected with the body," it is attracted to the invisible, divine, or rational world. On the contrary, "the soul which has been polluted, and impure at the time of departure, and always the servant of the body, enamoured and fascinated by it and its desires and pleasures," is by the force of its "craving for the corporeal," after a time, "dragged down again into the visible, until it is imprisoned finally in another body." Plato's idea is that the spiritual evolution of the human soul depends altogether on the use, good or bad, made of the opportunities for progress afforded to it during each successive return to life in a human body. He even hints that perhaps the brutes may be animated by degraded human souls, souls which during their former human lives may have abandoned themselves to their brutal instincts and passions. But even such degraded souls, he suggests, might perhaps be able, after a prolonged period of punishment and probation, to regain their former status.

In his later writings, Plato calls mind "the mediator" between the apparent world of sense and the real world of spirit, and thus rather confuses the meaning attached to "soul" and "mind" in his earlier writings. His theory, derived apparently from Pythagoras, is that all abstract ideas, such as justice, beauty, goodness, are neither more nor less than "recollections" of the mind's intuitive knowledge before it gained experience in human bodies. In all its higher flights of thought, therefore, the mind is, as it were, going deeper into *itself.* He says that the soul, "having been born again many times and seen all things that exist, whether in this world or in the world above, has knowledge of them all: and it is no wonder that she should be able to call to remembrance all that she knows about virtue: for, as all nature is akin, and the soul has learned all things, there is no difficulty in eliciting, or as men say learning, out of a single recollection all the rest, if a man is strenuous and does not faint: for all inquiry and all learning is recollection."

The word "idea," as Plato uses it, is synonymous with generalisation or abstraction. Objects are perceived by the senses, but the mind only can perceive ideas. In everyday talk we speak of the things that we can see and handle as "real." But Plato, like Heraclitus before him, calls nothing "real" but the lasting. Things beautiful fade and die, but beauty is everlasting. As in the world of matter things evolve from the simple to the complex, so, in the world of mind, or in the world of pure form, ideas evolve from the elementary to the abstract, and at last culminate in the ideas of "the Beautiful" and "the Good." Professor Caird, writing from the theological point of view, says: "For Plato the Idea of Good is the unity of being and knowing; it is the idea which sums up all other ideas in itself, or it is the intelligence in which all other intelligences are embraced: but, as such, it is essentially separated from the finite world and from the physical as well as the corporeal existence of man." Plato sometimes, indeed, speaks of the ideal world as the "Divine Intelligence," and the "Universal Mind." But he tells us that this Universal Mind is intuitive and contemplative only, and is devoid both of individual consciousness and of memory.

The material world is looked upon by Plato as a living entity having a soul of its own. He calls it "the second God," and the "only begotten" of the God. In the *Timæus*, he says that the physical world is "a god manifested to sense, the greatest and best, the most beautiful and perfect of all creatures, even the one, the only begotten universe." He adopts the Pythagorean theory that space and primordial-substance are one and the same, and calls it, indifferently, the "Imperceptible," the "Formless," the "Unlimited," the "Mother," and the "Nurse of Genesis." He postulates Substance as being co-eternal with Idea, or Creative Impulse, which, by acting upon it, gives it limitation and form. The creative act is dual. Idea gives the impulse; but it is the nature of matter to offer passive resistance to every attempt to limit its illimitable formlessness, and by so doing it actually co-operates in the creative act. Thus Plato seems to say that the hidden deity is revealed, or, in other words, the physical universe is evolved by the union of the active and passive forces of nature. As the principle of unity in the physical world must be similar to that in the ideal world, of which it is the manifestation, Plato regards the sun, the source of physical life and growth, as the material representative of the Good. The Good, therefore, is the basic idea of all life, mental or physical. But Plato has to bridge over the gulf between the world of mind and the world of matter, and so he postulates a mediator whom he calls the "demiourgos"—architect or creator—who is supposed to model things on eternal ideas. Plato fails, however, to explain whether his imaginary demiourgos depends for his creations on ideas, or whether the demiourgos is himself the sum or synthesis of all ideas or creative impulses, by which all things are fashioned

Plato's chief contribution to ethical thought is to be found in his *Republic*, which is more or less a modification of the Pythagorean idea of brotherhood.

Pater, in his picturesque language, describes the *Republic* as "a protest against the principle of flamboyancy and fluidity in things and in men's thoughts about them," and he points out that two opposing lines of development—the Ionian and the Doric—are clearly traceable throughout Greek history. "The Ionian or Asiatic tendency throws itself forth in endless play of undirected imagination, delighting in colour and brightness, moral and physical, in beautiful material, in changeful form everywhere—in music, in poetry, in architecture: its restless versatility drives it towards the assertion of individualism, of separation." But Plato saw clearly that social and political life must suffer from excessive individualism, and therefore he held up to the admiration of Athens the ideal of Sparta, and showed the beauty of disinterested manliness in private and public action. As Pater puts it, justice as Plato conceived it was "the execution by everyone of his own part—neither more nor less—in a 'musical exercise'; . . . it is harmony, it is health." Plato nowhere, in so many words, condemns the orthodox religion of his time, but he talks scornfully of men who worship gods whom they imagine they can bribe by offerings, or persuade by prayers to forgive their sins. He says: "When anyone prefers beauty to virtue, what is this but the real and utter dishonour of the soul? . . . When a person is willing to acquire dishonest gains, does he honour his soul by this gain? Far otherwise: he sells her honour and glory for small pieces of gold. But, all the gold that is under the earth or upon it is not enough to get in exchange for virtue." "There is nothing but the soul which causes each and all of us to be in this life the very thing that we are. . . . Know that if you become worse you will go to the worse souls, or if better to the better, and in every succession of life and death, you will do and suffer what like may fitly suffer at the hands of like. This is divine justice. . . . One who is injured ought not, as the multitude thinks, to return the injury. . . . A good man cannot harm any human being, no, not an enemy. . . . To conquer oneself is the first and most excellent of all conquests, while to be worsted by oneself is the most infamous of things. . . . A man's care ought to be, not to seem good but to be good, in private and public life, alike. . . . He who commits injustice is ever more wretched than he who suffers it. . . . The right punishment for one out of tune, is to make him play in tune."

Plato's most celebrated pupil was Aristotle, who was the son of the court-physician to Amyntas II., king of Macedon, and was born at the Ionian city of Stageira, near Macedon, in 384 B.C. At the death of his father, Aristotle went to Athens to study philosophy under Plato, and at the death of Plato, he returned to Macedon as tutor to Alexander, the grandson of Amyntas II. He once more went to Athens when Alexander became king of Macedon, and there he lived for the next thirteen years, writing voluminous works on philosophy and science, the latter being largely based on the careful records and reports made by the men of science who accompanied Alexander in his expeditions, and which Alexander sent home to his old tutor. But directly after

Alexander's untimely death, at Babylon, the Athenians brought against Aristotle a charge of impiety, which caused him to flee to Chalcis, in Eubœa, where he died shortly afterwards, at the age of sixty-two. Aristotle has been called the first of the encyclopædists, and he certainly seems to have spared neither time nor trouble in collecting and collating facts. These he classified with much cleverness; but his own original observations from nature are not very reliable, although he asserted his opinions very positively.

Aristotle refused to accept the theory, current at the time, that the brain is the organ of thought, on the ground that the sole function of the brain is to cool the blood. "Some persons," he says, "believe that the air is a kind of food, and that it is inhaled to feed the internal fire, but their theory would involve the absurd consequence that all animals breathe, because all have some heat." This apparently was intended as a slap at Anaxagoras and Diogenes, who both held this opinion: Diogenes, indeed, going so far as to explain that fish breathe though their gills by absorbing the air held in solution in the water. The atomic theory of Democritus is ridiculed by Aristotle, as is also Plato's suggestion that perhaps the rotation of the earth may be the cause of the apparent rotation of the sun. The moon, says Aristotle, always turns towards us the same face, proving that the moon, at least, does not rotate on its axis. Democritus thought that time is required for the transmission of light from a distance, but Aristotle asserts that the passage of light is instantaneous.

Following the idea of Plato, Aristotle defines soul to be the organising principle of all life: neither plants, animals, nor man can exist without soul. But he uses the word soul as synonymous with idea or form. Matter and form, or idea, he holds to be correlative conceptions, each of which implies the other; force or motion is the mediator between them which translates the one into the other; form is the end, or goal, towards which matter eternally evolves. Motion, says Aristotle, must be eternal. "How," he asks in the *Metaphysics*, "can there be a beginning of motion without some cause that is ever active? It is not the timber which constitutes a building, but the principle of carpentry; nor is it the passive element in procreation which generates, but the active semen." Matter and form, or idea, being equally eternal, there can, he holds, be no such thing as chaos; therefore the cosmos cannot be imagined to have either beginning or end. Time, he thinks, is nothing but a measure of motion: it is a mere fiction, which has existence only in the human mind. "Chaos and Night cannot have endured for an indefinite time, but there must always be the identical universe, either in recurring cycles, or in some other way."

Motion is the mainspring of all, but "there must always be some central thing which causes motion, while itself unmoved, an Eternal Substance which is ever active." This "central thing" he supposes to be the Divine Mind (Nous), and he defines it as being "the object of its own thought," as "the law and the law-giver," and as "the absolute Good." He further explains that "this Being of whom we speak has neither parts nor magnitude, but is indivisible. . . . Nor has it passions, nor possibility of change; for no change is prior to locomotion, and the cause is prior to the effect." Nous is said to be "immanent in all things," and also to be "transcendent to the universe," so that it is impossible to understand what he means, even if he knows himself. As Zeller remarks, the God imagined by Aristotle is a purely contemplative being, shut up in himself, who can neither act on the universe, nor even take cognisance of it. A still more recent commentator, on the theological side, Professor Caird, asks "how such pure thought, directed only upon itself, can become a determination of anything else than itself," and he adds: "But a still greater difficulty remains. . . . The whole process of the finite, with all its divisions and fluctuations, the continual conflict of its parts, and the marred and distorted existences which the conflict produces—seem to lie beyond the sphere of the contemplative reason, which cannot see anything but an ideally complete whole, in which every element is in complete harmony with every other." Professor Caird therefore concludes that "the central thought" concerning God which Aristotle seeks to elaborate in his *Metaphysics* is "that God must be conceived as living a life of pure contemplation," and consequently that his activity is "a purely ideal activity without movement and without change"—whatever that may mean. The Professor quotes Aristotle himself in support of his conclusion, as saying: "The life of God is like the highest kind of activity within us; but, while we can maintain it but for a short time, with him it is eternal; for it is an activity which is at the same time the joy of attainment. . . . Contemplation is the best and happiest of activities, and if all we could say were that God's life is like our life in the highest moments of contemplative thought, it would be worthy of our admiration: but if it be better with him than with us, it must be still more worthy of it. And so it is indeed. In him is life: for the activity of intelligence is life, and he is that activity. Thus his essential activity constitutes a perfect and a blessed life" (*Metaphysics*, 1072 B, 15).

It is amusing to find a philosopher like Aristotle assuming to know, with the self-confidence of a theologian, all about the inner life of God. But the fact that Aristotle did postulate a God made his teaching acceptable to the mediæval Church, and he is still the Greek philosopher most read by Catholics. Shortly before his death, Pope Leo XIII. is said to have ordered that the words of St Thomas Aquinas, a diligent student and translator of the philosophy of Aristotle, should be reprinted for the use of Catholic colleges. The intellectualism of Aristotle, as Professor Caird remarks, seems to divide the contemplative life altogether from the practical, and it is possible that his teaching lies at the basis of the false idea of the Christian Church that the monastic life is the highest a man can lead. "Thomas Aquinas," he says, "was only following out the principles of Aristotle, when he exalted the contemplative life above the moral virtues."

Aristotle becomes more intelligible and more sure of his own meaning when he discourses about the soul. Soul, he says, is "the energy of the organism," and "the internal formative principle of the body, which may be perceived by the senses, and is capable of life." Apart from a body, however, the existence of soul is only "potential." All organised beings have soul. But soul is of a double nature—the animal soul and the rational soul. The former man has in common with the brutes, but the latter, which Aristotle calls "nous poeticos," is the attribute of man only. It is the divine and immortal element in man, the connecting-link between the animal and the divine, which, at death, is reabsorbed into the divinity, and is therefore only relatively immortal. The animal soul is assumed to exist in the human ovum, and to it the rational soul is communicated at the instant of impregnation by the seminal fluid. But how so immaterial an entity as the rational soul can be involved in anything so essentially material as the virile semen, Aristotle gives us no hint. Without the experience which life in a body alone can give it, the "nous poeticus" is a mere "possibility of thinking." It is because of the double nature of the human soul that man can evolve morality. The animal cannot become moral, because it cannot control its instincts; nor can the deity be a moral being, because it has no passions to control. Man, however, is the balance, the pivot, the turning-point of the universe, the link between the material and spiritual worlds; therefore the soul of man is the battle-field on which the higher and lower forces of nature fight for mastery. A perfect human creature, says Aristotle, is one in whom the double nature—the physical and psychical

—is harmoniously balanced. This state of perfect "equilibrium" he calls "virtue." Thus, we see that Aristotle holds up to us no ideal of life, like Plato, but, like any Buddhist philosopher, preaches to the world the excellence of the "Middle Path." Is this perhaps the reason why no Hellenic philosophy appears to have been so generally studied and so generally popular in the West as that of Aristotle?

In 342 B.C., twenty years before the death of Aristotle, a thinker named Epicurus was born at Samos, of Athenian parents, and, after many years of travel and study at Colophon, Mytelenæ, and Lampsacus, settled, at the age of thirty-six, at Athens. Here Epicurus bought a garden and established a school of thought, which perhaps more than any other has been misunderstood and misrepresented. Although Epicurus lived a life so frugal and temperate as to be almost ascetic, his theory of living has been denounced as synonymous with self-indulgence. He taught that the aim of every sensible man should be to be happy; but he explains that happiness is no mere sensuous enjoyment, still less is it dissolute indulgence, which he warns his pupils must end, sooner or later, in the misery of exhaustion. "Happiness" consists, he says, in æsthetic enjoyment, in the pleasures of the mind, and above all in perfect contentment and undisturbed peace of mind. "Virtue" is not the end to be aimed at, but it is a chief means towards that end, and therefore excess in any direction is to be carefully avoided. Epicurus held that true friendship results in more real happiness to most men than marriage; and it is recorded that throughout Greece the disciples of Epicurus were remarkable for the strength and fidelity of their friendships for one another. Although known to have been a voluminous writer, but few of the writings of Epicurus have come down to us. His school of thought was never a large one, but two centuries after his death it was brilliantly revived, for a time, by the Roman poet, Lucretius. The chief work of Epicurus was a treatise, in thirty-seven books, *On Nature.* He taught the theory that the primordial substance of the universe is composed of infinitesimal and indestructible atoms which are in eternal motion. The human soul, he said, being, like all else, material and entirely dependent on the body, cannot be immortal. As proof of this he argues that in childhood the mental faculties are weak, that they increase in strength as the body develops, are not generally strong before the body is mature, and in old age decay. The complete influence of the body upon the mind is shown, he says, in fainting, in anæsthesia, and in delirium. Epicurus held that the belief in the soul's immortality, and the consequent fear of what may follow after death, is the greatest obstacle to that perfect peace of mind which should be aimed at by every wise man. He used to say to his disciples: "Where we are, death is not; where death is, we are not. Death therefore is nothing to us, and the pleasures of life are no loss, because we shall not feel the want of them."

During the lifetime of Epicurus, the teaching

perhaps most opposed to his was that of Zeno, who was a native of Citium, in Cyprus, and was probably of Phœnician descent. There is no exact record of the date either of his birth or death, but he is known to have been living, at a very advanced age, during the 130th Olympiad (260 B.C.). The system of philosophy taught by Zeno is best known as the Stoic, from the fact that it was his habit to walk up and down the "stoa," porch, or colonnade at Athens, which, being adorned with paintings by Polygnotus, was popularly called the "stoa poecile." Here Zeno taught the ethics of Socrates, learnt from Diogenes "the Cynic," a man of very noble character, whose courage, honesty, and serenity, it is said, nothing could upset. Epictetus, a later follower of Zeno, speaks of Diogenes as "the ideal athlete of righteousness." Zeno taught pantheism pure and simple, like any Indian philosopher. He accepted the idea of Heraclitus that all being is becoming, and also the atomic theory of Democritus. The universe, he says, is one, mind and matter being but different manifestations of one "Divine Substance," which he also calls "the Soul of the Universe" (Psyche tou Kosmou). Within this Divine Substance there is a motive-power which is the cause of all the various phenomena of nature. This motive-power Zeno calls "Nous," or "Universal Reason." Nous has a double aspect—a physical aspect, called "pneuma," and a psychical aspect, called "logos." From pneuma (the equivalent of the fiery breath or plastic fire of Heraclitus) all things evolve; and, after a cycle of manifested existence, to pneuma all things, including even the soul of man, ultimately return.[1] An impulse of expansion and differentiation within the Soul of the Universe alternates with an impulse of contraction and integration. The evolutionary process begins with the spontaneous activity within primordial substance of innumerable centres of force—an idea which, it will be seen, suggests the modern theory of "vortices." Zeno calls these centres of force "seminal manifestations" (spermatikoi logoi). Thus, we see that the deity postulated by Stoicism is neither outside the universe nor antecedent to it, but immanent in it. Professor Caird thinks that the whole gist of the Stoic system lies in "the combination of two ideas, which appear at once to be essentially opposed, and yet necessarily related to each other. The first is the idea of the self-centred individuality of the particular things and beings which make up the universe, and above all of man as a self-conscious being. The second is the idea of the unity of the universe as a whole, as the realisation of the one divine principle which makes the individuality of all particular things and beings, and even the individuality of man himself, into its expressions and instruments. In the antithesis and synthesis of these two ideas lies the whole interest of Stoicism."

Although the Stoic system of philosophy had but little attraction for the many, its ethical teaching influenced the minds of the best men in the Greek

[1] The Stoic theory is that, at death, the physical atoms of the human body are dispersed, and revert to the Universal Soul, to form, after a time, other combinations; whilst the "pneuma" which animated these atoms is reabsorbed into the Universal Reason.

and Roman world from about 300 B.C. to about 200 A.D. Marcus Aurelius, Cicero, Cato, Brutus, and Seneca all called themselves Stoics. The Stoic idea of virtue was practically the same as the old Roman idea of true manliness, or "virtus." Tacitus says that, in the first century of our era, the Stoics were the only men who were honest and disinterested in their public lives. No wonder that such tyrants as Vespasian, Domitian, and Nero showed their dislike and fear of such men by sending them to exile and death! Professor Caird says that "the Stoic doctrine of independence ceased to be a doctrine of revolt, and became a positive consciousness of the dignity of man as a rational being. . . . Withdrawing himself from all the entanglements of life, from all the special connections of society, and realising to the full his individual selfhood, and his separation from every other thing or being, he found that, . . . in the inmost secret of his soul, he was at one with mankind." The conscious self in man is the equivalent of the Divine Reason in the universe as a whole. Cleanthes, the pupil of Zeno, taught that the virtuous man is he who lives in harmony with the nature of the universe. Stoicism aimed at training the mind to acquire complete control of the body, so that a man should remain uninfluenced and undisturbed by the events and accidents of life. The Stoic theory is that each man has work of some sort to do in the world—work the nature of which is decided for him by circumstances beyond his control—and that all that concerns him is to do that work well. Epictetus, about the close of the first century A.D., says to his pupil, Arrianus: "Remember that you are to act in any drama that the manager may choose. . . . Your business is to act well the character that is given to you; to choose is the business of another. . . . Remember that you ought in life to behave as if you were at a banquet. Suppose some dish is carried round and is placed before you; stretch out your hand and take a portion with decency. Suppose that it is carried past you; do not detain it. Suppose that it has not yet reached you; do not send your desires forward to it, but wait quietly till it comes. Do so with respect to children; do so with respect to a wife; do so with respect to the honours of office; do so with respect to wealth: and so you shall one day be a worthy partner at the banquet of the gods." Earlier in the first century A.D., Seneca, who was murdered by Nero in 65 A.D., says: "It was not only of ivory that Pheidias could make statues, but of bronze as well; had you offered him marble, or some material cheaper still, he would have carved the best statue possible out of that. So the sage will show his virtue in wealth . . . or in poverty, . . . in his own country or in exile, . . . as a general or as a soldier, . . . in bodily vigour or in weakness; whatever fortune be granted him, he will make it the means of some memorable achievement." It was a Stoic axiom that the intention counts for more than the act, and that the wish is equal to the intention. Each man alone knows his own secret desires and the motives of his own actions; therefore he alone can truly judge whether those actions are right or wrong. Epictetus says: "Our happiness must consist solely in a righteous will. There is no pleasure a perfect man will not renounce, no pain he will not endure, rather than leave duty unfulfilled."

One of the most typical of Stoic thinkers was Marcus Aurelius, who was Roman emperor from 161 A.D. to 180 A.D. He says: "Always define and clearly picture to yourself the object presented to you, so that you may see exactly what kind of thing it is, discriminating it in its totality from all other things, and in your own mind assigning to it, and all the elements into which it will be ultimately resolved, the name that properly belongs to each." Speaking of the emptiness of fame, the emperor says: "He who is greedy for fame perceives not that of those who remember him every one will soon be dead: and so, in due course, will it be with each of their successors, till the last flicker of memory, through flutterings and failings, dies altogether out. . . . Why then wilt thou be so foolish as to neglect nature's present gift, and cling to what one or another says hereafter?" . . . "Why wait, O man! Do what nature demands. Make haste and look not round to see if any know it, nor hope for Plato's Republic, but be content with the smallest progress, and consider that the result of even this will be no little thing." . . . "He who is loyal to his own indwelling mind and god, and a willing votary to that inward grace, makes no scene, heaves no sighs, needs not a wilderness, nor yet a crowd. The best is his, the life that neither seeks nor shuns." . . . "Things of the body are but a stream that flows, things of the soul a dream and vapour; life a warfare and a sojourning; and after-fame oblivion. What then can direct our goings? One thing, and one thing alone, philosophy: which is to keep the deity within inviolate and pure from scathe, superior to pleasure and to pain, doing nothing at random, nothing falsely or disingenuously." Marcus Aurelius calls this "deity within" also his "ruler and guide," his "lawgiver," his "pilot," and also "the most precious organ we possess," so that it is difficult to avoid the conclusion that the "deity within" of the Stoics is what we now speak of as conscience.

In any case, there can be no doubt that to Stoic ethics and Stoic modes of thought we owe much that is best in our Western civilisation. Professor Rendall, in his translation of the diary of Marcus Aurelius, eloquently says: "The Stoic monism, . . . noble, far-reaching, and on its own lines exhaustive, not merely held for centuries a more active and commanding sway over the minds and hearts of men than the metaphysics of Plato and Aristotle, not merely interwove itself with Christian discipline and doctrine, and found reconstruction in Spinoza, but, at this day, alike in poetic and scientific imagination, enjoys a wider currency, and exercises a more invigorative appeal in the field of natural religion, than any other extra-Christian interpretation of the universe."

CHAPTER VIII

ALEXANDRIAN THOUGHT

THE most active centres not only of the world's thought but of the world's life, during the time immediately before and after the commencement of our era, were Rhodes, Antioch, and Alexandria. The powerful war-fleet of Rhodes secured the safety of all commercial vessels sailing under the flag of the Rhodian league from the corsairs of Crete and Asia Minor. Rhodes became, in consequence, the great banking-centre of the time. So important, indeed, was the commercial and political supremacy of Rhodes considered to be, that, when the city was almost destroyed by an earthquake, its customers and allies, Seleucus, Ptolemy, Antigonus, and Mithridates, all helped in its reconstruction with money, material, and ships. Antioch, with its port-town of Seleucia on the Orontes, was also a busy centre of trade between Eastern Asia and the Mediterranean, and a formidable rival of Alexandria itself. As early as the time of Alexander the Great, the Jews had acquired the reputation of being very keen traders, and were therefore encouraged by him, and afterwards by the

Ptolemies, to settle in Alexandria; whilst the Jews, on their part, were quick to see the facilities for lucrative trade which the situation of the city afforded. Josephus tells us that when Alexander's half-brother, Ptolemy "Soter," succeeded to the sovereignty of Egypt, he not only induced more Jews to settle in Alexandria, but brought captive Jews from Palestine to swell the population of his capital. Later, when Ptolemy liberated these Jewish slaves, he paid their masters one hundred and twenty drachmas for each Jew. Thus Alexandria became the largest Jewish centre in the world, one-fifth of its whole population being Jews.

By this time Greek had become the common language, not only of commerce, but of culture, and was universally spoken by the cosmopolitan inhabitants of Alexandria. During the forty years' reign of Ptolemy "Philadelphus," the brilliant son of Ptolemy "Soter," Alexandria was the favourite residence of men of culture. "Philadelphus" established there a university, or "museum," attached to which were a great library of seven hundred thousand volumes, an astronomical observatory, an anatomical school, a botanical garden, and a zoological collection. Here "Philadelphus" welcomed and entertained, at his own cost, thinkers, scholars, and students from Rome, Egypt, Greece, Persia, and India. But of the magnificence of Alexandria in those days scarcely a trace remains. The city was built largely of stone brought from the ruins of Saïs, and became, later, in its turn, a quarry for the stone used in the building of Cairo. The famous "Pharos" has long since vanished from the harbour, and the sole visible relic of Alexandria's ancient splendour is Pompey's Pillar, which was itself hewn out of a far more ancient obelisk. But should the ruins of Alexandria ever be thoroughly excavated, we may imagine that many a treasure of plastic art will be unearthed; for, at the epoch of Alexandria's greatness, Greek sculptors were carving such works as the noble "Venus" of Milo, and the beautiful "Niké" of Samothrace, wrought by Eutychides of Sicyon to commemorate the victory of Demetrius of Macedon over Ptolemy Soter of Egypt. The so-called "Dying Gladiator," and the "Apollo" in the Belvedere at the Vatican, also belong to this epoch, both being votive statues, erected in memory of Hellenic victories over the Celtæ and Galatæ, who overran Greece half a century after the death of Alexander. The Rhodian sculpture of this period was indeed less beautiful than the Greek, but it had the merit of spirited action, as the "Laokoon," in the Vatican, and the "Toro Farnese," at Naples, show. One of the most striking monuments of art of this epoch was the "Colossus of Rhodes," which was destroyed by an earthquake. It represented Helios, the sun-god, and was the work of Chares of Lindus, a pupil of Lysippus of Sicyon. The Hellenistic sculptors of this time aimed mostly at size and dramatic effect, and their ambitious self-confidence culminated in the proposal of Dinocrates to carve a vast figure, representing Alexander the Great, out of Mount Athos itself. Strabo tells us that this frantic idea was to have included a town of ten thousand inhabitants resting on the palm of one of the hands of the colossus, whilst from an urn in the other hand rushed a mountain torrent.

In a time so strenuous as this, all kinds of schools of thought, mostly long since forgotten, flourished in the Hellenistic world. But the philosophic system which has since exercised perhaps the most far-reaching effect of any on the subsequent thought of the world was the Stoic. Blending, as it does, much of the thought of the East with the thought of the West, it largely influenced the thinkers of Alexandria. It reflected the imagination of the East in its pantheism, in its allegory, and in its calm resignation to fate; whilst its doctrine of self-denial and unflinching devotion to duty foreshadowed the loftiest thought of the West. Philo, one of the most prominent thinkers at Alexandria during the earlier half of the first century A.D., was an especially earnest student of Stoic doctrine, and appears to have derived from it his own theory of the Logos. Philo was a Jew, a man of such social importance that he was chosen to head the Jewish deputation which went to Rome to entreat Caligula to excuse the Jews from paying divine honours to his statue at Alexandria. His nephew (Tiberius Julius Alexander), although also a Jew, was a Roman eques. He was married to a granddaughter of Herod the Great, and was appointed by Nero, for a time, governor of Egypt. Philo, who wrote in Greek, was a very voluminous writer. His philosophy was founded on the Jewish Kabbala, but he incorporated in his eclectic system ideas borrowed from Zoroastrianism, Platonism, Stoicism, and Gnosticism. As Professor Caird remarks, "it was Philo who more than any other writer prepared the way for that marriage of Greek thought with Christianity, which was the main agency in the development of theology in the early Church." His method was to interpret the Hebrew Pentateuch by means of Greek thought. For instance, we find that in writing of the creation-story, in Genesis, he explains the earth to mean "sensibility" and the heaven to mean "intelligence," and from this deduces the argument that "intelligence is prior to sense." Adam, he thinks, is a personification of "Divine Life," and Eve a personification of "Divine Wisdom." He says: "The 'Mother' is the knowledge appertaining to the Creator, with whom God united—not as man unites—and sowed the seed of genesis. And she, 'the Mother' received into herself the divine seed, and brought forth her only 'Son,' perceptible to the external senses, that is to say, the very Kosmos." The allegory of Adam hiding from God in the recesses of the Garden, after eating the fruit of the tree of knowledge, means, he suggests, that, escaping from God, man takes refuge in his own mind. On the other hand, he says that "he who escapes from his own mind, flees to the Mind of the Universe, which is God; . . . while he who seeks to escape from God, declares, by so doing, that God is not the cause of anything, and looks on himself as the cause of all that exists."

It seems, therefore, that God, in the idea of Philo, is synonymous with what he calls the "Mind of the Universe." He says: "God is not a being of the form of man, nor is the human body of the form of

God, but the resemblance is spoken of with reference to the mind, which is the sovereign of the soul. For the mind which is in each, was made after the likeness of and in relation to the One Mind of the Universe, its archetype, being in some sort the God of the body which bears it. 'Nous' is a very short word, but a most perfect miniature thing, a fragment of the Soul of the Universe, or, according to those who follow the philosophy of Moses, a faithful impression of the divine image."

Philo teaches that the material universe is evolved from primordial substance, which, although devoid of all faculty for thought, has yet somehow the power of generating the Logos. The Logos, he explains, is the synthesis of all the forces of nature, and may therefore be said to be the creator of the universe. He says: "Now the most ancient Logos of the living God is clothed with the Kosmos as with a garment. For it clothes itself in earth and water and air and fire, and in that which proceeds from these." He speaks of the Logos as "the First-born," the "Son of God," "Highest Archangel," and as the "Mediator" between God and man. Man, he says, as regards his reason, is "the image of the Logos." Philo's definition of soul is quite Pythagorean. He says that the soul of the wise man is "sown in the field of the body, where it sojourns as being in a land not its own. . . . The soul of the wise man considers the house of wisdom its own home, but the house of the body a lodging only in which for a time it proposes to sojourn." He imagines that souls exist which have never yet entered human bodies. He says:

"Some among souls descended into bodies, while others have not ever deigned to adapt themselves to any quarters of the earth. . . . But, the others, descending into the body as into a river, are at one time carried away and swallowed up by the sweep of a most violent whirlpool, while, at another time, they strive with all their power to resist the current. . . . The little housings in the lower world bring bondage and sad humiliation on the soul. For, in very truth, the passions of the body are false and foreign to the mind, being produced by the flesh. . . . Life is two-fold: one, in the body, corruptible, the other without the body, incorruptible. Therefore, the wicked man dies the death, who even yet, while breathing among the living, has already been buried, by reason of retaining in himself no inner spark of true life, which is perfect virtue. . . . The real 'Hades' is the life of one who is in a state of wickedness—a life which is an avenger." Philo held the Pythagorean theory of the soul's transmigration. He says: "Of these souls, some descend to be bound up in mortal bodies, such namely as are nearest the earth and most fond of the body. . . . Some yearn for the associations and habits of mortal life, and go back to it again; others charge it with much folly and trifling, and pronounce the body to be a prison-house and a grave, and, flying from it, as from a prison or a tomb, have raised themselves up on high, on light wings, to the æther, and for their æon engage themselves in things sublime." This "æon," or cycle, refers to the Stoic and also Indian theory that souls exist only so long as the universe continues in a state of manifestation.

But there are, says Philo, " still other souls, the most excellent and pure, who have succeeded to greater and diviner minds not even reaching out for any of the things of earth, . . . having all things in their view. . . ." The highest state of self-evolution that a man can attain, according to Philo, is that of a seer. This is the state of self-induced trance, or " ecstasis," in which he is said to be " possessed " by the deity, and thus obtains direct personal revelation of the Most High. " As long," says Philo, " as our mind still shines around us and revolves, pouring as it were a noontide light on the whole soul, we are masters of ourselves, and not 'possessed.' But, when it comes towards setting, then, in all likelihood, there falls upon us a trance, or divinised and most passive madness. For indeed, when the divine light shines, the human light sets, and when the divine light sets, the human rises and dawns."

About a generation later than Philo lived another Alexandrian Jew, who is known to us by his assumed name of " Hermes Tris-megistus." This writer is mentioned by several of the " Fathers " of the early Church, Justin, about 165 A.D., quoting verbatim a remarkable passage from his chief work, the *Poemandres* (the Shepherd, or Leader). He also was a student of Pythagorean and Platonic philosophy as well as of the Jewish " Septuagint " and " Kabbala," and was apparently also acquainted with the Fourth Gospel. In a work which the French Academy " crowned " in 1867, Dr Louis Ménard says that the writings of " Hermes Tris-megistus " belong at once to the philosophy of Greece and to the religion of Egypt, and in their mystic exaltation they impinge already on the Middle Age. . . . In them the beliefs which were being born and the beliefs which were dying met, and clasped hands."

Like Philo, Hermes holds the doctrine of a Universal Soul. "All things," he says, "are full of soul and are properly moved by that. . . . Life is the union of soul and mind, and the dissolution of their union is death. . . . Nothing is more comprehensive, quicker, or more potent than the incorporeal." In illustration of this last statement he says: "Command thy soul to go to India, and, quicker than thy command, it is there: command it again to proceed to the ocean, and there again it will quickly be; not as if having *passed* from place to place, but as if *being there*. . . ." Nothing is impossible to mind. . . . "Having supposed in thyself nothing impossible, *think* thyself immortal and able to understand all things—every art, every science, the habit of every animal—become loftier than every height, lower than every depth: collect in thyself all the sensations of all things made of fire, water, dry, and moist, and at the same time be everywhere in earth, in sea, in heaven. . . . Thou wilt be able to understand the God, . . ." for "there is nothing that does not image the Divinity." This, it will be seen, is nothing else than an Alexandrian version of Brahmanic thought. And when Hermes comes to define the human soul, he shows how intimately acquainted he was also with Pythagorean and Platonic ideas. The soul, he says, "is an eternal and intelligent essence," the basic element of which is "perpetual motion, the spontaneous movement of thought." At death, the human soul is "separated" from its physical body, but "endures in the Ideal World" as an "independent" entity. When again "emerging into life" from the Ideal World, it is "the property of the soul to assimilate other things to her own character." In the process of the "re-generation" of the soul, "essential spirit, reason, intelligence, perception, conjoin . . . to become a single form which is that of the soul."

It is not unlikely that the term "re-generation" comes to us from these thinkers of old Alexandria, for it is a very frequent and characteristic expression of Hermes Tris-megistus, who is an emphatic believer in the theory that the human soul can only attain to spirituality by means of repeated "re-generation" in a physical body. "Ah, my child," he exclaims to Tatios, "how many bodies must we pass through, that we may hasten to the one only God!" He postulates three kinds of soul—"divine, human, irrational." There are also the souls of "inanimate creatures," which he supposes to be "outside the bodies actuated." The souls of animals consist only of desire and passion. The human soul is "bound to the irrational elements—passion and desire, which are indeed undying, because they are energies." But, "when the divine part of the soul enters into a mortal body and therein meets the irrational elements, she becomes, by means of their presence, a human soul." Hermes teaches that the aim of a wise man should be to "become wholly mind." For "mind," he says, "is the very essence of the God, if indeed there is any essence of God." Mind is "united to the Godhead just as light to the sun; . . . the mind in men indeed is God. . . . In whatever souls the mind presides, to these it shows its own Light, practising against their proclivities, as a good physician pains the diseased body by cutting and burning, for the sake of health. In the same way also, the mind pains the soul, extricating it from pleasures by which every disease of the soul is generated. . . . If a man uses mind and soul as he ought, he will differ nothing from immortals. . . . We have the power of choice; it depends on us to choose, by our own will, either the worst or the best. The choice of evil approximates us to the corporeal nature and subjects us to Destiny." This last idea of Hermes is clearly his version of the Hindu doctrine of Karma—fate, the law of cause and effect. Hermes uses the word "Logos" in a sense slightly different from Philo. To Philo the word means the synthesis of the powers of nature; to Hermes it means the creative faculty of the deity. He says, speaking of the origin of the universe: "The Mind, the God, being masculine-feminine begat by the Logos, . . . for imagination is nought else than generation." Probably Hermes is the first Western thinker who postulates a Trinity. He says: "And three therefore are these—the God and Father and the Good, and the Kosmos, and the Man. The Kosmos is indeed the generated Son of God; but the Man is, as it were, the offspring of the Kosmos—the great and perfect animal, the Kosmos."

He too postulates an eternal substance of the

universe. He says: "O my son, matter *becomes*: formerly it *was*, for matter is the vehicle of becoming. Becoming is the mode of activity of the uncreate and foreseeing God. Having been endowed with the germ of becoming, matter is brought into birth, for the creative force fashions it, according to the ideal forms. Matter, not yet engendered, has no form: it becomes, when set in motion. . . . The sun is the only one of all the creatures that changes not, and which remains the same. . . . I recognise in it, after the First Unity, the creator. . . . The sun is the image of the creative and celestial God. For as God has created the Kosmos, so the sun creates animals and plants and governs fluid things." Hermes evidently accepts the theory of the eternal recurrence of the life of the Kosmos and of all things in it, and also, it seems, teaches the Vedantic doctrine of the unreality of all things. He says: "Dissolution is the condition of births. All that is brought forth dissolves, in order to be again brought forth. It is necessary that out of a dissolution life should come into existence, and that, in its turn, life should decay, in order that the generation of creatures should never cease. . . . Creatures born of dissolution are but shadows: they become at one time this, at another time that; for the *same* they cannot be; and how is it possible for that which is not identical with itself to be a real thing? Such then, my son, must be called appearances, and man must be regarded as an appearance of Humanity. . . . For, how shall it be said that a man is a man, a child is a child, a youth is a youth, a grown man is a grown man, an old man is an old man, since by incessant transformations they deceive us, both as to what they were and what they have become? Behold then, in all these things, my son, only the illusive appearance of a higher Reality. And since indeed this is the case, I define Illusion as the expression of the Real." [The above extracts from the writings of Hermes Tris-megistus are taken partly from the work of Dr Louis Ménard, partly from the *Eclogues* of Stobæus, a philosopher living in the fifth century.]

Although, at this distance of time, it is almost impossible to distinguish clearly between all the various systems of eclectic thought current in Alexandria in the first centuries A.D., there seems no doubt that Gnostics, Essenes, Therapeutæ, and Christians had many doctrines in common. The learned Alexandrian Jew, Epiphanius, who became Christian Bishop of Constantia, in Cyprus, in 369 A.D., says, indeed, in so many words, that the Essenes were Christians. It is also suggestive that the very city—Antioch—where "Christians" are said first to have been so called, was the headquarters of Gnosticism. Many of the "Fathers" of the early Church were certainly Gnostics, though some of them, in later life, wrote against the so-called "heresy." There were many phases of Gnosticism. The Syrian Gnostics of Antioch inclined to the teaching of Zoroaster, whilst the Gnostics of Alexandria gave preference to the teaching of Pythagoras, Plato, and the "Kabbala." All Gnostic sects, however, accepted the fundamental idea of the emanation of the visible universe from an unseen deity.

Jewish tradition assigns the compilation of the esoteric teaching contained in the Kabbala to Simon Ben Jochai, about the time of the destruction of Jerusalem by Titus. The critic, Franck, considers that in no case can the Kabbala be earlier than the last century B.C. The doctrine of the Kabbala is that the mystery of the First Cause cannot be fathomed by the human mind. It calls the First Cause "the One" (Ain = No-Thing). This, in Alexandrian Greek, is the "Monad." From the Monad emanates the "Duad," which is the postulated male-female principle of nature, and is called "Christos-Sophia." From this dual principle emanate "the Energies" (Dunameis, or Æons), which are apparently identical with the "Ideas" of Platonism and the "Angels" of the Christian Church.

We find the term "Gnosis" (secret wisdom) in the Greek Septuagint translation of the Hebrew Scriptures; and in the letters which Paul of Tarsus wrote, at a later date, to his disciples, we find not only the term "Gnosis," but also the terms "Æon," "Christos," and "Pleroma." This last is the name given to the synthesis of the "Dunameis" or Energies which emanate from the Duad. As applied to a sect, the term "Gnosticos" is said to have been used first by the Ophites, in the second century A.D. As a formulated phase of thought, Gnosticism appears to antedate Christianity. Clement of Alexandria uses the term "Gnosticos" to signify "the perfect Christian." Gnosticism was first introduced, it is said, into Antioch from Alexandria by Simon Magus, who speaks of the First Cause as "the Boundless

Power" and the "Root of all things." The Gnostic, Basilides, who flourished about 120 A.D., calls the First Cause "the Unknown," "the Incomprehensible," "the Non-Existent." Nothing, he says, can be predicated of It, and yet It created "the germs of all things." Another thinker of Alexandria, named Valentinus, taught the Gnosis at Rome from 138 A.D. to 160 A.D. Fragments of the writings of this teacher have been preserved to us by his pupils, Tertullian and Clement of Alexandria, who ranged themselves later among his opponents, because Valentinus declined to accept the idea of a physical and crucified Christos. The Christos he held to be the perfect self-manifestation of the Good. It can have no actual physical form of its own, but is purely psychic and pneumatic. There are, he says, three distinct types of humanity, viz.: the "hylic" or carnal man, who is hopelessly sensual; the "psychic" or moral man, who may certainly attain to goodness, if he will; and the "pneumatic" man, in whose nature traces of the divine already exist. The "Christos" is the Higher Spirit of Humanity, which dawns first in the psychic man and leads him to attain to the knowledge of the world and of himself; whilst in the pneumatic man it leads him ever nearer to the divine life, until, at last, the human is merged into the "Pleroma" and enters the "Kingdom of Light." Valentinus looked upon the so-called "Christians" of his time as psychic men who followed an exoteric doctrine. The true Gnosis, he maintained, is esoteric teaching which can only be communicated to and received by pneumatic or spiritually-minded men. The teaching apparently is that the Godhead gradually reveals itself in a rhythmic scale of celestial powers, or Æons, which constitute the links of a chain connecting the divine with the human. The Æons are respectively called: (1) Nous, (2) Aletheia, (3) Logos, (4) Zoë, (5) Anthropos (the Ideal Man), (6) Christos-Sophia, and (7) the Pleroma, which is the synthesis of all the divine energies.

The Gnostic teacher Cerinthus, who, according to Eusebius, the Church Father, flourished in the time of Trajan (98–117 A.D.), certainly made a distinction between the Christos of the Gnostics and the Christos of the Alexandrian Christians, whose miraculous birth he considered to be a fiction. According to Epiphanius, another of the Church Fathers, who as a young man was a Gnostic, Cerinthus accepted only a part of the gospel of Matthew as the truth. Another Gnostic teacher, Cerdo of Antioch, taught in Rome, about 140 A.D., that the Christos is not a real incarnation of the deity, but an apparent incarnation only. The only Christian Scriptures accepted by Cerdo were the letters of Paul. Marcion is said to have been a follower of Cerdo. Justin—known after his death as "the Martyr"—was born in 103 A.D., and taught at first, certainly, something akin to the Gnosis. He says: "In the beginning, God before all the works produced from himself a certain power (Dunamis) which is called sometimes "son," sometimes "wisdom," sometimes "angel," sometimes "God," "Kuros," and "Logos." Irenæus, born about 130 A.D., at Smyrna, was also in early life a teacher of the Gnosis. In his version of the creation of the universe, he says: "Ildabaoth looked into Matter, and with it united his concupiscence, whence was born a "son": this is Mind. . . . The Pro-Pater is invisible and everlasting, unborn in silence and in boundless cycles of time. . . . The Pro-Pater is known only to the "only begotten son," which is Mind. . . . Ennoia (Intelligence) is the mother, and Nous (Mind) is their son." Irenæus, after writing in this way, joined the party of Peter, and denounced the "heresy" of those Gnostics who held to the idea of the spiritual Christos, and refused to adopt Peter's new doctrine of a Christ of flesh and blood.

There is no evidence whatever that the idea of a physical Christ was taught in Alexandria or anywhere else before the middle of the second century A.D. But we have the evidence of Philo, certainly written before 40 A.D., that the exact kind of life which was afterwards called "the Christian life" was scrupulously led by several thousand ascetics, known as Essenes and Therapeutæ, in Egypt and Syria. Agreeing with many other writers, Dean Mansel suggests that Essenism was the result of the many Buddhist missions which visited Egypt "within two generations of the time of Alexander the Great." Philo tells us that there were at his time about two thousand Essenes, who were so called on account of "the holiness of their lives." He says that they "dwell in villages, and avoid cities on account of the wonted licentiousness of the citizen class. . . . Some of them cultivate the land, and others follow such handicrafts as are co-operative of peace. . . . They lay up no treasures of silver and gold. . . . They dream not even of trade, . . . rejecting with abhorrence every outlet to greed. . . . Of their love of virtue they give proof in their contempt for riches, pleasure, or glory, in their steadfastness and self-control, also in their contentment with little, simplicity, cheerfulness, freedom from pride, observance of law, and healthy calm. . . . Of their love for men they give evidence in their benevolence, equality, and in their community of goods, . . . and make of their own service a common benefit to all. . . . Their fellowship transcends description, and is a pattern of life perfect and most blessed." Of the Therapeutæ Philo says that they are "Essenes, who are in greatest number in Egypt, especially around Alexandria, and who embrace the life of contemplation. . . . The aim of these philosophers is shown at once by their name, for both men and women are called Therapeutæ in the true and literal sense of the word, because they possess an art of healing superior to that usual in cities, for that heals bodies only, whilst this heals souls also, which are brought near to death . . . by lusts and pleasures, griefs and fears, greeds and follies. . . . Self-mastery they lay down to be, as it were, the foundation of soul, and on this they build other virtues. Not one of them would take food or drink before sunset, inasmuch as they judge the pursuit of wisdom to be the work worthy of the daylight." Josephus, in his *History of the Jews*, which he published at Rome in 93 A.D., also speaks of the Essenes. He says that "there are three sets of philosophers among the Jews: the first are called Pharisees, the second Sadducees, and the third, who really seem to follow a holy discipline, are called Essenes. . . .

They condemn riches, and have a marvellous system of holding things in common. . . . Each gives of his own to anyone in need. . . . Everything that is said by them is of more force than an oath. . . . They despise danger, and regard death, if it come with honour, as better than deathlessness. . . . For the opinion is strongly held by them that though bodies are perishable, souls endure for ever, untouched by death. Proceeding from the finest æther, they are involved in bodies, as it were in prisons, drawn to them by some physical spell; but, when they are set free from their bonds of flesh, they have joy." And Pliny, who perished at Herculaneum during the eruption of Vesuvius in 79 A.D., notes regarding the Essenes that "this Eremite sect lives on perennial," although children were rarely born among the Essenes, "because daily is the throng renewed . . . by men resorting to them in numbers, driven through weariness of life and the surges of ill-fortune to their manner of existence."

That Essenes and Christians may have been in the early centuries of our era convertible terms seems likely from a very remarkable admission made by no less a person than Eusebius, who was Christian Bishop of Cæsarea in 315 A.D. He says: "It is highly probable that the ancient commentaries which Philo says they (the Essenes) have, are the very writings and gospels of the Apostles." We also get a glimpse, from Eusebius, of the way the so-called "logoi" or sayings of Jesus were handed down by the earliest Christian teachers and gradually collected by the Church. Eusebius quotes Paphias, who was Bishop of Hierapolis from 120 to 130 A.D., as having said: "If pupils of the elders came, I used to ask about the sayings (logoi) of the elders," which leads us to infer that the "logoi of the Lord" were neither more nor less than traditional precepts derived from various sources and handed down verbally from one teacher to another.

Clemens of Alexandria—the St Clement of the Catholic Church—was, like Philo, an eclectic thinker. He says: "There is one river of Truth, but many streams fall into it on this side and on that." Clement adopted many Stoic ideas, like Philo, and like him asserts that in the state of ecstatic trance (ecstasis) only can the devout mind enter into communion with the divine. "Only the pure in heart see God," he says: "he that would enter the fragrant shrine must be pure, and purity is to think holy things." Clement defines the "Gnosis" to be "the apprehensive contemplation of God in the Logos." His definition of God given in his "Miscellanies," or *Stomateis*, is interesting. He says: "Stripping from concrete existence all physical attributes, taking from it, in the next place, the three dimensions of space, we arrive at the conception of a point having position. . . . This is the Monad: this is God. . . . He is formless and nameless, though sometimes we give him titles, which are not to be taken in their proper sense—'the One,' 'the Good,' 'Intelligence,' 'Father,' 'Creator.' . . . The 'God,' being undemonstrable, is not the object of knowledge." The Gnostics called the synthesis of all the powers of the divine nature "Pleroma," whilst Clement says that "all the powers of the divine nature gathered into one complete the idea of the 'Son.' He is one, as all is one. Hence, he is all, for he is a circle, all the powers being orbed and united in him." Clement therefore may be said to symbolise the Logos or the Son as a circle and the Father as the central point within the circle, in a manner quite Pythagorean. God, he adds, has no "consciousness" of the universe except as it is "mirrored" in the Son.

Clement's famous pupil, Origines, or Origen, was an Alexandrian Copt, who filled Clement's post of cathechist of the Church of Alexandria after the departure of Clement. He was a man of intense convictions, who followed with extreme rigour every self-denying ordinance of the Church, and, to carry out literally the precept that any of a man's members which "offended" should be cut out and cast from him, he had the fanatical courage to mutilate himself. All the same, in 232 A.D., Demetrius, the Christian Bishop of Alexandria, excommunicated him for heresy. The "heresies" of Origen were published in his work *Peri Archon*, or *De Principiis*, which boldly asserts the freedom of man's will. Origen refuses to accept the doctrine that human nature is originally corrupt, and asserts that no punishment for sin can possibly be eternal. He also maintains that many passages in the Pentateuch and Gospels alike are allegorical. He wrote an essay *Against Celsus*, defending Christianity, in which he frankly admits that the "Fall of Man," described in Genesis, is pure allegory, that "Adam" is the generic name of humanity, and that the sin of Adam is symbolic merely of souls falling away from God. Further, he suggests that the "coats of skins" which Adam and Eve wore after they were driven out of paradise are emblems representing the human bodies with which all souls are clothed who prefer physical to spiritual joys. After some time spent in Palestine and at Cæsarea in Cappadocia, Origen went to Greece. During the persecution of Christians at the time of the Emperor Decius, 249–251 A.D., Origen was on one occasion so horribly tortured that, in 253 A.D., he died from the effects, at Tyre.

Origen teaches a conditioned God, omniscient and omnipotent, who is perfectly wise and perfectly just. His theory is that the "Father" begets the "Son" by a continuous process of generation. He says: "The Father did not beget his Son and let him go from himself, but he always begets him," and he uses the simile of the torch and the ray to illustrate his meaning. Origen postulates the "Ideal World" of spirits, all "free," all of "the same nature," and clothed in bodies of "ethereal texture," as existing at the beginning of the universe. Then these spirits begin to differentiate. Some are content to remain in their "first estate," but others evolve into "souls," which vary in character as mind or sense predominates in them. All souls are born into life on earth; each soul "comes into life with its spermatic germs of good and evil." The "germinative principle" of the universe is the Logos, and the soul of man possesses "a germinative principle, a vital assimilative spark, which lays hold of suitable matter, and shapes it into a habitation fitted to its needs. . . . Wherefore will no one think that birth, happy or unhappy, is ruled by chance." Thus it seems that the Christian writer, Origen, adopts not only the Stoic idea of progress by means of the discipline of life, but also the Indian idea of the invariable working of the law of cause and effect.

The most spiritual and at the same time perhaps the most logical of the Alexandrian thinkers was Plotinus. He was born in 205 A.D., at Lycopolis, on the Nile, a town half-way between Memphis and Thebes, and studied philosophy at Alexandria, under Ammonius "Saccas." In his thirty-ninth year Plotinus went to Persia with the Emperor Gordianus III., and two years afterwards to Rome. Here for the next quarter of a century he taught philosophy to numerous pupils—amongst whom we find poets, physicians, rhetoricians, senators, and the Emperor Gallienus (260–268 A.D.) and his wife. But it was not until urged to do so by the most distinguished among his pupils, Porphyry (born 233 A.D.), that Plotinus wrote down the essence of his verbal teaching. Porphyry afterwards arranged the fifty-four lectures written by Plotinus into six books, each containing nine discourses, and known consequently as "the Enneads."

The philosophy of Plotinus is generally spoken of as the Neo-Platonic, because it is based upon the teaching of Plato. But it contains also much Pythagorean and some Indian thought, and it incorporates such ideas as the "Nous" of Aristotle and the "Anima Mundi" of the later Stoics. He ascribes the origin of all life and all thought to a Divine Being, or Unknown Force (Dunamis), which can have neither qualities nor attributes, for the simple reason that it *is* all things. "It is," he says, "in truth unspeakable; for, if you say anything of it, you make it a particular thing. Now, that which is beyond everything, even beyond the most venerable of all things, intelligence, and which is the only truth in all things, cannot be regarded as one of them; nor can we give it a name, or predicate anything of it. But, we try to indicate it to ourselves, as we are able. When, therefore, in our difficulties about it, we say that it neither perceives itself, nor is conscious of itself, nor knows itself, it must be considered that, in using such language, we are getting at it through its opposites. . . . We speak indeed about it, but itself we do not express, nor have we any knowledge of it." To the student of Indian philosophy, this description of the Divine Being is very suggestive of that of the "Unconditioned Brahman." Plotinus also adopts the idea of the Indian mystics when he says that thought is lost in union with the divine unity, that in all intense meditation on the abstract deity active thought is merged in contemplation and adoration, which culminates in union with the divine. Incorporeal things, says Plotinus, are not kept apart by corporeal obstructions, but by difference of nature only. If their natures are in harmony, each is at once present to the other. Therefore, when we "direct our gaze" to the One, "we attain to the end of our desires and to the rest of our souls." We rise, in fact, "from thought to vision." Thought can lead us only to the outer temple, but Oneness with the Divine (Enosis) only can open to us the sanctuary.

Although he adopts the Stoic idea that spirit is the only real and permanent thing in the universe, Plotinus hesitates to accept the theory that mind and matter are merely different aspects of the same thing, and, like Plato, he finds it necessary to postulate a link or "Mediator" between them. This he calls the "Universal Soul." His explanation of the origin or evolution of all things is, however, to say the least, vague. The idea apparently is that the life of the universe, physical and psychic alike, radiates from the One, as light and heat radiate from the sun. He says: "The first genesis of being is this. The One overflows, and in its superabundance produces another; but that which is produced turns itself towards the One, and being fulfilled by it and contemplating it becomes . . . at once being and intelligence." Elsewhere Plotinus calls this first "production" of the One the "Mind of the Universe." The Universal Mind then evolves the Universal Soul, which, in its turn, evolves the Material Universe, into which individual souls—the component atoms of the Universal Soul, ultimately descend. He defines the Universe, or Kosmos, as a living organism, of which no part can act without reaction on the whole. The Universal Soul is one and indivisible, just as sunlight, considered as an entity, is one and indivisible, although its rays penetrate everywhere. As light emanates from the sun, as heat emanates from fire, so life in the universe emanates from the Absolute Life, each wave of life becoming, as it were, less and less divine the more distant it is from the divine source.

The first emanation from the One he calls the

Universal Mind, defining it as a duality composed of "Nous" and "Kosmos nöetos" (Mind and Mental World), each of which is apparently to be imagined as included in the other. In other words, Plotinus seems to say that the mind and its ideas are inseparable. He speaks of Nous as "the One-many," from which it may be inferred that Nous is to be considered as being the totality of all ideas existing in the universe. Ideas he holds to be the only realities, sense-forms being but images stamped by mind on matter. Human minds are picturesquely described as sparks emitted by the central fire of the Universal Mind. The second emanation proceeds from the first. It is called Soul (Psyche), and seems to be identical with the Anima Mundi or Universal Soul of Stoic philosophy. But Plotinus says that, properly speaking, the Kosmos cannot be said "to have a soul," for the reason that "it lies *in* soul, which sustains it, and no part of it is destitute of soul, being *moistened with life*, like a net in water." With Plotinus, as with Plato, life and soul seem to be synonymous. His term "Psyche" seems to indicate the hypothetical primordial substance, or undifferentiated matter, before the evolution of any qualities such as shape, size, temperature, texture, or colour. If so, it is suggestive of the ether postulated by modern science. "Matter," says Plotinus, "cannot give form to itself: hence it is necessary that there should be something which is the supplier of life. . . . There will be no *body*, if there is no psychical power; . . . nothing would be generated, if there were nothing to invest matter with form." And then he argues: "How can a body be full of productive power, except this is imparted to it by that which makes it *hot or cold*? . . . How can it increase at certain times, or to a certain extent, except so far as the power of growth is assumed in the mass of matter?"

Plotinus calls the human soul the "epitome of the Kosmos," and the "microcosm of the macrocosm." Like Plato, he is of opinion that the soul is no mere material product, because it is unthinkable that life and thought can result from any aggregation of senseless "atoms" only. Nor can the soul be "extended substance" merely, for the reason that, wherever the soul's activity reaches, our consciousness is instantly present as an individual entity. Souls, he thinks, are bodiless up to a certain stage in evolution, when, because of its development of an overpowering self-will, "the soul deviates from the One and falls into number and multitude." Thus the soul becomes an individual entity; it becomes self-conscious, and, by means of life in a physical body, it gains the knowledge of evil and of good, and evolves all its latent powers. But consciousness of self induces self-assertion and self-seeking, so that, incarnated time after time in a physical body, the human soul must for ever strive against selfishness, passion, and temptations of all kinds, until, ennobled at last by self-conquest, it is fitted to return to "its former abode." Thus we see that Plotinus fully adopts the Pythagorean and Brahman theory of the soul's repeated life on earth. And in answer to the objection that, if ever we had lived before in a human body, we should be able to remember the fact, he explains that such remembrance is impossible, because memory is of a double kind—the memory which pertains to the "higher" or spiritual soul, and the memory which belongs to the "lower" or animal soul. The higher soul looks inward, concentrates itself, and contemplates ideas; the lower soul expands, diffuses itself, and creates *its own emanation*, the body. With the death of the body vanishes the memory of everything material: it is all washed away in "the River of Lethe." So that, when next the soul "becomes situated in another body," all matters relating to the lower soul in former lives are absolutely forgotten. But, if the soul, when in another body, *consciously* strives towards spirituality, memories acquired by the higher soul in former lives will gradually be recovered. In descending into a mortal body, the soul, he thinks, leaves something of itself above, the consciousness of which may in certain circumstances be revived. Plotinus teaches the solidarity of all souls. Our separate bodies hinder us, indeed, from perceiving that we are all "one with another," because we all participate mutually in the Universal Soul, although this participation is the cause of man being able to feel sympathy with man. The senses, indeed, separate us, but reason should unite us. Dialectics, he argues, give clear evidence of this union of souls. For example, when Socrates and another, after long logical discussion, have reached an agreement, it is a proof that the two opposing minds are, after all, nothing but two different manifestations of the same Universal Mind. The number of individual human souls which work out their evolution during each period of cosmic manifestation Plotinus holds to be limited, and he thinks that the immortality of the individual soul ceases at the close of the manifested universe of which it forms part. Thus his theory of the alternate evolution and dissolution of the visible universe appears to be identical with the Indian idea of the alternate days and nights of Brâhma.

Plotinus follows Plato in his insistence that it is the love of the beautiful and the good only that can help the union of the human with the divine. "What then," he asks, "is the way?" and then answers that, as long as we are lured by material beauty, which is but "the image" and "the shadow" of the reality, we shall never be able to gaze upon the ineffable beauty enshrined in the "Sanctuary." He says: "For if one hastens to embrace as true the fair image reflected in the water, like Hylas, he sinks into the stream, and is seen no more. So, he who sets his affection on earthly beauty, and will not let it go, falls, not with the body, but with the soul, into abysses dark and terrible, and will dwell in Hades with the shadows which he clung to here. Let us then fly to our dear fatherland . . . even as the Master says, in a parable, that Odysseus fled from the witch Circe, or from Calypso, not *willing* to stay for any visible delights or any sensual beauty." Every man must carve out his own ideal for himself. Therefore, "if thou findest that thou art not yet beautiful, as the sculptor of a statue that is to be beautiful chips and files away, making this smooth and that pure, till he brings out a lovely face on his statue, so do thou chip off what is superfluous, straighten what is crooked, cleanse what is dark and make it bright, and cease not to labour at thy statue until the divine radiance of virtue shine forth, until thou beholdest self-control mounted on her holy pedestal."

Plotinus himself tried to act up to his ideal. He lived the life of an ascetic, and thereby developed the power of self-hypnosis, which at times enabled him to pass into a state of ecstatic trance, and so attain to union with the divine. Professor Caird calls him "the mystic *par excellence*," and says that "it was mainly through him and through St Augustine, as influenced by him, that mysticism passed into Christian theology, and became an important element in the religion of the Middle Ages and of the modern world." This union with the divine can only be attained, says Plotinus, by the man who leads a pure life and who has trained himself to cast out all desire from the heart, all fear and all hope from the mind. In this state of "enosis" the perceiver is "one with the thing perceived." It is "not vision, but union." He who passes from the "Outer Temple," where he leaves behind him "all the statues of the gods," will find "nothing visible" when he reaches the "Adytum," or Holy of Holies. But "there is another mode of perception, namely ecstasy, an expansion and accession of *himself*. Nothing is present to him in any other way." It is recorded that, when Plotinus felt himself to be dying, he threw himself into this state of ecstatic trance, saying to the friends around him: "Now seek I to lead back the self within me to the All-self."

CHAPTER IX

CONFUSION OF THOUGHT

In his attempt to explain what he calls "the confusion of thought which Christianity produced," Dean Stanley points to "the fluctuating state of the Greek language" in the early centuries of the Christian era. That there was, at this epoch, much confusion of thought at Alexandria and other chief centres of culture seems certain. And it is not unlikely that "the fluctuating state of the Greek language" may have added to the confusion, but it is scarcely conceivable that it produced it. The confusion seems rather to be due to the extraordinary eclecticism of the founders of the Christian Church. To the student of religion, who tries to understand the origin of the Christian cult, nothing is more striking than his discovery, that on the simple story of Jesus of Nazareth there have been grafted doctrines so mutually incongruous as Alexandrian Gnosticism, Buddhist humanitarianism, Jewish theocracy, and Roman Stoicism; and he wonders what else but confusion could be the result. Could any two ideas, for instance, be less in harmony than the idea of a

God of love, and a jealous God of battles? or, than the Jewish teaching of a life for a life and a tooth for a tooth, and the Buddhist idea that evil should be requited with good?

It is customary, no doubt, to accept as literally and historically true the accounts given in the Christian gospels of the origin of Christianity. But, when one comes to consider the fact that the writers of these gospels are absolutely unknown, that their original manuscripts have never been discovered, and that even the earliest copies of them now extant have been repeatedly copied and recopied, and probably as often more or less amended and revised, an honest searcher after truth has to admit that we have no certain knowledge of the actual genesis of Christian thought. The sect of Christians was, we are told, first heard of in Antioch. But it seems at least as likely that the cult may have arisen in the neighbouring city of Alexandria, which was the chief centre where the thought of the East met and mingled with that of the West. The earliest Christian documents now extant are supposed to be letters written by the teacher Paul of Tarsus to his disciples. From these epistles we gather that, from the very first, the Christian community contained a Greek and a Jewish element. The Greek Christians believed in the theory of the spiritual Christos, whilst the Jewish Christians held the theory that a material Christ was the divine founder of Christianity. As the scattered communities of Christians gradually developed into the Catholic or Universal Church of Christ, those in authority seem to have adopted, one by one, from very various sources, a number of doctrines, legends, symbols, and ritualistic observances, and to have grouped them around the central idea of a Saviour. We find that so many Christian doctrines are so similar to those of Buddhism, that we cannot avoid the inference that they probably had their origin in those Buddhist missions from India which, not long before the time ascribed to the rise of Christianity, were welcomed with such sympathy in Western Asia; so much so that, under the influence of these Buddhist teachers, communities of ascetics settled on the shores of the Dead Sea, in Palestine, and by the Lake Mareotis, near Alexandria.

These ascetics are known to history as Essenes and Therapeutæ (Healers), and they certainly led a life of self-denial and brotherly love, which closely resembled the Christian ideal. In the Roman Empire, at this epoch, there flourished also other cults which have strong resemblances to Christianity, especially Serapism, Mithraism, and Gnosticism. Serapism was a late form of the earlier Egyptian cult of Isis and Serapis. We learn from Plutarch that the mysteries of Serapis and Isis, as they were celebrated at his time, resembled the Greek mysteries of Dionysos and Demeter, and that "the Greeks consider Dionysos to be, not only the patron of wine, but also of the entire moist or generative principle in nature." He also speaks of the "mystic symbols" which were shown tc those who were initiated into "the sacred orgies of Dionysos." Among these emblems were "the egg and the serpent," the egg being symbolic of the primordial substance of the universe, and the serpent of generation and life. It must be remembered that the Egyptian Isis, the Greek Demeter, and the Roman Ceres are all goddesses who personify the passive productive force of nature. A very interesting letter, which was written in the first century of the Christian era by the Emperor Trajan to his brother-in-law, Servianus, has been preserved to us by the historian Volpiscus. In this letter Trajan says: "Those who worship Serapis are likewise Christians; even those who style themselves Bishops of Christ are devoted to Serapis. The very Patriarch himself, when he comes to Egypt, is forced by some to adore Serapis, by others to worship Christ."

The analogy between Christianity and Mithraism is still more remarkable. Mithraism was a later phase of the old Zoroastrian cult of Mithra. In the earlier cult, Mithra was adored as "the Friend of man," who blessed the world with light and heat, and who waged war against darkness and error: he was the "Companion" of Ahura Mazda, the One God, and was the "Mediator" between him and humanity. During the Roman Empire, Mithras was no longer thought of as the "Companion," but as the earthly incarnation of the One God, and was adored under the form of a hero, ever young and ever victorious. He was called "invictus" and "insuperabilis," and is represented on the Mithraic monuments kneeling with one knee on a vanquished bull, and attended by two torchbearers. One of the torches is held upwards, symbolising the sun's course through the heavens; the other is held downwards, emblematic of the sun's course through the underworld. The followers of Mithras were called "soldiers," because, at his initiation, each took an oath to war against evil. So well was this vow kept, that we find the Christian father, Tertullian, in a homily written about 200 A.D., holding up the "temperance" and "steadfastness" of "the soldiers of Mithras" as an example to be followed by the wavering and self-indulgent Christians.

Like Gilgamesh of Babylonia and Herakles of Hellas, Mithras was fabled to have performed twelve heroic "labours," one of which was the slaying of the bull, an allegory of the control acquired by the spiritual man over his animal nature. From the blood of the slain bull sprang the sacred "vine," the fruit of which was the chief element in the celebration of the Mithraic mysteries. At the end of his twelve labours, Mithras was said to have partaken of a supper in the company of Helios and other companions, and it was in memory of this supper that periodical love-feasts were held by the soldiers of Mithras. We find on a bas-relief discovered at Konjica, in Bosnia, celebrants of this supper represented holding a cup and a flat round cake which is stamped with the solar cross ⊕. The Church Father, Justin Martyr, who died in 165 A.D., tells us that bread and water were the symbols used in the celebration of the Mithraic mysteries; and St Jerome tells us that initiates into these mysteries passed through seven degrees of initiation. Inscriptions on the Mithraic monuments found up and down the Roman Empire—at Rome, Ostia, Bologna, Modena, Milan, Arles, Aix, Friedberg in Hesse, Hedderheim near Frankfurt, and Osterbrucken in the Odenwald—show us some facts about these initiations. We find that before he took the "sacramentum," or vow of secrecy, the soldier of Mithras was called "Corax" (raven); after taking the vow, he became a "Mystic." Passing into the third degree, the initiate first became "a soldier of Mithras." He had then to prepare himself by fasting and ablution, and to submit to serious tests of his courage and endurance before he attained the fourth degree of "Leo" (lion), when he received on his body the mystic marks of "the sword and the crown." In the fifth degree, the initiate became a "Persian" (Perses), and had the right to wear the Phrygian cap—the cap which Mithras himself wears on the monuments. On passing to the sixth degree, he became "Heliodromus." This term has been translated "a runner of the sun"; but the translation is not very satisfactory nor explanatory. "Helios," of course, is the sun-god, and "dromos" was the Spartan race-course. Perhaps, therefore, we might paraphrase the term as "the illumined." In the seventh degree, the initiate became a "Father" (pater), whilst the chief of all the initiates was called "Father of the fathers" (pater patrum).

These seven degrees of initiation were held to have an occult relation to the seven spheres, through which it was supposed that the soul passed after death. The spheres were imagined to be under the influence of the sun, moon, and five planets, and the theory is that, as it passes successively through each sphere, the soul puts off something of its human attributes. The faculty of nutrition is left behind in the sphere of the moon; the combative instinct passes from the soul in its passage through the sphere of Mars; the sexual impulse vanishes in the sphere of Venus, ambition in the sphere of Jove; and finally the intellectual faculty is absorbed in the sphere of the sun. Mithras, "the Helper," was imagined as guarding and guiding the soul in its passage through the seven spheres to its final rest.

All men were equals within the Mithraic brotherhoods, whatever they were outside — aristocrats, freedmen, or slaves. We find among the initiates tribunes, prefects, legates, and even emperors. The figure of Mithras is seen on the reverse of bronze coins of the Emperor Gordianus II., dated early in the third century; and Aurelian, who died in 275 A.D., officially recognised Mithraism; whilst Diocletian built the best preserved of all the Mithraic temples, which is still to be seen at Carnutum, near the Danube; and Julian, who died 305 A.D., is also reputed to have been an initiate. At Rome, Mithraism came sometimes into such sharp rivalry with Christianity, that each cult in turn accused the other of imitating its doctrines or its ritual. We find Tertullian, the Church Father, saying: "The devil, whose business it is to pervert truth, mimics the exact circumstances of the divine sacraments in the mysteries of idols. He himself baptizes some, that is to say, his believers and followers; he promises forgiveness of sins from the sacred font, and thereby initiates them into the mysteries of Mithras. Thus he marks on the foreheads of his own soldiers, he celebrates the oblation of bread, he brings in the symbol of the resurrection, and wins the crown with the sword." This language is rather amusing when we remember that Tertullian praised the steadfastness of the soldiers of Mithras, and held them up as examples to the soldiers of Christ. But Tertullian ignores the fact that, long before the introduction of Christianity, flat wheaten cakes of a circular form, marked with the solar cross, and a cup of wine were the two chief emblems used in the celebration of the mysteries of Dionysos. In the mysteries of Mithras, flat cakes were also used, which were called "Miza," and resembled the "wafer" afterwards adopted by the Catholic Church. Placed on the rim of the wine-cup, the "Miza" stood as the symbol of the union, or "marriage," of the elemental forces of nature—active and passive.

There are many external similarities between Mithraism and primitive Christianity, but it is especially when we compare the spirit which animated these two cults that we cannot help the surmise that the one may perhaps have been the outcome of the other.

It is assumed, on quite insufficient evidence, that the doctrine of a Christ of flesh and blood was taught by the Gnostic Paul of Tarsus, and theologians point to several passages in his epistles which seem to bear out this assumption. But we must not forget that no single epistle of Paul's exists in its original text, and that the copies which have come down to us have been repeatedly transcribed. There is therefore the possibility that these particular passages may have been inserted in the text at a later date; and this possibility seems to be a probability, because no thoughtful student can read even our present translation of Paul's letters to his disciples without perceiving that the passages which allude to Jesus as a living personage are in direct contradiction to the general drift of Paul's teaching. No theological ingenuity, in fact, can harmonise these passages with Paul's emphatic condemnation of those disciples of his who appeared to accept the teaching of certain Alexandrian Jews, who by their doctrine of a material Christ, a man of flesh and blood, corrupted the Gnostic theory of the spiritual "Christos"—that "Light which lighteth every man that cometh into the world," and by means of which every man, if he will, may rise above his animal nature; thus, as Paul puts it, "foolishly changing the glory of the incorruptible God into an image made like corruptible man." In fact, Paul explains to his disciples, in so many words, that the Christos is a "mystery"; it is "the Christ *in you*"; it is "the Lord of Light, *which no man hath seen, or can see.*" And again Paul exclaims: "Know ye not that *ye* are the temple of God, and that the spirit of God dwelleth in you!" Passages such as these seem altogether to dispose of the idea that Paul was a "Christian," otherwise than in the Gnostic sense of the term. His teaching is similar to much of the teaching which we find in the Gnostic gospel which is popularly attributed to John, whilst both are very suggestive of the Buddhist and Vedantic teaching, which at that epoch was well known in Alexandria. Indeed, Paul is preaching pure Vedantism when he says: "Every man who striveth for the mastery is temperate in all things. . . . Every man shall bear his own burden. . . . Whatsoever a man soweth that shall he also reap. . . . Let us not be weary of well-doing, for in due time we shall reap, if we faint not." In very many passages in his letters to his disciples, we find Paul condemning the reactionary teachers, who, he says, "changed the truth of God into a lie." He warns his friends in Crete against "giving heed to Jewish fables," and he urges them to "avoid foolish questionings and genealogies," such as were invented in the endeavour to trace the lineal descent of this supposed human Christ from King David. In spite of Paul's warnings, some of his pupils in Galatia appear to have accepted the false teaching, for we find him writing to them: "I marvel that ye are so soon removed from him that called you into the grace of Christ unto another gospel. . . . O foolish Galatians, who hath bewitched you!" He also seems to have been doubtful of the steadfastness of his disciples at Corinth, for he writes to them: "I fear lest, by any means, your minds should be corrupted from the simplicity which is in Christ."

Others among the earliest Christian teachers, besides Paul of Tarsus, rejected the idea of a material Christ. Chief amongst these were Cerinthus, Tatian, and Marcion; and when, in the year 144 A.D., the Church decided that only certain specified writings should be accepted as the genuine "Word of God," these three teachers left the Christian community, and we find that the Marcionite churches were opposed to the Catholic churches up to the end of the third century A.D. It is remarkable also that the Church Father, Irenæus, who was Bishop of Lyons in 177 A.D., addressed a homily to the members of his Church who doubted the doctrine of a Christ of flesh and blood, in which he maintains that not only did Jesus live, but that he lived to be an old man, and allowing the inference that he died a natural death. Irenæus says that Jesus "passed through every age, becoming an infant for infants. . . . So, likewise, was he an old man for old men, that he might be a perfect master for all, not merely as regards the setting forth of the truth, but as regards age also, sanctifying at the same time the aged also, and becoming to them likewise an example. Then, at last, he came to death itself." Seeing what harmony exists between the teaching ascribed to Jesus and the teaching of Philo Judæus, the historian of the persecution of the Palestine Jews by Pontius Pilate, and of the life and doctrines of the Alexandrian Essenes, it seems strange that Philo makes no allusion whatever to any such person as Jesus. This is all the more remarkable, because Philo's own nephew, also a Jew like himself, was not only a Roman "eques," who was for a time governor of Egypt, but was actually married to a relative of the very King Herod who, according to the story of the Gospel, ordered the massacre of the young children in the hope of getting rid of the infant Christ. In fact, the only scrap of historical evidence that the Christ of the Gospels was a real being is the following short passage in Josephus:

"At that time there appeared a certain Jesus, a wise man, and he drew to him many Jews. And when, at the instigation of our chief men, Pilate condemned him to the cross, those who had first loved him did not fall away. To this day the sect of Christians, called after him, exists." But Canon Farrar says that there are "two reasons, which are alone sufficient to prove that this passage is spurious—one, that it was unknown to Origen and the earlier Fathers, and the other, that its place in the text is uncertain."

It seems strange that a man like Marcus Aurelius, who became emperor in 161 A.D., and who, as John Stuart Mill reminds us, was not only "the gentlest and most amiable of philosophers and rulers," but even "a better Christian in all but the dogmatic sense of the word than almost any of the ostensibly Christian sovereigns who have since reigned," and whose own ethical writings "embodied the Christian ideal," altogether failed to see that "Christianity was to be a good and not an evil to the world." It was during his reign, indeed, that the philosopher Celsus published his essay, *A True Word against the Christians*, which the Church Father, Origen, did his best to refute. In this essay Celsus showed that, even at that time, there was no valid evidence of either the birth or death, still less of the resurrection, of the alleged founder of Christianity. There seems some justification for the contention of Celsus, when we find that it was much more than three hundred years after the birth of Christ was said to have taken place that the Church decided to celebrate it annually on the 25th day of December.

Chrysostom, Archbishop of Constantinople, tells us in his 31st Homily that this date was fixed upon because it would allow Christians to "perform their holy rites in peace," whilst their opponents were engaged in the celebration of the rebirth of the sun at the winter solstice. It is not a little suggestive that not only the celebration of the birth, but also of the death and resurrection of Christ are coincident with the sun's passage of the winter solstice and the sun's ascension at the vernal equinox. Writing in 367 A.D., Epiphanius, Christian Bishop of Constantia, in Cyprus, tells us that the festival of the rebirth of the sun was held in an underground sanctuary, and that, at the moment of the sun's passage of the solstice, the officiating priest proclaimed the glad tidings with the significant words, "The Virgin has brought forth, the Light begins to grow!"

By Teutonic Christians the festival of the resurrection was called after their ancient goddess, Ostara, Eostre, Eastre, whilst the Latin Christians named it "Pascha," from the Hebrew "Pesach." Until the Church Council met at Nice in 325 A.D., the Eastern churches celebrated the resurrection on the same day as the passover, but the Western churches held their celebration a day earlier. It was decided by the Nicean Council that this important festival must be held thenceforth by all the churches on the same day, and that this day must be the Sunday which happens to fall "most nearly after the full moon of the vernal equinox." The "Table of Golden Numbers" was then compiled, to enable each church to find out the proper date, which may be any day between the

22nd of March and the 21st of April. In other words, we find that the celebration must take place during the passage of the sun through "Aries," the first of the *ascending* "signs" of the zodiac. Therefore, even by this elaborate device, the Church has been unable to dissociate the idea of the ascension of Christ into heaven from the idea of the ascension of the sun into the upper sky at the spring equinox.

That eminent Catholic and Oriental scholar, Emil Burnouf, thinks that "most of the Christian sacraments are originally Vedic," and that a careful study of the ancient missals of the Catholic Church clearly shows that "all the rites and hymns, the records of Easter Sunday, are celebrations of the event which took place the night before, and which continued till dawn." This event is no doubt, he says, "a double one: it is at once and indissolubly both the resurrection of Christ and the resurrection of the fire." On the morning of the spring equinox the sun rises at six o'clock above the horizon, and it is "during the second nocturne, that is, between three and six in the morning, or at dawn," that "the great Paschal candle is lighted." Burnouf further points out that this candle, symbolic of the resurrection, is lighted by fire produced for the express purpose from the friction of stones—as in the East the sacred fire is produced by the friction of wood—and that as it is lighted the priest exclaims: "The Light of Christ!" The term "Agnus," which the Catholic Church translates as "Lamb" of God and applies to Christ, is, according to Emil Burnouf, a corruption of the Vedic "Agni," or Sacred Spark; and he considers that the ancient Church text,

"Corporis Agni margaritum ingens" (the Great Jewel of Agni's body), is synonymous with the far earlier Sanskrit text, "Agni Kaya mâtra ratam." In the ancient crucifixes of the Church this "Jewel of Agni's body" was always placed in the centre of the cross, at the very spot where the sacred spark was generated by friction in the Vedic "arani." It is only in later crucifixes that we find this jewel replaced by the figure of a blazing sun. At the epoch when Christianity arose there was no novelty in the idea of tracing the origin of a religion back to a saintly teacher who had been miraculously born of a virgin-mother. The legendary Indian teacher Krishna, and Gautama, "the Buddha," were both said to be the sons of virgins, and there can be no doubt that these legends were well known in Alexandria at the beginning of the Christian era. We even find the Church Father, Hieronymus, or St Jerome, who was presbyter in 379 A.D., relating the legend that, after seven days of seclusion and fasting, the Virgin Mâyâ dreamed that she was carried by angels to heaven, where the infant Buddha entered her womb. The legend of the birth of Krishna is remarkably similar to that of the birth of Christ. It tells how Kansa, the Rajah of Madura, being, like Herod in the Gospel narrative, warned in a dream that his niece, the Virgin Deva-Naguy, would give birth to a son, who was destined to supplant him on the throne of Madura, took the precaution to shut her up in a tower, where he left her to starve. But the Holy Virgin was fed by angels until, in due time, Krishna was born; and at the infant's first cry a mighty wind arose and blew down the prison wall.

Mother and child were carried by angels to a cowshed belonging to Nanda, which stood beyond the territory of Kansa, and at the same time Nanda himself was warned in a dream of the danger to Deva Naguy and the Holy Child, and hastened with his servants to their rescue. Nanda brought up the young Krishna as his adopted son, and, in after-life, Krishna is said to have been called "Govinda," or cattle-owner, in allusion to his foster-father.

The virgin-mother idea is also found in Persian thought. The three legendary mediators, or divine messengers, known as Oshéda-bani, Oshéda-mâh, and Sosiash, are all supposed to have been born of virgins.

Nor is the idea of the resurrection anything new. The allegories of the revival of life each spring, the awakening of nature from its winter sleep by the genial warmth of the spring sunshine, or, in more poetical words, by the fervid kiss of the youthful sun-god, are of very early date. In Babylonia the renewal of life was celebrated as the union of Ishtar and Dumuzi. From the Euphrates the mythos passed into Syria as the marriage of Ashtoreth and Tammuz; whilst in Greece it was commemorated as the wedding of Venus and Adonis. In colder climes the annual return of the genial heat of the sun to generate life on the earth was welcomed by the lighting of great fires, which were always kindled from a spark struck from flint. These fires were lighted at the time of the spring-equinox, though in some districts the celebration was deferred till the summer-solstice, and called the "Fires of

St John." In his *Golden Bough* Frazer recites numerous records of the lighting of the "Easter fires" in Catholic countries, in some of which, he says, it was customary to kindle them in the ancient Vedic manner, by the friction of wood. The mystic rite was thus performed in Routhenia by the village elders, in solemn silence, until the birth of the sacred spark, which was greeted with a burst of song. When the fire blazed up, the youths and maidens of the village leaped, hand in hand, through the flames; and, when it died down, the cattle were driven through the glowing embers, so that they also might be fruitful.

In early times the regeneration of life, especially of vegetal life, was closely connected in men's minds with the idea of corn- and wine-gods, who were fabled to be incarnations of the deity, and were annually sacrificed to ensure a prolific harvest. One of the best known of these divine incarnations was that of the Egyptian Osiris. On the wall of the little temple, built on the roof of the great temple at Denderah, a representation of the resurrection of Osiris from death may still be seen.

As there was nothing new in the Christian dogma of the birth of a redeemer from a virgin-mother, neither was there any novelty in the later dogma of the Holy Trinity, which, in historical times, brought about the first great schism in the Christian Church. The theory of a triad of gods, co-eternal and co-equal, had been formulated long ages before, both in Babylonia and Egypt, where the elemental forces of nature were personified as the Divine

Father, Mother, and Son, the joint sources of all that is. The latest and best known of these trinities was that of Osiris, Isis, and Horus. Horus, "the Son," symbolises the everlasting renewal of life, and was held, as in all the earlier triads, to be identical with both "the Father" and "the Mother." The Christian dogma of the Trinity simply changes the three persons—Father, Mother, Son—into the less logical idea of Father, Son, and Spirit, whilst it retains the idea of their co-eternity and co-equality. The introduction of the new teaching was strongly opposed by a very important section of the Christian community, headed by Areios (Arius), the presbyter of the church at Alexandria. In a letter to Bishop Alexander, Areios set forth the point of view of those Christians who maintained that God is "One" (Monas). So numerous and so influential were the opponents of the dogma of the Trinity, that in 325 A.D. a council of the whole Christian Church was summoned to meet at Nicæa, to discuss this and other questions. At this council, Athanasius argued in favour of the new theory that the Son is "of the same substance" as the Father, and is therefore "very God of very God," and carried the majority of the council with him, so that the contention of Arius that "God is one" was declared to be "heretical." Athanasius was subsequently promoted to the bishopric of Alexandria; but nevertheless the more logical theory of Arius continued to be widely held, especially in the West. Alaric, who died in 410 A.D., Genseric, who died in 477 A.D., and Theodoric, who died in 526 A.D., were all "Arian" Christians.

Even the first Teutonic version of the Scriptures was made by an Arian, named Ufilas, whilst up to the time of Clovis Lombardy and the south of France remained Arian.

Ten years after the first Church-Council met at Nice, a second council of the Church formulated the orthodox form of Christian belief. This first "Credo" of the Church is known as the Athanasian Creed. It was modified by certain additions and omissions, at the council which met later at Chalcedon, but in its original form it ran thus: "We believe in One God, the Father Almighty, maker of all things, both visible and invisible; and in One Lord Jesus Christ, the Son of God, begotten of the Father only, begotten, that is to say, of the substance of the Father, God of God, Very God of Very God, begotten not made, being of one substance with the Father, by whom all things were made, both things in heaven and things in earth, who, for us men and for our salvation, came down, and was made flesh, and was made man, suffered, and rose again on the third day, went up into the heavens, and is come again to judge the quick and the dead: and in the Holy Ghost. But, those who say 'there was when He was not,' and 'before He was begotten,' and that 'He came into existence from what was not,' or who profess that 'the Son of God is of a different person or substance, or that He is created, or changeable or variable, are anathematised by the Catholic Church." Thus it appears that the Christian Church, starting from the idea of a God of love, the brotherhood of man, and universal charity, ended by cursing, in its very first Credo, those Christians who dared to think for themselves. "Confusion of thought" here surely reaches its climax!

That the origin of Christianity is so completely hidden is due largely to the practice which at that time prevailed of imparting all teaching in the form of allegory and under a pledge of secrecy. The Jews of Alexandria called their secret doctrine "Apocrypha" (Things hidden), and the Alexandrian Christians spoke of their own esoteric teaching as "the Unveiling" (Apocalypse). Thus we cannot trace to its very source the stream of Christian thought. Indeed, we may well ask the question whether we should to-day know anything more about Christianity than we know of the two rival cults of Gnosticism and Mithraism, had not Constantine chosen it for his state-religion. The Church claims Constantine as the first Christian emperor, although the records of his life reveal him, at best, as a Christian only in name. Just about the time when the first Church-Council met at Nicæa, he put to death his eldest son, Crispus, on a mere suspicion of treason; and on his own death-bed, immediately after his formal baptism by Eusebius, he dictated an order to another son to execute six members of his family whom he suspected of a conspiracy to poison him. That Constantine was but a nominal Christian is shown also by his coins. Many of these bear indeed on one side the name of Christus, but on the other they show the figure of the sun-god, with the inscription "Sol invictus." His latest coins show the sun-god standing before a solar cross, crowned with solar rays, and bearing in one hand the symbolic apple of life, whilst the other hand is raised in benediction in the well-known manner of the Catholic bishops. In the forum of his capital Constantine also placed a colossal statue of the sun-god, and decreed a weekly festival or day of rest, under the name of "Dies Solis." It seems evident that Constantine's Christianity was a simple matter of policy. The Roman Empire was made up of a number of different nationalities, each with a religion of its own. Constantine was shrewd enough to see that not only must all these religions be tolerated, but that the adoption of a state-religion would greatly help to weld the empire into a whole. He appears, therefore, to have selected Christianity because its catholic or universal character rendered it less likely to offend the religious instincts of the various nationalities than any other religion available.

Christian writers tell us that, as Constantine marched from Treves to Rome with his Gallic legions, he saw in the sky a vision of the Holy Cross. But we may take this as pure legend. Indeed, it seems doubtful whether at any time the Christian cross ever adorned his battle-standards. His Gallic legionaries, who were his most reliable soldiers, were sun-worshippers, and the emblem borne on their standards was the ancient sun-wheel, or sun-cross. The cross was indeed adopted about this time as the chief Christian symbol, instead of the fish, and is the most prominent instance of the practice of the Church to adopt and adapt any earlier emblem, ritual, or legend that seemed suited to its purpose. The cross, in fact, is quite one of the oldest symbols in the world, being the emblem of the sun's beneficent influence on life and of its apparent rotation in the sky. We find it engraved on pottery in the lake-dwellings of the later Stone Age in Central Europe, and on the breast of the god Khem, "the Generator," in early Egyptian monuments: we find it among the archaic ruins at Mykene and Hissarlik; and we know that it was symbolically used in India five hundred years before it was adopted as a Christian emblem. Long before it was used in Christian baptism, the cross was certainly traced on the foreheads of youthful Buddhists, and regarded, as Max Müller tells us, as "the emblem of life, health, and wealth."

Interesting as all the facts collated in this chapter undoubtedly are, they do not completely explain "the confusion of thought which," as Dean Stanley says, "Christianity produced." But at least they help to throw some light upon the confusion, and they give a suggestion of what may possibly have been the process of the evolution of Christian thought. The basis of the whole of this complex system of thought seems to be the beautiful Greek idea of the "Christos"—that spiritual light "which lighteth every man that cometh into the world," which light will lead the man who follows it, on an ever-ascending path, from the animal, through the human, up to the divine. But naturally, an idea so subtle was unfit for general acceptance, and therefore, one after the other, there were grafted on it other ideas. First, apparently, certain Jewish members of the Christian community materialised the spiritual idea of the Christos into a

Christ of flesh and blood, by adopting the familiar mythos of a divine incarnation in the person of a teacher, supposed to have been miraculously born of a virgin-mother. The second stage of the evolution seems to have been the revival of the idea, common to many of the earlier religions, of a Mediator or Divine Messenger between God and man, who passes continually between heaven and earth, and of whom till then, the sun had been the symbol. Of such mediators, we know at least of three postulated by Persian thinkers, and it is possible that the idea may have been borrowed from Persia. With this idea the Christian thinkers associated the Jewish idea of the coming of an earthly Messiah, and the earlier Jewish idea of the scapegoat who took upon him the sins of the whole community, and also the far more ancient idea of the corn- and wine-gods, who were slain for the good of the world. Then, not only much of the ethical teaching current at that epoch, but also many a legend, was adopted and adapted from Indian and other sources, and woven into the story of the life and teaching of the incarnated God, the mythical founder of the religion. Much ritual and symbolism was also gradually borrowed from older religions, and lastly perhaps, to make the new faith more popular with the unthinking many, the birth, death, and resurrection of the God-man were commemorated at the same time as the so-called birth, death, and resurrection of the sun, with which everyone was familiar. It was, possibly, in this way that the Christian festivals became in course of time as popular as the solar festivals, which they ultimately supplanted.

It cannot be denied that much confusion of thought was caused by Christianity; nor can it bc denied that the onward progress of thought was hindered during all the centuries in which the Church dominated men's minds. But, on the other hand, it must not be forgotten that, during the rough times which followed the break-up of the Roman Empire, it was only in the monasteries of the Christian Church that men of thought and culture in Europe could find a refuge.

CHAPTER X

THOUGHT IN WESTERN EUROPE

Of thought in Britain we have but little record until after the introduction of Christianity by Augustine, towards the end of the sixth century. From 55 B.C. to 410 A.D., when the Roman legions were recalled to save Italy from the Goths, Britain had been a province of the Roman Empire, with York as the centre of its government. The country people appear to have worshipped Thor and Woden, and to have retained their native language and customs, whilst the dwellers in the chief towns spoke Latin, and were more or less Romanised. Diodorus Siculus, writing in the latter half of the last century B.C., refers to a famous temple of Apollo, of which it is thought we see, to-day, the remains at Stonehenge, the great stone monoliths of which experts think were probably first erected as early as 1500 B.C. The Roman historian says: 'Hecateus and others assert that opposite the Celtic provinces there is an island, not less in size than Sicily, on which is a magnificent enclosed circle (temenos) of Apollo, and a famous temple of circular form, abundantly adorned with votive offerings." Pliny, writing in the first century A.D., says: "At this day Britain celebrates the magic rites with so many similar ceremonies, that one might suppose them to have been given them by the Persians"; whilst Strabo, in the second century A.D., says: "Ceres and Proserpine are venerated in an island close to Britain with rites similar to those of Samothrace." Speaking of the Druids in Britain, Julius Cæsar says: "They dispute largely concerning the power of the immortal gods, and instruct their youth in their doctrine. Of all the gods they most honour Mercury, whom they represent as the originator of the arts." Under whatever name he may have been invoked, there seems to be no doubt that the Druid temples in Britain were dedicated to the sun-god, or that the thirty great monoliths at Stonehenge symbolised the days of the month; whilst the "Circle of Revolution" (Caer Sidin), which measures 360 paces in circumference, symbolised the course of the sun through the zodiac. At the festival called "Nollig" in Celtic, "Nolach" in old Irish, and "Noel" in modern French, great fires were lighted on the mountain-tops to celebrate the annual rebirth of the sun. The deity who was worshipped as the active principle in nature was invoked in Celtic as "Æsar," a name which is not only suggestive of the Greek and Latin "Æther," but curiously resembles the Sanskrit "Æswar." We read in the Bhagavad Gîtâ that "Æswar by his magic power puts in motion all things which circle in the wheel of time." The worship of Hu, the chief deity of the Druids, who seems to be identical with Apollo, the sun-god, was always associated with that of the goddess Kêd, or Ceridwen, who has all the attributes of Isis and Ceres. The sun was the symbol of the god Hu, whilst the moon and an ear of wheat were the symbols of the goddess Ceridwen, as many ancient British coins show. Davies tells us that there is authentic proof that the mysteries of Ceridwen were celebrated in Wales as late as the middle of the twelfth century, and that Hywel, son of Owen Gwynedd, Prince of North Wales, who died in 1171, was an initiate of these mysteries. Our knowledge of early British thought in general and of the mysteries of Ceridwen in particular is derived chiefly from fragments of the songs of three bards, named Taleisin, Aneurin, and Merdiner, the last being best known by his modernised name, Merlin, who lived in the sixth century A.D. In these poems the god Hu is described as "riding on the sunbeams. . . . The smallest of the small is Hu, the mighty in the world's judgment, yet is he the greatest and Lord over us. . . . Our God of mystery. His course is swift and light, his chariot is a particle of lucid sunshine." Hu is also called "the ethereal One who has for his girdle the rainbow," also "the gliding King, presiding over the earthly circle of stones." Two of the poems, known respectively as the "Great Song of the World" and the "Little Song of the World," are quite Pythagorean and socialistic in character. "All men," says the bard, "are born free, therefore no man has the right to assume authority over his fellows. . . . All things not produced by human art are the common property of all." From even these few specimens of early British thought it may be assumed that it was in a fairly advanced state at the time when Christianity was first established in Britain by the baptism of Æthelbert by Augustine, in 598 A.D. From that time onward during many centuries the only records of thought come to us from the monasteries of the Catholic Church. About the middle of the ninth century an Irish monk, John Scotus Erigena, not only dared to think for himself, but published his thoughts in an essay, entitled *De Divisione Naturæ*. In this Erigena maintains the pantheistic thesis that "God is everything, and everything is God." God, he says, is a mystery, and can be but faintly indicated by such words as Truth, Light, Goodness; and the human soul is equally a mystery, because it is identical with God. From God emanates the universe as light emanates from the sun: creation is a continuous process, of which we can imagine neither the beginning nor the end. In his ethical teaching Erigena urges us to follow virtue, which will lead us at last to the "vision of God," but wrong doing and wrong living is "hell," which is best defined as "remorse." There is nothing to show that Erigena in any way suffered for such bold and unorthodox views during his lifetime, although we find that, long after he was dead, his works were declared in Paris, in 1209, to be heretical.

Anselmus of Aosta, who died Archbishop of Canterbury in 1109, is the next thinker after Erigena who stands out from among his fellow-monks. In his *Monologium* Anselmus speaks of God as "the most real entity" (ens realissimum) and the causeless cause of all. God, he says, is eternal Truth, Justice, and Goodness; nevertheless all the qualities attributed to God are mere figures of speech. Anselmus adopts the Platonic theory that all things existed as "ideas" from all eternity, but, like a good churchman, he teaches that God created the universe "out of nothing" (ex nihilo).

Platonic thought was now once more beginning to stir men's minds, and Pierre Abelard of Nantes, a monk of the Abbey of St Denis, dared even to assert that the ethics of Plato are more in harmony with true religion than the ethics of Moses, and that the lives and teaching of the Greek sages are "truly evangelic and apostolic." Abelard teaches also that we should not call the natural impulses which prompt us to self-indulgence sinful, because, unless we had these impulses, we could not evolve virtue by resisting them. The sinful desire is as bad as the sinful act, for the real sin consists in the wish to indulge an evil passion, even if it be not actually consummated. Abelard also published a treatise on the Trinity, which was publicly burnt in 1122 by order of the Church-Council of Soissons, because it maintained the theory that the Holy Trinity consists simply in Power, Wisdom, and Goodness, which together make up the "tota perfectio boni." All the divine acts, he maintains, are acts of necessity. God, being the ultimate cause, "in whom we live and move and have our being," must necessarily be the cause of man's thoughts and man's actions: God, in fact, acts through man. For such heretical doctrines Abelard was imprisoned in 1140, and died two years afterwards.

It was at about this time that the remarkable commentaries on the philosophy of Aristotle written by Ibn Roshd of Cordova, whom Dante compared to the old Greek sages, and who is better known to us as "Averroes," were being studied at the universities of Padua and Bologna. Other Arabian scholars were employed by Roger, King of Sicily, and Frederick II., Emperor of Germany, to translate the works of Aristotle into Latin, and copies of these translations were presented to the universities of Paris and Oxford. Many treatises were also written on the *Metaphysics* of Aristotle by the monk Thomas Aquinas, and thus the thoughts of this thinker gradually became once more current.

In 1267 the Franciscan monk, Roger Bacon, at that time lecturer at the University of Oxford, published his *Opus Majus*, in which he recorded the result of his scientific researches during twenty years. This caused Bacon to be condemned by the ecclesiastical authorities to twelve years' imprisonment for unorthodox free-thought, and he died two years after his release from prison.

Duns Scotus of Northumberland, another Franciscan monk, lectured on theology at Oxford in 1301, and at Paris in 1304, with the aim of proving by logic the truth of the holy faith of the Catholic Church. But in this he failed, because all his arguments were founded on the theory that all thought is free. Ecclesiastical influence was greatly weakened by the influx into Florence, in the middle of the fifteenth century, of large numbers of Greek thinkers, who fled from Constantinople when that city was taken by the Turks. But perhaps the greatest blow was struck against the tyranny which the Church at this time exercised over men's minds, when, in 1543, Copernicus dared to demonstrate the discovery that the earth is not the centre of the universe, as till then had been assumed, but a mere planet, circling round the sun. Copernicus died shortly afterwards, and thus escaped the censure of the Church. But when Galileo, a generation later, ventured to publish the further discovery that the earth also revolved on its own axis, he was threatened with death by burning unless he recanted this heretical doctrine.

Nevertheless, the new heliocentric system was so enthusiastically accepted by the Dominican monk, Giordano Bruno, born in 1548 at Nola, near Naples, that he had the courage publicly to lecture on it successively at Venice, Brescia, Milan, Geneva, Lyons, Toulouse, and Paris. Henri III. offered Bruno a chair at the Paris University, and it was to him that Bruno dedicated the very unorthodox treatise which he called *Shadows of Ideas* (De umbris idearum). Soon after this, with a letter from the French king recommending him to Michael Castellan, his ambassador at the court of Elizabeth, Bruno went to England. During his stay—from 1583 to 1585—he lectured at Oxford on "The Rotation of the Earth," and on "The Endless Evolution of Nature," with the result that the university condemned his teaching as heretical. Nothing daunted, Bruno, on his return to London, published a still more unorthodox treatise on cosmogony, entitled *Del infinito Universo e dei Mondi*. In this he advances the theory that the earth is a living organism (organum), that all that exists is but a manifestation of the One Life, and that the stars are probably inhabited by beings of a higher order than men. In another treatise, which he calls *Della Causa principio et uno*, Bruno maintains the idea that "the Universal Soul" is the one creative force from which all proceeds and to which all reverts. Returning to Paris, Bruno, in his lectures at the Sorbonne, upheld still more emphatically the teaching of Copernicus, and showed how contrary to science are many theories advanced by Aristotle, whose philosophy had by this time been accepted by the Catholic Church. For this he was driven from France by the ecclesiastical power, and for two years Bruno lectured at the University of Wittenberg, and then passed on to Prague, where he dedicated to the Emperor Rudolph his essay *Against the Philosophy and Mathematicians of to-day.* At Frankfort on the Main, Bruno published his work on *Monads*, and then he had the temerity to go once more to Venice, where he was at once thrown into prison by the Holy Inquisition, and after two years' captivity was burnt at the stake for heretical teaching, "in the year of our Lord" 1600.

Bruno teaches that life is a rhythmical whole, of which the higher forms evolve naturally from the lower, the Infinite Being thus unfolding itself in innumerable genera, species and individuals. God is in all things, all things are in God, and have life because of God's real presence everywhere in the universe. Bruno sometimes speaks of God as synonymous with matter. Matter, he maintains, is immaterial in its essence and the origin of all things: it contains the germs of all forms, and evolves them all in succession. Things change their forms, but essentially they are the same. For instance, a grain of wheat, put into the ground, becomes an ear of corn, then bread, which, eaten by animal or man, passes successively through the phases of chyle, blood, semen, embryo, and animal, and in due course returns again to earth. In all these changes of form, essential matter is practically the same, because it is eternal. Death is no more than change, caused by the recombination of the elements of other combinations that are dissolved. The highest evolution of universal life is the human soul, which, however, is produced from universal substance by the same agency as the plant is produced from seed. All things are living monads, each, after its own nature, reproducing God, the Monad of monads. The variety of forms assumed by universal substance are due to the differentiating force, which Bruno calls "Dyas," existing within the monads. Dyas, he says, has two poles, positive and negative. The expansive force of the monads evolves body, the concentrative force of the monads evolves the mind, and life lasts as long as this double movement of expansion and contraction continues. God is the primal idea of which the world is the reflection or shadow. Man is able to harmonise with nature just because man is an integral portion of the divine. God is the source of all light—physical or mental. But man's mind cannot bear the brilliance of the pure light of truth, which therefore must be veiled in shadows or symbols. Christ is the spiritual light, the

Logos of God; Christ mediates indeed between God and man, but is not the materialised God taught by the Church.

In 1605, five years after the martyrdom of Bruno, appeared the English translation from the Latin of Francis Bacon's remarkable work, the *Novum Organon Scientiarum.* Bacon chose this title because the collected treatises of Aristotle (with many of whose methods and theories Bacon disagreed) had been called the "Organon (Instrument)." The Scholastics, says Bacon, dispute about words instead of trying to understand things. They begin by assuming final causes, which are purely the products of their own imagination, and thus they confuse science with theology. But, if we desire scientific truth, we must forget all these scholastic traditions, and must work on the experimental and deductive system. It is useless, moreover, merely to enumerate a number of facts, or to imagine that any useful conclusion can be drawn from the observance of a few facts only. But we must study facts with great care and patience, until, little by little, we are able to discover laws. "We must not stop at actual discoveries, nor, with careless grasp, catch at shadows and abstract forms," because we shall inevitably find that "peculiar abstract opinions on nature and the principles of things are not of much importance to men's fortunes."

Bacon's younger contemporary and friend, Thomas Hobbes, looks at things from Bacon's point of view. After a residence of thirteen years in France, he published his first work on philosophy in 1642, defining philosophy to be "the reasoned knowledge of effects from causes and causes from effects." To philosophise, he says, is simply to "think correctly," whilst to think "is to compound and resolve conceptions." Perception being altogether subjective, he argues that the apparent objectivity of phenomena must be an illusion. For instance, light is not an external object, it is not a thing perceived, but it is a motion, or a modification, which takes place in the brain of the perceiver. As a proof of this, Hobbes instances that a smart blow struck on the eye excites the optic nerve and produces the *effect* of light. Thus, it is a mere illusion of our senses which leads us to imagine that either light, colour, or sound exists outside us. There is, he thinks, no fundamental distinction between matter and spirit. He says: "By spirit I understand a physical body refined enough to escape the observation of the senses. An incorporeal spirit does not exist." Nor will he allow that there is such a thing as free-will. It is true that "a voluntary action is that which proceedeth from the will," but it is no less true that willing itself is not voluntary, because there must be "a sufficient reason" for every act. Without sufficient reason there is no act, and sufficient reason is the same as "necessity." All men are subject to necessity, which, if we like, we may call "the Will of God." Hobbes maintains that good and evil are relative ideas only, and that absolute good, absolute evil, absolute justice are mere empty phrases coined by theologians and metaphysicians.

René des Cartes, born in 1596 in Touraine, was educated by the Jesuits of La Flèche, and, after serving as a lieutenant in the army of the German emperor, retired to Amsterdam, where, in 1650, he published his first work on philosophy. In all his writings the influence of his early training is apparent. Des Cartes loves to systematise, to start from axioms and definitions, and to reach results as rapidly as possible. He was also most anxious to say nothing unorthodox. Very likely he was thinking of the price which Bruno had to pay, half a century earlier, for daring to differ from Holy Church, when we find him, in the preface to his chief work, addressing the Theological Faculty of the Sorbonne in these words: "Whatever force my reasons may possess, because they belong to philosophy, I have no hope that they will influence men's minds unless you take them under your protection, your Faculty being held in so great esteem, and the name of the Sorbonne having such authority."

Like St Augustine before him, Des Cartes founds his philosophy on doubt. He begins his arguments with the assumption that one thing at least is certain —that he doubts! and then he goes on: "To doubt is to think. Therefore I think." He could not think, he argues, if he did not exist; therefore, the fact that he is able to think is sufficient proof of his existence; and so Des Cartes formulates his well-known axiom, "Cogito, ergo sum" (I think, therefore I exist). After this start, he goes on to ask, Is thought subjective, or objective? Are the objects of our thoughts within us or without? Whilst he is considering this question, it occurs to Des Cartes that one thought at least must come to him from without, namely, the idea of God. He argues that his mind is finite and limited, and that, as a limited cause cannot produce an unlimited effect, his finite mind could not possibly conceive the existence of an infinite God, and therefore that the idea of God could only have been implanted in his mind by God himself. In this easy way Des Cartes succeeds in proving, to his own satisfaction, his own existence and the existence of God. And he says that, instead of saying that God exists because our mind conceives Him, we ought rather to say that we conceive God because He exists, and because God reveals Himself to us in our *innate idea* of infinity. Then Des Cartes defines God as "the Infinite Substance, on which everything depends, and which Itself depends on nothing, and which needs no other thing in order to exist"; and then he proceeds to demonstrate the existence of the "corporeal world."

Nature, say Des Cartes, often deceives us. We are deceived by the apparent rising and setting of the sun, and may therefore be deceived when we assume the reality of all the things which are perceived by our senses. Our idea of an external world might well be an illusion of the mind unless we had the idea of God. But, God's existence being proved, it follows that the world also exists, "because God is the creator of all things and, being a perfect Being, is incapable of deceiving me." Such are the arguments which seem sufficient to Des Cartes to prove the existence of what he calls "the three realities"—the ego, the universe, and God. God, "needing no other thing in order to exist," he calls

"Infinite Substance," the universe and the bodies in it "extended substance," and the human soul "thinking substance." But his theory is that soul and body are entirely opposed to each other, and therefore no real union between them is possible. "Those," he says, "who never philosophise, and only use their senses, have no doubt that the soul moves the body and that the body acts upon the soul." This, he maintains, is not so, although in his treatise on the Passions, published at Amsterdam in 1650, he expresses the opinion that not only is the soul united to all parts of the body, but that soul and body act upon each other through the medium of the "pineal gland" and the "animal spirits."

Half a century after the Catholic Church had burnt Bruno for his heretical teaching, another free-thinker, Baruch de Spinoza, a Portuguese Jew, living at Amsterdam, and better known to us as Benedict Spinoza, bravely carried forward the attempt to emancipate thought. In his treatise on the Jewish scriptures, Spinoza shows that they have been compiled after the time when Alexander the Great reigned in Babylon, and that the so-called Psalms of King David, and much of the prophetical writings, are composed of fragments put together without any chronological order. He also points out that the writings of Ezekiel were only declared to be canonical by the Great Synagogue after they had been carefully edited and remodelled. The Jewish rabbi at Amsterdam naturally objected to such heretical teaching, and accused Spinoza of impiety. "What!" he cries, "our knowledge of God to depend upon perishable things . . . such as the first tablets of stone, which Moses can dash to the ground and break to pieces, or of which the originals can be lost, . . . which can come to us confused, imperfect, mis-written by copyists, tampered with by doctors! And you accuse others of impiety! It is *you* who are impious to believe that God would commit the treasure of the true record of Himself to any substance less enduring than the heart." Such language could not, of course, be tolerated by the orthodox, and consequently Spinoza was "placed in anathema" by the synagogue of Amsterdam, in the year 1656, with these words: "We anathematise, execrate, curse, and cast out Baruch de Spinoza, the entire Holy Community assenting, . . . pronouncing against him the maledictions written in the Book of the Law." Therefore, from that time Spinoza signed his name "Benedict" instead of "Baruch," and retired to the Hague, where he lived a most abstemious life, supporting himself by his skill in grinding and polishing lenses, until his death in 1677, at the early age of forty-four.

Spinoza's chief work, the *Ethics* (Ethica more geometrico demonstrata), was first published by his friends after his death. The postulate on which his whole philosophy is based is the eternal imperishability of substance. He says: "I understand by 'Substance' that which is self-contained, the conception of which requires the conception of no other thing whence it has to be derived. . . . The absolutely infinite entity or being which I designate 'Substance' is to be defined as constituted by an infinity of attributes, each of which expresses an eternal and infinite essence, existing necessarily. . . . Substance is not manifold, or multiple, but exists singly, and is ever one and the same nature. . . . Beyond it there is and there can be neither essence nor existence. Thus it accords most exactly with the essence of the alone supreme God. . . . All things are in God, and all that happens, happens in accordance with the laws of the infinite God of nature alone, following from the necessity of his essence. . . . In the human sense of the words, neither understanding nor will pertains to God." Spinoza speaks of God regarded as the "Free Cause of all that is," as "active nature" (natura naturans), whilst "all that follows from the necessity of the divine nature" he calls "natura naturata" (passive nature). All this train of thought is summed up by Spinoza in his phrase, "Substantia sive Deus." As Substance and God are one, so are mind and body "one and the same thing, conceived now under the attribute of thought, now under that of extension." And the "human soul or mind" is also part of nature, "inasmuch as I hold," says Spinoza, "that in nature there is inherent an infinite power of thought." There is no such thing as freedom of will: "men deceive themselves when they suppose that they are free." We are conscious of our acts, but not of the causes by which our acts are determined. "The idea of freedom comes, therefore, of men not knowing the causes of their acts." Some causes are adequate, whilst other causes are inadequate. "An adequate cause is that, the effect of which can be distinctly perceived through it; an inadequate cause is that, of which the cause cannot be understood through it alone." The mind may be said "to act" only "so far as it has adequate ideas," whilst it "in some way necessarily suffers" so far as it has "inadequate ideas." Spinoza thinks that "the passions depend upon inadequate ideas alone," and that what we describe as "appetite, desire, will, impulse, or emotion" are all one and the same thing. "Desire is the very essence of human nature, in other words, of the effort man makes to continue in his state of being." There is "nothing of a positive nature" in good or evil "as applied to things considered in themselves," because the same thing may be both good and evil: "a thing is necessarily good, as far as it accords with our own nature." All men are of the same essential nature. Therefore those of us who live "under the rule of reason," or, in other words, "by the laws of his own nature," desire "nothing for themselves which they do not desire for others," because "the highest joy of those who live virtuously is to know God, in other words, to enjoy a good common to all. . . . The self-content alone which springs from reason is the highest that is possible. . . . Beatitude is not the reward of virtue, but virtue itself; nor do we enjoy true happiness because we restrain our lusts; on the contrary, it is because we enjoy true happiness that we are able to restrain our lusts. . . . The wise man scarcely knows what mental perturbation is, but, conscious of himself, of God, and of that special, eternal necessity of things, never ceases from being, but is always in possession of true peace of mind."

Spinoza had been dead thirteen years when John

Locke published, in 1690, his *Essay concerning Human Understanding*. In this he maintains, in direct opposition to Des Cartes, that we have no "innate ideas" at all. All thought may be traced back to sensation more or less directly, and, "when we examine it closely," much of our assumed knowledge turns out to be nothing more than "probable presumption." Locke points out how early a child's mind may be impressed in any way its teachers choose, with the result that, later on, when children "so instructed" come to have the power to reflect and reason, "they cannot find anything more ancient in their minds than those opinions, and therefore they imagine (like Des Cartes) those propositions are the impress of God and nature, and not things taught them." All these "ancient preoccupations of our minds are to be examined, if we would make way for truth," because we can no more "know by another man's understanding," than we can "see by another man's eyes."

All our knowledge of external things comes to us from sensation, all other knowledge comes from reflection. All ideas are derived either from one source or the other: no ideas are innate. "Even the most abstruse ideas, how remote soever they may seem from the senses, and the operations of our minds, are yet no other than what the mind may and does attain by the ordinary use of its faculties." Then Locke classifies all ideas as either "simple or complex," and explains "simple" ideas to be such as the ideas which we have of "light, heat, softness, hardness, etc." The mind, he says, is a mirror, which must reflect, without alteration, any simple idea presented to it by the senses. In doing this, it is in a passive state, but becomes active when it compares, unites, repeats simple ideas, and by so doing forms "complex ideas" in endless variety. The functions of the mind brought into play in forming complex ideas are classified by Locke as "perception, retention, comparison, composition, and abstraction." Retention, however, is a twofold faculty of the mind. It has the power to keep before the mind for a time the ideas derived from sensation: this we call "contemplation"; and it has also the power to revive and recall ideas once impressed upon the mind; this we term "memory." The power of abstraction is that which most differentiates the human mind from the mind of an animal.

We observe that a series of simple ideas, imprinted by the senses on the mind, always come together, when we form complex ideas, such as those of a man, horse, tree, sun; and thus we come to think of such a group of ideas as a thing in itself and give it a name. Thus, what we call "the sun" is the aggregate of the ideas of light, heat, roundness, and regular motion. But, if we consider the sun, or anything else, as a "thing in itself," or a "substance," not merely as a combination of qualities, we must admit that it is nothing more than our own "idea" of it, and that we have no real knowledge of it. Locke therefore concludes that "the idea of corporeal substance, or matter, is as remote from our apprehension as that of spiritual substance, or spirit." Such ideas also as those of infinite space, eternity, or immortality are at best "negative." Our notion of infinite space, for instance, is due to the power of the mind to "extend its idea of space by an endless number of new additions": it is not a "positive" idea at all. "Species" and "genera," again, are mere names for things that have no real existence. But how then, it may be asked, do we get general ideas such as these? and Locke explains that, to begin with, we have no general ideas at all. All our ideas are particular. As an instance of this, the only idea a young child has of such things as a mother or a father, are his particular mother and father. But by degrees the little child perceives that there are other beings similar to his own parents, and thus the general idea of fathers and mothers is evolved in his mind. To put it differently, the child *abstracts* from his original idea of mother or father all the particular qualities characteristic of his own parents. We understand how very valuable this power of abstraction is, when we reflect that it would be impossible for the mind to retain *distinct* ideas of *all* that it perceives. It being then evident that all abstract or general ideas are pure creations of the mind, Locke points out that genera, species, and essences all "appear upon a more wary survey to be nothing but an artifice of the understanding" and to have no real existence in the organic world, in spite of the imagination of "philosophers who mistake words for things."

There are indeed cases, says Locke, in which we are able to "perceive a truth as the eye doth light, only by being directed to it by bare intuition." All knowledge of this kind is "irresistible, and leaves no room for doubt or examination, but the mind is presently filled with the clear light of it." Locke calls this "common sense," the faculty which enables us intuitively to perceive such facts as that three are more than two, and equal to one and two.

All that Locke ventures to say about the idea of immortality is that "it seems probable that there should be some better state somewhere else, to which men might arise, since, when one hath all that this world can afford, he is still unsatisfied."

Locke bases his conception of a Supreme Mind, very much as Des Cartes does, on his perception of his own existence as a self-conscious being. He says: "We cannot want a clear proof of God, as long as we carry ourselves about with us," because mind "can be explained only by Mind." But he adds: "Though I call the thinking faculty in man, mind, yet I cannot, because of this name, equal it in anything to that infinite and incomparable Being, which, for want of right and distinct conception, is called 'the Eternal Mind.'" Nevertheless, Locke will not deny that the only thing we can do, "when we would frame an idea, the most suitable we can, for the Supreme Being," is to "enlarge every one of our simple ideas with our idea of infinity," and unite them into "our complex idea of God," because it is impossible for us to have any other "idea of God but a complex one of existence, knowledge, power, happiness—infinite and eternal."

Gottfried Wilhelm Leibniz, when librarian to the Duke of Hanover, published in 1714 his work on atoms or monads, entitled *La Monadologie*, which he says combines "whatever is good in the hypotheses of Epicurus and Plato." Leibniz starts with the dictum that extension and resistance are the chief characteristics of matter. Extension is only an abstraction, however, which presupposes something which extends, whereas, everywhere throughout the universe, we are conscious of force or action. We see the effects produced by this force on matter, but force itself is something hidden and immaterial. This idea somehow leads Leibniz to his paradoxical theory that matter itself is immaterial, by which he, as it were, obliterates the difference between the material and the immaterial worlds. Force, he maintains, is not an entity, as Spinoza's *Substantia sive Deus* assumes it to be; but we see active force in all things, therefore everything must be itself a centre of force. Consequently Leibniz advances the theory that the universe is made up of an infinite number of infinitesimal "points of substance," or "monads." These monads have no visible extension, and therefore they may be thought of as "metaphysical points," although each monad is a self-acting entity, having, in however slight degree, perceptive power or soul. No monad, however, can perceive anything but itself, or, as Leibniz picturesquely says, the monads "have no windows." The monads imagined by Leibniz are consequently quite unconscious. Even we, who are the highest of all monads, can perceive nothing but our own being: what we think of as the outside world is nothing but "the involuntary projection of what takes place within ourselves." So that we may call each monad "a microcosm of the macrocosm," reproducing in miniature what occurs outside it. There are, however, monads and monads, and the lower monads group themselves around the higher, which is, as it were, "the soul" of plant, animal, or man. The reason why a man has notions of the world outside so much more distinct than an animal, is because the human monad, or soul, *is* itself so much more complete an image of the universe. In inorganic bodies, such as rocks and liquids, there is no "higher monad." Therefore, all the monads forming such aggregates being equal and of like nature, they only hold each other in equilibrium in the "inanimate mass" of matter.

After postulating this theory of the grouping of lower monads around the higher, Leibniz might be expected to make some suggestion as to the interaction of soul and body. But he only says that the monads "have no windows," and therefore that neither sensation nor experience can be imagined to pass from one to another. Each higher monad, like the lower, is itself *both soul and body*. The question then arises, How can we move our limbs by an act of will if no communication can pass from the higher monad to the lower monads grouped around it? But all Leibniz can say in explanation is, that the lower monads act in accordance with the higher monads, because of "a pre-established harmony," like "well-regulated clocks." So complete, indeed, does he imagine this pre-established harmony to be, that there is no need for any intervention of a creator in the working of the universal machinery. "Mr Newton," he says, "and his followers have a curious opinion of God and His work. According to them, God must wind up His watch from time to time, otherwise it would cease to go, because He had not insight enough to make it go for ever." The pre-established harmony is so complete that each soul may be said to build up its own body, each monad being, "as it were, a little divinity in its own department." The monads are all at least "as old as the universe," but the higher monads are unconscious until they are surrounded by the lower monads which ultimately form their bodies. The "primitive units," or monads, "are born, so to speak, from moment to moment by continual fulgurations of the Divinity" in "the original simple substance" of the universe.

This "Divinity" is imagined as distinct from the universe and as "the sufficient reason for its existence." Our idea of God, "the Monad of monads," must necessarily be, at first, but confused and contradictory, just as a plant can have—if any—but a confused perception of an animal, or an animal a confused perception of a man. Then, after saying this, Leibniz, like any other theologian, sets about an elaborate definition of the nature and attributes of God.

To understand thoroughly the point of view which Dr Berkeley maintains in his *Treatise on the Principles of Human Knowledge*, which was published in Dublin in 1709, a few years before the *Monadology* of Leibniz, we must remember that, like his German contemporary, Berkeley was an enthusiastic theologian, and that he hoped to stem and confound the sceptical thought of the time, by proving that unperceived and unperceiving matter, or substance, with all the mysterious forces latent in it, has no real tangible existence. Just then, the Archbishop of Dublin was liberal-minded enough to admit that, "strictly speaking, goodness and understanding can no more be assumed of God than that He has feet and hands." But, in direct opposition to his Archbishop, Berkeley maintained that "God is an understanding, wise, and benevolent Being in the strict and literal and proper meaning of these words," and that the very existence of the world around us is a proof of the existence of this "wise and benevolent Being." And, after this, Berkeley does his best to prove that nature is nothing but an unsubstantial show, the mere creation of man's brain, and that nothing exists unless it is perceived.

Berkeley founds his philosophy on Platonism. "The Pythagoreans and Platonists had a notion," he says, "of the true system of the world." . . . "They saw that a mind, infinite in power, unextended, invisible, and immortal, governed, connected, and contained all things. They saw there was no such thing as real absolute space: that mind, soul, or spirit really existed: that bodies exist only in a secondary and dependent sense: that the soul is the place of form." From Neo-Platonism also Berkeley borrows some ideas. He says: "Plotinus acknowledgeth no place but soul, or mind, expressly affirming that the soul is not in the world, but the world in the soul. And farther, the place of the soul, saith he, is not body, but soul is in mind, and body in soul." Therefore Berkeley will not accept Locke's theory that substance is a combination of primary qualities that exist outside us and secondary qualities that have existence only in our sensations, but he maintains that nothing whatever exists outside the perceiving mind, and that all existence consists in perceiving and being perceived.

A friend puts the doctor in a corner by writing to ask: " If there be nothing but spirit and ideas, what make you of that part of the six days' creation that preceded man ? " and all Berkeley can find to say is: " I do not deny the existence of the sensible things which Moses says were created by God. They existed from all eternity in the Divine Intellect, and they became perceptible in the same manner as described in Genesis." Then Berkeley, the thinker, feels that Berkeley, the theologian, cannot quite shelter himself behind Moses, and so suggests that, even if there were not then human minds on earth to see the things created before man, " 'tis possible that other spirits besides man might have perceived this visible world, as it was successively exhibited to their view before man's creation." When we read, however, that " corporeal substance " is carefully defined by Berkeley as " a combination of *sensible* qualities, such as extension, solidity, weight, and the like," we are inclined to ask whether Berkeley himself quite understood what he did mean.

He is most emphatic in denying the existence of any such thing as " abstract substance," and asserts that " abstract ideas " cannot be formed by the mind. " Abstract ideas," he says, are " a fine, subtle net which has miserably entangled the minds of men." His argument is, that " qualities or modes of things do never really exist, each of them apart by itself," and that, for instance, we cannot conceive "the idea of colour exclusive of extension, or of motion exclusive both of extension and colour." We are told, says Berkeley, that the mind makes itself "an idea of colour in the abstract which is neither red, nor blue, nor white, nor any other determinate colour," by retaining only "that which is common to all colours," and also that "by considering motion abstractedly . . . the abstract idea of motion is framed; . . . and, after this manner, we come to the abstract idea of man, or if you please humanity, or human nature." But Berkeley insists that, though he "can imagine a man with two heads, or the upper part of a man joined to the body of a horse," he "cannot by any effort of thought conceive the abstract idea of a man," any more than he can "form the abstract idea of motion distinct from a body moving." Such a simple idea as a triangle in the abstract, which most of us think of merely as a flat space bounded by three straight lines, which may be of equal or unequal length, is mystified by Berkeley as being necessarily "neither oblique, nor rectangle, neither equilateral, equicrural, nor scalenon, but *all and none* of these, at once."

Replying to an imaginary objection that the sun, moon, and stars cannot be mere "apparitions of the mind," because we certainly see them a long way *outside* us, Berkeley says that the mere sense of sight "does not suggest nor in any way inform you, that the visible object you immediately perceive exists at a distance." On the contrary, "the *outwardness* of things is unintelligible, apart from the experience we have . . . when we touch them." We do not see distant things, but we only "*fore-see*" them, for the things we think we see at a distance are merely signs of the coming sensation of touch. "Seeing becomes predicting," because all that we see outside us is nothing but so many "signs and ideas of God."

David Hume, whom Kant recognised as one of the clearest thinkers of his time, published his *Enquiry concerning the Human Understanding* in 1748. The system of Des Cartes, is, he says, "scepticism antecedent to all study"; it is, in fact, a scepticism which not only doubts our principles, but the very faculties which are the only means by which it is possible for us to "arrive at a conviction on any subject." Berkeley's attempt to explain away the very existence of the material world strikes Hume as being absurd, because, "by a natural instinct, and without any reasoning, or almost before the use of reason, we suppose an external universe which depends not on our own perception, but would exist though we and every sensible creature were absent."

If, however, we consider the world we live in merely from a metaphysical point of view, we may say that the images which are formed in the mind under the stimulus of the senses are nothing more than representations of external objects. But how can this possibly do away with the objects themselves? "This very table which we see white, and which we feel hard, is believed to exist independently of our perception, and to be something external to our mind which perceives it. Our presence bestows not being on it: our absence does not annihilate it." And yet some philosophers pretend that nothing exists beyond an *image* of the table which our senses of sight and touch enable us to perceive, and as a proof of their assertion they point out that "the table which we see seems to diminish as we remove farther from it." This is true enough, Hume replies; it does seem to get smaller; but the real table which exists independent of us "suffers no alteration." Speaking, of course, merely from the metaphysical standpoint, "when we say 'this house,' or 'that tree,' we speak of nothing but perceptions in our minds," which perceptions we may certainly call "fleeting re-presentations"; but that does not alter the fact that the actual tree and the actual house "remain uniform and independent of our perception of them." Hume is greatly amused by such "curious researches" as these, by which "a philosopher" may "throw himself or others into a momentary amazement and confusion"; but he predicts that all such "profound reasonings" will vanish before the most trivial events of actual life, so that, when the philosopher "awakes from his dream, he will be the first to join in the laugh against himself." In this life, he says, we have all to "act and reason and believe, though by our most diligent enquiry we are unable to satisfy ourselves concerning the foundations of these operations." And when Dr Berkeley argues that there is no material world at all, and that all we think we see is only an idea of God, Hume reminds him that he forgets that, "if the external world be once called in question, we shall be at a loss to find arguments by which we may prove the existence of the Supreme Being."

Nor is Hume satisfied with Locke's classification of primary and secondary qualities, and he observes that, when "Mr Locke maintained that all sensible qualities of objects, such as hard, soft, hot, cold, white, black, etc., are merely secondary qualities, and exist not in the objects themselves, but are perceptions of the mind," he quite lost sight of the fact that our ideas of what he calls "the primary qualities of extension and solidity are entirely acquired from the senses of sight and feeling." Therefore, Locke cannot say that solidity and extension are more "primary" than hard, soft, cold, hot, white, etc., if, at the same time, he maintains the theory that "all the qualities perceived by the senses are in the mind, not in the object."

By his annihilation of matter Berkeley "leaves only a certain inexplicable something" as the sole cause of our perceptions; therefore he should not suggest that we get our ideas of primary qualities by means of abstraction, especially after condemning all abstract ideas as "unintelligible and even absurd." Hume defines perceptions as being more or less lively or vivid. Everyone, he says, will admit that when he actually feels the pleasure of genial warmth or the pain of intense heat "the perception of his mind" is quite different from that which he gets when he afterwards recalls these sensations by memory, or when he anticipates them by imagination. The utmost that either memory or imagination can do, is to "represent their object in so lively a manner that we could *almost* say we feel or see it." But we all know that "the most lively thought is still inferior to the dullest sensation." Thought can, at best, mirror sensation, but its images are faint compared to the original sensation. The more lively perceptions or sensations, therefore, are classed by Hume as "impressions," and the less lively perceptions as "thoughts, or ideas," and it is when we "see, hear, feel, desire, will, love, or hate" that we have the more forcible perceptions or "impressions."

So great is the power of thought that we sometimes say it is "unbounded." It can indeed transport us, in an instant, "to the most remote regions of the universe," or even beyond, so that we can conceive things never seen or heard. But Hume points out that the actual limits, within which thought works, are very narrow, and that, in truth, "the creative faculty of the mind amounts to no more than the faculty of compounding, transposing, augmenting, or diminishing the materials afforded us by the senses and experience. . . . When we analyse our thoughts and ideas, however compounded or sublime, we always find they resolve themselves into such simple ideas as were copied from a precedent feeling or sentiment. Even those ideas which, at first view, seem most wide of this origin, are found upon a nearer scrutiny to be derived from it." For instance, "the idea of God, as meaning an infinitely intelligent, wise, and good Being, arises from *reflecting* on the operations of our own mind, and augmenting, without limit, those qualities." Thoughts and ideas are "less lively perceptions"; but the least lively are our abstract ideas. If we distinguish, as we should, between impressions and ideas, and "if we understand by innate what is original," in other words, not copied from any "*precedent* perception, then we may assert, that all our *impressions* are innate, and our *ideas* not innate."

One of the most important studies connected with any inquiry into human understanding Hume considers to be that of the "Association of Ideas," because, "even in our freest talk, or in our wildest reveries," our thoughts are always connected in one of three ways, either by resemblance, by contiguity (in time or place), or by cause and effect. For instance: "A picture naturally leads our thoughts to the original (resemblance). The mention of an apartment in a building, naturally introduces an inquiry or discourse concerning others (contiguity). If we think of a wound, we can scarcely forbear reflecting on the pain which follows it (cause and effect)."

Various theories concerning cause and effect had been much discussed about this time. Hume's theory is that our idea of cause and effect "arises entirely from experience." He explains that "all arguments from experience are in reality founded on the *similarity* which we discover among natural objects, and by which we are induced to expect effects similar to those which we have found to follow such objects." We are quite unable to draw any inference concerning matters of fact unless we are aided by experience, although we are accustomed to think that we can, because "no effect is discoverable in what we call its cause." Who, for instance, asks Hume, would "infer from its fluidity and transparency, that water would suffocate him? or, from its light and warmth, that fire would consume him?" Or, what is there to tell us beforehand that, when one billiard-ball strikes another, it will communicate to it its own motion? "No reasoning, *a priori*, can show us the result of one billiard-ball striking another, can explain the communication of motion by impulse, or the ultimate cause of electricity, gravity, or cohesion of parts." Therefore Hume maintains that all our conclusions about cause and effect are nothing more than the outcome of our experience. "From causes that are similar, we expect similar results." That is why a burnt child dreads the fire. No one supposes that the child is "led to this conclusion by any process of argument or ratiocination": it is just the result of the child's experience. We are accustomed to see two things constantly in conjunction, such, for instance, as flame and heat, solidity and weight, and we get into the habit of "expecting the one from the presence of the other." But that is no explanation of cause and effect. The great guide of human life, says Hume, is "custom." It is custom that makes our experience useful to us. Were it not for custom, we should know nothing "beyond what is immediately present to the senses and memory: we should never know how to adjust means to ends." From experience and custom, however, we learn that what we call the effect follows the cause, although we can discover no satisfactory reason *why*. For experience gives us no hint of the secret "connection" between them which renders cause and effect inseparable. We are conscious of our power "to move our body, or direct our thoughts." We say this is done "upon the command of our will," but we have no knowledge of "the means by which this is effected." We may very well ask, "Why has the will an influence over the tongue and fingers, and not over the liver and heart? All we know is, that it is so." Our philosophers carry on keen controversies concerning "Liberty and Necessity." But the result is "mere words." "That Necessity which we ascribe to matter" comes from observing "a certain uniformity in the operations of nature." Moral necessity is only a phase of physical necessity, and liberty of action, as opposed to necessity, is simply to act as our will determines. And if we ask, what determines our will? the answer is that to a great extent it is custom.

We find that "in all ages and among all nations there is great uniformity among the actions of men." Human nature, indeed, is ever the same; therefore, "the same motives always produce the same actions." This is the reason why "our experience of human nature enables us to regulate our conduct and our speculations." Our experience helps us "to discover men's inclinations and motives from their actions, expressions, and gestures; and again, from the knowledge of their motives and inclinations to foretell their actions." We could not possibly "engage in action of any kind without acknowledging the doctrine of necessity," and without "this inference from motives to voluntary action, from character to conduct." Hume is amused to find the very "philosophers" who deny the doctrine of Necessity "acknowledging it without hesitation in their whole practice and reasoning." How do these philosophers, he asks, define a cause? "If they say that a cause is 'that which produces anything,' we can reply that 'producing' is synonymous with 'causing.' If a cause be defined as 'that by which anything exists,' we ask, what is meant by the words '*by which*'?" Hume suggests that perhaps we may define 'Cause' as, "that *after* which anything constantly exists, for this is indeed all we know about the matter." This is "the very essence of Necessity."

To sum up: the result of Hume's "Enquiry" is to show the difference between perceptions and thoughts, and that both are due, directly or indirectly, to sensation; to show that all our knowledge is the result of experience; to show that what we imagine to be liberty of action is brought about by necessity; and to show that, although we can perceive the results of energy and force in the universe and in ourselves, we are quite unable to account for them. Finally Hume suggests that, until we are able to explain such simple things as *why* we can move our limbs, or *why* heat accompanies flame, or *why* an ivory ball when struck conveys the impulse to another ball, it is useless to puzzle our minds over such far greater mysteries as the origin of the universe, the human soul, and the Causeless Cause of all things.

It is interesting to note that Joseph Priestley, the discoverer of oxygen, published, in 1777, a *Disquisi-*

tion relating to Matter and Spirit, in which, after expressing his opinion that man's soul is entirely dependent on his body, and that it evolves with it to ever higher states of existence, he asks, why should the soul be associated at all with a body, if it could act independently without it? Then, Priestley suggests that the material element of the soul is perhaps the hypothetical ether, "that mysterious agent which we know only by its manifestations, but which we assume to be the basis of intellectual phenomena?"

Immanuel Kant's remarkable work, *Kritik der reinen Vernunft*, was published in 1781. He explains that it is not a system of philosophy, but only "a method of thought," which may be called "transcendental," because it goes beyond the usual forms of thought. In reading Kant, we are reminded of Socrates, for, like him, Kant saw that criticism is a better method of helping men to think than dogmatism. Kant starts from the same point of view as Hume, by saying "there can be no doubt that all our knowledge begins with experience"; but he qualifies this by saying that "it does not follow, however, that it arises from experience." The whole aim of Kant's criticism appears to be to find out "whether there exists a knowledge independent of experience, and even of all impression of sense?" And in the end he differs from Hume, and satisfies himself, apparently, that there is such a kind of knowledge.

Kant begins by distinguishing between two kinds of knowledge—"empirical knowledge" and "pure knowledge." Empirical knowledge is the result of experience, which he generally speaks of as "knowledge *a posteriori*," whilst the knowledge that does not depend on experience he calls "knowledge *a priori*." He defines "Pure Reason," or "die reine Vernunft" (which is the chief object of his whole "Criticism") as being "the faculty which supplies the principle of knowing anything *a priori*." Experience, indeed, teaches us what is, "but not that it necessarily must be *as* it is." Therefore, we have to "enlarge the sphere of our judgments beyond the limits of experience" if we want to arrive at "general truths," and to form concepts such as freedom, immortality, or God. Sensation and "the faculty of judging" are, indeed, the sole sources of our knowledge. But judgment is of two kinds—analytic and synthetic. By means of analysis we find out all about a thing or an idea; but synthesis extends and amplifies our ideas. Synthesis is "the result of the faculty of imagination," or of "the faculty of representing an object even without its presence in intuition." Sensations, intuitions, or perceptions are only the materials which the understanding works up into thoughts, concepts, and ideas.

The "blind feelings," which we call sensations, follow each other with the greatest rapidity, and must be synthesised and arranged before they can be used. This process of synthesis and arrangement is done, Kant thinks, by certain "forms of thought," to which he gives the name of "categories," borrowing the term from Aristotle. He arranges these categories into four classes, each with three subclasses, thus:—

QUANTITY.	QUALITY.	RELATION	MODALITY.
Unity.	Reality.	of Inherence and Substance,	Possibility—Impossibility.
Plurality.	Negation.	Causality and Dependence (or Cause and Effect).	Existence—Non-existence.
Totality.	Limitation.	Community or Reciprocity between the active and passive.	Necessity—Contingency.

These categories are the "conditions of thought" which, according to Kant's idea, "make experience possible." Some of them, he explains, are "dynamical," some are "mathematical," but all are "fundamental concepts of the mind," without which we cannot "think an object" at all. He points out that the third category in each class results from combining the first and second in that class: for instance, "Totality is nothing but Plurality, considered as Unity." Kant tells us that this table of categories gave him "the greatest trouble," and, indeed, the whole scheme strikes one, at first, as sufficiently perplexing. But it "appears upon a more wary survey," as Locke says, to be nothing more than a roundabout and elaborate way devised by Kant of saying that, as fast as perceptions come to us through sensation, the mind must, so to speak, at once docket each perception and put it into its proper pigeon-hole for future use. If our perceptions get into their appropriate pigeon-holes in the mind, we get knowledge, if not—not.

But there are, Kant maintains, "two original intuitions" of the mind, two "pure intuitions, which contain, *a priori*, the conditions of objects as phenomena," and without which we could have no perception of the world outside. These are our intuitions of space and time. Kant's theory, that space and time are mere "modes of perception," becomes at once intelligible, if we consider that every child has these intuitions long before it can possibly have any perception of what it learns later to know as space and time. We see an infant instinctively draw near to anything that pleases it, and as instinctively shrink back from anything that it fears or dislikes, showing thereby what Kant calls an "*a priori* intuition" that objects are in front, behind, or beside it. We notice also that the infant evinces just as instinctive an intuition of before and after, as regards time. Indeed, as Kant puts it, "through space alone is it possible that things should become external to us." We cannot even imagine that there is no space, although we can "very well imagine that there should be space without objects to fill it." And again, although it is impossible to eliminate time from phenomena in general, "we can well take away phenomena out of time." Thus Kant concludes that time and space are in reality nothing but the "*formal* conditions, *a priori*, of all phenomena": they are "nothing but the subjective conditions of our sensibility." We speak, indeed, of different times; but we find that they are only parts of one and the same time. Space and time, then, must be regarded not as realities, but as only "transcendental idealities," which have no existence apart from our intuitions. Carlyle, no doubt, had this theory of Kant's in his mind, when he says in his *Sartor Resartus*, "Where and when, so mysteriously inseparable from all our thoughts, are the warp and woof of the canvas whereon our dreams and life-visions are painted? Think well, thou too wilt find that space is but a mode of our human sense, so likewise is time: there is no space and no time. . . . Nature with its thousandfold production and destruction is but the reflex of our inward force, the fantasy of our dream." And it seems likely too that when Goethe makes the Earth-spirit, in his *Faust*, describe nature as "the living garment of God," which is woven in "the roaring loom of Time," he also was thinking of this theory of Kant's.

Although Kant defines nature as "not a thing by itself but a number of representations," and although he says that all the phenomena of nature are created by "the perceiving and thinking I," and that "it is reason which makes the cosmos," he will have nothing to do with what he calls Berkeley's "dogmatical idealism." He says: "The good Bishop Berkeley degraded bodies to mere illusion. But, if I say that the intuition of external objects and the self-intuition of the mind represent both (mind and objects) in space and time, as they affect our senses, that is, as they appear, I do not mean that these objects are mere *illusion*, I do not mean that bodies *seem* only to exist outside me. For objects, as phenomena, nay even the properties which we ascribe to them, are always looked upon as something really given: all we do is to distinguish the object *as phenomenon* from itself as an object by itself." . . . "The external sense gives us nothing but representations of relations": we cannot really know the "thing by itself," or the thing-in-itself.

Kant makes a clear distinction between the matter and form of phenomena. He says: "In a phenomenon I call that which corresponds to the sensation its 'matter,' but that which causes the manifold matter of the phenomenon to be perceived as arranged in a certain order I call 'form.'" And he adds that form may be "considered as separate from all sensations," because the idea of form exists "*a priori* in the mind."

All our perceptions of phenomena must be related to our self-consciousness, because in order to think at all one must have "the necessary consciousness of the identity of oneself," or of "the ego." The ego, as defined by Kant, is "a transcendental subject of thoughts, which is known *only through the thoughts*, and of which, apart from them, we can never have the slightest concept." He maintains, therefore, that the power to think is no proof of the existence of the soul as an imperishable entity, and that the "Cogito, ergo sum" argument used by Des Cartes is no better than "paralogism," a faulty and misleading chain of reasoning, and in fact is a mere "*a priori* judgment." To say "Cogito, ergo sum" is "tautological," because the "cogito (sum cogitans)" predicates reality immediately. . . . The 'I think' is an empirical intuition which contains within itself the proposition 'I exist': whereas my existence cannot, as Des Cartes supposed, be considered as derived from the proposition." We get, says Kant, so into the habit of drawing inferences, that we constantly "mistake inferences for perceptions." I am able, he says, to conceive things as being "different from myself, but whether such a consciousness of myself is even possible *without* things outside me, whether I could exist merely as a thinking being (without being a man), I do not know."

Hume had maintained that all we know about cause and effect is that, "from causes that are similar, we expect similar results." In criticising this theory, Kant says that "all change takes place according to the connection between cause and effect." Hume, before him, had spoken of the "secret connection" between cause and effect which renders them inseparable, and Kant makes no attempt to explain this connection, but agrees with Hume so far as to say that "the truth of the principle of causality is based on no knowledge," and consequently that "its authority rests on its general usefulness in *experience*." He defines experience as "knowledge by means of perceptions," which is possible only "through the necessary connection of perceptions." Whenever we see two phenomena one after the other, we imagine one to be the cause of the other. But this "concept of the relation" is nothing but "a pure concept of the understanding." The proposition that "each change must have a cause," is a proposition which, he says, "contains the concept of the *necessity* of the connection between cause and effect." This, however, is nothing but "a pure judgment *a priori*," and would be destroyed altogether if we accept Hume's theory that it is *custom* only which leads us to expect the one from the other. It seems, therefore, as if Kant cannot upset Hume's theory, although it is evident that he does not like it.

Hume had dismissed the whole dispute about

liberty and necessity as one of mere "words," and Kant admits that it is impossible to prove that there is any such thing as "freedom" in the true sense of the word. "In its cosmological sense," freedom "is the faculty of beginning a state spontaneously," whilst freedom, "in its practical sense," or "the freedom of our arbitrary will from coercion, is not a physiological problem but a transcendental idea, or fiction." And although Kant adds, "I may not know freedom, but that does not prevent me from thinking freedom," it seems that Kant practically agrees with Hume.

To investigate "the three ideas"—freedom, immortality, and God—is, Kant says, the real object of metaphysics: "everything else treated by that science is a means only in order to establish these ideas." Nevertheless, he feels obliged to admit that "in no way whatsoever can we know anything of the nature of the soul, so far as the possibility of its separate existence is concerned. All that reason can assume is "the empirical unity of all thought," and then, by representing that as "unconditioned and original, the concept is changed into that of a self-subsisting intelligence." So that it is only "hypothetically" that real existence can be attributed to the soul. The immortality of the soul is therefore only "a psychological idea," by which, however, Kant insists, "no windy hypothesis of generation, extinction, and palingenesis (rebirth) of the soul is admitted." "The three propositions" — freedom, immortality, God—"always remain transcendent to speculation," whilst any inquiry into the origin of the universe must ever be fruitless. It is, at best, but a "progressus ad infinitum," because it is as impossible to prove that "the world has a beginning in time and is limited also with regard to space," as it is to prove the contrary theory that "the world has no beginning and no limit in space." Nor have we any means of knowing whether substance "in its last analysis" is compound or simple. That it is simple is only a supposition—"a mere idea," because "the existence of the absolutely simple cannot be proved by any perception or experience, whether external or internal," whilst even "the proof of the infinite divisibility of matter is mathematical only."

But Kant evidently cannot quite recede from the theological point of view, so that even after his admission that "the three propositions must always remain transcendent to speculation," he feels it necessary to add that "it is the speculative interest of reason which makes it necessary to regard all order in the world, as if it had originated in the purpose of a supreme wisdom," because it it evident that, "if we once admit an absolutely perfect cause, there is no difficulty in accounting for all order, magnitude, and design which are seen in the world." Thus we come to "presuppose a something, of which we have no conception whatever as to what it is by itself, as a purely transcendent object." And then Kant at once passes over to the philosophical point of view and frankly makes the admission that "this Being demanded by reason (ens rationis ratiocinatæ) is no doubt a mere idea. . . . This unconditioned necessity which we require as the last support of all things is the true abyss of human reason." The so-called "ontological proof" of the existence of such a Supreme Being which was advanced by Des Cartes is criticised by Kant as "that unfortunate ontological proof which satisfies neither the demands of our natural and healthy understanding nor the requirements of the schools." And he adds: "Time and labour are lost on it. A man might as well imagine that he could become richer in knowledge by mere ideas, as a merchant in capital, if, in order to improve his position, he were to add a few noughts to his cash-account."

Towards the end of his remarkable *Criticism of Pure Reason*, Kant seems to realise that all his subtle and elaborate reasoning has thrown but little new light on the various problems of human knowledge, for he says: "The question, what can I know? is purely speculative," whilst the question, "what should I do? is purely practical." The laws of nature "tell us only what takes place, but reason gives us laws of freedom, or practical laws, which tell us what ought to take place." We gather that Kant's highest ideal is freedom in following the best impulses of man's nature—good will (die gute Wille). "A good will is that by which alone man's existence can have an absolute value." It is by freedom of will alone that morality becomes possible. Man's obligation to lead a moral life is "the Categorical Imperative."

CHAPTER XI

RECENT THOUGHT IN WESTERN EUROPE

A GENERATION after Kant had published his famous *Kritik*, Hegel, then a professor at the University of Berlin, published, in 1817, his *Encyclopædia of the Philosophical Sciences.* We must not think of the Absolute, he says, as only the principle or essence of the universe, but rather as Being itself, which becomes both nature and mind. The Absolute is not merely the cause of movement and life; it *is* itself life and movement. Therefore, mind and matter must be regarded as modes of the absolute reality. Reality is activity: a being exists only because, and as long as, it *acts* in some way: there is no such thing as absolute rest. The evolutionary process of the universe advances according to "Reason," or Law. This is not the mere human understanding of which Kant speaks, for "Reason" in nature is, at first, quite unconscious; it becomes conscious in animals, and self-conscious in man: it is the essence of evolution both in matter and mind: in a word, it is "the Absolute." We may define nature as the self-development of Reason, and Reason as nature conscious of itself. Being is infinite Becoming. The world may be said to be objectified thought, for the Infinite Reason, immanent in nature, defines itself when it becomes manifest. It is the very essence of life to manifest itself, to express itself in a series of phenomena. A thing consists in its properties: if we try to separate a thing from its qualities, nothing remains, for the qualities or attributes *are* "the thing itself." Substance is "not a substratum," as is sometimes said, but substance is the totality of all the modes of reality, activity, life, which only express or reveal substance.

Hegel insists that nothing in nature exists in isolation, and therefore that no cause, force, quality, or quantity is anything at all, apart from the whole to which it belongs. Thus, no cause can be absolutely absolute, but at most relatively absolute. Nor is it possible to separate cause and effect, for the simple reason that every cause is the effect of a preceding cause, whilst, in its turn, every effect becomes a cause. Rain, for instance, is the cause of moisture, and moisture is the cause of rain. Again, the character of a people is due to its form of government, and the form of government which every people adopts depends upon its character.

Hegel's theory is that the "ideal unity, from which all things proceed, and to which all things tend," is universal gravitation. This active force may well be called "the Soul of the world," for it may be said to realise the idea of proportion, and to make the world an organic whole, a moving, living unity, or "universum." The first phase of universal evolution is the differentiation by means of the force of attraction of individual stars. In its second phase, evolution advances from the quantitative to the qualitative differentiation of cosmic matter. Sidereal motion affects only the surface of the differentiated masses; their inner transformation is caused by chemism, through the reciprocal action of elementary forces. The chemic agencies produce the debris and ashes of terrestrial organisms, from which vegetable organisms arise. The appearance of life on the earth is the spontaneous effect of the same immanent power, which, as attraction and affinity, first differentiated the stars; but individuality proper is first realised by nature in animal organisms, which gradually evolve through zoöphytes, crustaceans, molluscs, insects, fish, reptiles, and mammals, up to man—the most perfect expression of animal form. Man, at first, is only potential mind, because consciousness can evolve only by degrees. In the earliest stage, man is little better than an animal, the essential egoism which is the characteristic of all animal life being swayed this way or that by blind instinct and passion. But, as reason gradually evolves, man recognises that other men are his equals, that nothing is his own exclusive right; and thus, by degrees, the freedom of others becomes the law of his own freedom, and society becomes possible. With the foundation of human society evolves an impersonal will, which is called right, or justice. When this impersonal will becomes the personal will of the individual, he attains to morality. "Morality is the legality of the heart," says Hegel, and subordinates the useful to the good.

Hegel's *Encyclopædia* deserves its name for its comprehensiveness. It is indeed a very complete synthesis of thought on most subjects of interest. Particularly suggestive are his admirable ideas on art, although they scarcely come within the scope of the present volume. But we may, at least, rapidly review Hegel's thoughts on religion. He points out that the predominant ideas in all Eastern religions are mystery, infinity, and pantheism, of which Brahmanism is the most complete expression. God is everything, man is nothing; God is omnipotent, man is so powerless that nothing is left him but complete submission to the will of God. But thought changes as we come westwards. There is no mystery in the religion of Greece. On the contrary, it is sunny, serene, and transparent: the divine unites with the human, and the religious instinct manifests itself in art: Greek art is the worship of humanity. The riddle of the Sphinx, for the Greek thinker, is man: humanity is adored under the form of gods: man's power is symbolised by Zeus, his intelligence by Athene, his art by Apollo, his beauty by Aphrodite. India bowed down at the shrine of the infinite: Greece worshipped at the altar of the finite. Later, the union of the infinite with the finite in human consciousness is symbolised by Christianity in its earliest stage, in the man-god, whose personality and teaching are imposed as an external authority on the human mind. Christianity and philosophy, says Hegel, "have the same *content*, though the *container* is not the same." With the philosopher it is reason, with the Christian it is imagination.

Arthur Schopenhauer's chief work, *The World as Will and Idea*, was first published at Dresden in 1818. Schopenhauer tells us that it will be best understood by those who are acquainted with the theories of Kant, Plato, and the Indian philosophers. "I confess," he says, "that next to the impression by the world of perception, I owe what is best in my own system to the impression made upon me by the works of Kant, by the sacred writings of the Hindus, and by Plato." He reminds us that Kant first of all conceived the idea that space and time are nothing more than modes of perception, that they are original intuitions of the mind; so that we may well say, "Before Kant we were in time, now time is in us." Kant, too, was the first thinker who clearly distinguished between the phenomenon and the thing-in-itself, and showed us the difference between knowledge *a priori* and knowledge *a posteriori*, or, in other words, between what we know by intuition and what we know by experience. Starting from "the eternal verities"—the foundation of all dogmatism—Kant investigates their origin, and "finds it in the human mind."

Schopenhauer expresses the highest appreciation of the mind and work of Kant, and frankly admits that Kant's distinction between the phenomenon and the thing-in-itself helped him to his own conception that the thing-in-itself is "will," and the phenomenon is "idea." But he will have nothing to do with the elaborate "Table of the Twelve Categories," which he calls "that strange, complicated machine with which Kant has burdened the theory of knowledge."

It is clear, he thinks, that Kant distrusted the working of his own "machine," because, whenever he "wishes to give an example for the purpose of fuller explanation, he almost always takes for this end the category of '*causality,*' and then what he has said turns out correct: for causality is indeed the real form of the understanding, but it is also its only form." After dismissing all the remaining eleven categories as being "only blind windows," Schopenhauer defines causality as "the law, according to which the conditions or states of matter which appear determine their position in time." Therefore, cause and effect are "just two successive states of bodies, and it is only because the state A precedes in time the state B, and their succession is necessary, and not accidental, *i.e.* no mere sequence, but a consequence—only because of this is the state A cause and the state B effect." He points out also that because Kant nowhere "clearly distinguishes perception from abstract knowledge" he is constantly "involved in irresolvable contradictions with himself": he puts "the procedure of our faculty of knowledge just upside down," simply because he "sees in things only concrete conceptions": he also often confuses his readers by his wordiness. Schopenhauer gives, as an instance of this, the seven different definitions which Kant gives in different places of understanding or reason. Then Schopenhauer himself defines reason as being simply "the faculty of framing conceptions."

Kant, like Des Cartes, Locke, and Berkeley, starts from self-consciousness. Schopenhauer, by distinguishing between "two completely different data of immediate knowledge in self-consciousness—the idea and the will," claims to have advanced philosophical thought. His theory is that consciousness must be regarded as two-sided, as being "a consciousness of our own selves, which is the will" and a consciousness, through perception, of things outside our selves. As thing-in-itself, every object is will, whilst, as phenomenon, every object is matter. Schopenhauer defines matter as being "that whereby will becomes capable of being apprehended." Matter can only become perceptible when it takes on some quality or form. The forms and qualities of matter are innumerable, but matter itself is one. "Matter can only be thought of *in abstracto* and not perceived, for to perception it always appears already in form and quality." We must necessarily postulate abstract matter, because its changes or "conditions presuppose something permanent whose changes they are." Matter, as such, is "merely the vehicle of the qualities and natural forces which appear as its accidents; and, just because I have traced these back to will, I call matter the mere visibility of the will. . . . What objectively is matter, subjectively is will."

After premising that his theory of "the world as Will and Idea" does not pretend to explain "the existence of the world in its ultimate grounds," for the good and sufficient reason that "the nature of things before and beyond the world is open to no investigation," Schopenhauer commences to explain his system by saying: "No truth is more certain, more independent of others, and less in need of proof than this, that all exists for knowledge, and therefore this whole world is only object in relation to subject-perception of a perceiver, in a word, idea. . . . All that exists, exists only for the subject. Everyone finds himself to be the subject, yet only in so far as he knows, not in so far as he is an object of knowledge. But his body is object, and therefore, *from this point of view*, we call it idea." Directly a man can understand the theory, "the world is my idea," it is clear to him that "what he *knows* is not a sun and an earth, but only an eye that sees a sun, a hand that feels an earth; that the world which surrounds him is there only as idea, *i.e.* only in relation to something else—the consciousness, which is himself." So that the world, as we know it, is only a thing perceived, only a "phenomenon of the brain," whilst the real world to everyone is just what *he* conceives it to be. It follows, therefore, that the phenomenal world is "akin to dreams, and indeed must be classified with them. For, the same function of the brain which, during sleep, conjures up before us a complete, objective, perceptible, and even palpable world, must have just as large a share in the presentation of the objective world of waking life."

The world as idea, then, is the one aspect of the universe. In its other aspect it must be considered as "the objectification of will," or, in other words, as "the will passed into perception." What, then, is will? Schopenhauer seems to consider will and action to be synonymous, for he says, "To will and to act are one." What do we know, he asks, about all the mysterious forces of nature? Must we not confess, if we are honest with ourselves, that we really "know no more of the inner nature of the universal forces, than of the inner nature of an animal? And is it not, as a matter of fact, "just as inexplicable that a stone should fall, as that an animal should move itself?" This being so, may it not be probable that "the inscrutable forces which manifest themselves in all nature," different as they are in degree, may be identical in kind with "what in ourselves we know as will"? Therefore Schopenhauer advances the theory that "the lowest grades of the manifestation of will" are to be recognised in the forces known to us as "gravity, impenetrability, rigidity, fluidity, elasticity, electricity, magnetism, and chemical properties of every kind." From these lowest manifestations, will advances in an ever-ascending scale from matter to mind, showing itself in the animal world first of all as "irritability." It is irritation which compels the plant to grow towards the light: it is irritation which inclines the animal to bask in the sunshine. The plant, in so doing, is conscious of nothing; but, just because it has a more highly organised body, the animal *is* conscious of the pleasant sensation of warmth.

What, asks Schopenhauer, "makes the chicken in the egg? Some power and skill coming from without, and penetrating through the shell? Oh no! The chicken makes itself, and the force which carries out and perfects this work, which is complicated and well calculated and designed beyond all expression, breaks through the shell as soon as it is ready, and now performs the outward actions of the chicken, under the name of will." In the mineral and vegetable world will is a mere blind force, as it is also in the animal world until a brain is evolved; and even "in the vegetative part of our own life will still remains only a blind force." No sooner, however, is the mind active enough to conceive the idea of a world outside itself, than the will becomes conscious of its own willing and of *what* it wills. Thus we see that every voluntary action is a manifestation of will. But if we ask why we will, or why we will to exist, we find no answer, for the simple reason that we ourselves are "nothing but will," and life is only "the manifestation of the will to live." In fact, matter, "with all its physical, chemical, electrical properties," is itself "latent will." Matter is the All-Mother of the universe, "the true 'Mater Rerum,' from the obscurity of whose womb all phenomena come forth," only to fall in due course "into it again," for the origin and annihilation of matter are alike unthinkable.

We know so well that without using our brains *we* could not contrive all the wonders that we discover in the universe, and therefore it is very difficult for us to imagine that all the apparent design we see in it is due to nothing but "blind will-power." Nevertheless the only reasonable and logical explanation of evolution is that all action, all change, is the result of that mysterious force inherent in matter which in ourselves we recognise as will. Will therefore must be regarded as "the thing-in-itself, the inner true and indestructible nature" of all things. Until it has a brain to function in, will remains a mere blind force. Therefore we must consider "consciousness, which is a function of the brain," to be only "a secondary phenomenon," whereas will, of which consciousness is the manifestation, is "the primary phenomenon." We may say that "the will is the matter, the intellect is the form." Will then, the thing-in-itself, the inner essence of the man, "becomes idea, and is that unity which we express by the word 'I.'" But it must not be supposed that the real ego is "the knowing I, which wearies in the evening, vanishes in sleep, and in the morning shines brighter with renewed strength." The mind cannot work healthily without intervals of rest, but the will, which sets the mind going, needs no rest, because "activity is its very essence." Nor must it be imagined that knowledge "fundamentally determines will," for to think that is "like believing that the lantern which a man carries by night is the 'primum mobile' of his steps." The intellect may be compared to the calm reflecting surface of a lake, and the will to the force, the vibrations of which disturb the clearness of the reflections in the watery mirror. "The will is warmth, the intellect light," as is evident in all discussion. We can discuss matters with coolness as long as the will does not come into play; directly it does, the arguments wax warm. The intellect curbs the will, as bit and bridle curb an unmanageable horse, and, like the horse, the will sometimes takes the bit between its teeth and bolts.

It is evident that, the will being primary, "the secondary world of idea" is necessary to produce the ego, and therefore that the ego is "not a substance, or soul, but a condition, or state." Directly an animal is able to apprehend its immediate surroundings, the world as idea begins dimly to dawn on it, and motives for its actions gradually arise; but, not until the human stage is reached, does "the pure separation of willing and knowing" take place. Will reveals itself to every man as "the in-itself of his own phenomenal being," and from this immediate knowledge of his own being man gets the false idea of freedom. The will indeed, *as will*, is free, but the individuals who are "its manifestations in time" are certainly not free, but are "determined by the will-to-live." All the same, we all think ourselves to be free in our individual actions, until we find out by experience and reflection that "our actions take place with absolute necessity from the coincidence of our motives with our character." No doubt this false idea of freedom of will accords perfectly with that other false idea, that the real ego is "a *knowing*, and indeed abstract-thinking," entity, or soul, which "enters the world a moral cipher, comes to know the things in it, and thereupon determines to be this or that, to act thus or thus." But, if will is "first and original," and knowledge only "an instrument belonging to the phenomenon of will," it follows that man must be "*what* he is, once for all, through his will." In course of time, helped by this knowledge and experience, man gets to know what he is, and in consequence often "modifies his conduct," though he cannot alter his original character. Man's choice of action is not freedom of will; it only offers "the possibility of a thoroughly fought out battle between conflicting motives," the strongest of which in the end determines his action, so that the power to choose often adds to the misery of man's existence.

Every man should know what he wills and why he wills it. If he also finds out his strength and weakness, and then cultivates chiefly those faculties and talents that are natural to him, he has some chance of happiness. But "nothing can be more perverse" than, by means of reflection, to endeavour to be something other than he is, because "the whole man is only the phenomenon of his will." Whatever his life may be, no man can make a nobler resolve than to live that life heroically. "Das höchste was der Mensch erlangen kann ist ein heroischer Lebenslauf!" Still, the best cannot be got out of life, unless its course be "interrupted" by one of two things—"the æsthetic demand for contemplation, or the ethical demand for renunciation." The first step towards insight into "the inner meaning of life" being "contemplation," Schopenhauer's theory is that this meaning can be best perceived by the saint, or by the artist, taking the word in its broadest sense. The more self-conscious we are, the less are we able to perceive other things: "we only apprehend the world in a purely objective manner when we no longer know we belong to it. All things appear the more beautiful the more we are conscious merely of them, and the less we are conscious of ourselves." Any intelligent man "with more or less trouble" may master a science, but "from art everyone gets only as much as he brings latent within him, for, unlike science, art has not to do with a man's reason only, but with his inmost nature, where every man counts only for so much as he really *is*." To give oneself up to the intense contemplation of the beautiful is to rise, for the moment at least, above self-consciousness and above willing, and to get glimpses of that deep delight which springs from "denial of the will." This rare joy is fully attained only by the saintly ascetic. We find that "the mystics of all religions ultimately attain to a kind of ecstasy, in which all, any, every knowledge with its whole fundamental form, object and subject, entirely ceases." This state is variously known as "illumination," "union with the divine," and "Samadhi." Brahmanism, Buddhism, Sufism, and Christianity alike teach "the need of deliverance from an existence which is given up to sufferance and death," and they all alike agree that such deliverance can be secured only by "a denial of the will, thus by a decided opposition to nature." The natural man imagines happiness to be the end and aim of life, and, as long as he continues to think this, life and the world must necessarily seem to him "full of contradictions." But man has only fully to understand what life really is, and then "he wills it no more." This is the case with the saintly ascetic. From his eyes "the veil of Mâyâ," the "principium individuationis," is so far lifted that he ceases to make "any egotistical distinction between his own life and that of others; he recognises himself—his will—in everything"; all the miseries of the world are his, and, knowing that all misery is the result of willing, he determines in future to will nothing. The body is the objectification of his will; therefore he resolutely mortifies it by abstinence and fasting, and at length he welcomes death as a happy release from life.

This point of view of the saintly ascetic is naturally quite unintelligible to the average man. In him the will-to-live is paramount; he looks upon life as "the *summum bonum*," and consequently, when he dies, the will which animates him must again manifest itself as a phenomenon in time. This is not the case at the death of the saintly ascetic, who has resolutely "denied" the will to live. Considered as a phenomenon in time and a phenomenon of empirical knowledge, every man "ceases to be" at death. It is, however, evident that "no more can be destroyed by death than was produced by birth; thus not *that* through which birth first became possible." Why then should we fear death? "Ceasing to be ought to disturb us as little as not having been." Consciousness, of course, ceases with life, simply because it is due to the perishable brain: not so the will, the indestructible principle of life, which must reappear in a new individual. In its turn, this new individual evolves a new brain, and with it a new consciousness. This is why no "bridge" can be shown to connect the various phenomenal appearances of the will as it passes through "a succession of life-dreams," until at last it reaches that stage of evolution in which "knowledge has, as it were, burnt up and consumed the will," so that no further desire remains for individual existence.

So logical is this idea of the continued rebirth of the will, says Schopenhauer, that, like an axiom of Euclid, it must be accepted "directly it is understood," as it was accepted not only by the thinkers in ancient India, but by the Pythagoreans and by Plato. This he considers to have been the esoteric meaning of the myth of the transmigration of souls, according to which the uncultured were taught that "wicked conduct involves a future life in lower castes," whilst good conduct is rewarded by "rebirth in better and nobler forms, as Brahmans, wise men, or saints," and the highest reward which awaits the noblest deeds and the most perfect resignation is never to be born again but to attain to "Nirvâna," that state of bliss in which neither birth, sickness, misery, age, nor death exists.

The "true nature," however, of every individual exists, says Schopenhauer, only in the species, or type, or idea, as Plato calls it, whilst the species itself has no other existence but that of the individuals which compose it. To understand the relative value of the individual compared to that of the species, we have only to notice the extreme care shown in the preservation of the species and the utter carelessness for the safety and preservation of the individual. The permanence of the species is sufficiently assured by such means as the extraordinary superfluity of seeds and germs, the extreme vehemence of the sexual instinct, and the remarkable devotion of the mother to her offspring. But no individual plant, animal, or human being is in any way protected or preserved; their lives are, on the contrary, a never-ending struggle for existence, so that we must admit that for most of us life is scarcely "worth having," and that nothing but an irrational will-to-live "holds us firmly on the scene of the tragi-comedy." This will-to-live is rooted in the species. "Therefore Plato attributed true being to the Idea alone, . . . and to the individual only a ceaseless arising and passing away."

Between 1830 and 1842 Auguste Comte first published his *Philosophie Positive*, which he tells us is to be understood simply as "a mode of reasoning on all subjects open to human investigation." Starting with the theory that, like everyone who thinks for himself, humanity has had to pass through three distinct phases of mental evolution, Comte points out that in the race's childhood, before any laws of nature were discovered, man could not help imagining that the world was ruled by wills like his own. This rudimentary stage of mental evolution passed through three sub-stages—fetichism, polytheism, monism—and was the real beginning of theology. In its highest development it became star-worship. In polytheism, at its best, we also trace the remains of fetichism, for "the gods of Greece—Earth and Ocean—issued from the two principal fetiches," and it is only "under a later monotheistic view that the ancient gods came to be regarded symbolically." In the fetich stage of man's evolution objects are imagined to have some sort of mysterious influence or power: in the next stage the world is supposed to be dominated by a number of deities whose existence is only later assumed to be merged in that of one omnipotent power—the idea of "Fate" being the "stepping-stone from polytheism to monotheism."

Theological philosophy indeed "was suitable to the needs of a primitive state of society." Its function in the evolution of thought has been "to stimulate man's moral courage, and to awaken and direct his intellectual activity," by means of the theological fiction about "the supremacy of man and his unbounded empire over nature." Therefore the rise of a priestly class in Chaldæa, Egypt, and Persia was an element towards progress in the early epochs, because it gave thinkers time and opportunity to think, and helped them to distinguish "between practice and theory." But priests became the bitter opponents of progress directly they began to use their influence and power for the purpose of maintaining their own supremacy. Happily for the world, Greece escaped altogether from this sacerdotal domination. Perhaps the remarkable independence of thought in Greece may be explained by the physical formation of the country itself: the deep gulfs which run far up into the land, and the lofty mountain-ranges, prevented any single state either from expanding itself or from dominating its neighbours. Thus "the Athenian people, triumphant in the Archipelago, in Asia, and in Thrace, was confined to a central territory so small, that there was little or no outlet for political activity." Consequently, the quick Greek brain was forced into intellectual and artistic development, and so we find that "thirty centuries ago in Greece the positive spirit began to manifest itself in the appearance of mathematical ideas." Before astronomical observation had revealed the existence of natural laws, these early Greek thinkers, in their eagerness to escape from theology, were searching for explanations of the origin and order of the universe "among rudimentary mathematical conceptions." Later on, the thinkers in Alexandria distinguished between natural and moral philosophy, and by their speculations about the Supreme Good entirely freed themselves from theological philosophy.

As the human mind evolved its powers, and as one natural law after another was discovered, men gradually gave up "the idea of the sovereign direction of events by an arbitrary will," because they perceived clearly that many events could not only be foreseen, but could even be modified by human forethought. Theology then fell back upon the notion of a Universal Providence, combined with special laws which this Power was supposed to have imposed on itself. At this point of mental evolution metaphysical philosophy steps in, and "by its mobile character helps to sustain speculative activity, and seems, for a time, to reconcile the radical opposition of theological and positive thought." Phenomena were now no longer explained by the actions of conscious wills, but by abstractions, which were assumed to be realities. By allowing the "scholastic compromise" that the Creator makes the laws which nature is left to execute, the Church was able to explain the laws of nature as so many revelations of divine wisdom. This negative doctrine is, however, the last phase of the ancient philosophy which assumed absolute knowledge in its explanations of those mysteries which modern philosophy knows to be beyond the reach of human inquiry. Even that attractive metaphysical speculation of the ego, "the idea of unity in the human being," is a direct outcome of theology, which makes morality to consist in a care for the salvation of the individual, whereas no "personal calculation" of any kind enters into the "positive" conception of morality. We find, "as the good sense of Sophocles had already foreseen," that the metaphysical spirit is radically unfit to be a basis even of mental, much less of social organisation, and that therefore each school of metaphysics "from Socrates to Epicurus" has ended in nothing but universal doubt.

Scientific thought in Europe began with the revival of Greek philosophy, much of which was translated into Latin by Arabian students. It seems strange that, although the tendency of the teaching of Plato is almost theological, whilst that of Aristotle is almost positive, it was the philosophy of Aristotle which found most favour with the Roman Catholic Church. Arabian thinkers also advanced mathematical and astronomical research, invented algebra, developed trigonometry, and thus led up to celestial geometry. The study of chemistry formed the link between inorganic and organic research, and even alchemy and astrology rendered to science the service of spreading the idea that all phenomena are subject to invariable natural laws. The speculations of the mediæval alchemists were based on Aristotle's doctrine of the four elements which made it seem to them as if the transmutation of metals was quite as possible as "the transformation effected by modern chemistry among vegetable and animal substances through the identity of their constituent principles." Science at that time would have been far more oppressed by the Catholic Church had not the clergy themselves indulged in astrological and alchemical speculations. But religious prejudice long delayed the study of anatomy, which at length numbered physicians among the speculative thinkers "and extended the study of the universe to the study of man himself."

Free inquiry is necessary and wholesome, but we cannot stop there, "always examining and never deciding," so that we must be content to take some things on the authority of experts—such things, for instance, as astronomical, chemical, and physical questions—because it is evident that society could not exist "if it were dependent on the arbitrary and variable decisions of the less competent minds." The tendency, therefore, of the social spirit to-day is to make government "less and less philosophical and more and more moral," because thoughtful men begin to understand that "the vague and stormy discussions about rights should be replaced by the calm and precise determination of duties. Society must always continue to "vibrate between the conservative and progressive tendencies of thought," for both are necessary. Indeed, society "exists only in their mutual neutralisation," because without the one we should lose the feeling for order, without the other the desire for progress. "Therefore order and progress are the chief features of the positive social science."

The modern systems of metaphysical philosophy are little more than variations of the ideas of the Greek or scholastic philosophers. Even "the illustrious Kant with all his logical power has not adequately fulfilled the conditions of philosophical *generality* in agreement with the present state of intellectual progress." One of the most decisive manifestations of the advance of thought is the contrast which thinkers now make between the relative and the absolute, who see that the vain desire for absolute knowledge can only force the mind "back into theological fictions and metaphysical entities." The mind which has "reached the positive stage of evolution" gives up the vain search after "the origin and destination of the universe" and "final causes." Therefore the Positive Philosophy does not "pretend to explain the real causes of phenomena, as this would only throw the difficulty further back; it only tries to analyse *correctly* the circumstances of their production and to connect them together by the normal relations of succession and similarity." It accepts, for instance, Newton's law of gravitation as the explanation of the general phenomena involved, leaving to "the imagination of theologians or the subtleties of metaphysicians" the further explanation of either gravitation or weight. "Any notion of creation must be put aside altogether as unintelligible": nor can we form "any reasonable conjecture about the formation of suns." So far, the cosmogony of Laplace seems to Comte to be "the most plausible theory of any yet proposed," having the great merit of "requiring for the formation of our planetary system only the simple agents of weight and heat." And he considers that we cannot regard our planetary system as stable, but must imagine "that, by the continuous existence of the general medium, our system must at length be reunited to the solar mass from which it came forth, till a new dilation of this mass shall occur in an immensity of a future time and organise in the same way a new system to follow an analogous career."

The thinkers of the early world were able to cultivate all the known branches of knowledge, just because so little was known. But, as knowledge grew, thinkers devoted themselves more and more to one special branch, to the great advantage of the individual sciences. But, in so doing, thinkers, for a time, lost sight of the fact that the different sciences are only parts of one great whole—"the general system of positive knowledge." Therefore Comte suggests "a new class of students whose business it shall be to take the respective sciences as they are, determine the spirit of each, ascertain their relations and mutual connection, and reduce their respective principles to the smallest number of general principles." This general study of positive knowledge seems to Comte "the only natural means of showing the logical laws of the human mind," for the modern science which goes by the name of psychology is nothing more than "the illusory last phase of theology," which thinks it can discover "the laws of the human mind by contemplating it in itself; that is, by separating it from causes and effects," ignoring, all the while, the self-evident truth that "the mind may observe all phenomena but its own." It is said that a man may study his own passions, "but it is certain that there can be nothing like scientific observation of the passions except from without, because the stir of emotions disturbs the observing faculties more or less. It is yet more out of the question to make an intellectual observation of intellectual processes. The observing and the observed organ are here the same. . . . In order to observe, your intellect must pause from activity, yet it is this very activity that you want to observe. If you cannot effect the pause, you cannot observe; if you do effect it, there is nothing to observe."

The more general and simple they are, the more phenomena are "removed from man's ordinary sphere," and can therefore be studied in a calmer and more rational frame of mind than phenomena with which we are more closely concerned. The study of positive philosophy should commence, therefore, with inorganic physics, which consists of astronomical and terrestrial phenomena, including chemical phenomena; and then we may proceed to the study of organic physics—physiology, the general laws of life, and social physics or sociology, which is dependent on it. Mathematics should be the basis of all our natural philosophy, not because of the knowledge of which it consists, valuable as it is, but because mathematics is "the most powerful instrument that the human mind can employ on the investigation of the laws of natural phenomena." We may indeed say that, "through its simplicity, abstracteuness, generality, and freedom from all disturbance of human passion," mathematics is "the natural basis of all logical education." Then it must also be admitted that "mathematical existence is the simplest and most universal, and, in a geometrical form first and then in a mechanical form, is the only kind of existence cognisable by us in the many and important cases in which our investigation can proceed only on visual evidence." A study of mathematics is necessary also for the development of "a sense of logical laws, without which physical laws could not be conceived of." Geometry too, Comte reminds us, "is more general than mechanics, for we can conceive of existence without motion, as in the case of the 'fixed stars,' which come under only geometrical conditions, and to geometry we owe the earliest conception of laws of agreement."

Comte therefore suggests as the most useful order of scientific study, (1) mathematics, (2) astronomy, (3) physics, (4) chemistry, (5) physiology, which will all lead the student logically up to (6) sociology; and, as a preface to this course of study, he gives us a most exhaustive and masterly review of the first five, which are to form the basis of the sixth. Sociology must be studied on the positive basis to enable us to arrive at the desired "social reorganisation which must terminate the great political and moral crises of existing society"; for it is sufficiently evident that, "in spite of all political palliatives," the nations must remain in that essentially revolutionary state caused by "the existence at once of three incompatible philosophies"—theological, metaphysical, and positive —"until we are agreed upon a certain number of general ideas capable of forming a common social doctrine." We must not "subordinate real life to an imaginary one," as theological philosophy does, nor must we "sanction egotism," as does metaphysical philosophy, but must make "social morality the basis of the positive philosophy." Comte contends that "the only really universal point of view is the social," and that it is of but "little importance to popular interests in whose hands capital is deposited, if its employment is duly useful to society at large," because the use of wealth depends "more on moral than on political methods." Under the theological régime the social sentiment can only exist in an indirect and contradictory fashion because theology "gives a character of exorbitant selfishness to all moral acts," and metaphysical philosophy also "bases morality on self-interest." But "positive morality teaches us the habitual practice of goodness without any other recompense than internal satisfaction." Consequently "morality must become more practical than it ever could be under religious influences, because *personal* morality will be seen in its true relations—withdrawn from all influences of personal prudence. . . . The restriction of our expectations to actual life must furnish new means of connecting our individual development with the universal progression, the growing regard to which is the only possible, and the utmost possible, satisfaction to our natural aspirations after eternity."[1]

Much as John Stuart Mill admired the *Philosophie Positive* of Comte—so much, indeed, that he induced several of his friends to join him in making such an

[1] All the quotations from Comte's works are taken from Harriet Martineau's translation, which so pleased Comte that he called it "this unexampled translation." The italics are also Comte's.

annual allowance to Comte that he might work free from financial worry—he differed from many of his political and social theories. In his thoughtful essay *On Liberty*, which he published in 1867, Mill begins by saying that "the first duty of a thinker is to follow his intellect to whatever conclusion it may lead." He must beware of letting himself be frightened by those timid or half-hearted persons who object to any argument "being 'pushed to an extreme,' not seeing that unless reasons are good for an extreme case, they are not good for any case." It is in the discovery of "the grounds for the opinions we hold" that the cultivation of our minds chiefly consists. When Socrates "came into collision with the public opinion of his time," it was the men who shirked discussion of opinions who thought it necessary to put him to death, although he is described by those "who best knew him and his age as being the most virtuous man in it." In all his discussions on life and philosophy Socrates had but one aim, which was to convince anyone "who had merely adopted the commonplaces of received opinion that he did not understand the subject—that he, as yet, attached no definite meaning to the doctrines he professed; in order that, in becoming aware of his ignorance, he might be put in the way to obtain a stable belief, resting on a clear apprehension both of the meaning of doctrines and their evidence."

It is only in proportion as each man's individuality is evolved, that he becomes valuable to himself and others, and it is certain that only "in an atmosphere of freedom" can originality, much less genius, be evolved. No good can possibly come to us by "wearing down into uniformity" all in us that is "individual." On the contrary, human beings can "become noble" only by calling forth their individuality "within the limits imposed by the rights and interests of others." Individuality is not only "one of the elements of well-being," but it is "the origin of all wise and noble things." We must beware lest we become the slaves of custom. Whenever, as in the East, it becomes the final appeal in all things, the despotism of custom is complete. Up to the time when the sway of custom became omnipotent the Chinese and Indians were progressive, but all progress stopped directly they ceased to "possess individuality." Custom is the ceaseless "antagonism to that disposition which aims at something better than customary, which is called, according to circumstances, the spirit of liberty or of progress." The greatness of England to-day can only be called "collective." Being individually small, we only appear capable of anything great by combining; and with this our moral and religious philanthropists are perfectly content. "But it was men of another stamp than this who *made* England what it has been; and men of another stamp will be needed to prevent its decline." Let us take warning by the Chinese. They are "a nation of much talent, and in some respects even wisdom, owing to the rare good fortune of having been provided, at an early period, with a particularly good set of customs." Their rulers and sages devised an excellent "apparatus for impressing, as far as possible, the best wisdom they possessed on every mind in the community, and securing that those who have appropriated most of it should occupy the posts of honour and power." In this way the Chinese government "succeeded, beyond all hope, in what our English philanthropists are so industriously working at—in making a people all alike."

Mill describes his essay as one about "Civil or Social Liberty," as treating of "the nature and limits of the power which can be legitimately exercised by society over the individual." He points out that there is "the government of each by himself," and also "the government of each by all the rest." The difficulty is to bring the two kinds of government into harmony. If "society itself is the tyrant," the liberty of the separate individuals who compose it is lost. Therefore "a limit must be fixed to the legitimate interference of collective opinion with individual independence." But where then shall we fix "the rightful sovereignty of the individual over himself? and where does the authority of society begin?" Mill admits that utility is the last appeal in ethical questions, but it must be "utility in the largest sense, grounded on the permanent interests of a man as a progressive being." He admits further that "general rules" must be observed in the conduct of human beings towards one another, so that "people may know what they have to expect." The mere fact of "living in society" and receiving a certain amount of protection justifies society in "enforcing its conditions," at all costs to the individual, on all who try to evade their obligations. But, in all those matters which concern nobody but himself, the individual is not accountable to society, and therefore the only way in which society has the right to express its disapprobation or dislike to his actions is by "advice, instruction, persuasion, or avoidance." When we consider that "the existing generation is the master of the training of the generation to come," the simple justice of this is evident; for it must be the fault of society itself if it does not train the young to be "reasonable citizens." The only purpose for which "power can be rightfully exercised over any member of a civilised community, against his will, is to prevent harm to others: his own good, either physical or moral, is not sufficient warrant."

So long as he does no harm to others, everyone has not only the absolute right to enjoy liberty of thought "on all subjects, practical or speculative, scientific, moral, or theological," but he has also the right of "publishing his opinions." He has the right, though others should think him wrong, to "lead the life suitable to his own character." Lastly, all individuals have the right to "unite for any purpose not involving harm to others." By suffering each other "to live as seems good to themselves," mankind are greater gainers than by compelling each "to live as seems good to the rest." Indeed, no society can be called "free," whatever may be the form of its government, in which "these liberties are not respected." Not only the ambition of a hierarchy, or the narrow spirit of Puritanism, have each in turn aimed at moral and social repression, but we find that many modern reformers, whilst strongly antagonistic to the religions of the past, "have been in no way behind either churches or sects in their assertion of the right of spiritual domination." We even find that the carefully thought out social system which is "unfolded by Comte in his *Système de Politique,* aims at establishing (though by moral more than by legal appliances) a despotism over society" more rigid than any advocated by ancient philosophers. It is therefore necessary for us to oppose "a barrier of moral conviction" against the tendency which the best as well as the worst of us have to impose our own inclinations and opinions "as a rule of conduct on others."

The state is bound, whilst respecting the perfect "liberty of each in what specially concerns himself," to keep "a vigilant control over all its citizens in their mutual relations." This is "at present disregarded" in the case of the family relations, which in their "direct influence on human happiness are more important than all the others put together." The state should see that all wives enjoy the same rights and the same protection of the law as all other persons, and also should compel all parents to educate their children up to a certain standard. The education should be at the expense of the parents, and only in the case of the poorest children at the expense of the state. But Mill strongly opposes the idea that "the whole or any large part of the education of the children should be in state hands." His theory is that a general education, "whether it be under the influence of a priesthood, an aristocracy, or a democracy," the more efficient it is, exercises the greater "tyranny" over both mind and body. It is, he says, at best but "a mere contrivance for moulding people to be exactly like one another"—the last thing to be desired!

"Government interference in all affairs which do not involve the infringement of liberty" should, says Mill, be persistently avoided, even if, as is possible in many cases, individuals may not be able "to do the particular thing as well, on the average, as the officers of government." And this, because it is the "practical part of the political education of a free people to let them manage their own affairs." The doing of this not only gives them opportunities of mental education and of exercising their judgment," but enables them to rise beyond "the narrow circle of personal and family selfishness," and to understand the meaning of "joint interests." Unless a people acquires habits and powers such as these, "a free constitution can neither be worked nor preserved." It is evident that, the more numerous the functions exercised by the government, the greater will be the desire of the active and ambitious members of the public to become the employés of the government. The different enterprises now managed by the public would be managed by men appointed and paid by the government, to whom they would look for every rise in life. Under such circumstances, "not all the freedom of the press and popular constitution of the legislature would make this or any other country free otherwise than in name." And the evil would be the greater, the better the administrative machinery worked; because the bureaucracy would have absorbed the best culture and all the most practised intelligence of the country, "except the purely speculative."

Doubtless the great difficulty of the art of government is "to determine the point at which evils so formidable to human freedom and advancement begin to predominate over the benefits attending the collective application of the forces of society under its recognised chiefs." But Mill thinks that the ideal to be kept in view is "the greatest dissemination of power consistent with efficiency," combined with "the greatest possible centralisation of information," and the general "diffusion" from the centre of this knowledge and experience.

In the long run the worth of any state consists in "the worth of the individuals composing it." Therefore, every state which "dwarfs its men," in order that they may be "more docile instruments in its hands," however benevolent its intentions may be, must discover, sooner or later, that "with small men no great thing can be really accomplished."

Herbert Spencer defines philosophy as "completely unified knowledge," and in his *Synthetic System of Philosophy*, published in 1862, he shows that the evolution of the universe is caused by the "instability of the homogeneous," which brings about the "unceasing redistribution" of matter and motion. At the beginning, evolution is simplicity itself, but the process soon becomes complicated by the "differences in the circumstances of the different parts of the aggregates," so that, as these differences increase, what began as "homogeneous, becomes more and more heterogeneous." Of this fact we see evidences everywhere—in the evolution of the far-off nebulæ, in the stars, in our planetary system, in the organic mass of the earth, and in every organism, vegetal or animal, on the earth. Finally we see evolution become still more complex "in mind, in society, and in all products of social activity." The process of evolution thus set in motion by "the instability of the homogeneous" goes on until the action of outside forces, "to which all parts of any aggregate are exposed," becomes balanced by the forces within, whose tendency is to resist all change. This state of equilibrium once reached, the process is reversed, and evolution passes into dissolution, either suddenly or gradually, until each aggregate of matter becomes dissipated, by the increase of its own "contained motion." Each aggregate, be it vast or infinitesimally minute, must undergo this alternate process of integration and disintegration, and it is to the action of this rhythmic process, set going by "an unknown and unknowable power, which we are obliged to recognise as without limit in space and without beginning or end in time," that are due all the phenomena of the universe. All things "emerge from the imperceptible to the perceptible, and then again disappear into the imperceptible." All that philosophy can do is to study the series of changes which they pass through in the process, but any attempt to explain such "ultimate scientific ideas" as space, time, matter, or motion can only bring us to "alternative impossibilities of thought."

This being so, it is hopeless to expect ever to be

able to read the riddle of the universe, ever to discover the causeless cause of its existence. Suppose we postulate, as the solution of the mystery, the "self-existence" of the cosmos. This gets rid of "the idea of any antecedent cause," but it also does away with the idea of any "beginning," because, to postulate a time when existence had not begun, is to admit that its beginning depended on something not itself. Again, the idea of the "self-creation" of the cosmos is just as unthinkable, because it is impossible to imagine "potential existence passing into actual existence by some inherent necessity"; besides which, we have to answer the question, "Whence the potential existence?" Being unable to explain to himself how this wonderful universe came into being, man's impatience or his timidity leads him to the theistic conception of an external agency, as being the easiest solution of the problem. Thus the world is imagined to be the work of "the Great Artificer"; but it is not so easy to say "how there came to be a Great Artificer," or to account for the origin of the materials used by this Great Artificer, or to explain whence come these "pre-existing elements"; for that something can be made out of nothing is quite unthinkable. So that it must be admitted that the idea of a self-existent creator is quite as inconceivable as the idea of a self-existent universe, and that therefore the solution of the great mystery is as far off as before.

When we speak, as we must do, of either time, space, matter, or motion, our words are only symbols of unknown realities. We are compelled to think of them as existing, but, because they have no attributes, we cannot "bring them within those conditions under which existences are represented in thought," and have really no idea whether they are objective entities or things, or whether they are subjective creations of our minds. Sometimes, indeed, we say that extension is an attribute of space, but, in so saying, we forget that space and extension are convertible terms, and, therefore, when we attribute extension to space we merely "identify the object with its attribute." We can attribute to time and space neither "limitation nor the absence of limitation." Then, what do we understand by matter? Newton's theory is that matter consists of "solid atoms not in contact," which "act upon each other by attraction and repulsion" as they float in a medium called the "luminiferous ether." Leibniz advanced the theory that matter consists of "unextended monads," whilst Boscovich defined matter as an aggregate of "centres of force," or "points without dimensions, which attract and repel in such wise as to be kept at specified distances apart." But can we imagine such a thing as "a centre of force which exists in a point, having position only"? And must we not admit that, "in its ultimate nature," we are as ignorant of matter as of motion, space, or time? Again, what *is* motion? We may say, perhaps, that motion is "change of place," forgetting that "in unlimited space place cannot be conceived." Or, what is meant by "transference" of motion? When one body strikes another, *what* has been "transferred"? Surely neither a thing nor an attribute is transferred to the body struck. Then, what is consciousness? "What is it that thinks?" If we say that "the successive impressions and ideas which constitute consciousness" are affections of "that something which we call mind," we infer that the mind is the real ego, and therefore "an entity": in other words, we make the admission that "the conscious self exists as a permanent continuous being." How do we know that it does? We analyse our mental actions and we find that they are based on our sensations; but we cannot give any account "either of the sensations themselves, or of that which is conscious of sensations." We ask, we cannot help asking, What is life? And we may answer that life is "the continuous adjustment of internal conditions to external conditions," and the definition holds good, whether we consider life in its physical or in its psychical aspect, because, as intelligence progresses, it merely establishes "more varied, more complete, or more involved adjustments" of inner to outer conditions. But, nevertheless, we can form "no approach to a conception of what underlies the phenomena" of life—of the "noumenal nature" of life we know absolutely nothing.

Hume said that it is impossible to conceive the Absolute. Kant urged that by means of our "synthetical judgment" we could "pass beyond our concepts"; and Spencer, in a measure, seems to side with Kant, for he says that, although we have, and can have, no "definite consciousness" of the nature of the Absolute, we have, at least, an "indefinite consciousness," which it is impossible for us to formulate, for, when it reaches "the limit of intelligence" thought tries in vain to form "a new relation" beyond. Thought cannot "pass into the unknowable," so that we are for ever baffled by the mystery which is "beyond our comprehension." Even if the theologian can be induced to look at things from this point of view, he will perhaps object that science postulates "a power to which no emotion whatever can be ascribed." Science admits, of course, that this is so, and adds that "the belief in a community of nature between himself and the object of his worship has always been to man a satisfactory one," and consequently man has "always accepted with reluctance those successively less concrete conceptions which have been forced upon him," age after age, as thought evolved and science grew. The various phases of religion have existed one after another just because, in each stage of progress, "men must think in such terms of thought as they possess." Sooner or later, the unknown power postulated by science will also have to be accepted. Meanwhile, for many men—perhaps for most—religion is still a necessity, and unhappily even for some, indeed, a religious system founded on the theological idea of "future punishments and rewards," because, at present, "the great mass of men are unable to trace out with clearness those good and bad consequences which conduct brings round through the established order of things."

The knowable world, says Spencer, is one great whole. Not only the physical and mental worlds, but also the social world, the industrial world, and the world of science and of art all combine to form one grand synthesis. Nothing in the cosmos stands alone: every thought involves a whole system of thoughts, and ceases to exist if severed from its various correlatives. We can no more isolate a thought, "and deal with it as though it had a life independent of the rest," than we can isolate an organ of a living body. And then, he treats of the phenomenal world more or less in detail, beginning with "impressions, or ideas." These "manifestations" of the unknowable, he says, may be either "vivid or faint." We get vivid manifestations of places, persons, and things; and, having once had these vivid "impressions," we get fainter manifestations of them which we call "recollections." These two kinds of manifestations we keep distinct in our minds, except during sleep, when the two kinds become more or less confused. For convenience, we speak of the sum of the recollections or faint manifestations of the unknowable as "the self, or ego," whilst we allude to the vivid manifestations, which have independent conditions of existence, as the "not-self." In our everyday talk, we assume that appearance and reality are "one and the same," and therefore are accustomed to call all external objects "real." But the metaphysician uses the word "real" to express "persistence in consciousness," because he knows that we are conscious only of "the appearance of reality." This persistence in consciousness may be "unconditional, as is our consciousness of space," or it may be "conditional, as is our consciousness of a body whilst grasping it." This conditioned effect is, however, sufficiently "real" to us, so long as the conditions "persist."

In all our investigations of the phenomena of the world we have to admit three postulates—(1) the indestructibility of matter, (2) the continuity of motion, (3) the persistence of force. Because it may vanish beyond the range of our perception, matter does not cease to exist: it undergoes merely a "change of state": evaporation is an instance of this. (1) We must conceive matter to be indestructible, because we cannot imagine that an atom of matter, however minute, can be compressible into nothing. (2) We must imagine motion to be continuous, because we know that visible motion often disappears from view: for instance, the molar motion, or motion of the mass, which disappears when a bell is struck by its clapper, "reappears in the bell's vibrations and in the waves of air which it produces." Similarly, the motion of a moving mass, which seems to be stopped when it strikes a mass at rest, is changed into "molecular motion." (3) We must postulate the persistence of force, because experience shows us that "force is the ultimate of ultimates." And we have to distinguish between two kinds of force, viz. "the intrinsic force by which a body manifests itself as occupying space," and "the extrinsic force, or energy," which is the active power which works change, and which shows itself alike in the movement of masses or of molecules. Then, as physicists affirm that action and reaction are equal and opposite, we must further assume that force "not only persists but remains unchanged in amount."

Whenever we are able to trace motion to its origin we find that it has always "pre-existed as some other mode of force." Under different circumstances, arrested motion produces either "heat, electricity, magnetism, or light"; conversely, "motion may again be reproduced by the forces which have emanated from it." All this we know from experience, but what we do *not* know is what force is in itself. We cannot conceive of matter "except as manifesting the forces of attraction and repulsion," but we are quite unable to explain the origin of these two mysterious forces. Motion is rarely, if ever, straight: the planets of our system, for instance, move in rhythmical curves, because of the "unsymmetrical distribution" of the forces of attraction and repulsion; and we even observe rhythmic motion in that spiral arrangement which is characteristic of "the more structured nebulæ of the sidereal system itself." The movements of the atmosphere and ocean, and the precession of the equinoxes, are also rhythmical, and rhythm is shown too in the various phenomena of physical life. All locomotion consists of oscillatory movements; the blood pulses rhythmically; the lungs alternately expand and contract. "All motion alternates—be it the motion of planets in their orbits or ethereal molecules in their undulations—be it the cadences of speech, or the rises and falls of prices." . . . "This perpetual reversal of motion between limits is inevitable."

Spencer gives two striking illustrations of his theory that all evolution is the natural result of the "instability of the homogeneous." What, he asks, can seem more absolutely homogeneous than a mass of calm water—more absolutely quiescent and motionless?

It appears to be of "exactly the same density throughout." Nevertheless, there is a "constant radiation of heat from neighbouring bodies," which differently affects the different parts of the mass, producing inequalities in the density of the water, and thus currents are formed. Likewise, a piece of metal appears to us to be absolutely homogeneous. But, if we expose it to the influence of air or water, it becomes "coated with a film of oxide, carbonate, or other compound." Or, suppose we heat a mass of matter until it is red-hot. It is only for a moment that the heat is quite even throughout the mass, because "the exterior cooling faster than the interior will become different in temperature." Again, the germ of an as yet unorganised but organisable being appears to the eye quite homogeneous; but, wherever that germ may be placed, "whether immersed in water or air, or contained within a parent-organism," certain parts of the surface of the germ are "more exposed to surrounding agencies than other parts—in some cases more exposed to light, heat, or oxygen, and in other cases to the maternal tissues and their contents. Hence must follow the loss of its original equilibrium." Further, what happens in the total mass happens also in its parts, so that "the uniformity of each part must, as inevitably, be lost in multiformity, as was that of the original whole." In all organic development, "each organ, as it is developed, serves by its actions and reactions on the rest to initiate new complexities," and thus to advance the process of evolution. Evolution is invariably a change "from a less coherent to a more coherent form," as we see, not only in all physical organism, but in all social organism, and in such things as language and art, for instance. We can, indeed, point to no evidence that our human speech was ever quite so homogeneous as to consist in mere exclamations, which conveyed vague ideas by single sounds, but we are able to trace language back to the stage of simple nouns and verbs; we can see how verbs differentiated into active and passive, and nouns into abstract and concrete; we can watch the evolution of mood, tense, person, and number: and, as language became more and more heterogeneous, we can follow the gradual use of adjectives, adverbs, pronouns, prepositions, and articles. Then, again, we can see how picture-writing passed through the phases of symbol-writing, hieratic-script, and cursive-script, until at length it evolved into printing. It is sufficiently evident also how wall-painting evolved into picture-painting, and bas-relief into sculpture. We know also that there was a time when "rhythm in speech, rhythm in sound, and rhythm in motion" formed part of one and the "same thing," and that they only gradually evolved into the separate arts of poetry, music, and dancing. Thus, whichever way we look, we see that evolution is changed from the relatively homogeneous to the heterogeneous state, and that it is, at the same time, a progress from the indefinite to the definite, "an advance from confusion to order."

Thus, integration and differentiation lead up to "segregation," which is the cause of that "orderly heterogeneity" which the process of evolution invariably displays. Segregation may be defined as the separation of the "unlike units or groups of units of which the aggregate consists." Segregation is caused by "likeness in the incident forces," just as differentiation is caused by unlikeness. This is clearly seen in the process of mental evolution. We can think only in relations; "no thought can express more than relations," because every "act of knowing is the formation of a relation in consciousness, answering to a relation in the environment." Thus, the mind forms "groups of like objects and like relations." In fact, all mental evolution consists in the differentiation in our thoughts of the various things originally confused together in the mind, followed by their segregation into different groups and orders. The mind arranges things into classes, and then into "sub-classes and sub-classes," until the once confused aggregate of objects known to it is resolved into an aggregate which unites "great heterogeneity among its multiplied groups with complete homogeneity among the members of each group."

After passing through concentration, differentiation, and segregation, the process of evolution at length reaches "equilibration," balance, or a state of rest. All motion is from its beginning met everywhere by resistance. From this resistance, motion "suffers increasing deduction," which results finally in its "cessation." Equilibration is visible in the minor changes of state which occur in our solar system. "Each planet, satellite, and comet exhibits at its aphelion a momentary equilibrium between the force which urges it away from its primary and that force which retards its retreat. In like manner, at perihelion, a converse equilibrium is momentarily established." We now recognise that the force known to us in solar radiations is the changed form of some other force of which the sun is the seat, and that by the emission of these radiations this other force is being slowly exhausted, "and thus it is supposed that this constant contraction of its mass causes the emission of the light and heat which we get from the sun." Helmholtz thinks that a yearly contraction of only "one twenty-millionth of the sun's diameter" would generate all the light and heat necessary for us, and he calculates that during the next million years the diameter of the sun will only be diminished "by something like one-twentieth." Calculations such as these of Helmholtz and others can be, of course, but "rude approximations" to truth. But still they show that, according to our present theory, "all the relative motions of the masses which constitute our solar system will ultimately be transformed into molecular motion, and all the molecular motion dissipated." Therefore it may be assumed that, at some period infinitely remote, not only will the solar system, but the sidereal system as a whole, arrive at the stage of equilibrium, and be again dissolved into nebulous matter.

But, on the theory, now held by our scientists, that the energy which animates the universe "remains undiminished," and admits of "no limitation in thought," Spencer suggests that, though we dare not perhaps affirm with the Indian philosophers that "in the totality of things" vast periods of evolution alternate with equally vast periods of rest, we may reasonably infer that "what we know happens to parts will eventually happen to the whole," and consequently that, as evolution goes back to an immeasurable past, it will also "fill an immeasurable future." We cannot, in our deepest researches after truth, get "beyond our experience of the relations of matter, motion, and force," which we have had to admit are but symbols used to express the unknown and unknowable Reality behind them. It is clear that, whatever explanation of the origin of the universe we incline to, whether to the theistic, pantheistic, or atheistic, we are inevitably forced, at some point, to make "the unthinkable assumption of self-existence," and thus to come face to face with "the Unknowable." Then, why not do this at once? Spencer asks, and why should not science and religion become reconciled by their mutual acceptance of the fact that the origin of all things *is* "unknowable"?

CHAPTER XII

ABSTRACT OF THE INHERITANCE

FROM the very nature of the subject, this short review of the world's thought is, at best, but a series of scraps. And yet I make no apology for this fragmentary treatment, simply because I know that, with all its shortcomings, I would so gladly have welcomed just such a collection of the thoughts of the world's thinkers at the time when I first began to take the trouble to think for myself. But, it seems to me that even these disjointed fragments that I have gleaned in the boundless field of philosophical and ethical thought should now be summed up, so that some sort of an estimate may be reached as to the net value of our inheritance.

The first fact, then, that stands out from the rest is the idea, postulated, perhaps more than seven thousand years ago, by the old Akkadian thinkers on the lower banks of the Euphrates, that the universe is dominated by a multitude of nature-spirits — good and bad. From this idea the thinkers of Babylonia, higher up the river, gradually advanced to the conception of a Supreme Spirit, who is supposed to dwell in "Highest

Heaven," the region of the fixed stars. Next, they imagined that between this all-powerful God and men there must be some sort of a "Mediator" or messenger, who passed continually between earth and heaven, and they fabled that this mediator was the great spirit who dwelt within the sphere of the sun, and of whom they looked upon the sun itself as the visible manifestation. They also symbolised the everlasting renewal of life on the earth by the poetical allegory of the love of the ever-youthful Sun-god for the "All-Mother," Nature.

The second great fact that stands out from the mass of thought of the distant past is that, quite three thousand years ago, the thinkers of ancient Egypt anticipated our modern idea of conscience by their theory that every man, at death, becomes the judge of his own past life, and must truthfully decide whether the balance of good over evil in that life justifies the passing on of his soul to everlasting rest by "the Pools of Peace." The records which we have of the moral code, according to which this momentous judgment had to be made, show us that the ethical thought in ancient Egypt was at least of as high an order as the code adopted later by the Jews, and through them by ourselves, and known as "the Ten Commandments."

According to the ideas of the Egyptian philosophers, the universe has evolved by the agency of moisture and heat from a primordial essence which they termed "the Nu." Heat and moisture, as well as all the other great natural forces, were personified as gods. Thus, the god "Khem" was the symbol of the generative force in nature, and the goddess "Maat," or "Mut" (Mother), later adored under the names of "Hâthor" and "Isis," symbolised nature's passive productive force. Somewhat later, Egyptian thinkers endeavoured to explain the origin of all things by the idea of triads or trinities of gods, which they called "Father, Mother, Son." In these trinities the Son was the symbol of the eternal renewal of life, and was held to be "identical" with both "Mother" and "Father." But, as a matter of fact, any of the attributes ascribed to any of the great gods in the Egyptian pantheon were supposed to be interchangeable; and thus the deities themselves gradually came to be looked upon, less as individual gods, than as attributes of one "Unknown God." To this Supreme God no altars were ever raised in Egypt: the inscriptions declare: "He is not seen. He doth not manifest his form. Vain are all representations."

Early thinkers in Persia also evolved the idea of one Unknown God who rules the world, and in Persia no temples were ever dedicated to "Ahura Mazda," the Spirit of Truth, because the whole earth was held to be the great temple of the deity. To account for the presence of evil in nature and in man the Persian philosophers postulated "Angrô-mainyu" (the Dark Spirit), who is ever at war with "Ahura Mazda"; and Persian ethics are based on the idea that every man may choose on which side he will range himself in the eternal strife between good and evil. It seems not unlikely that it was to Persian thinkers that the idea first occurred that one short human life is all too short to give a man the chance of conquering in this desperate strife. They therefore imagined that a frequent renewal of life on earth was necessary to enable the human soul to spiritualise itself. The teaching attributed to the legendary Zoroaster is that only by a resolute persistence in "good aims, good desires, and good deeds" during repeated lives on earth can the soul of man gain that complete knowledge of good and evil which renders life in a body unnecessary. The sole symbol used by the Persians to suggest "the Spirit who is all Life" was fire, which was always kindled by means of friction, and nourished on the household altar only by purified and sweet-scented wood.

Thinkers in India, both Brahman and Buddhist, also held the theory that it is not possible for the human soul to evolve complete spirituality unless it gains that thorough experience of good and evil which can only be attained by passing many lives in a human body. But this idea is differently formulated by the two great systems of Indian philosophy. The Brahman teaching is that the "Âtman," or soul, is a metaphysical entity which continues to exist from one incarnation to another. The Buddhist theory is that "the Self," or soul, is not a persistent entity, or ego, at all, but is nothing more than the synthesis of the "Samkaras." In other words, the Buddhist philosopher imagines that a man's soul is simply the aggregate or sum-total of his sensations, aspirations, and desires. The teaching attributed to Gautama, "the Buddha," or "the Enlightened One," is that the soul must be considered to be a series of different causes, each of which must, sooner or later, inevitably work out its own result, according to the natural law of cause and effect. "The Self" being but the sum of the "Samkaras," it follows that the nature of the desires, motives, and actions of the Self during one incarnation decides the nature of the advantages or disadvantages into which the Self is born in the next incarnation. Each human life, therefore, is the just and logical result of the use—good or bad—made by the man of previous lives. Therefore man's life is compared to the fruit of seed, which, once sown, must go on germinating, and must produce seed after its own kind. In the words ascribed to "the Buddha," "All that we are is the result of what we have thought. . . . By oneself evil is done, by oneself one suffers. . . . Purity and impurity belong to oneself: no man can purify another. . . . One may conquer a thousand men in battle, but he who conquers himself alone is the greatest victor. . . . Let a man overcome anger by kindness, evil by good: let him conquer the stingy by a gift, the liar by truth. . . . Never in this world does hatred cease by hatred. . . . Your low yearnings are within you, and the outside ye make clean. . . . The real treasure is that which is laid up by a man through charity and piety, temperance and self-restraint: this treasure a man takes with him. . . . Those who are in earnest die not: those who are thoughtless are as if already dead." It is worthy of note that these teachings, attributed to the Buddha, are at least three centuries earlier than similar teachings attributed to Jesus of Nazareth.

The most subtle of the many systems of Indian thought is the Vedânta, which teaches that "Karana

Karya." or cause and effect, are one and the same. The argument is, that its effect is latent in every cause, and that every effect must necessarily, in its turn, be the cause of some further effect. Therefore, says the Vedânta, "they are not other, are not different from each other." Thus Brâhman is one with the visible universe, for the reason that one is the cause of the other. It is, however, admitted that the mind can only realise this idea when the thinker is in the state of ecstatic trance known as "moksha." In this state of self-hypnotisation the mind instinctively perceives that it is "one with Brâhman," and that the phenomena which constitute the material world are mere "Mâyâ," or illusion. The consciousness, or "Self," is held to be the only "reality," because through all the changes of life that alone remains unchanged.

There seems to be more than a probability that Pythagorean thought, which had so great an influence in Greece from about the fifth century B.C., may have had an Indian origin. Plato speaks several times of Pythagoreanism, but never once mentions Pythagoras as a personality; and it may be that the name is nothing but a personification of a system of thought. There is indeed no more reliable record that Pythagoras ever lived and taught than there is that either Zoroaster, Krishna, Buddha, or Homer—to say nothing of Moses—were historical personages. But the legend is that Pythagoras was born at Samos, and that, after long wanderings in Egypt, Persia, and India, he settled at Crotona, where he founded a mystic brotherhood and disappeared during a popular emeute. What is certain, however, is that Pythagoreanism teaches that the soul of man is a "spark" of the "Divine Fire," an integral atom of the "Universal Soul," whose immortality it shares. Like Brahmanism, it teaches that to become spiritual the soul must pass through many lives on earth, and therefore that a system of self-discipline is necessary to evolve character, and to enable a man to become self-reliant, self-restrained, and self-possessed. The Pythagorean watchword was: "No man is free who is not master of himself."

But most of the Greek thinkers of this epoch inclined more to the solution of physical than of psychical problems. Of these, Heraclitus of Ephesus was the first who clearly perceived that eternal flux or change—in a word, evolution—is the inherent quality of the universe. He imagined that all the elements might be transmuted, one into the other, and he seems almost to have reached the conception of our modern postulate of the ether. A little later Anaxagoras of Clazomenæ advanced the theory that the universe consists of germs which combine under the stimulus of a powerful elementary-force; and he was also the first Greek thinker who surmised that the moon and the stars are solid bodies, and that moonlight is merely reflected sunlight. Democritus of Abdera followed with his very suggestive conjecture that the universe is made up of atoms, all vital and self-moving. It is interesting to note that among the many ethical sayings recorded of Democritus, he gave, four hundred years before the Christian era, utterance to such an idea as that "a charitable man is he who looks not for return, but deliberately purposes to do well," and also that "the whole world is the fatherland of a noble soul." It was only a little later than this also that Socrates laid down his life, as we may say, for an idea—too proud to plead for pardon for teaching what he thought to be right, for teaching men to free themselves from the slavery of custom, habit, and superstition, and to dare to think things out for themselves, and thus reach a loftier idea of life. For, Socrates was persuaded that all vice and all crime are the natural result of ignorance and error, and that goodness, when once *understood*, must inevitably draw all men to itself.

On the lines laid down by his revered master, Socrates, Plato afterwards founded his theory of an ideal "Republic." We get glimpses of Plato's beautiful ethical teaching in such ideas as: "All the gold that is under the earth, or upon it, is not enough to get in exchange for virtue. . . . A good man cannot harm any human being, no, not an enemy. . . . A man's care must be, not to seem good, but to be good, in private and public life alike." Plato's metaphysical teaching, which may have come to him through Pythagoreanism, undoubtedly suggests an Indian origin. He speaks of the material universe as "the God manifested to sense," like any Brahman philosopher; and he teaches that all that has life has soul, because soul and life are one and the same thing. He says that the perceptions of the mind are the only realities, and defines the mind as "the mediator" between the world of phenomenal appearances and the "real world" of ideas. Plato also frankly adopts the theory of the repeated rebirth of the soul. He says: "At one time the soul has an end, which is termed dying, and at another is born again, but is never destroyed." The soul, he explains, is impelled to incarnate time after time because of its intense craving for physical existence and for that experience which life in a human body only can give. But his idea is that, as soon as the soul has once attained to a true conception of "the Beautiful and the Good," it no longer needs to incarnate. Life and soul being one, all that has life must have soul; but soul itself is a complex thing; it consists of the "animal soul," which man has in common with the brutes, and of the "spiritual soul," which is the attribute of man only. Soul is "ever in motion," and therefore it must be immortal. All abstract ideas, such as justice, beauty, goodness, Plato considers to be "recollections" of the intuitive perceptions of the soul whilst existing on the spiritual plane. He says: "Having been born many times, . . . it is no wonder that the soul should be able to call to remembrance all that she knows about virtue; for, as all nature is akin, and the soul has learned all things, there is no difficulty in eliciting, or, as men say, learning, out of a simple recollection all the rest, if a man be strenuous and does not faint; for all inquiry and all learning is recollection."

Plato's idea of the human soul is more or less accepted by his pupil, Aristotle, who defines soul as "the energy of the organism," and as "the formative principle of the body." Aristotle imagines that, at death, the soul is re-absorbed into the divine, and he argues that the mind of man (nous poeticos) must be immortal because it is able "to conceive the universal and the divine." But mind without body can be but a "possibility of thinking," and can have but "a potential existence." Like Plato, Aristotle looks upon soul as the connecting-link between the two worlds of matter and spirit, which causes it to be the battle-field of the animal and spiritual powers. He defines virtue as the state of balance between man's lower and higher impulses. He does not say, with Plato, that soul and life are synonymous, but he calls soul the organising principle of life, and says that it is the "idea" or "form" which is the end and object of all evolution, the goal towards which, under the impulse of the "mediator," motion, matter is ever approaching. It is clear, says Aristotle, that all motion in the universe must have had a beginning: and he asks: "How can there be a beginning without some cause which is ever in motion?" To account for the commencement of motion, therefore, he postulates "Nous," or mind. This he defines as being "both Law and Law-giver," and also as being "the subject of its own thought." It is not easy to understand what Aristotle means by this entity which he terms "Nous," and which he conceives to be a power outside the universe, but which he explains has neither knowledge of the material universe, nor power to act upon it. Nevertheless, this postulate of the Divine Mind—"the subject of its own thought" —was enough to make the philosophy of Aristotle far more acceptable to the mediæval Church than the philosophy of Plato, although the ethical teaching of Plato is far more in harmony with Christian thought.

But of all the systems of Greek thought the Stoic was the one which exercised by far the greatest influence on men of culture in the Roman Empire, from about 300 B.C. to about 200 A.D. Tacitus, indeed, tells us that the only honest and disinterested men in public life, during the first century of the Christian era, were all Stoics. This name was given to the disciples of Zeno because it was the custom of that philosopher to discourse with them as they walked with him to and fro in the "stoa pöecile," at Athens, the colonnade adorned with the famous paintings of Polygnotus. Zeno taught pantheism pure and simple, like any Indian philosopher, basing his cosmology on the idea of eternal evolution. His theory is that everything in the universe proceeds from primordial substance, which he calls the Universal Soul, and that, after manifestation, all things again return to this universal essence. Inherent in the Universal Soul is a mysterious motive-power, which he terms "Nous," or Universal Reason. Nous is active both on the physical and psychical plane: when it manifests its energy on the physical plane, Zeno calls it "Pneuma," but he calls it "Logos" when it manifests on the mental plane. His idea of the beginning of the process of evolution of the material universe is, that it is due to the spontaneous activity of what he calls the "spermatikoi logoi," or seminal manifestations, and which he supposes to be countless centres of force latent throughout primordial substance.

It will be noticed that this idea is not unlike the theory of vortices, suggested by some modern thinkers.

But it was not so much the material as the ethical teaching of Stoicism which had so far-reaching an effect on human thought, especially the doctrine that, as the conscious self in man is identical with Divine Reason, or Nous, it is within the power of everyone to become virtuous who will take pains to train his mind to be in harmony with reason. The aim of the true Stoic was to gain complete control over himself, his passions and desires, and thus to fit himself to do his duty and his proper work in the world, unmoved by the trials and accidents of life. This is the drift of the teaching of Epictètus, whose discourses, delivered during the first century A.D., shadow forth the later sermons of Christian teachers. Epictetus says: "Our happiness must consist solely of a righteous will. There is no pleasure a perfect man will not renounce, no pain he will not endure, rather than leave duty unfulfilled." Life is compared to a drama, in which every actor has to play his part to the best of his ability. No matter what a man's work may be, he must do it well. "Remember," says Epictetus, "that you are to act your part in life's drama in any character that the manager may choose—your business is to act well the character that is given to you." Life is also likened to a banquet, at which every decent guest helps himself to whatever is placed before him "without haste and without greed." In 65 A.D., the Stoic teacher Seneca points out that, just as Pheidias would carve the best statue possible out of any material given to him, so the wise man will show his virtue equally in poverty or in wealth, in sickness or in health, as a general or as a mere soldier in the ranks, in his fatherland or in exile. In short, "whatever fortune is granted to him, the virtuous man will make it the means of some memorable achievement." The Stoics held that a man's own conscience is the only true judge whether his actions are right or wrong, because the intention counts for more than the act, and therefore no one but the man himself knows the motives of his actions. The Stoic emperor, Marcus Aurelius, writes during the second century, in his diary: "He who is loyal to his own indwelling mind and God, and is a willing votary to that inward grace, makes no scenes, heaves no sighs, needs not a wilderness, nor yet a crowd. The best is his, the life that neither seeks nor shuns. . . . Things of the body are but a stream that flows, things of the soul a dream and vapour, life a warfare and a sojourning, and after fame oblivion. What then can direct our goings? One thing, and one thing alone—philosophy, which is to keep the deity within inviolate and pure from scathe, superior to pleasure and to pain, doing nothing at random, nothing falsely and disingenuously."

It is interesting to compare this "deity within" of Marcus Aurelius, which he also calls his "law-giver," his "pilot," and his "ruler and guide," with the "Christos" of the Gnostics—that divine Light "which lighteth every man that cometh into the world." Valentinus, the Gnostic, who taught in Rome about the middle of the second century A.D., defined the

Christos as the higher spirit of humanity and as the perfect manifestation of the Good. It dawns, he says, in the "psychic man," and shines forth in "the pneumatic man," leading him ever nearer to the divine, until the human is merged in "the Kingdom of Light," or "Pleroma." This, it will be seen, is the equivalent of "the Universal Reason" of the Stoics. The well-known writer who assumed the name of "Hermes Tris-megistus" defines the human soul as "an eternal and intelligent essence" whose basis is "perpetual motion," which causes its repeated incarnation in a human body. "How many bodies," he exclaims, "must we pass through that we may hasten to the only God!" All things, he says, are "full of soul and properly moved by that." His theory is that animal-souls consist only of passion and desire. Human souls are also "bound to these irrational elements, which are undying because they are energies." Every wise man, therefore, must strive to "become wholly mind, which is the very essence of the God, if indeed, there is any essence of God. . . . The mind in man is indeed God."

Philo, the Alexandrian Jew, writing a little earlier, says that "souls descend into a body, as into a river." The whirlpool of passion sweeps many away, but a few strive against it. The man who is content to lead a material life only "dies the death even while yet breathing among the living." Hades, he explains, "is the life of one who is in a state of wickedness—a life which is an avenger." It is interesting again to compare this with the writing of the Christian Father, Origen, in the third century A.D., who maintains that all spirits in the Ideal World are originally "of the same nature," and are all "free to remain in their first estate." But the strong self-will of some of these spirits evolves souls which vary in their nature as sense or mind predominates in them. Each soul, says Origen, comes into life with its "spermatic germs of good and evil," and, laying hold of "suitable matter, shapes it into a habitation fitted to its needs." No "birth, happy or unhappy, is ruled by chance."

Among the mystic thinkers of the early centuries of the Christian era, no one is more suggestive than Plotinus, whose philosophy is to a large extent a revival of Plato's. He maintains that the universe is one living organism, and therefore that no action can take place in any part of it without causing reaction on the whole. The world of matter and of mind he conceives to be the result of waves of energy emanating from "the divine centre of life," each wave, as it recedes from the centre of force, becoming less and less spiritual. Life, he says, radiates from the Absolute Life as light radiates from the sun, as heat radiates from fire. He calls the first emanation from this centre of energy the Universal Mind, and also the "One-Many." It is, he thinks, the totality of ideas existing in the universe. The second emanation Plotinus calls the Universal Soul. But he explains that, strictly speaking, the universe cannot be said to have a soul, because "it lies *in* the soul which sustains it, and no part of it is destitute of soul, being moistened with life, like a net in water." The soul of the universe he conceives to be one, just as sunlight is one. The human soul is an epitome of the Universal

Soul, and is *en rapport* with all the forces in the universe. That is why the human consciousness is able to be instantly present, *as an individual entity*, wherever the activity of the human mind can reach.

Plotinus appears to have been the latest of the Greek thinkers to maintain the ancient theory of the necessity of the soul's repeated rebirth in a body, in order to become spiritual; and he seems to have been replying to some objections raised by one of his pupils, when he explains that there is nothing in the argument that, if men had lived before, they would remember their previous lives, because memory, as we generally understand it, is a faculty of the brain, which perishes with the body. But he suggests that memory is of a twofold nature. All the memories stored up by the physical soul are indeed "washed away in the River of Lethe"—the body; but the memories belonging to man's spiritual soul may be revived, little by little, in each human soul as it becomes more and more spiritual. Aim at a beautiful ideal, he says, and strive to live up to it: "and, if thou findest that thou art not beautiful, as the sculptor of a statue that is to be beautiful chips and files away, making this smooth and that pure, till he brings out on his statue a lovely face, so do thou chip off what is superfluous, straighten what is crooked, cleanse what is dark, and cease not to labour at thy statue until there shine forth the radiance of virtue."

So far, we have a very rough summary of the most suggestive thoughts that have come down to us, through the ages, from Babylonia, Egypt, Persia, India, and Greece. We have seen that a strong Mongolian element was at the basis of early Akkadian thought, but we have no other evidence that Chinese thought ever filtered through into India or Greece. It is only in late years that we have come into our heritage of Chinese thought, which we now know was active at a very remote epoch. As one of the many indications of this, we find King Khang, who lived a thousand years before the Christian era, reminding one of his viceroys, who is about to leave for his distant province, that "the end of all punishment is to make an end of punishing." This man is only one of many similarly enlightened monarchs. But perhaps the most interesting Chinese thought belongs to the time of the Pythagorean epoch in Greece. At that period we find a thinker, known as Lao-Tsze, teaching that an unknown spiritual force, latent in every molecule of matter, is omnipotent throughout the universe. This force he calls "Tao," and says that, as we can ascribe to it no attributes, it can be thought of only as "No-Thing." It can only be described as "the Way"; it is the eternal Path along which the whole universe moves. He who "walks in the way," he who is strong enough to conquer passion and desire, he who is pure in thought as well as in deed, becomes "one with Tao"; he is in harmony with the spirit of the universe, and to him Tao is revealed. As a means of attaining to this blessed union with Tao, Lao-Tsze advises his disciples to cultivate the faculty of throwing themselves, by meditation, into the state of ecstatic trance.

But the next notable Chinese teacher, Kung-fu-Tsze, better known under his Latinised name, Confucius, condemned this practice of self-hypnotism. During the latter half of the sixth century B.C. Confucius taught that, in order to lead a true life, a man must get a thorough knowledge of himself, so as to be able to purify and to brighten his mind, which is ever "dulled by desire." He says: "The perfect man behaves towards his friends as he expects his friends to behave towards him, but the foolish man swerves from 'the path,' doing either too little or too much." His conviction was that the only way to prevent crime is to educate the people. Kindness must, of course, be repaid with kindness; but, for the sake of society, all injury must be met with justice, however much a good man may be inclined to forgive an injury done to himself. "Remember always thou art a man," says Confucius, "and that human nature is weak, and that thou mayest easily fall, and thou shalt never fall. But if, happening to forget what thou art, thou chancest to fall, be not discouraged: remember that thou mayest rise again. . . . To conquer thyself is to do what is agreeable to reason."

When one thinks how many of our ideas about cosmology, religion, and ethics came to us originally through Jewish sources, it is rather humiliating to find that ancient Jewish thought was on a comparatively low level. The idea of the God of Abraham and of Jacob, for instance, was not nearly so grand as the the idea of the Unknown God of the Egyptian and Persian thinkers. Yahveh, indeed, was obviously nothing more than a tribal god, "jealous" of the worship of any other tribal deity, a "god of battles," and a "god of vengeance," just like Baal, "the Lord," the rival Semitic deity. The chief command given by Yahveh to his "chosen people" is to "increase and multiply," to slaughter their enemies, and to "possess the land." He is supposed to insist on the mutilation of all male children, in token of allegiance, and to demand the sacrifice of the first-born. The barbaric idea of justice ascribed to Yahveh is "an eye for an eye, and a tooth for a tooth"; and in the case of his contemptible "friend" Jacob, the "man after God's own heart," he is supposed actually to condone falsehood and deceit. Nor is any trace of the doctrine of a future life to be found in the Torah, or Jewish Book of the Law, better known to us as the Pentateuch, or Five Books. These, indeed, are popularly attributed to Moses, but were originally composed by the Jewish Rabbi in Babylonia, about six centuries B.C., and revised by Ezra about two centuries later. The Persian theory of the persistence of the soul seems to have been adopted first by the sect of the Pharisees, during the first century A.D., at the time when Philo, at Alexandria, was expounding the Jewish scriptures by the light of Greek thought. But the rival sect of the Sadducees continued to hold the Mosaic teaching that all rewards and punishments take place on earth. The Talmud is a collection of explanations of the teaching of the Torah which were originally given by word of mouth to their pupils by a succession of rabbis, and were only first put into writing, from memory, in the fourth century of our era. The result is described by a learned Jew as "a literary wilderness." We find the Talmud to be a mixture of Jewish, Persian, Greek, and Gnostic thought, amongst which, however, are some few fine sayings—such, for instance, as that attributed, about half a century B.C., to Rabbi Hillel, who, on being asked to sum up the whole Law, replied: "Whatever is not pleasant to thee, do not unto thy fellow-man. This is the substance of the Law and the Prophets: all the rest is commentary thereon. Go, and reflect on it!" Other suggestive sayings in the Talmud are: "Never put thyself in the way of temptation." . . . "Let thy nay be nay, let thy yea be yea." . . . "The trouble sufficeth for each hour." . . . "Judge not thy neighbour so long as thou art not in his place." . . . "Charity is more than sacrifice." . . . "With the measure with which a man measures, men will measure him." . . . "Whosoever is quick in forgiving, his sins also shall be forgiven him. . . ."

Of all the various commentaries on the Jewish Law, the most interesting is that of Rabbi ben Maimon, better known to us as Maimonides. Towards the end of the twelfth century A.D. he published his chief commentary, which he calls "A Guide to the Perplexed," and which he addresses "specially to thinkers who have studied philosophy." He explains that the written Law is intended "for the instruction of the young, of women, and of the common people," and therefore is written in language they can understand. But the sciences, he says, are "mysteries" (sodeth) veiled in allegories and riddles which are unveiled only to "the wise." He picturesquely compares the "hidden meaning" of a symbol or allegory to "a pearl hidden in a dark room." The pearl is always there, but cannot be found until "light is kindled." Like other thinkers, Maimonides has his theory of the universe, which he considers to be "one individual being," composed of five spheres, one outside the other. The innermost sphere is the earth, beyond which are successively the spheres of water, air, fire, and a fifth element which, as he describes it, seems very like the "primordial substance" of the Greek thinkers, or the "Akâsa" of the Indian philosophers, or the hypothetical "ether" of our modern scientists. He suggests that motion in the universe has its origin in the eternal activity of this fifth element, "in the same way that action in the human body has its origin in the pulsation of the human heart." And Maimonides also surmises that all the elements may be transformed one into the other by the activity of the fifth element. The universe is controlled by "a certain force" without which existence would be impossible: "that force is God, blessed be His Name!" He uses the word "One," he says, in reference to God, "to express that there is nothing similar to Him." Then he indulges in a laugh at the foolish vanity of the theologians of his time who undertake to explain God: "Those foolish persons, extravagant in praise, fluent and prolix in the prayers they compose, and in the hymns they make in the desire to approach the Creator. They describe God in attributes which would be an offence if applied to a human being. Treating the Creator as a familiar object, they describe and speak of Him in any expression they think proper: they eloquently continue to praise Him in that manner, and believe that they can influence Him and produce an effect on Him."

We see that, up to the time of the Roman Empire, thought was clear and continuously progressive. Then came that "confusion of thought" which was due to the eclectic system known as Christianity, which materialised the beautiful teaching of the Christos, the spiritual light in man, and combined with it so many discordant ideas. The Emperor Constantine, for political reasons, had adopted Christianity as the state religion, and, after the fall of the Roman Empire, the Roman Church, by means of the subtle influence it exercised over the minds of the many, gradually secured more and more of the political power which had once belonged to the state. During the "Dark Ages" which followed the break-up of Græco-Roman civilisation, men of culture sought refuge more and more in the Christian monasteries, and the continued use of the Latin language by the Catholic Church formed, for a long time, the only link with the literature of the past.

Towards the end of the fourth century A.D., Siricius, Bishop of the Church at Rome, assumed the title of "Holy Father," or Pope, the Ecclesia became more and more complete, and gradually began to exercise temporal as well as spiritual power. This power was exercised by the Church with increasing tyranny, until, in 1233, Pope Gregory IX. formally established the Inquisition, or "Holy Office," to stamp out all heretical thought. Agents of the

Inquisition were appointed in every district to hunt down heretics; torture was freely used to extort evidence of their heresy, and conviction was frequently followed by burning the heretic at the stake. In Italy, Spain, and France the Holy Office was for a time omnipotent, but in England no Inquisitor seems actually to have been appointed—under that name, at least; nor was the Holy Office ever firmly established in Germany, where, in 1520, Martin Luther boldly stood up for freedom of thought, and burned the papal bull of his excommunication before his pupils at Wittenberg. "Confusion of thought" had indeed reached its climax when the Church of Christ, which preached universal brotherhood and love, tortured and burned men and women for no other reason than that they declined to accept its doctrines.

One is glad to remember that, even in such times as these, there were always men who dared to think for themselves. Such a man was the Irishman, John Scotus Erigena, who was chief teacher at the Palatine Academy about the middle of the ninth century. In opposition to the doctrine of the Church, Erigena maintained the pantheistic theory, that "God is everything and everything is God." But, what God is, he confesses to be a mystery too deep for the human mind to fathom, nor do we, he says, get any nearer to its solution when we speak of God as "Light," "Truth," "Goodness," or "Love." Erigena argues that, if we admit that God is everything, it follows that the human soul is identical with the deity. Thus, being in harmony with God, the man who is really virtuous may attain to "the vision of God." Anselmus of Aosta was perhaps the next very prominent speculative thinker. He entered the monastery of Bec, in Normandy, became abbot, and died as Archbishop of Canterbury in 1109. It is true that he says that doubt is a temptation of Satan, and that no one must doubt the dogmas of the Church; but, all the same, he thinks it necessary to prove the existence of God. He argues, like Des Cartes at a later date, that we have in ourselves the idea of an absolutely perfect Being, that perfection implies existence, and that it follows that God exists. Anselmus also dares to say that all attributes ascribed to God are mere figures of speech.

About this time dissertations concerning the Holy Trinity were not uncommon. Rocellinus of Compiègne, among others, showed the difficulty of accepting this dogma of the Church; and somewhat later Abelard, influenced by a slight knowledge of Greek philosophy, which, as he says, he only knows at second hand from the works of St Augustine, explains the Trinity to consist of the divine attributes of power, wisdom, and goodness, not of Father, Son, and Holy Spirit, as the Church teaches. This heretical teaching of Abelard's was previous to the formal institution of the "Holy Office," which had, we know, its own Christian way of dealing with heretics. One of such "heretics," to whom the modern thinking world owes a deep debt of gratitude for his assertion of the freedom of thought, was Giordano Bruno. Summed up in a few words, his teaching is that life is a rhythmical whole, the higher forms evolving from the lower. All that exists is the manifestation of the "One Life." From this all proceeds, to this all returns. Universal Substance is vivified by Universal Soul, both alike being indestructible; but the forms which result from the action of soul upon substance are transitory and incomplete, and it is this state of incompleteness which is the cause of evil and death. Until all transitory forms evolve into a higher state of being, death and evil are inevitable. Soul acts upon substance by means of a differentiating force, which Bruno calls "dyas." His idea is that the expansion of "dyas" produces material forms, whilst thought is evolved by its concentration. In speaking of the universe, he employs many synonyms, calling it, indifferently, "substance of substances," "monad of monads," "universal life," and "God." All life emanates from God as radii from a centre: God is the sole source of light, both physical and mental: God is the primal idea, reflected in the material world, whilst Christ is spiritual light, not the materialised God, as the Church tells us. It is not surprising, perhaps, that teaching so heretical as this, together with Bruno's persistent and unflinching demonstrations of the new theory that the sun is the centre round which the world revolves—one of the most damaging blows ever dealt to the authority of the Catholic Church,—should have brought Bruno to the stake, in the "year of our Lord" 1600, a few years after Shakespeare had published his *Venus and Adonis* and Bacon had published his *Essays*.

Five years after the martyrdom of Giordano Bruno,

Francis Bacon issued the English edition of his great work, originally written in Latin, under the title of *Novum Organon Scientiarum.* In this Bacon shows the folly of disputing about words, as do the Scholastics, when the only way to reach true knowledge of any kind is to try to understand things. He contends that it is useless to start our study of nature by assuming final causes, but that we must begin by investigating facts, which will lead us little by little to the discovery of laws.

Bacon's younger friend and secretary, Thomas Hobbes, who during his thirteen years' residence in France had been mathematical teacher to the young prince, afterwards Charles II., looked at things from Bacon's point of view. He ultimately came to the conclusion that good and evil are only relative ideas, and that absolute good and absolute evil are mere empty metaphysical phrases.

Two generations later, John Locke published his very thoughtful *Essay concerning Human Understanding.* In this he maintains, in opposition to Des Cartes, that there are no such things as innate ideas or freedom of will, but that all our knowledge of external things comes to us through the medium of our sensations, whilst our knowledge of internal things is simply and purely the result of our own reflections. From the one or other of these two sources proceed all our ideas, which may therefore be classified as either "simple or complex." Simple ideas he defines as those of hardness, softness, light, heat, etc.: these ideas reach our minds through our senses, the mind being in a passive state to receive them. When the mind is in a state of activity it forms for itself complex ideas in endless variety. We can, Locke thinks, have no possible knowledge of what either matter or spirit actually is. Such ideas as those of space, eternity, or immortality he defines as "negative ideas," and such ideas as genera, species, or essence are, he says, a mere "artifice of the understanding." He thinks that a future existence is probable, because, "when one hath all that this world can afford, he is still unsatisfied," and he infers the existence of God from the fact of the human mind. He says, "We cannot want a clear proof of God as long as we carry ourselves about with us, because mind can only be explained by mind." But he goes on to say that we can have "no other idea of God than a complex one of existence, knowledge, power, happiness infinite and eternal. . . . All which, being originally got from sensation and reflection, go to make up the *complex idea* we call God."

Bishop Berkeley did his best to counteract the free-thought of his time by his endeavour to prove, something after the manner of Plato, that the material world has no actual existence. But he thoughtlessly upsets his own argument, by pointing to the wonderful design evident in the world around us as the best proof of the existence of God. This lays him open to the banter of David Hume, who, in his *Enquiry concerning Human Understanding*, published in 1748, laughs at the "curious researches" by which "a philosopher may indeed throw himself and others into a momentary amazement and confusion." But Hume admits that, if we consider things from the metaphysical point of view only, "when we say 'this house,' or 'that tree,' we speak of nothing but perceptions in our minds"—perceptions which may indeed be described as being "fleeting representations." Nevertheless, as Hume says, this does not do away with the actual tree and the actual house, which "remain independent of our perception of them." Hume agrees with Locke, that all our ideas may be traced ultimately back to sensation, and that the most we can do is to "arrange" the ideas which we get from our "outward and inward sentiment." He classifies all our perceptions according as they are more or less "lively," and calls the lively perceptions which we have when we see, hear, feel, desire, love, or hate "impressions," whilst the less lively perceptions he calls "ideas, or thoughts." After saying that "the most lively thought is still inferior to the dullest sensation," Hume adds that the least lively of all are those indefinite ideas which we call abstract. "All our impressions are innate," but "our ideas are not innate." It is useless to dispute about cause and effect, because "no effect is discoverable in what we call its cause." We are so accustomed to see things constantly in *conjunction*, that we get into the habit of "*expecting*" the one from the presence of the other. But of cause and effect we know, in fact, nothing.

All our knowledge being due to experience, Hume asks how we can hope to solve the mystery of the soul, or the origin of the universe, when we cannot explain such simple things as why heat accompanies flame, or even why we are able to move our limbs.

Kant agrees with Hume so far, that "there can be no doubt that all our knowledge begins with experience." But he thinks that it does not necessarily "arise from experience," nor end with experience; and therefore he wrote his *Critique of Pure Reason* to show that there is a kind of knowledge "independent of experience," which we arrive at by means of what he calls "synthetical judgments." Kant points out that "the blind feelings," which we call sensation, must be synthesised and arranged before we can use them to form concepts. He therefore makes the distinction between *a priori* knowledge and *a posteriori* knowledge. *A posteriori* knowledge is obtained from our experience, but *a priori* knowledge deals with "general truths," and goes, therefore, "beyond the limits of experience." To prove his point, Kant carries his readers on through the most subtle and intricate arguments. But, in the end, he practically admits that there is, after all, no such thing as "*a priori* knowledge," or knowledge *previous* to all experience. He says that it is as impossible to prove that "the world has a beginning in time and is limited also with regard to space," as it is to prove the contrary; that the real existence of the soul is "nothing more than a psychological idea"; that the ego is "a transcendental subject of thought which is known only *through* the thoughts, and of which, apart from them, we can never have the slightest concept." Kant admits, indeed, that "the three ideas"—God, freedom, immortality—to investigate which, he says, is "the real object of mathematics," are and must "always remain transcendental to speculation." In the course of his remarkable *Critique* Kant propounds the helpful theory that time and space are not realities, but are simply "two original intuitions" of the mind, without which we could have no possible perception of the world outside us. This theory, which Kant supports with very clear arguments, was afterwards adopted both by Goethe and Carlyle. Like Hume, Kant smiles at "the good Bishop Berkeley" when he tries to do away altogether with the material world. Kant explains that, when he says that "the mind represents objects in time and space as they affect our senses, that is, as they appear, I do not mean that these objects are mere illusion, I do not mean that bodies *seem* only to exist outside me." Kant distinguishes between the matter and the form of phenomena, calling "that which corresponds to sensation" its matter, but that which causes the matter to be perceived by us "as arranged in a certain order" its form. He thinks that form may be "considered as separate from all sensations," and that the *idea* of form exists "in the mind *a priori*." After all the elaborate thinking in his *Critique of Pure Reason*, Kant concludes: "The question, What can I know? is purely speculative," but the question, "What should I do? is purely practical," a question of what a man *wills* to do: "A good will is that by which alone man's existence can have an absolute freedom."

A generation later we find Hegel asserting that activity is the only reality, and that a being exists only because, and as long as, it *acts* in some way, and that everything evolves according to "reason," or law. Reason, as Hegel understands it, is not the mere human faculty treated of by Kant. But reason is explained to be the very essence of evolution both of matter and mind: nature is the self-development of reason. At first, reason in nature is quite unconscious: it becomes conscious in animals, and self-conscious in man. Nothing in nature exists in isolation. Therefore, no cause, force, quality, or quantity is anything at all apart from the whole of which it forms part. Consequently, no cause is absolutely, but only relatively, absolute; nor can we ever separate cause and effect, for the simple reason that every cause is the effect of a preceding cause, and every effect must itself become a cause. As reason in man gradually evolves, he recognises that other men are his equals, that nothing is his own exclusive right, and thus, by degrees, society becomes possible. Society evolves an impersonal will: this impersonal will becomes, in its turn, the personal will of the individual, and man becomes moral: law regulates the material interests of life, and morality subordinates the useful to the good.

A year after Hegel had published his *Encyclopædia of the Philosophical Sciences*, Schopenhauer gave us his treatise on *The World as Will and Idea*, written to prove his theory that "the inscrutable forces which manifest themselves in nature, different as no doubt they are in degree, are probably identical in kind with what in ourselves we know as will." Schopenhauer enforces his hypothesis with a series of cogent arguments. Our earth, which has been formed into a sphere by the conflict of the forces of repulsion and attraction, furnishes us, he says, with an example of "the very lowest grade of will," for every force in nature is a manifestation of will, which shows itself in an ever-ascending scale from matter to mind. "The lowest grades of will are gravity, impenetrability, rigidity, fluidity, elasticity, electricity, magnetism, and chemical properties of every kind." Will shows itself first in the organic world—in plant or in animal—under the guise of "irritability."

To ask why or how the world exists is useless. The only sensible question is: What is it? The best answer Schopenhauer can find to this question is the Indian theory that the real world to every man is just what *he* conceives it to be—no more and no less. The world, he says, is merely a thing perceived—"a phenomenon of the brain." To Schopenhauer this seems to be so self-evident a proposition, that, like an axiom of Euclid, "it must be recognised directly it is understood." It is absurd, he says, "to attribute to the material world, as such, an existence apart from all idea, and independently of the knowing subject," because what each man knows is not a sun or an earth, but only an eye which sees a sun and a hand which feels an earth." He reminds us that thinkers in India and Greece discovered long since that "this world which appears to the senses has no true being, but only a ceaseless becoming." But although the world of phenomena is an illusion, primordial substance, "with all its physical, chemical, and electrical properties," is not an illusion, but is "the true 'Mater rerum' from the obscurity of whose womb all phenomena come forth, to fall back into it at some time again." The material world is the result of the action of unconscious forces or will. We know that "*we* could not contrive such things without using our brains," and we therefore postulate a Divine Will to account for them. But some of us are beginning to discover that the evolution of the universe may be accounted for by the action of the forces which are inherent in matter, and which act according to laws of which as yet we know but little. Will and action are in reality one and the same. Until brain is evolved, will remains a blind force in nature, and a blind force it still is "in the vegetative part of our own life." We can find no answer to the question why we will, or why we will to exist at all, just because we ourselves are "nothing but will" Schopenhauer is perhaps thinking of Hegel when he says that our relation to the outer world leads us to imagine that the ego is "the knowing 'I,' which wearies in the evening, vanishes in sleep, and in the morning shines brighter with renewed strength": whereas "the true self is what is behind that, and knows nothing but willing and not willing, being content and not content." We can no more say that will is the result of knowledge than we can say that the light carried by a man in a lantern "is the 'primum mobile' of his steps." But we may liken the intellect to "the reflecting surface of a calm lake," and the will to "the force whose vibrations disturb the watery mirror"; or we may say. "The will is warmth, the intellect light." The self-denying saint whose will has reached "perfect self-knowledge" may indeed attain to "that peace which is above reason," which the Indian sages speak of as Nirvâna. But to the ordinary man, who still cherishes "the will to live," death is not the end of life, and therefore it is probable that "after the sleep of death" most of us will wake again, "refreshed and fitted out with another intellect as a new being," although just because of this "new intellect" we cannot possibly have any remembrance of an earlier existence. We cannot "show the bridge between them," indeed, but the two existences may be said to be continuous, and the ego to be a manifestation of "the indestructible will" as it passes through "a succession of dreams." These "dreams" Schopenhauer thinks must continue, until the ego has been so thoroughly educated by experience gained "in a constantly new form" that "knowledge has, as it were, burnt up and consumed the will, so that no desire remains for individual existence."

Comte describes his *Philosophie Positive*, which he published in successive volumes between 1830 and 1842, as "a mode of reasoning on all subjects open to human investigation." The vain desire for absolute knowledge, he says, forces the mind back into theological fictions and metaphysical entities; therefore the Positive Philosophy does not "pretend to explain the real causes of phenomena, but only to analyse correctly the circumstances of their production and to connect them together by normal relations of succession and similarity." Comte starts with the theory that, before reaching the positive phase of thought, every nation passes, as does each individual thinker, through two previous phases—the theological and the metaphysical; and, in a masterly and exhaustive review, he traces the progress of the world's thought through these stages up to the positive stage of thought. This he does as a preface to a system of study which will enable thinkers in future to unite in the introduction of a social organisation which shall ensure the happiness of mankind. Nothing can be done, he says, without free inquiry, but "it is useless to be always examining and never deciding." Therefore it is the duty of thoughtful men to see that "the vague and stormy discussions about rights should now be replaced by the calm and precise determinations of duties."

Comte therefore suggests that the student of the Positive Philosophy should begin his study of science "with the review of the most general and simple phenomena, going successively to the more particular and complex." The most general of all the sciences is astronomy, and the most particular is sociology. The student must therefore start from "inorganic physics," which, Comte explains, "consist of astronomical and terrestrial phenomena, including chemical phenomena." Only after obtaining a sufficient knowledge of these should the student pass on to the study of "organic physics," which include physiology and the general laws of life, ending with the study of "social physics, or sociology." A logical education must be based on mathematics; not so much on account of the knowledge of which mathematics consists, but because of "its simplicity, abstractedness, generality, and freedom from all disturbance of human passions." It is these qualities which make mathematics "the most powerful instrument that the human mind can employ," developing in the student "the sense of logical laws without which physical laws could not be conceived of." But the "practical value" of the Positive Philosophy, says Comte, is that, the whole system being founded on "social morality," it is "the only solid basis of the social reorganisation which must terminate the great political and moral crises of existing society. Theological philosophy "gave a character of exorbitant selfishness to all moral acts"—men were good in order to save their own souls, and even metaphysical philosophy still "bases morality on self-interest." But positive morality teaches "the habitual practice of goodness without any other reward than internal satisfaction." It is to be regretted that the detailed scheme of social regeneration which Comte intended should follow his course of Positive Philosophy was never written.

Twenty years after the publication of the *Philosophie Positive*, Herbert Spencer, in his *Synthetic System*, defined philosophy to be "completely unified knowledge." Like Comte, Spencer is convinced that "the deepest truths we can reach are simply statements of the widest uniformities in our experience of the relations of matter, motion, and force," and that even what we know as matter, motion, and force are at best but "symbols of an unknown and unknowable reality." The whole of that vast and apparently never-ending process which we speak of as the evolution of the universe is due, Spencer points out, to "the unceasing redistribution" of motion and matter, which arises from "the instability of the homogeneous." At first, evolution is exceedingly simple, but the process becomes ever more and more complicated as differentiation increases between the parts which make up the whole, or, in the language of Spencer, "as the homogeneous becomes more and more heterogeneous." Once started, evolution must go on until the action of the forces outside, "to which all parts of any aggregate are exposed," is balanced by the action of the forces within those parts—action which tends to resist all change. But when this state of equilibrium, or rest, is reached, the process is reversed, and evolution changes to dissolution; its own "contained motion" increases gradually or suddenly, until it dissipates and destroys the aggregate. In this way, every force in the universe is decomposed into "divergent forces."

Spencer therefore also adopts the theory of certain Indian and Greek thinkers, that the universe is for ever in alternate states of evolution and dissolution, and says that, "remote as must be the time when the relative motions of the masses composing our solar system will be transformed into molecular motion, and all the molecular motion dissipated," that time must inevitably come. But he thinks that we may infer that "what we know happens to parts will eventually happen to the whole," and therefore that it is probable that, after the universe that we now know has passed through its period of dissolution, it will again begin to evolve and will once more "fill an immeasurable future, as it has already filled an immeasurable past." As it is thus impossible for the mind to imagine either end or beginning to this eternal process of becoming, we are forced to say that the origin of all things is not only unknown but unknowable.

In its attempt to explain the phenomena of this never-ending process of evolution, philosophy has to postulate such "ultimate scientific ideas" as time, space, matter, motion. But when we try to explain these abstractions themselves, we arrive only at "alternative impossibilities of thought," and find that we use them only as "symbols of unknown realities" behind them. We cannot even explain what life and consciousness are. Thought is based on sensation, we say. But, what *is* sensation? *What* is it that is conscious of sensation? What is it that *thinks*? We may say that "the successive impressions and ideas which constitute consciousness" are affections of "that something which we call mind." And we may infer that the mind is the real ego, and that the ego is "an entity," and that "the conscious self exists as a permanent continuous being." But all this is pure supposition, of which there is no proof whatever.

This, however, we perceive, that "nothing stands alone"—not even a thought. Every thought we think involves a whole system of thoughts, and ceases itself to exist if severed from its various correlatives. "We can no more isolate a thought than we can isolate an organ of the living body and deal with it as though it had a life independent of the rest." And we see, too, that nothing in the universe can ever be at rest, but that it undergoes from instant to instant some alteration of state. All things around us integrate and disintegrate, and in all living aggregates, especially in animals, we know that the conflicting processes of integration and disintegration go on rapidly because of the absorption of "motion latent in food." We also perceive that all evolution is change "from a less coherent to a more coherent form," that it is a change from chaos to order. To illustrate this fact, Spencer describes at length and very lucidly the gradual growth not only of the physical world, but also of language, writing, art, and society. He shows further that the evolution or progress from chaos to order is revealed in "the tendency of all European nations to form alliances, in the restraining influences exercised by governments over one another," and that, "in the system of settled international arrangements by congresses, as in the weakening of commercial barriers, and in the increasing facilities of communication, we see the beginnings of a European federation—a still larger integration."

Hume said that it was impossible to conceive the Absolute, whilst Kant asserted that by means of what he terms "synthetical judgments" it is possible "to pass beyond our concepts." Spencer, the apostle of synthesis, seems at first to agree with Kant, for he admits that, although we can have no "definite consciousness," of the nature of the Absolute, we yet have of it an "indefinite consciousness." But he says that we cannot in any way formulate this indefinite consciousness, because thought cannot "pass into the unknowable," which is "absolutely beyond our comprehension." It seems therefore that, after all, Spencer agrees with Hume rather than with Kant, for he says that in our deepest researches we cannot get beyond "our experience of the relations of matter, motion, and force," which are and must ever remain to us "the symbols of an unknown and unknowable reality."

The book is finished. Perhaps some reader may say: "Yes! But you have come to no conclusion." That is so. But, is any conclusion possible when we consider how vast is the subject and how slow the process of assimilating even so much of our great Heritage of Thought as I have been able to pass in review? As the ideas of the thinkers of the distant and more recent past unfolded themselves, little by little, before me, I naturally drew from them many an inference, as I hope each of my readers will do for himself. But I may say that quite the most helpful suggestion that has come to me from my study of past thought is, that we must accept nothing at second-hand which we can possibly think out for ourselves.

Among all the great thinkers since Heraclitus there seems to be a consensus of opinion that the universe is for ever in flux. The world evolves, and with it evolve the minds of men—from age to age, from year to year, from day to day. This being so, let us resolutely keep our thoughts from running into grooves, so that our minds may not fossilise as our bodies grow old. We can, indeed, no longer accept the plausible axiom "Cogito, ergo sum"; but we may transpose the words of Des Cartes, and say:

"SUM, ERGO COGITO."